Comparative Perspectives in Scottish and Norwegian Legal History, Trade and Seafaring, 1200–1800

EDINBURGH STUDIES IN LAW

Volumes in the series:

Andrew R C Simpson and Jørn Øyrehagen Sunde (eds), *Comparative Perspectives in Scottish and Norwegian Legal History, Trade and Seafaring, 1200–1800* (2023)

Jonathan Hardman and Alisdair D J MacPherson (eds), *The Floating Charge in Scotland: New Perspectives and Current Issues* (2022)

Hector L MacQueen (ed), *Continuity, Influences and Integration in Scottish Legal History: Select Essays of David Sellar* (2022)

Guido Rossi (ed), *Authorities in Early Modern Law Courts* (2021)

John W Cairns, *Enlightenment, Legal Education, and Critique: Selected Essays on the History of Scots Law, Volume 2* (2015)

John W Cairns, *Law, Lawyers, and Humanism: Selected Essays on the History of Scots Law, Volume 1* (2015)

Paul J du Plessis and John W Cairns (eds), *Reassessing Legal Humanism and its Claims: Petere Fontes?* (2015)

Remus Valsan (ed), *Trusts and Patrimonies* (2015)

Eric Descheemaeker (ed), *The Consequences of Possession* (2014)

Neil Walker (ed), *MacCormick's Scotland* (2012)

Elaine E Sutherland, Kay E Goodall, Gavin F M Little and Fraser P Davidson (eds), *Law Making and the Scottish Parliament* (2011)

J W Cairns and Paul du Plessis (eds), *The Creation of the* Ius Commune*: From* Casus *to* Regula (2010)

James Chalmers, Lindsay Farmer and Fiona Leverick (eds), *Essays in Criminal Law in Honour of Sir Gerald Gordon* (2010)

Vernon Valentine Palmer and Elspeth Christie Reid (eds), *Mixed Jurisdictions Compared: Private Law in Louisiana and Scotland* (2009)

John W Cairns and Paul du Plessis (eds), *Beyond Dogmatics: Law and Society in the Roman World* (2007)

William M Gordon, *Roman Law, Scots Law and Legal History* (2007)

Kenneth G C Reid, Marius J de Waal and Reinhard Zimmermann (eds), *Exploring the Law of Succession: Studies National, Historical and Comparative* (2007)

Hector MacQueen and Reinhard Zimmermann (eds), *European Contract Law: Scots and South African Perspectives* (2006)

Elspeth Reid and David L Carey Miller (eds), *A Mixed Legal System in Transition: T B Smith and the Progress of Scots Law* (2005)

https://edinburghuniversitypress.com/series/esil

EDINBURGH STUDIES IN LAW
VOLUME 18

Comparative Perspectives in Scottish and Norwegian Legal History, Trade and Seafaring, 1200–1800

Edited by
Andrew R C Simpson and
Jørn Øyrehagen Sunde

EDINBURGH
University Press

Edinburgh University Press is one of the leading university presses in the UK. We publish academic books and journals in our selected subject areas across the humanities and social sciences, combining cutting-edge scholarship with high editorial and production values to produce academic works of lasting importance. For more information visit our website: edinburghuniversitypress.com

Edinburgh University Press Ltd
The Tun – Holyrood Road
12(2f) Jackson's Entry
Edinburgh EH8 8PJ

Typeset in New Caledonia by
Cheshire Typesetting Ltd, Cuddington, Cheshire and
printed and bound by CPI Group (UK) Ltd,
Croydon, CR0 4YY

A CIP record for this book is available from the British Library

ISBN 978 1 3995 0385 3 (hardback)
ISBN 978 1 3995 0387 7 (webready PDF)
ISBN 978 1 3995 0388 4 (epub)

Contents

Acknowledgments

We wish to thank the many people and institutions who have supported the publication of this book in various ways. First and foremost, we are most grateful to the Barony Rosendal, and to the Stiftinga Hardanger og Voss Museum for generously providing subventions towards covering the costs of publication. We also wish to thank both institutions for hosting the seminar in August 2019 which led to the decision to edit the papers presented. All of the contributors have very fond memories of the hospitality of the Hardangerfjord. Secondly, five of the chapters in this volume – those by Erik Opsahl, Per Norseng, Andrew Simpson, Jørn Sunde and Miriam Tveit – were brought to completion whilst the contributors were research fellows at the Centre for Advanced Study (CAS) in Oslo. Their fellowships formed part of the project *Social Governance through legislation*, which Erik Opsahl and Jørn Sunde led and CAS hosted during the academic year 2021–2022. Andrew Simpson and Jørn Sunde also wrote the introduction to the book during this period. We wish to express our sincere gratitude to CAS for its generous support of this project. Thirdly, we are very grateful to Alexandra Braun and the Edinburgh Studies in Law series for taking such a strong interest in the project, and for agreeing to publish the book; Laura Quinn, Sarah Foyle and the team at EUP have also been extremely helpful throughout. Fourthly, we would like to express our sincere thanks to Andrew Simpson's wife Philippa Simpson for her help with aspects of the language editing of the book. We are also very grateful to Jørn Sunde's research assistant, Johanne Harstad, for her help in dealing with matters of house style in the volume. Any editorial infelicities that remain, whether linguistic or stylistic, are wholly the responsibility of the editors.

Finally, we wish to thank our families for their very kind and unceasing support. Andrew would like to thank his wife Philippa, who took such a genuine interest in the project, and his son Peter, who so enthusiastically and happily threw himself into the radically different world of Oslo after lockdowns in Laurencekirk. Jørn would like to thank his wife and companion in life through thirty years, Elisabeth, and their two daughters Anna Elisabeth and Sunniva, for endless trips around Scotland and Norway exploring historical sites to discover the mysteries of the past.

Andrew R C Simpson
Jørn Øyrehagen Sunde
Oslo
May 2022

List of Contributors

Dauvit Broun is the Professor of Scottish History at the University of Glasgow.

J D Ford is the Professor of Civil Law at the University of Aberdeen.

Sören Koch is Professor in Legal History at the University of Bergen.

Steve Murdoch is a Professor of Military History at Försvarshögskolan, the Swedish Defence University.

Per G Norseng is Professor Emeritus in History at the University of South-Eastern Norway and project manager in the Norwegian Maritime Museum.

Erik Opsahl is Professor of Medieval History at the Norwegian University of Science and Technology, Trondheim.

Andrew R C Simpson is Professor of Scots Private Law at the University of Aberdeen.

Jørn Øyrehagen Sunde is Professor in Legal History at the University of Oslo.

Alice Taylor is Professor of Medieval History at King's College, London.

Miriam Jensen Tveit is Associate Professor in History at Nord University, Bodø.

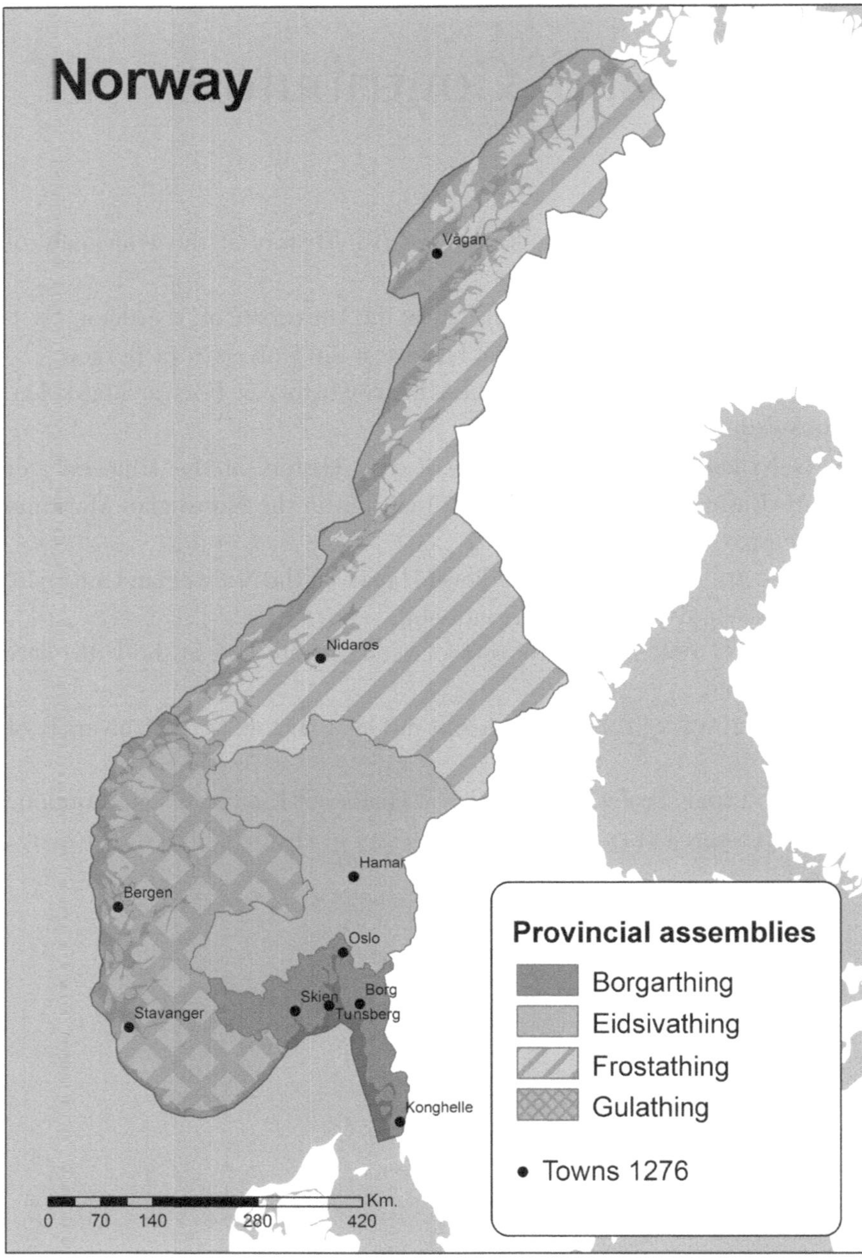

Norway
Vågan
Nidaros
Hamar
Bergen
Oslo
Skien
Borg
Tunsberg
Stavanger
Konghelle
Provincial assemblies
Borgarthing
Eidsivathing
Frostathing
Gulathing
Towns 1276
Km.
0 70 140 280 420

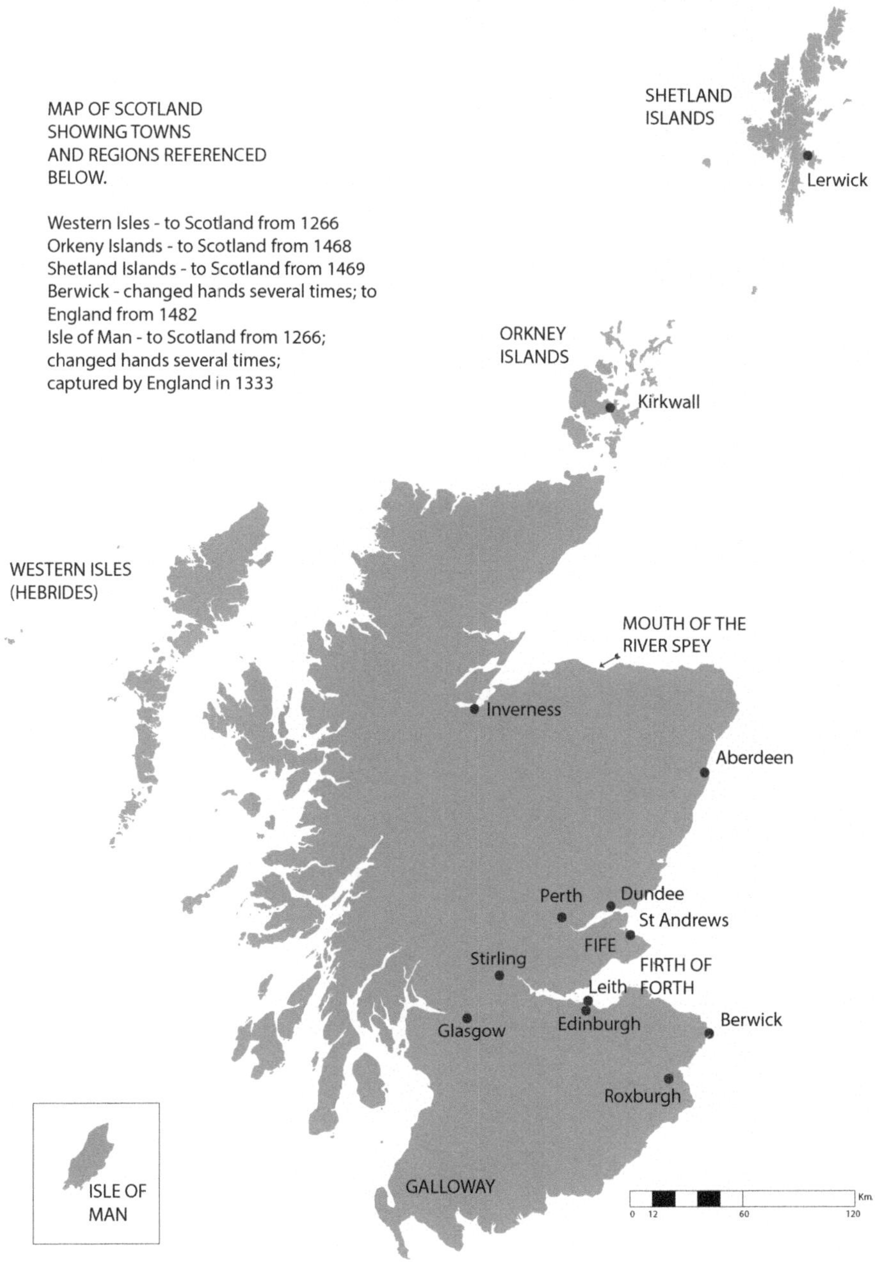
MAP OF SCOTLAND
SHOWING TOWNS
AND REGIONS REFERENCED
BELOW.
Western Isles - to Scotland from 1266
Orkeny Islands - to Scotland from 1468
Shetland Islands - to Scotland from 1469
Berwick - changed hands several times; to
England from 1482
Isle of Man - to Scotland from 1266;
changed hands several times;
captured by England in 1333
SHETLAND
ISLANDS
Lerwick
ORKNEY
ISLANDS
Kirkwall
WESTERN ISLES
(HEBRIDES)
MOUTH OF THE
RIVER SPEY
Inverness
Aberdeen
Perth
Dundee
St Andrews
FIFE
FIRTH OF
FORTH
Stirling
Leith
Edinburgh
Glasgow
Berwick
Roxburgh
GALLOWAY
ISLE OF
MAN
0 12 60 120
Km

Introduction

*Andrew R C Simpson and Jørn Øyrehagen Sunde**

A: 1266 AND ALL THAT?

1266 is not as famous a year as 1066 in the history of the British Isles.[1] Nonetheless, it is one useful point of departure for any attempt to compare the legal and political histories of Scotland and Norway.[2] In that year, a long-running conflict between Scotland and Norway came to an end. This culminated in the Treaty of Perth, which was agreed between the representatives of the respective kings of the two countries – Magnus VI of Norway (r. 1263–1280) and Alexander III of Scotland (r. 1249–1286). Both kings shared certain assumptions about what it meant to exercise kingship. Both

* This article was written whilst the authors were partners in the project *Social governance through legislation* at the Centre for Advanced Study in Oslo.

1 The title alludes to W C Sellar and R J Yeatman, *1066 and All That: A Memorable History of England* (1930). Regrettably, the present volume contains fewer jokes.

2 See E Opsahl, 'The Treaty of Perth: union of the realm and the king's law' (Chapter One below in the present volume) and D Broun, 'The Treaty of Perth: union of the realm and the kingdom' (Chapter Two below in the present volume).

wanted to articulate the territorial boundaries of their realms – something that the Treaty of Perth helped to achieve. Within their territorial boundaries, they sought to articulate their kingship in similar ways. For example, they both reformed the coinage, in Alexander III's case by establishing a remarkable number of mints across the kingdom during the 1250s, and in Magnus VI's case during the two succeeding decades.[3] In addition, they both cultivated the idea that their realms possessed unitary laws. In the Treaty of Perth, it was provided that the people living in islands ceded by Norway to Scotland would thereafter be governed by the "laws and customs of the kingdom of Scotland and be dealt with and judged according to them from now into the future".[4] This indicates that Alexander III and his advisers could at least appeal to a unitary law of the realm as an ideal.[5] In Norway, Magnus VI's political efforts after the Treaty of Perth were directed towards unifying the law of the realm, including the law in the Northern Isles and the Faroes, Iceland and Greenland. This reinforced the older idea that the king might issue law for the whole of the realm, and simultaneously created a standard of unified law for the whole kingdom.[6]

Considering these points about Alexander III and Magnus VI together is a helpful way to introduce the present volume, which is concerned with comparative legal history, and specifically comparing the legal histories of Norway and Scotland. The stories of their reigns illustrate that some of the elements essential for any effective comparison are present. Ostensibly, there are similarities in the historical developments of both kingdoms as their rulers sought to forge political and legal identities within their territorial realms. Nevertheless, what has just been said shows that there were differences too. Magnus VI promoted the goal of legal unification through wide-ranging codifications of the law, replacing the individual laws of the things with a potent symbol of legal unity – the *Landsloven*, or Code of the Realm.[7] By contrast, Alexander III articulated his conception of the legal unity of Scotland in a very different context. What he and his elite nobles and clergymen seem to have done was to promote the notion that Scotland existed as a unitary jurisdiction, drawing on a recently-articulated national

3 Opsahl, 'Treaty of Perth' 44–45 below; Broun, 'Treaty of Perth' 65–66 below.

4 Broun, 'Treaty of Perth' 72 below, citing A A M Duncan (ed), *Regesta Regum Scottorum*, vol v, *The Acts of Robert I King of Scots 1306–1329* (1988) no 24 at 308–309.

5 Broun, 'Treaty of Perth' 63–94 below; see also A Taylor, 'Law and administrative change in Scotland, twelfth–fourteenth centuries' (Chapter Four below in the present volume).

6 Opsahl, 'Treaty of Perth' 35–53 below; see also J Ø Sunde, 'Law and administrative change in Norway, twelfth–fourteenth centuries' (Chapter Three below in the present volume).

7 Opsahl, 'Treaty of Perth' 40–43 below; Sunde, 'Law and administrative change' 103–107 below.

history and the widespread experience of royal and aristocratic courts. These courts were all – ultimately – manifestations of royal authority.[8] Therefore, if there are similarities between the political and legal histories of Norway and Scotland in the thirteenth century – and in later periods – there are also very significant differences; and this raises the question of what comparison of the legal histories of the two realms can achieve.

The aim of this introduction is to explain why we believe comparison of the histories and the legal histories of Norway and Scotland might prove to be illuminating. At the outset, we will say something about the origins of the book, and the basic methodological assumptions that underpin it. We will then consider each of the contributions of the book, and explain how we think each contributes to a comparative legal historical discourse concerning Norway and Scotland. One of the issues that emerges from the book taken as a whole relates to the difficulties inherent in comparing different legal histories when the meaning of "law" and related terms were themselves developing during the medieval and early modern periods. We will draw this point out fully in our conclusion, where we will make suggestions about how the research presented here might lay a foundation for future research.

B: ORIGINS, METHOD AND THEME OF THIS BOOK

(1) Origins and methodological assumptions

This book emerged from papers presented at a seminar held at Agatunet and the Barony Rosendal in the Hardangerfjord, Norway, on 20 and 21 August 2019. The papers were given in the inspiring surroundings of the Lagmannsstova, a thirteenth-century building once used as a court by a medieval Norwegian lawman, and the Barony at Rosendal, a manor house dating from 1665. The aim of the seminar was to explore possible connections between Norwegian and Scottish history, with a particular focus on legal history and related questions of trade and population movements. To that end, each Scottish speaker and each Norwegian speaker was asked to explore what seemed – at first sight, anyway – to be a historical phenomenon or theme common to both nations. To give some examples, Erik Opsahl and Dauvit Broun were both asked to consider the Treaty of Perth from Norwegian and Scottish perspectives respectively. Jørn Sunde and Alice Taylor considered the development of institutions and structures used in the

8 Broun, 'Treaty of Perth' 80–81, 92–94 below.

administration of the law in Norway and Scotland during the thirteenth and fourteenth centuries. Miriam Tveit and Andrew Simpson considered the extent to which there was a connection between the provisions of town laws and legal practice in urban settings in Norway and Scotland respectively. During the seminar, it became clear that there were a range of prima facie similar historical phenomena that could be observed in the histories and legal histories of both countries, and it also became clear that these phenomena were, on closer inspection, marked out from each other by a range of differences. Exploring the historical factors that caused these similarities and differences promised to be a very rewarding academic exercise. For this reason, we decided that the work presented in the seminar merited further work with a view to publication; the present volume is the result.

The account of the origins of the book just given will make it clear that speakers were not asked to follow a specific methodology of comparative legal history. Questions of what such a method might look like have attracted significant attention over the past few years; John Hudson and William Eves have recently published a most helpful overview of the growing literature.[9] We will not attempt to replicate that sort of overview here; but we will allude to the relevant methodological literature in so far as it is relevant to our discussions of the individual contributions below. However, it is helpful to outline here two of the broad methodological assumptions that come through all of the contributions to the volume.

First, all of the contributions to this volume are studies of the past for its own sake; our book is consciously historical in its focus. When we look at a text from the past, we want to understand what its author might have meant to communicate to a contemporary audience in light of the assumptions and linguistic conventions that they shared.[10] Lawyers may – quite legitimately – look to the legal past as a body of "old principles" and "old phrases" that are gradually "charged with new content", and think of this as "an evolution of the true intent and meaning of the old law".[11] Historians, by contrast, with

9 J Hudson and W Eves, 'Introduction: Situating, Researching, and Writing Comparative Legal History' in W Eves, J Hudson, I Ivarsen and S B White (eds), *Common Law, Civil Law, and Colonial Law: Essays in Comparative Legal History from the Twelfth to the Twentieth Centuries* (2021) 1–24. For stimulating and important discussions of the methodology of legal history, see too the essays in OMoréteau, A Masferrer and K Å Modéer (eds), *Comparative Legal History* (2020).

10 For this approach, see, for example, J Tully (ed), *Meaning and Context: Quentin Skinner and his Critics* (1988); Q Skinner, *Visions of Politics*, 3 vols (2002), vol 2.

11 F W Maitland, *Why the history of English law is not written: An inaugural lecture delivered in the Arts School at Cambridge on 13th October, 1888* (1888) 14.

their aim of understanding the past on its own terms, will see this "almost of necessity as a process of perversion and misunderstanding".[12] Maitland put the point very well when he said that "[w]hat the lawyer wants is authority and the newer the better; what the historian wants is evidence and the older the better".[13]

Secondly, the contributions to this book focus on "national" histories; each contribution is predominantly concerned with either Scottish or Norwegian history. Nevertheless, the assumption that runs through the whole volume is that the medieval and early modern legal histories of both countries may receive some light from the comparison. Maitland again puts the point very well; "[h]istory involves comparison" and, he continued, "the English lawyer who knew nothing of and cared nothing for any system but his own hardly came in sight of the idea of legal history".[14] For example, comparison makes historians conscious of the possibility that things could have been done differently. If law was changed to deal with a particular problem in one way in one jurisdiction, and it was changed in a different way to deal with the same problem in another, one might want to try to explain the factors that caused the different approaches.[15] Precisely what will be learnt as a result of the exercise cannot be predicted in advance; however, we undertook this project on the assumption that something might be discovered from the comparison that would allow us to look at our own "national" legal histories again with fresh eyes. In other words, we assumed that the comparison might enable us to further the historical goal of better understanding the past on its own terms.[16] We think that assumption has been vindicated, as we will explain in more detail shortly; and it has been vindicated to the extent that we believe further research comparing the histories of Norway and Scotland may prove to be illuminating.

12 Maitland, *Why the history of English law is not written* (n 11) 14.

13 Maitland, *Why the history of English law is not written* (n 11) 14; a similar point is made very clearly in A W B Simpson, 'The Common Law and Legal Theory' in A W B Simpson, *Legal Theory and Legal History: Essays on the Common Law* (1987) 359–382, particularly at 366–370. See also the helpful discussion of legal historical method in J H Baker, 'Reflections on "doing" legal history' in A Musson and C Stebbings (eds), *Making Legal History: Approaches and Methodologies* (2012) 16–24.

14 Maitland, *Why the history of English law is not written* (n 11) 11.

15 See the discussion in D Ibbetson, 'Comparative Legal History: A Methodology' in A Musson and C Stebbings (eds), *Making Legal History: Approaches and Methodologies* (2012) 131–145 at 143–145.

16 Valcke says that the point of any comparison must be to generate meaningful information; obviously enough, not all comparisons will achieve this (see C Valcke, *Comparing Law: Comparative Law as Reconstruction of Collective Commitments* (2018) 61–70). The sort of meaningful information that one might expect from a genuinely *historical* comparison is indicated here.

(2) A theme of the book

Before considering the contributions to the volume, it is worth introducing a theme – or at least a recurrent question – that we believe emerges from reflection on several of the essays printed below; and this is related to what it means to do comparative "legal" history. It was mentioned above that Alexander III wanted all of his subjects to be governed by the "laws and customs of the kingdom of Scotland".[17] What did he and his advisers mean by this phrase, and what did they mean by "law"?

Legal historians are well aware of the difficulty of answering this question for past generations (and indeed for themselves); part of the problem is that their usage of the word depended on certain assumptions that were rarely fully articulated. David Ibbetson illustrates some of the problems here in an article on the subject matter of legal history. He begins by distinguishing external from internal legal history, describing the former as "the history of law embedded in its context, typically its social or economic context" and in this he includes "the history of courts, of literature, of the legal profession".[18] By contrast, internal legal history "deals with the law on its own terms" and "[i]ts object, if we do our history right, would seem to be the law that would have been recognised by lawyers in its time".[19] Having drawn these distinctions Ibbetson then focuses on internal legal history and notes that here "the real problem is to decide what we mean by *law*".[20] He notes that many readers will have a Hartian model in mind of "law as a system of rules, rules susceptible of identification by reference to some more or less determinate Rule of Recognition".[21] Ibbetson then proceeds to point out four difficulties with using this model when talking about the history of "law" as "rules". First, it is sometimes difficult to identify an articulate rule of recognition in the past that is much more sophisticated than "the law was what the lawyers thought it was". Secondly, the rule-based model can exclude from consideration certain standards not based on rules that are nevertheless influential, such as the background beliefs of society. Thirdly, identifying the existence and operation of these beliefs can be extremely difficult, particularly where the assumptions in questions were essentially lawyers' concerns

17 See Broun, 'Treaty of Perth' 72 below.

18 D Ibbetson, 'What is Legal History a History of?' (2004) *Law and History Review* 33–40 at 33.

19 Ibbetson, 'What is Legal History?' (n 18) 34.

20 Ibbetson, 'What is Legal History?' (n 18) 34.

21 Ibbetson, 'What is Legal History?' (n 18) 34, citing J Austin, *The Province of Jurisprudence Determined* (1832) and H L A Hart, *The Concept of Law* (1961).

about how legal rules were to be organised and categorised. The latter types of assumptions can help to shape perceptions of the scope and limits of individual rules, and so the historian has to be alive to their possible existence. Fourthly, lawyers are – and have been – keen to emphasise that the law "is" something at a given point in time; but legal historians must be wary of any such pronouncements, because law can be genuinely ambiguous for a long period of time before disagreements about its content are resolved in an authoritative manner. If this is true of legal rules, then it can also be true of the conceptual frameworks that lawyers use to organise them.[22]

While Ibbetson would probably locate several – if not all – of the contributions to the present volume largely within the field of external legal history, his comments provide a very helpful introduction to the difficulties of talking about "law" and, indeed, to the consequent difficulties in talking about comparative "legal" history. Our volume is not written to provide any sort of silver bullet, but several of the contributors do grapple with this issue. The approach to the problem taken by the contributors in question seems relatively uniform and it is already articulated in the first of our methodological assumptions as stated above. All the work in this volume is written to understand the past in its own terms, and this includes difficult terms like "law", through rigorous study of the assumptions and linguistic conventions of those who used them in communication with one another. Sometimes, as will be explained shortly, that entails consideration of the assumptions and conventions of political elites and the institutional structures that they sustained and within which they operated. There are certainly a range of ways of answering the question of what was meant by "the laws and customs of the Scots" in 1266. However, the contributions to this volume are methodologically consistent with Broun's approach to the question, where he states his desire to "explore what the Treaty of Perth might have meant to the Scottish ruling elite at the time in terms of the kingdom's unity and identity".[23] We believe that the comparative structure of the book helps to throw the resulting plurality of historical approaches to the meaning of terms like "law" into relief. By juxtaposing the ways in which different ideas of law developed in Norway and Scotland, and by reflecting on the different factors that caused those developments – including political and economic factors – the volume

22 Ibbetson, 'What is Legal History?' (n 18) 34–36; for a detailed study of the importance of this last point concerning the ambiguity of conceptual frameworks used to organise the law, see A M Godfrey, *Civil Justice in Renaissance Scotland* (2009) and, in particular, the conclusions drawn at 449–453.

23 See Broun, 'Treaty of Perth' 64 below.

sheds some light on the legal histories of Scotland and Norway respectively.[24] We will now attempt to justify that last claim by discussing the individual contributions to the book.

C: COMPARATIVE PERSPECTIVES ON LEGAL HISTORY, TRADE AND SEAFARING IN NORWAY AND SCOTLAND

Our book is divided into two broad sections. The first focuses on the medieval period, and includes six essays, by Erik Opsahl, Dauvit Broun, Jørn Sunde, Alice Taylor, Miriam Tveit and Andrew Simpson. The second section focuses on the early modern period, and includes four essays, by Steve Murdoch, Per Norseng, Søren Koch and John Ford. There is a structural difference between the two. The first fully preserves the device of pairing Norwegian and Scottish articles concerned with broadly similar themes; it will be recalled this was employed in the seminar at Agatunet and Rosendal in August 2019. As the contributions on the early modern period were edited, it became clear that the possible connections between the contributions of Murdoch and Norseng and Koch and Ford respectively were looser; however, it will be suggested below that they can also be seen as "pairs" of essays, albeit less closely connected than those concerned with the medieval period.

(1) The idea of law, political symbolism and state formation

Erik Opsahl wrote the first essay included below, and Dauvit Broun wrote the second. They both start from a common subject – the Treaty of Perth, which was agreed between Norway and Scotland in 1266. Both writers explore the theme of the relationship between law – or the idea of law – and political unity. Both writers see the Treaty as marking an important moment in the historical development of Norwegian and Scottish political and legal identities. For Opsahl, the Treaty was at least "part of a decisive phase in what we call state-building in Norway in the middle ages".[25] It was as much a boundary marker as a treaty, providing an opportunity for Magnus VI to establish part of the western frontier of his realm; he showed equal interest in articulating the territorial extent of his kingdom and also his *skattlands*

24 To some extent, the manner in which we articulate our approach is indebted to remarks in Ibbetson, 'Comparative Legal History' (n 15) 143–145; Ibbetson rightly emphasises the importance of the rigorous study of national legal histories as a prelude to, and in the course of, comparative work.

25 Opsahl, 'Treaty of Perth' 36.

(i.e. tributary lands) elsewhere. Magnus linked the idea that his kingdom was a united territorial entity with the idea that it possessed one set of laws, which he promulgated as the Code of the Realm in 1274; this was extended to the *skattlands* in the west, Orkney, the Shetland Isles and the Faroes, while Iceland and Greenland got a separate code of law based on the Code of 1274. Opsahl argues that these developments had significant repercussions for centuries. The idea that the kingdom of Norway was a defined territorial unit, governed by codified laws promulgated on the authority of the Norwegian monarch, reinforced the link between law and political identity. This symbolic idea that Norwegian law was unified was not necessarily reflected in legal practice. Nevertheless, it was a powerful idea, and Opsahl shows that it helped to maintain a sense of distinctive Norwegian identity even after the Union of Kalmar with Denmark and Sweden in 1397. Norwegians "could and did invoke the Code and Norwegian customs to protect Norwegian independence within the union".[26]

Broun's essay also commences with an examination of the Treaty of Perth. It seeks to answer the question of what the Treaty meant when it declared that the Western Isles ceded to Alexander III of Scotland in 1266 were thereafter to be governed by "the laws and customs of the kingdom of Scotland".[27] This might be taken to indicate some expectation that any distinctive laws and customs in the Western Isles would now be replaced with the laws of the Scottish kingdom – with the associated implication that the application of the law on the mainland was already unified. Broun shows that any such reading is problematic, for two reasons. First, he argues that "there was no expectation that the king's laws and customs – in the fullest sense that this was understood at the time – would be uniform throughout the realm". Secondly, he suggests that "in this period, it would have been so remarkable for a kingdom to be subsumed so completely by another that this would have been unthinkable in 1266".[28] Broun then surveys the evidence for the existence of significant legal diversity in the Scottish mainland, linking this with Taylor's account of how royal jurisdiction functioned.[29] In thirteenth-century Scotland, royal jurisdiction operated through aristocratic power; aristocrats had responsibility for the functioning of the royal courts that held sway over large territories within the realm and they also possessed their own territorial jurisdictions. In this context, Broun notes that

26 Opsahl, 'Treaty of Perth' 53 below.
27 See Broun, 'Treaty of Perth' 72 below.
28 Broun, 'Treaty of Perth' 73 below.
29 See A Taylor, *The Shape of the State in Medieval Scotland, 1124–1290* (2016).

> there was no conceptual difficulty in acknowledging that some of the most powerful lords, such as the lord of Galloway and the earl of Fife, exercised their judicial authority in particular customary ways referred to as the laws of Galloway and the laws of Clan Macduff.[30]

Broun acknowledges that medieval Scots did claim to possess a common law. However, he agrees with Taylor when she says that the

> common law of the land did not mean that all people interacted with the same judicial institutions in the same way, but that, regardless of jurisdiction, the common law or the law of the kingdom was supposed to be upheld.[31]

Nevertheless, there evidently was an idea of legal unity in Scotland; and so the question relates to how one is to explain this. While there was no figure like Magnus VI who united the laws of Scotland through codification, Broun does point out that contemporary Scottish histories and chronicles pointed to ancient monarchs such as the ninth-century Cinead mac Ailpín as the original Scottish law-givers. One chronicle proclaimed that Cinead was the often called the first king, not because he was, in fact, the first, but rather because he was the first to give the Scottish people laws. In other words, thirteenth-century Scots projected the idea of unified laws of the Scots (*leges Scoticana*) back into the distant past. At the same time, this came to be associated closely with another idea, which was that the territories ruled by the kings of the Scots in fact constituted one united territory. This territory came to be thought of as "Scotland" in the thirteenth century, whereas previously "Scotland" was simply the landmass north of the River Forth. There was also a sense that the territory constituted a single Scottish royal jurisdiction; but that jurisdiction manifested itself through aristocratic power in a way that made legal diversity almost inevitable. Elite aristocratic perceptions of legal reality – that they had responsibility for exercising royal jurisdiction and that they were answerable to the king where they failed to do so – helped to create an idea of a unified law of Scotland operating across a single territory ruled by the kings of the Scots. It was into this idea of Scottish legal and territorial unity that the Western Isles were to be incorporated in 1266.

What light, then, flows from the comparison of Opsahl's reflections on the Treaty of Perth, and those of Broun? For both Magnus VI and Alexander III, the Treaty was an opportunity for consolidation of their realms understood as territorial units – the Treaty was, as Opsahl puts it, a boundary marker. For both kings too, there was a belief that territorial consolidation of the

30 Broun, 'Treaty of Perth' 80 below.
31 Broun, 'Treaty of Perth' 90 below, citing Taylor, *The Shape of the State* (n 29) 247.

kingdom went hand in hand with legal unification. There was to be one king, one territorial realm and one law governing it. Here, however, these high-level similarities begin to break down and it is by attempting to explain the differences between what was going on in Norway and Scotland that one learns something rather intriguing about the different political conditions that resulted in different forms of legal unification at this time. In Norway, it was possible for the idea of legal unity to manifest itself in codifications of the law. Magnus VI negotiated his power directly with four provincial assemblies, which already possessed their own traditions of written law. As Sunde shows in his contribution to this volume, Magnus VI could simultaneously draw upon a tradition of a Norwegian monarch as legislator and present his unified code of the realm as amendments to the written laws of the provinces that were in the interests of those who dwelt there.[32] By contrast, in Scotland, as Broun explains, the provincial assemblies – in so far as they were ever comparable with the Norwegian equivalents – had been largely eclipsed by baronial courts or sheriff courts as the most important judicial fora by the early thirteenth century. Laws were promulgated by assemblies composed of aristocratic magnates and senior ecclesiastics. Therefore, "[a]n authoritative statement of the kingdom's laws would only have been conceivable . . . through the active involvement and self-interest of the ruling elite". Broun makes a compelling argument to the effect that any such project to unite the laws was not, in fact, in the interests of that elite.

This shows that similar ideas of law as a symbol, serving similar functions in territorial state formation in Norway and Scotland, could manifest themselves in radically different ways depending on the broader political and legal contexts. Juxtaposing Opsahl's reflections on Norwegian history with those of Broun on Scottish history throws into relief just how distinctive Norway and Scotland were in terms of its pattern of state formation, and in terms of what contemporary elites understood by "law". Law might have been a political idea, a symbol used in both countries to realise royal ambitions to consolidate power; but for Norwegian and Scottish elites, the unification of "law" meant different things. It may not be pushing the evidence too far to speculate that in Norway those around the king who aspired to create a political symbol of legal unity had to grapple with a simple problem. There were rival symbols of disunity – the laws of the provincial assemblies. Overcoming that problem necessitated the creation of a new symbol of unity – the Code of the Realm of 1274 – and lay at the heart of the idea of Norwegian law for

32 Sunde, 'Law and Administrative Change' below, 96–109.

centuries, as Opsahl demonstrates. By contrast, in Scotland, the idea of legal unity – of a Scottish common law – flowed from experience of royal Scottish jurisdiction manifested through aristocratic power. Scottish elites saw no pressing need to give that idea of legal unity greater substantive content, at least in the thirteenth century.

Note that both Opsahl and Broun suggest that the symbolic idea of legal unity expressed in the Code of the Realm and the Scottish common law did not go hand in hand with the experience of uniformity of the application of the law in practice. Indeed, both writers suggest that the image of legal uniformity was quite different from the practical reality; law as experienced was diverse. Sunde and Taylor develop this theme further in their contributions to the present volume.

(2) Law, regularisation of law and legal plurality

Sunde's essay is the third chapter printed below. It addresses an apparent paradox in medieval Norwegian history. Norwegian kings like Magnus VI established a political idea of the unity of Norwegian laws, and indeed there is evidence of regularisation of the administration and application of law in practice. However, there is also significant evidence for legal diversity and plurality too. The essay begins by developing themes introduced by Opsahl, explaining how the idea that the Norwegian king could make laws for the whole realm developed, probably from the eleventh century onwards. Sunde shows that this power was not unqualified. In the mid-thirteenth century, the Gulathing – one of the provincial assemblies – reduced the law concerning the defence of the realm to writing. However, one provision of this law stated that it was unclear whether or not the law was "right or wrong". The provision then said that if it turned out that the law was wrong, then the law that would be applied would be older written regulations "which Atle explained to the men in Gulen"; this would follow "unless the king wants to grant us other plans and we all agree to them".[33] Having used this example to explain the difficulties in talking about Norwegian legislative power in this period, Sunde then proceeds to explore its origins. It is thought that Olaf II – later regarded as St Olaf – organised some sort of law-making assembly at Moster in 1024, and that he promulgated some laws for the whole kingdom. Later, in the mid-twelfth century, the royal government of the infant Magnus V drew on this example to claim legislative authority over the whole

33 Sunde, 'Law and Administrative Change' below, 98.

of Norway. In doing so, they bypassed the traditional provincial assemblies and attempted to justify this on the basis that they were simply amending the laws of the holy St Olaf. Finally, in the mid-thirteenth century, Håkon IV and his son, Magnus VI, drew upon this legislative tradition in negotiating the reform of the laws with the provincial assemblies; this helped to bolster their authority to issue codes of written law as "amendments" to what had gone before. Sunde then traces in detail the negotiation of the codification project with the local assemblies. He notes that while the king wanted to achieve legal unification, he was prepared to negotiate exceptions from some of the provisions of the code for individual territories within the Norwegian kingdom. This acceptance of some diversity and plurality in the law was designed to secure broad compliance with the code as a whole across the kingdom.

Nevertheless, all this raises the question to which Sunde's article turns next. How much compliance was there, in practice, with the Code, and if there was compliance, how was this achieved?[34] Sunde agrees with Opsahl that the Code continued to enjoy respect – almost veneration – as an authoritative statement of Norwegian law for centuries; and he suggests that "its authority was probably due to the system for the application of law established within the code, which made plurality within unity possible".[35] Central to this system of application of the law were the lawmen, and the discretion that the Code of 1274 gave to the provincial assemblies when applying the law. Lawmen were originally charged with declaring the law; but disputes were decided by the provincial and the regional assemblies. A reform of ca. 1260 changed this; litigants could now bring disputes before the lawman directly, rather than one of the assemblies. By 1274, where the assemblies were involved in dispute resolution, the lawmen – increasingly understood as the king's lawmen – were required to negotiate the decision in each dispute with groups of six or twelve men chosen by the assemblies. In essence, the lawmen were required to establish the applicable law and the six or twelve men were required to establish the facts. There were at most sixteen lawmen. Through them the king exercised some control of the interpretation of the Code of the Realm; at the same time, he negotiated the application of the law with local elites.[36] Sunde gives several other examples of the way in which the application of the code was decided in consultation with such elites. For example, gaps in the law were to be filled

34 Sunde, 'Law and Administrative Change' below, 109–120.
35 Sunde, 'Law and Administrative Change' below, 109–110.
36 Sunde, 'Law and Administrative Change' below, 109–120.

by the lawmen and the six or twelve men acting together; and the lawmen and the six or twelve men could depart from the written law where it seemed to them too strict or too lenient. Sunde cites examples of this sort of negotiation happening in practice. By the fourteenth century, decisions that were seen as significant departures in the law would come to the king's attention, and he would then order them to be included in all books of the law thereafter.

Therefore, the political idea of Norwegian law as a unified entity did have practical consequences; it did influence the application of law in practice. Nevertheless, it is important to understand that the "law" that was to be applied was not viewed as the last word on the resolution of a dispute. There is nothing here like the principle of subsumption that is supposed to be followed in the application of the great continental codes promulgated from the early-nineteenth century onwards.[37] The "law" was an essential starting point for the negotiation of solutions to legal disputes in local communities; the king's sixteen lawmen probably helped to maintain some uniformity of application of the law within the system as a whole.

Taylor's contribution considers broadly comparable developments in Scotland between the twelfth and the fourteenth centuries.[38] However, her overall position is that the histories of Norway and Scotland in this period are quite dissimilar. In many ways, her work underlines just how important it is to question rigorously superficial similarities in comparative historical research. The danger is that such apparent similarities mislead scholars who are seeking to draw inspiration from "models" of development in one medieval polity when trying to make sense of their own. Taylor's aim is to "complicate . . . the narrative of the regularisation of justice over the twelfth and the thirteenth centuries" and to explore questions about the "trajectory" of legal development during the fourteenth century. In particular, she explores the extent to which these developments can be explained with reference to what she labels the "English model" of state formation, with its emphasis on institutional development and bureaucratisation, and with its associated emphasis on the development of the English common law. Taylor notes that there has been speculation as to the extent to which the reception of English institutions and ideas in the medieval

37 It will be very clear that the Norwegian codes of the thirteenth century were quite different from the nineteenth century codes and operated in quite different legal cultural contexts. For introductory remarks on the nineteenth century codes, see, for example, P Stein, *Roman Law in European History* (1999) 110–123.

38 Taylor, 'Law and Administrative Change' below, 123.

period can be characterised as a legal "transplant", of the sort described by Alan Watson.[39]

However, her arguments seriously complicate any such narrative. In discussing trends in the development of royal justice, she agrees with Hector MacQueen's assessment that one does witness some regularisation,[40] but she argues that this is more true of the thirteenth century than of the twelfth. There were royal officers who assisted the king in the administration of justice from the mid-twelfth century onwards, but they did not exercise jurisdiction over the whole of the kingdom. Some of these officials – who became known as justiciars – did come to exercise oversight in respect of the courts of other royal officials, known as sheriffs. In addition, chamberlains exercised oversight of the administration of justice in the courts of individual royal burghs (towns that had trading and jurisdictional privileges from the king). Writs or brieves could – in certain cases – be purchased from a writing office known as the king's chapel in order to instruct these royal officials to hear disputes. By the fourteenth century, literature was beginning to emerge about the scope of these brieves, and the ways in which litigants might respond to brieves in court. Taylor goes so far as to suggest that a "vernacular sort of expertise" may have developed around "common law procedure" – although she is careful to note that it must have been of a radically different nature than the sort of collective expertise developing in what Sir John Baker has termed the "little intellectual world" of Westminster Hall in England.[41] This is because there was no focal point for the communal development of legal expertise in the form of central courts in Scotland as there was in England.

If all this points towards regularisation of justice – and the possible relevance of the English model for medieval Scottish legal historians – other factors underline just how diverse the application of law must have been in

39 See H L MacQueen, *Common Law and Feudal Society: Classic Edition* (2016) 5, 264–267. MacQueen's use of the transplant metaphor is very careful and considered and some further comments about it will be offered below. For the transplant metaphor, see A Watson, *Legal Transplants: an approach to comparative law*, 2nd edn (1993); for the historical development of the metaphor in the twentieth century, see J W Cairns, 'Watson, Walton and the history of "legal transplants"' (2013) 41 *Georgia Journal of International and Comparative Law* 637–696. For a illuminating critical studies of the concept from a comparative lawyer's perspective, see M Graziadei, 'Comparative Law as the Study of Transplants and Receptions' in M Reimann and R Zimmermann (eds), *The Oxford Handbook of Comparative Law*, 2nd edn (2019) 434–473 and M Graziadei, 'Legal Transplants and the Frontiers of Legal Knowledge' (2009) 10 *Theoretical Inquiries in Law* 723–743; for a radical critique of the concept, see P Legrand, 'The Impossibility of "Legal Transplants"' (2017) 4 *Maastricht Journal of European and Comparative Law* 111–124.

40 See generally MacQueen, *Common Law and Feudal Society* (n 39).

41 J H Baker, *An Introduction to English Legal History*, 5th edn (2019) 209; Taylor, 'Law and Administrative Change' below, 136–137.

practice. The twelfth-century picture was much more "dynamic" and this continued to reverberate into the thirteenth century. The territorialised aristocratic lordship and jurisdictions of the thirteenth century replaced older structures of dispute resolution and law-making. These included Scottish assemblies that have a "superficial similarity" to their Norwegian equivalents.[42] However, considering the Scottish assemblies in light of their Norwegian counterparts throws into relief the distinctive aspects of both. In the Norwegian assemblies, in general terms the lawmen declared the law whilst the assemblies judged disputes; in the Scottish assemblies, *iudices* were trusted to know the laws and also to give judgments. In addition, the *iudices* appear to have been lawmakers at an early period. While in Norway the king had to negotiate law-making with the assemblies, in Scotland the king made some law alongside the *iudices* for a time, and gradually – in the late-twelfth century – developed the practice of promulgating other laws in assemblies of the new territorial aristocrats who held their own courts. If different forms of law-making existed alongside one another, so too did different legal orders. The legal world of the *iudices*, which was predicated on notions of communal "honour, injury and status" survived well into the thirteenth century, alongside the more "regularised" system of royal justice that was being developed through the exercise of territorialised aristocratic power, whether in the courts of royal officials like the justiciars and the sheriffs or in aristocratic courts. Taylor then seeks to explore the ways in which the more regularised system may have interacted with the older system. In fact, she suggests that "royal justice inserted itself into communal practice" in a rather "limited way", seeking to bolster forms of dispute resolution and proof of claims that could be dealt with in the localities without any real state intervention.[43] Taylor cites the brieve of inquest as having been of particular importance here.[44]

Taking a step back from the detailed and sophisticated argumentation of Sunde and Taylor, does the juxtaposition of their two articles shed any light on the histories – and the legal histories – of Norway and Scotland respectively? What Taylor calls superficial similarities between Norway and Scotland are just that – superficial. Even if more evidence about the operation of the Scottish assemblies, and the work of the Scottish *iudices*, were to

42 Taylor, 'Law and Administrative Change' below, 138.
43 Taylor, 'Law and Administrative Change' below, 146.
44 Taylor's arguments are somewhat reminiscent of those presented in J Wormald, 'Bloodfeud, Kindred and Government in Early Modern Scotland' (1980) 87 *Past and Present* 54–97, particularly at 90.

become available, it seems unlikely that they discharged comparable functions, or even operated in similar ways. In addition, it is true that the kings of Norway and Scotland both acquired more extensive functions as law-givers at roughly the same time, and that these legislative functions had to be negotiated with traditional elites. However, the elites in question were quite different, and – as has been explained already – the use of legislative power as a tool of legal unification (however symbolic) made much greater sense in a Norwegian context than would have done in thirteenth-century Scotland.

If the juxtaposition of the chapters of Sunde and Taylor serve to warn historians about taking superficial similarities too seriously, they also point to interesting questions. In Scotland and in Norway during the thirteenth century, one witnesses older frameworks for the resolution of disputes being supplemented by new administrative and judicial structures; and both frameworks interacted with one another and influenced one another over a long period of time. In addition, in both jurisdictions this interaction was marked by the invocation of both royal authority and the power of local elites in the negotiation of dispute resolution. Both Sunde and Taylor point to the fact that this interaction continued over the course of the fourteenth century and indicate that further research could be conducted to explore the consequences of this dynamic in later centuries.[45] What seems different about the dynamic in Norway, as opposed to Scotland, is the role of the king's sixteen lawmen in enabling royal authority to interact quite directly in determining the outcomes of legal disputes; and this presumably had some sort of effect on the uniformity of the application of the law in practice. In Scotland, Taylor makes the intriguing suggestion that "a vernacular sort of expertise" developed "around common law procedure" and this too may have resulted in some (indeterminate) level of uniformity in the application of the law.[46] Perhaps this informed both the development of Scottish legal literature during the 1300s and also the idea that there existed "a *book of law* for the kingdom of the Scots" by the end of the century.[47] Yet the Norwegian consciousness of precisely *who* had the capacity to maintain a level of legal uniformity after 1274 – the sixteen lawmen – underlines the need for historians of medieval Scots law to pay considerable attention to questions of who might have been

45 Ibbetson suggests that conflict between competing conceptual legal frameworks could cause change for internal legal history; it may be that the arguments made here support this proposition as regards external legal history too. See Ibbetson, 'What is Legal History?' (n 18) 36–40; see also Godfrey, *Civil Justice* (n 22) 449–453.

46 Taylor, 'Law and Administrative Change' below, 136–137.

47 Taylor, 'Law and Administrative Change' below 152.

in a position to develop a common body of expertise concerning common law procedures. Indeed, one would like to know why they might have wanted to do that. Taylor's related work in this regard is groundbreaking, and it is to be hoped that it will continue to shed light on these questions.[48]

This last point may also be recast in a slightly different way. As was explained above, in the past the metaphor of legal transplants has been used to explore the borrowing and adaptation of English legal ideas and institutions in Scotland during the twelfth and thirteenth centuries. MacQueen considered this idea in the course of the concluding remarks of his book *Common Law and Feudal Society in Medieval Scotland*. He noted that Watson thought that the transplantation of legal institutions and rules from one society to another, radically different society, was relatively straightforward, in part because there was no necessary connection between legal and social change. MacQueen noted that even if there was no such necessary connection, many of the legal changes that occurred in Scotland at this time were undoubtedly caused by social, political and economic shifts.[49] However, MacQueen pointed out that "Watson's view encompasses the possibility of external factors playing a role in legal development" and continued by remarking, "[h]is argument is that, even when these factors do operate, they generally operate within the legal culture of the system, which is the principal determinant of the nature of the change".[50] MacQueen then argued that there was no question that Scotland possessed such a legal culture, and that this legal culture was shaped by English influences and by canon law, and that it – more than anything – dominated legal development going forward.[51] Yet if there was such a culture – and if such a culture was connected with the apparent emergence of expertise concerning a procedural Scottish common law – then the question suggested by the Norwegian experience still must be answered. In whose minds did this "legal culture" and this "expertise" exist?[52] Were there Scottish equivalents of the sixteen lawmen in Norway?

48 See, for example, A Taylor, 'What does *Regiam maiestatem* Actually Say (and What Does it Mean)?' in W Eves, J Hudson, I Ivarsen and S B White (eds), *Common Law, Civil Law, and Colonial Law* (n 9) 47–85.

49 MacQueen, *Common Law and Feudal Society* (n 39) 264–267, citing (for example) AWatson, *Slave Law in the Americas* (1989) 1–21; A Watson, 'Legal change: sources of law and legal culture' (1983) 131 *University of Pennsylvania Law Review* 1121.

50 MacQueen, *Common Law and Feudal Society* (n 39) 266.

51 MacQueen, *Common Law and Feudal Society* (n 39) 266.

52 The formulation of this question owes a great deal to conversation with John Ford, but he bears absolutely no responsibility for the manner in which it is articulated here.

(3) Law in the books and legal outcomes in Norwegian and Scottish towns

Some further remarks about the identities of those who may have had responsibility for developing broadly "common" laws for the towns of Norway and Scotland are made in the next two chapters, by Tveit and Simpson respectively.[53] In her article, Tveit begins by considering the Norwegian Code of the Towns, promulgated by Magnus VI in 1276. Originally, this seems to have been enacted as law for Norway's largest town, Bergen but within decades it was adapted for use in the three other large Norwegian towns, these being Niðaros (Trondheim), Oslo and Tunsberg (Tønsberg). Tveit's account of the Code of the Towns shows that some of the laws were lifted from an older written compilation, called *Bjarkeyjarréttr*, but most of the provisions in the Code of the Towns were identical to provisions in the Code of the Realm. The only really distinctive section of the Code of the Towns was the extensive *Bøarskipings balkr*, or "Book of town regulations".[54] Tveit then acknowledges the fact that the limited surviving evidence makes it difficult to establish the extent to which the Code of the Towns was followed in practice. However, her work reveals some of the similarities and differences between the law as stated in the text and the law as applied. For example, the Code of the Towns envisaged a situation whereby "law would be conducted at or by the town assembly, the *mót*, both at regular intervals and ad hoc".[55] However, the functions of the *mót* were largely taken over by the members of the town council – originally made up of twelve men – who generally acted together with an urban lawman in the resolution of disputes. On the other hand, other aspects of the Code of the Towns were observed in practice and seem to have made a difference in practice. For example, crafts involving ovens and the use of fire were moved to the edge of towns, as required by the Code. Town planning regulations in the Code were also generally observed in practice. Tveit also surveys evidence of legally-enforceable agreements, and shows that some of the provisions in these agreements were consistent with provisions in the Code of the Towns. Property transactions in particular seemed to reflect those rules.

53 M J Tveit, 'Urban Legal Procedure in Fourteenth Century Norway' (Chapter Five below in the present volume); A R C Simpson, 'Procedures of the Scottish Common Law in a Medieval Town: A Fresh Look at the 1317 Court Roll of Aberdeen' (Chapter Six below in the present volume).

54 Tveit, 'Urban Legal Procedure' below, 157.

55 Tveit, 'Urban Legal Procedure' below,163.

Simpson pursues similar themes in his chapter.[56] He begins by considering the oldest surviving court roll from a Scottish town, the roll of the burgh courts of Aberdeen dating from 1317. He notes that there are references in that roll to *leges burgorum Scocie*, meaning "laws of the burghs of Scotland", and he considers what that phrase meant to contemporaries. He notes the possibility that they may have had in mind a collection of laws and customs sometimes labelled the "*Leges burgorum Scocie*"; versions of this text survive in a late-thirteenth-century manuscript and in three fourteenth-century manuscripts. However, historians are aware that this text developed significantly over time and that it is difficult to date many of the laws in the text. For this reason in particular, it is not regarded as secure evidence of what the laws of the burghs of Scotland may have been at any particular point in time. Even so, it is possible that the burgh courts of Aberdeen did have in mind a version of the text of the *Leges burgorum Scocie* when it referred to burgh laws of the realm.

In his paper, Simpson considers this possibility. His argument is presented in two stages. First, he suggests that there was some sort of link between the laws of the burghs of Scotland as they were conceptualised in Aberdeen, on the one hand, and the textual *Leges burgorum Scocie*, on the other. However, he suggests that that link calls for further comment. This is because while there are similarities between the *leges burgorum Scocie* attested in Aberdeen, on the one hand, and the textual *Leges burgorum*, on the other, they are also quite different in some important respects. This makes it unlikely that, when the people of Aberdeen referred to the burgh laws of Scotland, they were thinking of the textual *Leges burgorum* and nothing more. The second stage of Simpson's argument seeks to explain this phenomenon. He argues that both the *leges burgorum Scocie* as they were conceptualised in Aberdeen and the textual *Leges burgorum Scocie* are best understood as witnesses of a common law of the burghs of Scotland that fundamentally existed elsewhere. The argument is that

> the common laws of the burghs of Scotland in a real sense existed in the minds of a small group of royal administrators and clerks, headed up by a royal official known as the chamberlain, who supervised the administration of justice within the burghs by proceeding round the country on a progress known as an "ayre".[57]

In reality, it is likely that the merchant burgesses who generally made up the burgh courts of Scotland all had their own different views about

56 Simpson, 'Procedures of the Scottish Common Law' (Chapter Six below in the present volume).
57 Simpson, 'Procedures of the Scottish Common Law' below, 185.

precisely what constituted the common laws of the burghs. In this context, the ayre of the chamberlain and their clerks around all of the burghs of the realm was probably one of the few forces capable of generating some level of uniformity in the application of burgh laws across the kingdom. Simpson suggests that the chamberlain would not have been "working with a blank canvas" in articulating their views of the common burgh laws; the "echoes of the work of his predecessors would presumably have already found their way into burgh practice, and shaped the existing – if discordant – manuscript witnesses to the Scottish burgh laws".[58] In other words,

> [i]f the administrative practice of the chamberlain was the ultimate reference point for the "common" laws of the burghs" then that practice was perhaps "articulated . . . and negotiated with reference to the collective memories of those who operated the burgh courts *and* with reference to the existing manuscript witnesses to the laws.[59]

If this is correct, then the juxtaposition of Simpson's article with that of Tveit perhaps underlines the challenges inherent in any future attempt to compare the town laws of Scotland with those of Norway, or indeed any other jurisdiction. Assuming that Simpson's characterisation of the burgh laws of Scotland is correct, reconstructing them at any given point in time will require significant scholarly effort. One cannot simply take a text of the *Leges burgorum Scocie*, note some superficial similarity with a text in the Norwegian Code of the Realm, and then generate any sort of meaningful information that will actually shed light on the historical development of the law in Scotland or in Norway. One must take the effort to reconstruct the mind-sets of those entrusted with the development of town laws in Scotland – the chamberlain and their clerks – in order to talk sensibly about what the burgh laws of the realm might have been at any given point in time. This might be one reference point when thinking further about what MacQueen calls medieval Scottish "legal culture".[60] Only then will it be possible to conduct a *historical* comparison that has any chance of generating meaningful

58 Simpson, 'Procedures of the Scottish Common Law' below, 204.

59 Simpson, 'Procedures of the Scottish Common Law' below, 204.

60 MacQueen, *Common Law and Feudal Society* (n 39) 266. For illuminating guidance on the sorts of questions one might ask when interrogating the concept of "legal culture", see J Ø Sunde, 'Champagne at the Funeral: An Introduction to Legal Culture' in J Ø Sunde and K E Skodvin (eds), *Rendezvous of European Legal Cultures* (2010) 11–28. For other helpful introductions to the subject written from the perspective of comparative lawyers, see also, for example, R Cotterell, 'Comparative Law and Legal Culture' in Ms Reimann and R Zimmermann (eds), *The Oxford Handbook of Comparative Law*, 2nd edn (2019) 710–33; R Sacco, 'Legal Formants: A Dynamic Approach to Comparative Law' (1991) *Amercian Journal of Comparative Law* 1–34, 343–401.

information about similarities and differences in historical development in Scotland and elsewhere.

Perhaps the same is true of Norway. Norwegian historians do not have the same difficulties as Scottish historians in one sense; they know that there was a moment in the late thirteenth century when there emerged an apparently coherent legislative statement of laws. However, Norwegian historians do have a similar problem when compared to their Scottish counterparts, in that if there were levels of uniformity in the application of the laws in the towns in practice, this still calls for some explanation. In her contribution, Tveit expressed interest in the question of precisely how the Code of the Towns came to be applied in different urban centres across the realm. It seems likely that the royal lawmen mentioned by Sunde in his contribution to this book were highly influential in shaping whatever uniformity emerged in the practical application of law following the promulgation of the Code of the Realm in 1274. Perhaps the same might be said in connection with the extension of practices found in the Code of the Towns from Bergen to Niðaros, Tunsberg and Oslo. If so, then it is possible that a comparison of the work of such royal administrators in Norway with apparent counterparts in Scotland might, in time, be fruitful. It might also provide the necessary "legal cultural" context to make sense of any apparent similarities and differences between individual texts of the Code of the Towns, on the one hand, and the *Leges burgorum Scocie*, on the other. These reflections might also be useful to comparative legal historians thinking about relationships between "law in the books" – such as the laws found in the Code of the Realm and the *Leges burgorum Scocie* – and what Ibbetson calls "legal outcomes", the decisions in actual cases – such as the evidence preserved in the roll of the Aberdeen burgh courts of 1317.[61]

(4) Foundations for early modern comparative discourse: warfare, trade and law

The first six chapters in the book outline the parameters for future comparative discourse between historians and legal historians of Norway and Scotland. The next four chapters seek to achieve similar goals for the early modern period. Chapters Seven and Eight of the book – written by Steve

61 For discussion, see Ibbetson, 'Comparative Legal History' (n 15) 135–143. Ibbetson avoids the use of the phrase "law in action" because he is not talking about "all the ramifications of law in practice"; see Ibbetson, 'Comparative Legal History' (n 15) 135 footnote 14.

Murdoch and Per Norseng respectively – explore aspects of the political and economic contexts within which legal relationships between Norway and Scotland, and Norwegians and the Scots, operated during the sixteenth, seventeenth and eighteenth centuries.[62] Norseng's article in particular provides some of the context necessary for understanding Chapter Nine, written by Søren Koch, which explores the factors that caused a legal framework for North Sea trade between Norway and Scotland (and elsewhere) to fall apart.[63] The tenth and final chapter, by John Ford, is a study of the law and economy of shipwreck in sixteenth century Scotland. The editors have chosen to conclude the book with this essay because in many respects it returns readers to one general theme of this volume – which is to reflect critically on what contemporaries may have meant by "law".[64]

Steve Murdoch's essay reviews "key moments of Scotto-Norwegian interaction, particularly during periods of escalated tension" in order to "test the impact of these events against commercial and migratory patterns to see how, or even if, they impacted in any meaningful way upon relations between the two kingdoms".[65] The first substantive section of his chapter explores the legal and political background to relations between Norway and Scotland; in a sense, it carries on where the chapters by Opsahl and Broun left off. For example, Murdoch explains that the Treaty of Perth continued to be seen as a partial basis for relations between the two nations, in that it was renewed in 1312 and again in 1426. He also notes that Scottish and Norwegian relations changed in 1469, during the period of the Kalmar Union, when Margaret, daughter of Christian I, married James III of Scotland. This resulted in the "Norwegian transfer of Orkney and the Shetland Islands to the Scottish Crown as a pledge for the 4/5ths of Margaret's dowry that remained unpaid".[66] However, the sixteenth century witnessed a decline in relations between

62 S Murdoch, 'War and Peace: Scottish-Norwegian Relations in the Early Modern Period (c. 1520–1707)' (Chapter Seven below in the present volume); P Norseng, 'Traders and Immigrants: A Norwegian perspective on Scottish-Norwegian economic relations from the fifteenth to the early seventeenth century' (Chapter Eight below in the present volume).

63 S Koch, 'Norm and Fact: Timber trade in early modern western Norway (1530–1730)' (Chapter Nine below in the present volume).

64 J D Ford, 'The Law and Economy of Shipwreck in Scotland during the Sixteenth Century' (Chapter Ten below in the present volume).

65 Murdoch, 'War and Peace' below, 212.

66 Murdoch, 'War and Peace' below, 213. This incident should be familiar to Scottish lawyers, as well as historians, who will recall its importance in connection with the debate in *Lord Advocate v University of Aberdeen and Budge* 1963 SC 533. Some will also be fortunate enough to recall the prominence given to the case by the late Professor David Carey Miller in his lectures in property law.

Denmark-Norway and Scotland following internal strife within Scandinavia, in the course of which "Scottish support was split between Christian II and his usurping uncle Frederik I".[67] There followed "numerous cases of maritime predation" and indeed conflicts, but this did not stop population movements from Scotland to Norway; quite the reverse.[68] There was also an attempt to secure rights for Scots in Denmark and Norway and for Danes and Norwegians in Scotland as part of the marriage negotiations between James VI of Scotland and Anna of Denmark in 1589. Relations between the two countries were complicated when James VI succeeded to the throne of England in 1603, in part due to long-standing hostility between England and Denmark-Norway. Murdoch then traces in detail the changing international relations, and associated treaties, between Scotland, England, Denmark-Norway and indeed Sweden over the course of the seventeenth century. Simultaneously, he shows that Scots were actively involved in all sides of the various conflicts within Scandinavia during this period. However, the central point that emerges throughout the essay is that focusing simply on the "spectacular events" of international relations, wars and treaties should not be allowed to obscure remarkable continuities in patterns of trade and population movement between Scotland and Norway during the early modern period. Even particularly violent incidents such as the *Skottetog* or Kringen Massacre of 1612 seem to have had little real impact upon this.

This observation helpfully introduces the two essays that follow, by Norseng and Koch respectively. In his essay, Norseng focuses on "the origins, early development, character, extent, and impact of the Scottish-Norwegian trade relations up to the 1600s".[69] He begins by noting the Scottish demand for Norwegian timber, and the corresponding Norwegian demand for items that the Scots could provide as representatives of "a more advanced mercantile economy with extensive international commercial connections".[70] He then examines the Norwegian primary sources that allow us to explore these matters, including in his work a helpful account of relevant Norwegian and Danish-Norwegian royal privileges, Norwegian court records and customs accounts. Many of these privileges were designed to concentrate trade in particular areas, and in particular in the Norwegian towns. It was, in fact, the timber trade that made it particularly difficult to uphold these privileges in practice, since it was more convenient to ship timber from the locality

67 Murdoch, 'War and Peace' below, 213.
68 Murdoch, 'War and Peace' below, 213.
69 Norseng, 'Traders and Immigrants' below, 233
70 Norseng, 'Traders and Immigrants' below, 233.

of production than first transporting it to a town, a point that Koch considers in his contribution in more detail. Norseng notes that one other major issue that the Norwegian merchant classes faced in the towns was competition from the Hanseatic League; as the fourteenth century progressed, more and more of the trade between Norway and England was taken over by Germans. However, the Germans engaged in less direct trade between Scotland and Norway, leaving more opportunities for merchants from both countries to engage in commerce with one another. Norseng then surveys some of the evidence of individual Scots and Norwegians engaged in the timber trade from the fifteenth century onwards; in so doing, he develops Murdoch's related work on the subject in the present volume. The evidence is richer from the early-sixteenth century; while there were not significant increases in the numbers of Scots settling in Norway in this period, the Scots who came did often settle permanently, and probably disappear as "Scots" from the customs records thereafter. However, Norseng demonstrates that even the abundant evidence of Scottish trading activities in the Norwegian towns does not capture the full picture; Scots were very active in the rural areas too, again in connection with the timber trade. While the Scottish trade was capable of infringing a range of legal privileges, it was sometimes viewed as a means of countering the influence of the powerful Hanseatic League. Undoubtedly, the Germans resented the Scottish control of aspects of Norwegian commerce; by contrast, the re-emerging Norwegian mercantile classes seem to have welcomed it.

The question of what this sort of study of Scottish and Norwegian trade can reveal for legal historians in particular is taken up in Koch's contribution. Koch presents a detailed study of the legal regulation of the timber trade in western Norway between 1530 and 1730. He begins from the proposition that all timber trade was, in principle, supposed to be conducted through major urban centres such as Bergen and Stavanger. However, in practice the timber trade was frequently conducted in such a way as to "avoid the cities" and also often "to evade taxation".[71] Koch's paper is divided into two parts; first, he considers the "lawmakers' attempts to enforce a particular model of trade, and their failure to do so"; and secondly, he considers "some reasons causing the disparity between the normative and the factual".[72] The essence of his argument is that the regulatory framework failed because it failed to consider the economic interests of all parties who were involved in the trade

71 Koch, 'Norm and Fact' below, 272.
72 Koch, 'Norm and Fact' below, 274.

and, in particular, it came to be inconsistent with the interests of the Danish-Norwegian monarchy that was supposed to enforce it.

In exploring the normative framework regulating the timber trade, Koch begins with a decree (*rettarbot*) of Håkon V of 1299, which established Bergen as the proper location for the timber trade in western Norway. No merchant could trade directly with the rural population. Such prohibitions were repeated and extended several times throughout the medieval and the early modern periods. The rationales given for the principle that the timber trade should only operate through Bergen were twofold. The first was that the merchants of Bergen would ensure that the rural populations were not exploited by apparently ruthless foreign traders; and the second was that this arrangement would make it easier for the king to collect taxes connected with the trade. Such rationales were also used to target the timber trade with Scots in particular from the 1540s, when Norwegians were forbidden from trading with Scots "pirates". The prohibition on exporting timber was renewed in 1562 and then partially lifted in 1564, but again this was coupled with an insistence that trade should be conducted through Bergen and Stavanger. Even so, the Scots continued to trade with the countryside.

In 1561, some attempt was made to reconcile "norm and fact", as Koch puts it, in a judgment of a higher Norwegian court convened in Bergen by Erik Rosenkrantz, the Danish-Norwegian royal governor. Four lawmen in Bergen interpreted a relevant decree dating from 1302 and promulgated by Håkon V very narrowly – Koch suggests almost *contra legem* – in such a way as to accommodate direct trade between the Scots and the rural population. The lawmen maintained that the provision restricting trade between foreign merchants and the rural population only applied where the merchants were not prepared to pay official fees and taxes to the state. Koch suggests that while this outcome was not in the interests of the merchants of Bergen, it may have been consistent with royal interests. The crown was probably trying to ensure that it raised some revenue from a trade that was established in practice; legitimising the trade was a way of subjecting it to taxation. Tax posts were built outside Bergen, meaning that the timber trade could continue in the localities and the king could more easily ensure that tax revenues were collected from visiting merchants there. Again, the Bergen merchants protested, but again to little effect; one of their arguments seems to be borne out by other evidence, which is that the uncontrolled timber trade was causing extensive deforestation in western Norway, and consequently threatening the future of the trade itself. In 1661, they had some initial success in restricting the trade between foreign merchants and the rural population. However, the effects on royal taxation were so catastrophic that the older restrictions were finally replaced in 1665 with a rule that the rural population could sell timber to foreign merchants if the citizens of Bergen did not buy a reasonable amount of timber from them at a fair price.

Koch then proceeds to demonstrate the curious fact that the normative order, so often repeated and restated, but so little heeded in practice, was controlled by the Norwegian mercantile elites in part because of their direct influence in the Norwegian *Herredag*, the high council of the realm. Nevertheless, all other groups with an economic interest in the trade – the king, the nobility, the foreign merchants and the rural populations – benefited very little from the normative order. Even if the king gave the merchants of Bergen some support in maintaining the normative order in theory, the practical realities of the trade meant that he had very little interest in enforcing their privileges.

The fourth and final essay concerned with the early modern period, written by John Ford, does not consider a disjunction between a normative framework and practical realities in the same way, but it does deal with differences in what may perhaps be termed two different perceptions of the law of shipwreck in Scotland during the sixteenth century.[73] At the outset, however, Ford's contribution simply considers two different types of evidence. The first consists of "several treatises touching on aspects of the law of shipwreck, written by lawyers in the last quarter of the century"; and it is noted that the writers of this material "tended to draw their information from other books, and may not have provided an accurate account of how wrecks were dealt with in practice".[74] The second consists of "records . . . of litigation relating to the subject, sometimes in burgh courts and sometimes in central courts sitting in Edinburgh".[75] As regards the treatises, Ford begins by considering the works of two writers of the late-sixteenth century, Sir James Balfour of Pittendreich and Sir John Skene of Curriehill. Both attempted to articulate a view of the law of shipwreck through reflection on what were sometimes called the "auld lawes" and, in particular, on a passage in the medieval *Leges forestarum*. Ford considers the rather curious question of why provisions on shipwreck might have ended up in a tract ostensibly concerned with "the

73 Ford, 'Law and Economy of Shipwreck' (Chapter Ten below in the present volume).
74 Ford, 'Law and Economy of Shipwreck' below, 298.
75 Ford, 'Law and Economy of Shipwreck' below, 298.

regulation of activities in forests".[76] He then focuses on the interesting issue of how and why Skene chose to present the rules on shipwreck as an act of Alexander II of Scotland (r. 1214–1249) rather than as part of the *Leges forestarum*. Next, he considers how Scottish jurists sought to make sense of the relevant rules. These provided that if ships were wrecked and any creature from the ship survived and came to the shore, the ship was not to be treated as "wrak". Rather, everything washed ashore was to be preserved by the authorities so that they could be returned to anyone who appeared within a year and a day with lawful title to claim them. If no one claimed the salvaged property within that time, then it passed to the king as "wrak" unless the "wrak" had been granted to someone else. A charter of 1587 granted to the Scottish admiral allowed him to claim one third of the "wrak", and one third of the "wrak" that would have pertained to the king, leaving the remaining third to pass to the finders. This ignored the possibility that the king might already have granted a right to "wrak" – specifically, his third share – to a landowner where the shipwreck came ashore. Ford explores how Scottish jurists used the literature of the learned laws to interpret these rules, and to debate the question of whether or not "wrak" should, in fact, pertain to the king or the admiral. While some jurists defended the practice, others, like Alexander King, used texts drawn from the civil law to argue that the admiral should not take advantage of the misfortunes of others. He "reasoned . . . on the strength of his civilian learning, that the privilege" of laying claim to "wrak" introduced through a corrupt custom should be "allowed to fall into disuse".[77]

Ford then considers how shipwreck was handled in contemporary courts, and notes the frequent use of the action of spuilzie, which was linked in the minds of learned lawyers with the *actio spolii* of canon law. He notes that sometimes those pursued for spuilzie were quite innocent; sometimes what had happened was that the captains of ships wrecked on the shore had made bargains with local dignitaries to help salvage their vessels, in exchange for a third of the goods on board. The local dignitaries would then have dispatched people in their locales to help with the salvage operation, promising them some sort of reward for their effort. Those people then held on to the goods salvaged while waiting for their rewards. Salvage agreements like this are quite regularly attested in the records and Ford notes that there was legal literature on the subject. He comments that:

76 Ford, 'Law and Economy of Shipwreck' below, 299.
77 Ford, 'Law and Economy of Shipwreck' below, 308–309.

> While the people who appeared as litigants or served as judges and jurors in the burgh courts may not have had much familiarity with these or any other written sources, a vague awareness of the provisions they contained may nonetheless have informed a popular belief that rewards ought to be paid to salvors.[78]

Ford develops this theme by considering what the evidence reveals about the attitudes of ordinary people to rights of "wrak" and salvage. He comments that the "claims made in practice to "wrak" did not fit neatly with the written sources referred to by the lawyers in their treatises, although the practice may ultimately have been founded on those sources". There follows the critical point – while "the sources referred to by the lawyers may have come to influence the practice of the courts sitting in the coastal towns" it was "practice itself, or the accepted way of doing things, that was considered obligatory by the people who litigated there".[79] Ford distinguishes two approaches here; for jurists who wrote treatises that dealt with shipwreck there was a tendency to connect the practice of the courts with learned legal literature, and also to attempt to reform practice in the process. This makes considerable sense, given that these jurists tended to conceptualise the law as "a body of learning fashioned through expert debate".[80] By contrast, for lay people, "practice became law when it was established as custom, regardless of how closely it might have accorded with the law written down in the books".[81]

D: CONCLUDING REMARKS

Ford's comments bring the present introductory essay back to a point with which it began. Directly or indirectly, several of the essays in this volume are concerned with the question of how to interpret different uses of the word "law". Ibbetson posed the rhetorical question "What is Legal History a History of?" and answered it with one word: "Law".[82] He then proceeded to show some of the difficulties with that answer, remarking on the need for legal historians to think about law not simply as rules, or rules about rules, but rather as encompassing the conceptual frameworks lawyers use to make connections between rules. Ibbetson's focus was on internal legal history, as was explained above, and this volume is more concerned with

78 Ford, 'Law and Economy of Shipwreck' below, 313.
79 Ford, 'Law and Economy of Shipwreck' below, 319.
80 J D Ford, *Law and Opinion in Scotland during the Seventeenth Century* (2007) 5.
81 Ford, 'Law and Economy of Shipwreck' below, 320.
82 Ibbetson, 'What is Legal History' (n 18) 33.

external legal history. Nevertheless, several of the contributions underline the importance of being alive to the very different ways in which past generations could conceptualise "law". The essays where discussion of this point is most obvious are those of Broun, Simpson and Ford. Broun explores the question of what thirteenth-century Scottish elites might have meant by the "laws" of the kingdom in the Treaty of Perth; Simpson considers what fourteenth-century Aberdonians and Scots more generally might have meant by the laws of the burghs of Scotland; and Ford examines how jurists and lay people could conceptualise the "law" of shipwreck in quite different ways.

The point that past generations could conceptualise law in different ways than we do today is obviously trite. Yet thinking about how they conceptualised the "law" has underlined the importance of identifying in both Scotland and Norway the minds within which ideas and expectations of the law were made operational; and this is underlined and given fresh significance as a result of the comparative historical exercise undertaken here. Opsahl and Broun draw attention to the different types of elites with whom symbolic ideals of legal unity were negotiated in both countries. Sunde's contribution in particular underlines the importance of thinking further about the minds in which "legal culture" and "expertise" existed. This emerges from his discussion of the (at most) sixteen lawmen of the king, who were the people with the capacity to maintain a degree of uniformity in the application of the law following the promulgation of the Code of the Realm in 1274. Their work may also be the key to understanding the apparent success of the Code of the Towns of 1276, as traced in the work of Tveit. Furthermore, thinking about the literature that developed around the procedures of medieval Scots law, as discussed in Taylor's article, does raise the question of which group (or groups) of individuals developed this "expertise", and why. As was explained above, thinking about that question may help to develop MacQueen's insight that medieval Scotland possessed a "legal culture" of its own.[83] It is possible that Simpson's work sheds some light on this sort of problem for the burghs; but much more work needs to be done here, and Taylor's work – for example, on the origins of *Regiam* – is promising in this regard.[84] If there were some individuals, or groups of individuals, who were developing expertise in connection with legal procedures in medieval Scotland, Ford's contribution – which does, of course, deal with a later

83 MacQueen, *Common Law and Feudal Society* (n 39) 266.
84 See, for example, Taylor, 'What does *Regiam maiestatem* Actually Say?' (n 48).

period – reminds us that historians still need to be careful when thinking about the relationship between such expertise and the "law" as practised and understood by lay people. This too may be relevant to a comparison with Norway, where customary expectations of law continued to assert themselves even after the promulgation of the Code of 1274, as both Opsahl and Sunde show in their respective contributions. Understanding as much as possible about the influence of economic and social factors on law, and the interactions of ordinary people with the law in both countries will be necessary in future comparative legal historical work. Expertise can be an instrument for dialogue between society and law, framing the legal culture at any given time. Murdoch and Norseng show the sort of work that needs to be done in this regard; and Koch shows the potential it has to shed light on legal historical questions.

The juxtaposition of related essays on the histories and legal histories of Norway and Scotland here does point to the potential for a comparative discourse with the capacity to generate meaningful information. Such a discourse can throw into relief similarities and differences between comparable developments in both countries, and can offer historians of both Norway and Scotland models for thinking about how to explain those similarities and differences. Further comparative work on the medieval period in particular may well be illuminating. However, the potential for comparative legal historical research into the late-medieval and early modern periods should not be underestimated. The development of conciliar government in Norway prior to the Reformation might bear comparison with the development of conciliar government in Scotland at the same time.[85] This was a period when diplomatic links between the Kalmar Union and Scotland were strong, as shown by both Murdoch and Opsahl. In addition,

85 The literature on the role of the Scottish king's council in government is extensive; for some helpful introductions to the topic, see A L Murray, *The Exchequer and the Crown Revenue of Scotland, 1437–1542* (unpublished PhD thesis, University of Edinburgh, 1961); A L Murray, 'The Lord Clerk Register' (1974) 53 *Scottish Historical Review* 124–156; T Chalmers, *The King's Council, Patronage and the Governance of Scotland* (unpublished PhD thesis, University of Aberdeen, 1982); J Goodare, *The Government of Scotland 1560–1625* (2004) at 113–172 in particular; Godfrey, *Civil Justice* (n 22) 1–160; A Blakeway, 'The Privy Council of James V of Scotland, 1528–1542' (2016) 59 *The Historical Journal* 23–44; K Emond, *The Minority of James V: Scotland in Europe 1513–1528* (2019). For the Norwegian position, see, for example, L Hamre, *Norsk historie frå omlag år 1400* (1968); L Hamre, *Norsk historie 1450–1513* (1971); L Hamre, *Norsk politisk historie 1513–1537* (1998); Y Nielsen: *Det norske Rigsraad* (Kristiania 1880); E Albrectsen: *Fellesskabet bliver til 1380–1536*, bind 1 av *Danmark-Norge 1380–1536* (1997); S Bagge: *Cross & Scepter: Rise of the Scandinavian Kingdoms from the Vikings to the Reformation* (2014).

further rigorous research into the early modern legal cultures of both countries might help to make sense of territories that were strongly influenced by both: the Shetland Isles and the Orkneys.[86] Such questions must wait for future studies.

86 For discussion of this particular point, see, for example, J Ø Sunde, 'A Dubious Tale of Misfortune Revealing the True Nature of Udal Law on Shetland and the Schound Bill – Shetland Law at the Beginning of the Seventeenth Century' in A R C Simpson, S C Styles, A Wilson and E West (eds), *Continuity, Change and Pragmatism in the Law: Essays in Memory of Professor Angelo Forte* (2016) 150–174. See also B Smith, 'Shetland, Scandinavia, Scotland 1300–1700: The Changing Nature of Contract' in G G Simpson (ed), *Scotland and Scandinavia 800–1800* (1990) 25–37; J H Balantyne and B Smith (eds), *Shetland Documents 1580–1611* (1994); G Donaldson (ed), *The Court Book of Shetland 1602–1604* (1991).

PART 1
THE MEDIEVAL PERIOD, CA. 1200–CA. 1500

1 The Treaty of Perth: Union of the realm and the king's law

*Erik Opsahl**

A: INTRODUCTION – THE NORWEGIAN-SCOTTISH STRUGGLE OVER THE ISLANDS IN THE WEST

Every king in medieval Europe wanted to expand their realm. Kings tried to subjugate or conquer new territories and ethnic groups beyond their original core territory. New territories gave kings increased incomes in taxes and other duties from the subjects, together with trading opportunities and potential strategic gains over rivals. In the Norwegian case, the core territory of the kingdom was united during the tenth and eleventh centuries. A king's space of action in "foreign policy" could be affected or decided by the existence of domestic and foreign rivals.[1] The Norwegian kingdom had its

* The article was written while the author was a partner in the project *Social governance through legislation* at the Centre for Advanced Study in Oslo.

1 "Foreign policy" is here used as an analytic term. Halvard Leira has recently criticised medievalists for using the term "foreign policy", claiming that this gave no meaning for royal politics in

interests to the west, towards the territories to which ethnic Norwegians had emigrated; to the north, towards the arctic regions where different ethnic groups lived; to the east where there were disputed border regions with Sweden; and to the south and the Danish border territories.

The Treaty of Perth initiated, or was part of a decisive phase in, what we can call state-building in Norway in the middle ages. This article will discuss this process from the end of the thirteenth century into the first decades of the fourteenth century and then the further development into the late middle ages. The process created a political framework around Norwegian society, this being the Norwegian kingdom with its laws and this became a major catalyst for the emergence of Norwegian identity through the centuries. The Norwegian kingdom, with its laws, became even more important in the fourteenth and especially the fifteenth century when Norway had entered the Scandinavian Kalmar Union (from 1397). Politics, concepts and symbols became important realities when Norway as a political unit came under political pressure from stronger union partners. In a situation like that, Norwegians from different social groups filled political images and symbols with content that meant something for them in their daily lives.

King Håkon IV Håkonsson's reign (1217–1263) was characterised by the final defeat of domestic rivals to the throne and a systematic strengthening of the royal administration in Norway. A new law of royal succession was decided in 1260.[2] Here, an almost automatic hereditary kingship was established. The basic principles of the law were one king, legitimacy and primogeniture. The king also initiated in the same year a revision of the Law of Frostating, one of Norway's regional laws. Furthermore, King Håkon pursued an assertive, even sometimes aggressive foreign policy on several fronts, especially towards Denmark. The most enduring results of this policy were achieved in the west and southwest. Greenland, Iceland, the Faroe Islands, the Orkneys, Shetland, the Hebrides and Man had different social, economic, political, cultural and religious ties to Norway before Håkon IV's reign. All the bishoprics in this area were formally under the archbishopric in Nidaros (Trondheim). While canon law gave the Norwegian archbishop

medieval Europe, in H Leira, *Utenrikspolitikkens opprinnelse* (2020). Leira's criticism, however, misses its mark, because he reveals an insufficent knowledge of medieval policy and political systems.

2 S Bagge, S H Smedsdal and K Helle (eds), *Norske middelalderdokumenter* (1973) 104–111. The law was revised in 1273 and 1302; P A Munch and R Keyser (eds), *Norges gamle Love indtil 1387: Andet Bind* (1848) 24–32 (henceforth NgL, vol II); P A Munch and R Keyser (eds), *Norges gamle Love indtil 1387: Tredie Bind* (1849) No 14, 44–55 (henceforth NgL, vol III).

control over all of these episcopal seats, in practice his authority was quite limited in respect of some of the dioceses. Therefore, the Norwegian king and archbishop could co-operate to obtain a better foothold in the west.[3]

Neither in Greenland nor in Iceland did the Norwegian king have any nearby rivals for supremacy. Due to different factors, both the Greenlanders and the Icelanders swore loyalty to the Norwegian king and crown during 1261–1264. The situation was somewhat different further south. The challenges were more significant because both the Norwegian and Scottish kings sought supremacy in the region. The connections between the Norwegian king and the groups of islands north and west of Scotland differentiated in strength and content. The Faroe Islands and Shetland had the closest ties to Norway. Orkney was greatly incorporated into the Norwegian realm after earl Harald Maddadson's unsuccessful involvement in the Norwegian civil wars at the end of the twelfth century. The earldom survived, the earl thereafter being the Norwegian king's vassal. Nevertheless, the king's actual control over the earl varied. The earl of Orkney had considerable Scottish interests, both in terms of possessions and kinship.

Several of the chieftains both on Man and in the Hebrides carried the title of king, which indicated a looser connection with the Norwegian king, who was more of an overlord.[4] The area's population and culture were more predominantly Gaelic than in the Orkneys. The political situation was very similar to that of Iceland, with an intense and over-complex power struggle between chieftains. A significant difference was that the chieftains could appeal to different foreign monarchs' conflicting interests, first and foremost the Norwegian and Scottish kings' when it came to supremacy. However, even the interests of the English king and Irish princes were involved. All this together made it difficult for a Norwegian monarch to obtain firm and lasting control and supremacy.

The Scottish kings' determined policy to obtain control and supremacy over Scotland's northwest territories and the Hebrides included alliances

3 For a broad and updated review and analysis of the Norwegian king's "*skattlands*" in the middle ages, see S Imsen (ed), *The Norwegian Domination and the Norse World c. 1100–c. 1400* (2010); S Imsen (ed), *Taxes, tributes and tributary lands in the making of the Scandinavian kingdoms in the Middle Ages* (2011); S Imsen (ed), *'Ecclesia Nidrosiensis' and 'Noregs veldi': The role of the Church in the making of Norwegian domination in the Norse World* (2012); S Imsen (ed), *Legislation and State Formation. Norway and its neighbours in the Middle Ages* (2013); S Imsen (ed), *Rex Insularum: The King of Norway and His Skattlands as a Political System c. 1260–c. 1450* (2014).

4 G W S Barrow, *Kingship and Unity: Scotland 1000–1306* (1981) 107–108; see also D Broun's article in this anthology.

with local chieftains and building a fleet. The last was a necessity if the Scots were to control the isles. King Alexander III's (1249–1286) offer to buy the Hebrides was refused by King Håkon IV in 1261.[5] Alexander II (1214–1249) had met with a similar refusal from the Norwegians in the 1240s.[6] The isles were hardly of significant economic interest to the Norwegian kingdom, however, prestige could have played a role. One should consider that Håkon was older and more experienced than Alexander.

Moreover, Håkon's coronation in 1247 gave him the full royal status still denied to Scotland's rulers. Together, these facts might have given Håkon a feeling of superiority to Alexander. Still, besides prestige, strategic considerations motivated King Håkon to act. Scottish control over the Hebrides could threaten the earldom of Orkney. The Norwegian king could only hope to maintain control over the Hebrides if the local chieftains were under his allegiance. The Norwegians could not uphold military control by stationing military troops on the islands permanently, but demonstrating military strength to deter and pacify was something else. Therefore, when the Scots raided the islands in the summer of 1262, King Håkon's response was a major naval campaign. The Scots, however, gained the upper hand by avoiding open sea battles while the Norwegians were not prepared for land war. The Norwegian fleet had to be put into port before winter was coming, in the long run. After the skirmish at Largs in Scotland, King Håkon returned with his fleet to Orkney for the winter. The king became ill and died in Kirkjuvåg (Kirkwall) just before Christmas 1263.[7]

B: THE TREATY OF PERTH

Håkon's successor, King Magnus VI Lawmender (1263–1280) and his counsellors were unwilling to continue the war. The local population was not ready to support the Norwegians militarily, severely undermining Norwegian supremacy. Besides, the English king pushed for Norway and Scotland to

5 F Hødnebø, *Noregs kongesoger.* Bd 4 (1979) 308; A A M Duncan, *Scotland: The Making of the Kingdom: The Edinburgh History of Scotland Volume 1* (1978) 577–584; M Brown, *The Wars of Scotland, 1214–1371* (2004) 80–88.

6 F Hødnebø, *Noregs kongesoger* bd 4 (1979) 241; N Bjørgo, Ø Rian and A Kaartvedt, *Norsk utenrikspolitikks historie bind 1: Selvstendighet og union. Fra middelalderen til 1905* (1995) 72.

7 O G Moseng, E Opsahl, G I Pettersen and E Sandmo, *Norsk historie I 750–1537* (2007) 151–153; S Bagge, *From Viking Stronghold to Christian Kingdom. State Formation in Norway, c.900–1350* (2010) 86–87; E Opsahl, 'Der Schottlandfeldzug 1263 – ein militärischer Weckruf?', in E Oldach and T W Friis (eds), *Staat – Militär – Gesellschaft. Festschrift für Jens E. Olesen zum 65. Gebrurtstag* (2015) 27–50.

make peace because English-Norwegian trade suffered from the war.[8] In the Treaty of Perth of 1266, the king of Norway resigned the Isle of Man and all the Hebrides. The express condition was that the king of Scotland recognised that Orkney and Shetland remained Norwegian. A lump sum of 4,000 marks was to be paid in four yearly instalments and, after that, the annual sum of 100 marks was to be paid in perpetuity. The diocese of Man and the Hebrides was to remain under the archbishop of Nidaros.[9] The recognition of Norwegian supremacy over Orkney and Shetland and that the Western Isles remained under the archbishopric of Nidaros might have made the loss of the Western Isles less significant, because they strengthened the unity of the Norwegian church and what remained of the Norwegian realm. That the connection between the archdiocese of Nidaros and the dioceses north and west of Scotland would be virtually broken during the union monarchy from 1397 could not have been predicted in 1266. The obedience to Nidaros for the dioceses of the Orkney Islands and the Hebrides formally ceased in 1472 when the pope transferred them to the new Scottish archdiocese of St Andrews.[10]

Was the Treaty of Perth a result of "hard facts of geography" or an insufficiency of Norwegian military power? It was the result of neither, in my view. The sea was the most crucial fairway in the middle ages. Without the sea, there would have been no Norway. The Norwegians had few military alternatives to naval forces when it came to the defence of Norwegian supremacy in the Western Isles. The Norwegian king's willingness to resign Man and the Hebrides is better understood due to realistic strategic and political considerations that had the primary goal of consolidating and stabilising the unity of the Norwegian realm. The Treaty of Perth was a boundary stone for the Norwegian realm in the west. The treaty with Scotland, and the oaths of loyalty sworn by the Greenlanders and Icelanders to the Norwegian king, carried with them a consolidation of the Norwegian realm in the area. Greenland, Iceland, Orkney and Shetland became *skattlands*,

8 Bjørgo et al, *Selvstendighet og union* (n 6) 77–81; M Brown has another view on King Henry III of England's interests and position in the conflict, Brown, *The Wars of Scotland* (5) 81–82 and 85. See letter from King Henry III to King Magnus VI from 28 July 1264 in A Bugge (ed), *Norvegicum*, vol XIX (1914) no 276 (henceforth DN).

9 C R Unger and H J Huitfeldt-Kaas (eds), *DN*, vol VIII (1874) no 9 and Bugge (ed), DN, vol XIX (n 8) no 482.

10 S Imsen (ed), *Ecclessia Nidrosiensis 1153–1537; Søkelys på Nidaroskirkens og Nidarosprovinsens historie* (2003); S Imsen (ed), *Rex Insularum; The Norwegian King and His Skattlands as a Political System c. 1260–c. 1450* (2014); S Imsen, 'Nidarosnettverket' (2021) vol 3 *Collegium Medievale* 53–90.

meaning tributary lands/crown dependencies, territories that paid tribute to the Norwegian king, thereby acknowledging his overlordship. The *skattland system* at the end of the thirteenth century resulted from a centuries-long relationship between the Norwegian king and the inhabitants of the *skattlands* where Norse emigration had taken place. Based on an assumption of the common past, the inhabitants were considered the Norwegian king's potential or actual subjects. The system was based on tradition, law, rights and reciprocity and ensured both the king's and the local aristocracy's interests.[11] Here we can see clear parallels to the political culture of medieval Scotland.[12] The fact that the remaining parts of the Norwegian realm after 1266 were more unitary might have enhanced royal control and governance.

C: LEGISLATION AND DETERMINATION OF BORDERS

The Treaty of Perth resulted from King Magnus VI Lawmender's policies, which were characterised by cautious and peaceful foreign policy and strong domestic "state-building". The most prominent result of this state-building was the Norwegian Code of 1274 and the Code of the Norwegian towns of 1276. The laws have been characterised as a culmination of the state-building process in high medieval Norway.[13] Together, they laid the foundations for common legislation for the whole country, which was a rarity in Europe of that time. The Code of 1274 remained in force as Norwegian law, albeit in a Danish translation as Christian IV's Norwegian law from 1604, until Christian V promulgated his Norwegian law from 1687. Both the Code of 1274 and Code of the Towns of 1276 provisions seem to have been implemented quickly and extensively.[14] Historians have criticised this claim because it seems that Norwegian farmers have followed their own customary law in criminal cases in the late middle ages and early modern times. This customary law was quite similar across the country but deviated from the rules of the Code of 1274.[15] This historical critique overlooks the

11 See R B Wærdahl, *The Incorporation and Integration of the King's Tributary Lands in the Norwegian Realm c. 1195–1397*, in the series *The Northern World*, vol 53 (2011).

12 See D Broun's article in this anthology.

13 J Ø Sunde, 'Above the law – Norwegian constitutionalism and the Code of Law of 1274', in J Ø Sunde (ed), *Constitutionalism before 1789. Constitutional arrangements from the High middle Ages to the French Revolution* (2014) 165–185 at 166.

14 Sunde, 'Above the law' (n 13) 166.

15 F Næshagen, 'Folkets rettferdighet. Strafferett i senmiddelalder og tidlig ny tid' (2009) 22 *Collegium Medievale* 128–186.

national law's significance for changing the legal culture in Norway. Legal culture is the experience of community that arises through ideas about, and expectations of, the legislation and how these expectations apply in practice. A legal culture changes because the culture in general and politics change.[16] The Code of 1274 was also designed to function as a starting point that could be adapted locally through case law. The relatively large number of surviving manuscripts of the Code of 1274 also indicate that the Code was widely used.[17] Even in Scotland, there was a distinction between symbolic legal unity and legal unity in practice.[18] While Norway had given more substance to the symbolic idea that there was legal unity across the kingdom, the variation in practice may suggest that the situation did not differ greatly from that which prevailed in Scotland. Another study of the criminal process relating to murder in Norway in the period ca. 1300–1560 supports the view of the Code's flexibility and adaptation to local case law. The conclusion is that the process essentially followed the provisions of the national law and royal ordinances.[19]

At about the same time the Treaty of Perth was agreed, perhaps in 1273, a Norwegian-Swedish commission determined the border between the two kingdoms, from south and north to Norwegian Jemtland (today Swedish Jämtland) and Swedish Ångermanland.[20] Together with the Code of 1274, this border commission can be considered part of a process of establishing unity on different levels. Articulating boundaries and promulgating laws achieved unity on different levels. Large parts of the border between Norway and Sweden had probably been established long before the end of the thirteenth century. The oldest borders between the two kingdoms usually coincide with existing borders between settlements or land properties. When the farmers in a frontier area became loyal to a king or ruler of a kingdom, they probably immediately became interested in raising the old outer boundaries between settlements or landscapes to a border between kingdoms. A national border was the highest in the hierarchy of all borders. Therefore, such a border better protected the farmers' right of use in the field from invaders from outside. The connection between borders and

16 J Ø Sunde, *Speculum regale – rettsspegelen. Ein introduksjon til den norske rettskulturens si historie i eit historisk perspektiv* (2005) 14–26.

17 J Ø Sunde, 'Landslova ut til folket', *Adresseavisen*, 18 November 2015, 31; Sunde, 'Above the law' (n 13) 166.

18 See D Broun's article in this anthology.

19 S Imsen, 'Den gammelnorske drapsprosessen' (2009) 88 *Historisk tidsskrift* 185–229.

20 Munch and Keyser (eds), NgL, vol II (n 2) 489–491.

farmers' rights illustrates the link between borders and law and, in special cases like this, the link is obvious and very strong. Later, national borders could possibly be shifted because of pressure and the use of force by central authorities. Swedish Hälsingland's border with Norwegian Herjedalen (today Swedish Härjedalen) and Jemtland is an example of such a landscape border that was raised to become a part of the Norwegian-Swedish national border in the middle ages. Later, Norwegian pressure may have also pushed this border further east.[21]

Some of the surviving attempts to articulate the borders must date from the first years of the fourteenth century. Many of these accounts of the boundaries had a very firm and metrical character, almost like verses. The explanation for this is probably that the border marks were old and metrically shaped rhymes eased the memory.[22] Even though parts of the border might be older, it was symptomatic of broader trends in contemporary state formation that a more fixed and continuous border was established in the second half of the thirteenth and beginning of the fourteenth centuries. Still, Jemtland was a pronounced border landscape. It was brought under more substantial Norwegian royal control during the thirteenth century. The landscape was also the only mainland territory in the Norwegian realm subjected to the Swedish archbishop of Uppsala, not the archbishop of Nidaros. Jemtland can best be characterised as a skattland – tributary land – due to this and a relatively geographically isolated placement. Considering this and the fact that Isle of Man and the Hebrides remained under the archdiocese of Nidaros after 1266, despite coming under the Scottish crown, lack of ecclesiastical connection was less of a worry for the Norwegian king.

Unlike the southern border, the northern border was not firmly determined in this period. A peace treaty was concluded between Norway and Novgorod in 1326 that regulated their areas of influence on North Calotte. The Norwegian king was left with the actual demarcation. He was to divide the land according to the old boundaries as he would defend them before God.[23] Although there is a discussion about where the boundaries of these

21 O Holm, 'Den norsk-svenska riksgränsens ålder och hävd. En studie av rikssamlingsprocesser och gränsbildning i mellersta Skandinavien' (2003) 16 *Collegium Medievale* 135–237.

22 P Hovda, 'Rigsgrænse (Norge)', in *Kulturhistorisk leksikon for nordisk middelalder fra vikingtid til reformasjonstid*, vol 14 (1969) 210–211. One finds exactly the same on the Scottish isle of Lewis centuries later; A Wilson, A R C Simpson and A L M Wilson, *Scottish Legal History Volume One: 1000–1707* (2017) 91–92.

23 Unger and Huitfeldt-Kaas (eds), DN, vol VIII (n 9) no 80; Munch and Keyser (eds), NgL, vol III (n 2) 152–153.

areas of interest lay and what they fully entailed, there is agreement that there were overlapping spheres of interest between the powers, with different geographical centres of gravity.[24] The borders in the north thus still had a dominant character of "frontiers", that is, floating borders, while the borders in the south increasingly became physically determined borders, "boundaries".[25] At the same time, one must remember that these were not clearly demarcated boundaries in the modern sense. Besides natural boundary markers such as watercourses or lakes, one made use of points in the terrain that were marked with rocks, poles, or the like. The determination of the border was affirmed by farmers from each kingdom, often six from each side. The determination of national borders thus followed the same basic procedures and proceeded on the basis of the same fundamental assumptions as the many determinations of borders between farms known from Norway in the middle ages.[26]

D: LEGISLATION FOR THE NORWEGIAN KING'S DEPENDENCIES OR TRIBUTARY LANDS

The determination of the borders between Norway and Sweden and the Treaty of Perth were effects of the kingdoms in Norway, Sweden and Scotland being strengthened and consolidated. Nevertheless, Norway experienced from this point onwards more domestic stability and peace than the other two kingdoms due to uncontested royal succession and an existing power balance between the king and aristocracy. The Code of 1274 defined the limit of the Norwegian king's authority. To grasp the complexity of the Norwegian king's territorial domains one should distinguish "the kingdom" and "the realm". The Norwegian kingdom was the mainland, while the Norwegian king's realm encompassed the Norwegian kingdom and its dependencies or tributary lands ("*skattlands*"). The law stated that, "[o]nly

24 L I Hansen, 'Chapter 9: The Arctic Dimension of "Norgesveldet"', in S Imsen (ed), *The Norwegian Domination* (2010) 199–228; L I Hansen, 'Chapter 14: Norwegian, Swedish and Russian 'tax lands' in the North', in S Imsen (ed), *Tax, tributes and tributary lands* (2012) 295–330; L I Hansen, 'The successive integration of Hålogaland and Finnmǫrk into the realm of the king of Norway', in S Imsen (ed), *Rex Insularum*, 347–369; M Tveit, 'Chapter 2: The introduction of a law of the realm in northern Norway', in S Imsen (ed), *Legislation and State Formation; Norway and its neighbours in the middle ages* (2013) 41–54.

25 On the difference between "frontiers" and "boundaries", see F Kratochwil, 'Of systems, boundaries, and territoriality; An inquiry into the formation of the state system' (1986–1987) 39 *World politics*, 27–52.

26 E Opsahl and S Sogner, *Norsk innvandringshistorie; I kongenes tid 900–1814*, vol 1 (2003) 43–46; see also H Hovstad, *Gårdsgrenser. Et bosetningshistorisk hjelpemiddel?* (1980).

one person shall be king of the Norwegian king's realm, both domestic and the crown dependencies".[27]

The Norwegian king also demanded income from special royal rights – regalia. The privilege to mint coins was a royal monopoly that could provide income in seigniorage and devaluation. Coin production did not reach a certain extent until Harald Hardrada's reign (1046–1066). However, coin production seems to have been too small to have been among the largest sources of income for the Norwegian king. A modest coin production appears to have been something that the Norwegian and Scottish kingdoms had in common.[28] However, the Scottish coins became more plentiful from 1250 when the Scottish coinage was reformed. Earlier issues seem to have been withdrawn on a large scale and reminted. There was a further recoinage towards the end of Alexander III's reign.[29] In Norway, few coins are preserved, and we have no coins with royal names in the circumscription between King Sverre (1177–1202) and King Magnus VI. King Magnus is considered to be the great reformer of the coinage in the high middle ages. The king's extensive legislative work included several provisions on coins and monetary affairs, which indicates that these were priority tasks for the king. Recent research has also argued that King Magnus' coinage was of considerably greater scope than previously thought. Magnus carried out a comprehensive coin renewal in one of his first years on the throne. He struck two-sided coins of two values with the king's name in the circumscription, probably well into or towards the end of his reign. The direct model or inspiration for Magnus' coinage was England. However, even French coinage might have inspired the Norwegian king. The more plentiful Norwegian coins might have been minted in the last part of King Magnus' reign.[30] Pope Nicholas III (1277–1280) agreed in 1179 that the tithes collected in Norway for aid to the Holy Land should be converted into merchandise sold for silver abroad. The reason was that the Norwegian coin was so bad that it was not accepted abroad.[31] However, the privilege to mint coins cannot have been without importance. The fact that the archbishop had

27 M Rindal and B D Spøeck (eds), *Kong Magnus Lagabøtes landslov: del I* (2018) 176; Munch and Keyser (eds), NgL, vol III (n 2) 25; A Taranger (ed), *Magnus Lagabøters Landslov*, 5th edn (1979) 20.

28 Duncan, *Scotland – The Making of the Kingdom*, 517–518; K Skaare, *Norges mynthistorie Volume 1* (Oslo, 1995).

29 Duncan, *Scotland – The Making of the Kingdom*, 518.

30 S H Gullbekk, *Pengevesenets fremvekst og fall i Norge i middelalderen* (København 2009) 73–83.

31 Chr C A Lange and C R Unger (eds), *DN*, vol I (1849) No 68; Skaare, *Norges mynthistorie*, 76.

been granted mint privilege indicates both the economic and prestige value. King Håkon IV Håkonsson gave the right to the archbishop in the early 1220s and Magnus VI confirmed it in the agreement with the church in 1273 and 1277 (*sættargjerden*).[32]

The archbishop was the head of the other state-like or social power besides the monarchy in Norway as elsewhere in medieval Europe. The clerics constituted one part of the aristocracy. The other part was the secular aristocracy. Even though the clergy primarily constituted a separate group in society with unique functions and privileges, the clergy and secular aristocrats had significant common interests, not least economic ones. The groups also shared some of the same privileges, and they had common interests in protecting or perhaps even expanding them. Furthermore, the groups' members were linked mainly through family ties, as they, to a certain extent, had a common social origin. A clerical career at this time was one opportunity for a son from an aristocratic family. The foremost clergy, archbishops, bishops and abbots were either recruited from the secular aristocracy or became members of it.

The privileged secular aristocracy was still organised in the so-called *hirð* in the second half of the thirteenth century. The *hirð* had initially been the king's retinue or bodyguard.[33] In the latter half of the thirteenth century, however, the *hirð* was first and foremost a nationwide organisation for the country's secular aristocracy. Most of the *hirð's* members did not stay with the king permanently. Instead, they resided in local royal administrative positions or engaged in private activities. In either case, they had a duty to support royal officials in the king's affairs.

Moreover, new features had emerged that pointed to a dissolution of the *hirð* organisation. The *hirð* members were the king's immediate vassals who offered him their allegiance and service, particularly military service, in return for royal protection and other privileges. The *hirð* organisation was divided into different corporations, each with its internal ranking. King Magnus VI Lawmender decided in 1277 that the two highest rank titles should both be given the title of "lords" and also that those with the highest

32 Chr C A Lange and C R Unger (eds), *DN*, vol III (1855) No 1 and Chr C A Lange and C R Unger (eds), *DN*, vol IV (1858) No 64A; Keyser and Munch (eds), NgL, vol II (n 2) 462–467; *Skaare, Norges mynthistorie*, 73 and 76.

33 The word was probably a loanword from Anglo-Saxon, *híréd*, meaning "family", a (great) man's household; J Fritzner, *Ordbog over Det gamle norske Sprog. Første bind*, 4th edn (1973) 820–821; Bosworth Toller's Anglo-Saxon Dictionary online, *híréd*, available at *https://bosworthtoller.com/52556* (last accessed 11 July 2022).

rank, *lendmenn*, should be called "barons" and those with the second highest, *skutilsveiner*, "knights". The Norwegian barons were crown vassals like the English barons. They had fiefs directly from the king. However, the barons in Norway had no power of justice in their estates, in contrast to both Scottish and English barons. In Scotland, the barons stood below the earls, while in Norway, the barons were the highest rank of the higher nobility.[34] The Scottish historian Alexander Grant distinguished five tiers of Scottish nobility before about 1350: earls; "provincial lords"; "greater barons"; barons; and freeholders.[35] The Norwegian barons were never numerous. In 1308 Håkon V Magnusson (1299–1319) banned the appointment of new earls and barons in the future. The king's drastic decision was motivated by his experience of the baronial rule while he and his brother, King Eirik II Magnusson (1280–1299), were children.[36]

Furthermore, the *hirð* organisation dissolved during the first decades of the fourteenth century, probably due to its archaic character. Instead, the Norwegian secular aristocracy was organised following the standards of European chivalry. The ordinary *hirdmenn* had obtained the title "esquires". In order to be considered part of the privileged secular aristocracy, it was necessary first to become the king's vassal, and secondly to render particular types of military service. As in the other two Nordic kingdoms, the late-medieval members of the secular aristocracy were grouped into the two rank classes, i.e. "knights" and "esquires". It was necessary to be a member of this group in order to become a fief holder.[37]

However, legislation and administration varied inside the realm. The Shetland and Faroe Islands got the Norwegian Code of 1274 unchanged, which indicates a high level of integration in the realm. Unity of law was part of a general policy of unity in the Norwegian kingdom in the thirteenth and the first half of the fourteenth century. Brian Smith has argued that Shetland's political system was transformed under Magnus VI Lawmender and his son, Duke Håkon Magnusson, later Håkon V Magnusson. Shetland was part of Duke Håkon's ducal appanage (1280/1284–1299). Duke Håkon/King Håkon V transformed public institutions in Shetland. He and his servants replaced land assessments that had been devised in Orkney with local ones, modelled on a specific system for determining the annual use value of land (*markebol*) of southeastern Norway. The duke also reformed the

34 See Brown, *The Wars of Scotland* (n 5) 92–93.
35 A Grant, 'The development of the Scottish peerage' (1978) 57 *Scottish Historical Review* 1–27.
36 C E Unger and H J Huitfeldt-Kaas (eds), *DN*, vol XI (1884) No 6.
37 Moseng et al, *Norsk historie* I *750–1537* (n 7) 189–198.

taxation, streamlined Shetland's law courts and enforced the Code of 1274. The institutions that Håkon Magnusson reformed or introduced in Shetland nevertheless became peculiarly Shetlandic.[38] This also applies for the so-called *Saudabrevið* – the Sheep Letter – for the Faroe Islands from 1298, which reveals the flexibility and adjustment to regional conditions in the Norwegian king's legislation.[39] The letter made allowances for the nature of the economic life of the islands, which was based on hunting, fishing and sheep-keeping.[40] Legal practice and the country laws of Shetland indicates that the Sheep Letter was also applied there. However, Dauvit Broun, in his contribution to this volume, shows that we are speaking of legal concessions to legal unity of quite a different kind than those the Western Isles enjoyed under Scottish rule at this time.

As we have seen, Orkney was partly incorporated in the realm after 1193–1194 with its earldom and royal official. Nevertheless, due to a lack of sources we do not know enough about how the Code of 1274 and its administration worked in Orkney. The influence of Norwegian kings on local institutions seems to have taken longer to mature than in Shetland.[41] In 1425, Orcadians were begging the union Queen Filippa to guarantee that all officials in Orkney were, among other things, bound by King Olaf's "old laws".[42] We cannot know for sure which "King Olaf" this was. It might refer to St Olaf's old laws. The Code of 1274 speaks of St Olaf's laws in several paragraphs.[43] "King Olaf" might also have been King Olaf IV Håkonsson (1380/1381–1387).[44] Confirmation of current law in the Orkneys might have taken place when Olaf was acclaimed as Norwegian king in 1381 or in the wake of this tribute. During the acclamation in Trondheim in July that year the royal steward, on behalf of the king (then a minor) promised to abide by old law and justice in Jemtland.[45] A similar confirmation might have been

38 B Smith, 'Chapter 5: Hákon Magnusson's root-and-branch reform of public institution in Shetland, c.1300', in S Imsen (ed), *Taxes, tributes and tributary lands* (2005) 103–112.

39 Munch and Keyser (eds), NgL, vol II (n 2) 665–667.

40 S Imsen, 'Chapter 1: Law and justice in the realm of the king of Norway', in S Imsen (ed), *Legislation and State Formation* (2013) 15–40 at 30–31.

41 B Smith, 'Chapter 7: Dull as ditch water or crazily romantic: Scottish historians on Norwegian law in Shetland and Orkney', in S Imsen (ed), *Legislation and State Formation* (2013) 117–131; see also B Crawford, 'The Northern half of the Northern Earldom's lordship; A comparision of Orkney and Shetland', in S Imsen (ed), *Rex Insularum – the king of Norway and his "Skattlands" as a political system c. 1260–c. 1450* (2014) 143–161.

42 C R Unger and H J Huitfeldt-Kaas (eds), *DN*, vol VI (1864) No 423.

43 M Rindal and B D Spørck (eds), *Kong Magnus Lagabøtes landslov: del 1* (2018) 172–175, 186–191, 195–197 and 200–210.

44 Smith, 'Dull as ditch water or crazily romantics' (n 41) 117.

45 C R Unger and H J Huitfeldt-Kaas (eds), *DN*, vol XIV (1895) No 12.

issued for other "*skattlands*", including Orkney. Henrik Sinclair committed himself in his installation charter as Earl of Orkney in 1379, among other things, to defend the inhabitants of Orkney so that they got their rights. If Henrik killed or maimed someone or robbed someone of property within the area, he should stand trial before the king and his advisers and be judged according to the kingdom's laws.[46]

In 1262, the Icelanders had asked the Norwegian king for new Icelandic laws as part of the process of paying homage to and submitting to the Norwegian king. The agreement resulted from a long political process where the Norwegian king wanted to incorporate Iceland into his realm. King Magnus VI Lawmender met the request by sending a new lawbook in 1271. The lawbook has been characterised as an adaption of the two new provincial Gulating and Frostating compilations from 1267 and 1269 to Icelandic conditions, thus containing many features from Norwegian law.[47] Scholars have disagreed upon which of the two provincial compilations was the primary model.[48] The law code, called Járnsiða, was accepted in Iceland in 1271–1273.[49] However, there was dissatisfaction with the lawbook in Iceland and, as part of the introduction of the Code of 1274, Iceland received a new lawbook in 1281, Jónsbok. Therefore, this law book was not a simple copy of the Norwegian Code, but rather a new code of law that was particular for Iceland. However, Jónsbok was based on the Norwegian Code, as can be seen from section to section, chapter to chapter. Although the Icelanders were given many concessions, a large degree of legal unity with Norway was achieved. About 50 per cent of the Code of 1274 can be found in the Icelandic code. The essential elements in the Code of 1274 concerning the crown and judicial matters are found unaltered in the new Icelandic code. Both law reforms were met with heavy resistance, even though Jónsbok has been characterised as, without a doubt, the best-designed code of law within King Magnus VI's whole programme of law reform.[50] That might be the case. However, the Icelanders were not as

46 Chr C A Lange and C R Unger (eds), *DN*, vol II (1852) no 459.

47 A Taranger, *Udsigt over den norske Rets Historie* (1898) 47–48; K Robberstad, *Rettssoga* I (1976) 192.

48 A C Horn, 'Lovrevisjonene til Magnus Håkonsson Lagabøte – en historigrafisk gjennomgang' (2018) vol 110 no 2, *Maal og Minne*, 1–27; E Mundal, 'I kva grad kan forholdet til Island ha påverka den norske lovgjevinga som fører fram til Landslova 1274?', in A C Horn and K A Seip (eds), *Lov og lovgiving i middelalderen* (2020) 67–98.

49 Imsen, 'Law and justice' (n 38) 15–40; see also M M Lárusson, 'Járnsiða', in *Kulturhistorisk leksikon for nordisk middelalder fra vikingtid til reformasjonstid, vol* 7 (1981) 566–568.

50 M M Lárusson, 'Jónsbok', in *Kulturhisotrisk leksikon for nordisk middelalder fra viktingtid til reformasjonstid, vol* 7 (1981) 611–617 at 615.

happy with the legal unity as the king. They asked for, and got more, legal concessions in 1294, 1305 and 1314.[51] Nevertheless, the two law codes, and especially Jónsbok, together with the allegiance sworn to the king of Norway in 1261–1264, constituted the legal basis for the relationship between the Icelanders and the king of Norway. The acclamations of new kings renewed this basis until 1382/1383.[52]

When it comes to Jemtland, there has been a debate whether the region had its own lawbook or received Norse law. Today's dominant view is that Jemtland was under the Norwegian Code at the latest during Håkon V's reign (1299–1319), perhaps as early as in the 1270s.[53] Just as the Faroe Islands received their "Sheep Letter", Jemtland received its royal statute on elk hunting in 1301.[54] It is also worth noticing how King Håkon V clearly defined and claimed the Jemtlanders to be his subjects in the regulation. The king forbade Swedes from conducting hunting or other activities in Jemtland beyond old customs; he exempted from this ruling his "men" in Sweden. King Håkon advocated a principle of reciprocity. Swedes could hunt and do a range of things in Jemtland, corresponding to the Norwegian king's "men", and here must be meant that everyone under his rule was entitled to carry out the same activities in Sweden. It has been claimed that the ordinance allowed elk hunting on skis in Jemtland in contrast to the rest of the Norwegian kingdom. However, elk hunting on skis was not banned in the rest of Norway if it did not take place on other people's property. The Code of 1274 also threatened "men from the east" (Swedes) with the same

51 G Storm (ed), *Norges gamle Love indtil 1387 fjerde bind* (1885) 341–346 and 348–353 (henceforth NgL, vol IV); Lange and Unger (eds), DN, vol II (n 46) No 182.

52 Imsen, 'Law and Justice' (n 40) 30; G Storm (ed), *Islandske Annaler indtil 1578* (1888/1977) 282 and 414; P A Munch, *Det norske Folks Historie; Anden Hovedafdeling. Unionsperioden*. Anden Deel (1863) 245–246; see also Jón Viðar Sigurðsson, 'The making of a 'Skattland: Iceland', in S Imsen (ed), *Rex Insularum – the king of Norway and his "Skattlands" as a political system c. 1260–c. 1450* (2014) 181–225.

53 K Robberstad, 'Jemtland og Magnus Lagabøtes lovbok' (1961) 74 *Tidskrift utgiven av Juridiska Föreningen i Finland* 182–201; Imsen, 'Law and justice' (n 39) 31; M Njåstad, '"Det østre riket". Kongelig administrasjon i Jemtland ca. 1300–1500' (2014) bd 51 *Heimen* 297–306; M Njåstad, '"The eastern realm": the king of Norway and the border province Jemtland', in S Imsen (ed), *Rex Insularum, the king of Norway and his "Skattlands" as a political system c. 1260–c. 1450* (2014) 325–345. Njåstad's use of the term "the eastern realm/det østre riket" on Jemtland, is a traditional misinterpretation of this term, used in the aforementioned royal statute for Jemtland from 1301. However, the term "the eastern realm" refers to "Sweden" in this statute; Robberstad, 'Jemteland og Magnus Lagabøtes lovbok, 188, 193; O Holm, 'Kung Håkon Magnusson och "østra riket" i 1301'; S Bagge and A Nedkvitne (eds), *Regesta Norvegica*, vol III (1983) no 22; see also N Hallan, 'Svar til Nils-Erik Eriksson' (1976) vol 55 *Historisk tidsskrift*, 335–339.

54 A Bugge, Chr Brinchmann (eds), *DN*, vol XVIII (1919) no 2.

punishment as those who lived in the kingdom of Norway if they shot or killed something in the kingdom of Norway. Thus, it can be said that despite the statute's regional traits, it was nevertheless following the provisions of the Code.[55] Therefore, it cannot be said to be much of a deviation from the legal unity achieved.

A new and critical situation for the Norwegian king's rule over Jemtland arose in 1364. Father and son, Magnus VII Eriksson (1319–1355 /1374) and Håkon VI (1355–1380), had ruled both Norway and Sweden together since 1362. However, in February 1364, Albrekt of Meckleburg (1364–1389) was elected Swedish king instead of Magnus and Håkon. Nevertheless, the latter two retained control of parts of western Sweden, and several Swedish nobles remained loyal to them. In the winter of 1365, Magnus and Håkon lost a battle at Gataskogen, near Enköping. Magnus was captured, while Håkon continued the fight from Norway to regain all of Sweden.[56] In this struggle for the dominion of Sweden, King Håkon saw the need to secure his control over the border region Jemtland, which had close connections to Sweden.[57] In August 1364, King Håkon VI, probably as part of the preparations for his and his father's campaign during the coming winter, issued a royal statute with privileges for Jemtland.[58] The king declared that the inhabitants of Jemtland should be under old Norwegian law. There may have been a tendency towards the reception of Swedish law in Jemtland.[59] The king also exempted the Jemtlanders from all supply of soldiers and campaigns under the auspices of the royal army organisation, called *Leidangen*, dating back to the tenth century. But in case he had to mobilise the ordinary people in Norway for military service, the Jemtlanders were to follow the king's men wherever these men went. This arrangement was found useful for both the region (Jemtland) and the Norwegian kingdom. The statute is an example of a general European distinction in the middle ages between almost total

55 O Holm, 'Kung Håkon Magnusson och 'det östra riket' 1301. Kommentar til Magne Njåstad' (2015) 52 *Heimen* 190–192; Munch and Keyser (eds), NgL, vol II (n 2) 143–144; Taranger, *Magnus Lagabøters Landslov* (n 27) 155; M Rindal og B D Spørck (eds), *Kong Magnus Håkonssons Lagabøtes Landslov: Del 2* (2018) 828, note 6831. Due to Njåstad's continuation of the misinterpretation of the term "the eastern kingdom" in the regulation, he also misinterprets the ordinance to be a ban on Norwegians hunting elk in Jemtland; Njåstad, "'Det østre riket'", 301; Njåstad, "'The eastern realm'", 335. Rindal and Spørck (eds), *Kong Magnus Håkonssons Lagabøtes landslov: Del 1* and *Del 2* (n 54).

56 Moseng et al, *Norsk historie I 750–1537* (n 7) 321–327.

57 See N Ahnlund, *Jämtlands och Härjedalens historia. Första delen intill 1537* (1948) 256–261.

58 Unger and Huitfeldt-Kaas (eds), DN, vol XIV (n 45) no 9.

59 See C R Unger and H J Huitfeldt-Kaas (eds), *DN*, vol VI (1864) no 273; E Gunnes and H Kjellberg (eds), *Regesta Norvegica*, vol IV (1979) 843 and 1021.

mobilisation in extreme crises and general army service in "normal" periods. Furthermore, while the statute gives concessions, it assumes the existence of a unified system of Norwegian law, operating within the Norwegian king's realm.

In Europe, the duty of the free man to defend the country existed throughout the middle ages. In Norway, if the enemy was already in the country, a so-called *allmannautbud* or *mann-av-huse utbud* was sent out, mobilising the entire adult male population, which meant that all men had to meet with weapons. Everyone had to provide their own food. Ordinary total mobilisation of the royal army, on the other hand, was the whole or maximum mobilisation of the national royal army organised according to a system with a given number of men, ships and provisions from the individual districts.[60] It may seem somewhat strange that King Håkon in this situation did not order the Jemtlanders to serve in the royal army; but it is necessary to remember that the king's main goal was to maintain the loyalty of the Jemtlanders. If the king's demands were excessive, their loyalty would wane. Håkon, like his predecessors, discovered that the population was not always willing to provide the military service when the king mobilised the army. Moreover, it was said in the ordinance that the guarantees and reliefs which the king gave the Jemtlanders should, in return, make them all the more willing to defend their region against their enemies and those of the king. Håkon declared in his statute that his exemptions were given as a response to good men's requests. These men might have been representatives of Jemtland or royal counsellors who knew the situation and mentality in Jemtland. There was always an element of negotiation between the monarchy and the people in such cases. We saw the same when it came to Iceland. In any case, the Norwegian king used the law to obtain as much political unity as possible within his realm.

E: THE NORWEGIAN REALM IN THE THIRTEENTH AND FOURTEENTH CENTURY

The Treaty of Perth was essential in establishing the borders of the Norwegian realm in the thirteenth and fourteenth centuries. Within its borders, the Norwegian realm was a multi-ethnic community. Nevertheless, not later

60 M Rindal and B D Spøeck (eds), *Kong Magnus Lagabøtes Landslov del I* (2018) 225–231; Munch and Keyser (eds), NgL, vol II (n 2) 35–36; Taranger, *Magnus Lagabøters Landslov* (n 27) 30–31; Moseng et al *Norges historie* I *750–1537* (n 7) 206; E Bull, *Leding* (1920) 153; G A Ersland and T H Holm, *Norsk forsvarshistorie 1, krigsmakt og kongemakt* (2000) 82.

than the first decades of the fourteenth century, all Norse countries in the west and the eastern and northern borderlands of Norway were united by a common code of law, albeit with some regional differences, and a uniform legal system. Common king, law and military organisation (*Leidangen*) generated a Norwegian community inside the kingdom of Norway. However, not everyone in the Norwegian king's realm became or were Norwegians. Instead, there were Icelanders, Faroeses, Shetlanders (*hjaltlendingr*), Orcadians and Jemtlanders. Still, a sense of community existed between Norwegians and the other groups inside the realm, especially in respect of their relations with the outside world. It was fundamental that different laws applied depending on which side of the border one lived. Moving from one side of the border to the other meant going from one area of law to another. Jurisdiction, as well as duties such as tax and military service, followed national borders. The law in force depended on the territory in which one lived. The law did not follow the individual regardless of where they were. For example, as stated in the paragraph mentioned above of the Code of 1274 on elk hunting, it was to be applied "as far east as the kingdom of Norway stands".[61] Medieval people in Norway were fully aware of what boundaries meant for which law applied. For example, the Norwegian knight and royal counsellor, Sigurd Havtoresson, invoked both Norwegian law and the regional law of Värmland in Sweden when he protested against a verdict in Värmland that had deprived him of property in the region.[62]

It is easy to see similarities between the unifying structures in the Norwegian king's realm and the corresponding basic structures in the Scottish king's realm that Dauvit Broun outlines in his contribution. The fundamental legally binding element of the Scottish kingdom was that the royal administration, either directly or through barons and other regional nobles, took place based on the Scottish king's law, which varied from region to region. Although the law from the end of the thirteenth century was more uniform in the Norwegian king's realm than in the Scottish one, the essential factor was the king as the supreme law enforcer in a society. The king gained legitimacy among the population and thus power and influence, because law enforcement was the most crucial form of political power in the middle ages. Europe's great legislator and King Magnus VI Lawmender's contemporary, King Alfonso X of Castile (1252–1284), articulated this basic source for royal

61 Opsahl and Sogner, *Norsk innvandringshistorie* 1 (n 26) 45–46; see also Imsen, 'Law and justice' (n 40). See above (n 55).

62 Chr C A Lange and C R Unger (eds), *DN*, vol III (1855) no 308.

power in his great law code *La Siete Partidas* (ca. 1265), commenting "as the soul resides in man's heart and the body lives and is sustained by it, so justice, which is the life and sustenance of the people, resides in the king".[63] The king was the supreme judge and source of justice. Still, medieval state-building involved establishing judicial procedures, an appeal system and the definition of judicial authority to varying degrees in the various European kingdoms. Even though Norway with its Code of 1274 was an exception in medieval Europe, it was still not the case that kings in kingdoms without such a national code were not a unifying factor, as the Scottish example shows. In the Nordic countries, Denmark can illustrate the same. Although Denmark did not formally receive a nationwide code until 1683, the Danish king gave laws for the whole kingdom in the middle ages and, as in Scotland, the king was the guarantor in the last resort to enforce the law no matter what regional law was involved.[64]

However, the Norwegian Code of Law of 1274 became incredibly decisive when the kingdom entered the union with Denmark and Sweden in 1397, generally referred to as the Union of Kalmar. Norway became the weaker partner compared to Denmark's growing dominance within the union. The Danish-oriented union monarchs emphasised knowing Norwegian law and following it as far as it could be reconciled with their policy of centralisation. However, the Norwegian Code of 1274 gave Norwegians a fundamental cohesive national protection within the union independent of the king. They could and did invoke the Code and Norwegian customs to protect Norwegian independence within the union. The Norwegian political entity was partly upheld by the legal unity within the Norwegian realm.

F: THE UNION OF KALMAR

The Union of Kalmar stated that each kingdom should be ruled by its law. Likewise, the common king was to have the entitlements that belonged to him in each realm, respectively, as Norwegian, Danish and Swedish king. Furthermore, no law from one of the kingdoms was to be introduced in any of the other kingdoms. Outlawry in one kingdom was to mean outlawry in all three kingdoms. The Act declared that the three Scandinavian kingdoms from now on were to be ruled by one king and ruler and therefore be

63 J F O'Callaghan, *Alfonso X, the Justinian of his Age* (2019) 99.

64 See P J Jørgensen, *Dansk Retshistorie* (1947) 33–56; see also H Vogt, *Jyske Lov* (2019) 50–55; C Friisberg, *Kongemagten udfordret. På vej mod et konstitutionelt monarki i Danmark 1241–1340* (2020) 304–308 and 358–360.

regarded as one realm ("*rike*"). However, the fundamental principle behind all the other paragraphs was that the three kingdoms were to be equal and stay independent, with only the king in common. Moreover, the kingdoms agreed to establish a military alliance. An attack on one of the kingdoms was considered an attack on all three kingdoms.[65] Therefore, the Union of Kalmar did not establish *one* Scandinavian kingdom or crown.

On the contrary, the three Scandinavian kingdoms and crowns continued to exist independently even after 1397. Still, they were to be administered by the joint union monarch, as Norwegian monarch in Norway, Danish monarch in Denmark and Swedish monarch in Sweden. This fact constituted the context for all inter-Scandinavian politics in the late middle ages and inside each kingdom. The draft of a new union agreement in the wake of the union crisis of the 1430s shows how embedded was the intention of the aristocracies in the three realms that the union king should rule as the Norwegian king in Norway, the Swedish king in Sweden and the Danish king in Denmark. Here, a paragraph stated that "since there are three kingdoms and the year is counted for 12 months, the king shall make it so that he is four months in each kingdom".[66] One paragraph in the election charter for King Hans (1483–1513) as Norwegian and Danish king, where the intention was that the Swedes were to join later, from 1483, stated "when we [the king] are accepted as Swedish king, we shall stay one year in Sweden, the second year in Denmark and the third in Norway".[67]

Due to the design and material, historians have debated whether or not the Union Act from 1397 became current law; perhaps it was never more than a draft. *Stand der Forschung*, however, is that the Union Act was perceived as valid for how the union was to be organised.[68] In any case, the essential union principles of equivalence, independence and separate laws for the union kingdoms were confirmed and repeated in the Norwegian-Danish Act of Union from 1450 and in all Norwegian election charters (*håndfestning*) for the kings in the period 1449–1524.[69] However,

65 A Taranger (ed), *Norges gamle Love: Anden Række, 1388–1604: Første bind: a* (1912) no 22 (henceforth NgL 2, vol I).

66 Taranger (ed), NgL 2, vol I:a (n 65) no 88.

67 A Blom (ed), *Norges gamle Love: Anden Række, 1388–1604: Tredje bind: 1* (1966) 24–25.

68 A Taranger pointed out that the paragraphs on outlawry and military alliance, demanded a revision of the Norwegian national code; Taranger, *Norges historie*, tredje binds første del, *tidsrummet 1319–1442* (1915) 209.

69 O A Johnsen, O Kolsrud and A Taranger (eds), *Norges gamle Love: Anden Række, 1388–1604: Andet bind: 4* (1934) nos 4, 5 and 21 (henceforth NgL 2, vol II); G A Blom (ed), *Norges gamle Love: Anden Række, 1388–1604* (1966) 3 no 1; H Kjellberg (ed), *Norges gamle Love: Anden Række, 1388–1604: bind 4: 1* (1995) no 93 (henceforth NgL 2, vol IV). The only election charter

the union monarchs violated the original union agreement by conducting a policy that made Denmark the centre of the union and reduced the other two kingdoms' equivalence and independence within the union.[70] Of course, this did not mean that the union kings did not know and consciously use their rights as Norwegian kings and holders of the Norwegian crown. It seems that ratification of older privileges and treaties was issued separately for each kingdom, while future commitments and promises were given collectively for the union. That is why King Erik (1389–1442) renewed solely with the Norwegian Council of the Realm the Hansa privileges in Norway in 1398.[71] Additionally the renewal of the Treaty of Perth in 1426 took place on Norwegian soil in Bergen, and members of the Norwegian Council of the Realm agreed on behalf of King Erik as king of Norway.[72]

This deliberate constitutional practice is also evident when Christian I (1449/1450–1481) pawned Orkney to Scotland in 1468 in a marriage contract with King James III of Scotland. Christian acted as king of Norway, not Denmark, in every decision concerning Orkney's constitutional position. Only at the end of the contract does Christian promise to fulfil the agreement on behalf of himself and his "heirs and successors, kings of Denmark and Norway".[73] However, the last formulation was a consequence of the Act of Union mentioned above between the two kingdoms of 1450. The Act stated a perpetual union between independent, equivalent kingdoms, each governed by its own law and domestic officials. There is no doubt that Christian I acted on behalf of his Norwegian, and not his Danish, crown in 1468. It is disputed whether he consulted his Norwegian Council of the Realm, as the marriage contract claims, or not. The Danish nobleman and historian, Arild Huitfeldt, reproduces the content of the treaty faithfully in his history of Christian I's reign from 1599, stating both that the Norwegian Council of the Realm agreed upon the pawning and also that either King

that did not fully recognise Norway as an equal partner with Denmark in the union was the common Danish-Norwegian election charter for Christian II from 1513; Kjellberg (ed), NgL 2, vol IV: 1 (n 69) no 3.

70 Moseng et al, *Norsk historie* I *750–1537* (n 7) 318–400; S Bagge, *Cross & Scepter: The Rise of the Scandinavian Kingdoms from the Vikings to the Reformation* (2014) 248–289.

71 Chr C A Lange and C R Unger (eds), *DN*, vol V (1861) no 382. The agreement from the negotiation meeting of which the confirmation was a result, however, was issued by King Erik, Queen Margrete and the Councils of State of the three kingdoms on the one hand, and the envoys from the Hanseatic League on the other; Taranger (ed), NgL 2, vol I: a (n 65) 43.

72 C R Unger and H J Huitfeldt-Kaas (eds), *DN*, vol VIII (1874) no 276.

73 J Mooney (ed), *Charters and Records of the City and Royal Burgh of Kirkwall* (1950) 96–109. Despite the treaty text, the editor describes the treaty of 1468 as a treaty "between Denmark and Scotland"; Johnsen et al (ed), NgL 2, vol II: 4 (n 69) no 115.

Christian or his successors, the kings of Norway, were responsible for paying the dowry.[74]

Brian Smith has raised the possibility that Christian I and the Danes conspired with the Scots; perhaps the king never seriously contemplated the redemption of the mortgage.[75] Suppose this is a fact and not a misinterpretation by Smith of how the Danish-Norwegian union functioned. In that case, the king's violation of his obligation as a Norwegian king becomes even more severe. Christian I's Norwegian election charter explicitly stated that the king (as Norwegian king) should not do or negotiate anything concerning the Norwegian crown without the consent of the Norwegian Council of the Realm. Furthermore, the king had promised that he would not pledge or surrender any of the kingdom's castles, fiefs, or revenues, without it being essential and without the consent of the Norwegian Council of the Realm.[76] In short, Danish counsellors had no formal position or authority in the management of the Norwegian crown. In any case, after Christian died in 1481, the Norwegian Council of the Realm complained bitterly that the king had pawned Orkney and (in 1469) Shetland.[77]

The Norwegian Council of the Realm continued to claim, at every royal accession until Norway becamee subdued politically to Denmark in 1537, that the king should demand the restoration of the islands to the Norwegian crown. That this was a Norwegian, not a Danish issue, became evident when Fredrik I (1524–1533) became king of Denmark in 1523 and Norway in 1524. In contrast to King Hans and Christian II (1513–1523), Fredrik had to accept separate electoral charters as king, respectively, in Denmark and Norway. There were a lot of similarities between the two charters, but only the Norwegian charter had the clause concerning Orkney and Shetland.[78] The Norwegian historian Lars Hamre has interpreted this clause as part of the Norwegian Council of the Realm's conscious policy of marking Norway as an independent kingdom and restoring Norway's political independence within the union. Norway had experienced severe setbacks for its autonomy and equality with Denmark during Christian II's reign (1513–1523/1524).[79]

74 A Huitfeldt, *Danmark Riges Krønike. Christian I's Historie* (1977) 189–190.

75 B Smith, 'When did Orkney and Shetland become part of Scotland? A Contribution to the debate' (2011) vol 5 *New Orkney Antiquarian Journal* 45–62 at 47–48.

76 O A Johnsen et al (ed), NgL 2, vol II: 4 (n 69) 6.

77 O A Johnsen et al (ed), NgL 2, vol II: 4 (n 69) 300; no 116.

78 H Kjellberg (ed), NgL 2, vol IV: 1 (n 69) 218.

79 L Hamre, *Norsk politisk historie 1513–1537* (1998) 283. Regarding Christian II's reign and Norway's position within the union, see the commentary on Christian's electoral charter in footnote 69.

The Code of 1274, and the idea of distinctively Norwegian law and custom, came to be the foremost and best defence of Norwegian independence within the union throughout the late middle ages. This was understood at all levels of Norwegian society, including the levels of the political elites, the aristocracy, and the rest of the population. The idea that there was a distinctively Norwegian law also provided a sense of cohension and common discourse between these groups. The national law was increasingly called "St Olaf's law" after the kingdom's patron saint, and St Olaf became the foremost symbol of the Norwegian kingdom and its independence. The Norwegian political culture of the period, and its frame of reference for argumentation, complaints, mobilisation, etc. were generally based on referring to violations of St Olaf's law, whether by the union monarch or foreign officials in the Norwegian administration. The political discourse was also underpinned by a sense that Norwegians had a duty and a right to defend the Code of 1274.[80] The Swedes pursued a similar policy within the union based on their kingdom's constitution, law and traditions, with greater success than the Norwegians. After several temporary breaks with the union, Sweden finally broke out in 1521/1523, and a domestic royal dynasty was re-established under King Gustav Eriksson (Vasa).[81] On the other hand, Norway became politically subdued to Denmark and was deprived of its independence within the union through Christian III's (1536/1537–1559) coup-d'état in 1536–1537; this also brought the Reformation to both Denmark and Norway. Christian III had promised to reduce Norway from its status as a separate kingdom to become a Danish province in line with the original Danish provinces in his Danish electoral charter.[82] However, apart from a few examples shortly after 1536 where the king and his representatives referred to Norway as a "royal land", the monarchs consistently spoke of Norway as a kingdom, both domestically and also to the outside world.[83] According to the Danish

80 E Opsahl, 'Conflict and Alliance. The question of a national kingdom – political attitudes of Norwegian gentry and farmers in the Late Middle Ages' (2008) 33 *Scandinavian Journal of History* 161–182; E Opsahl, 'Nasjonal identitet i middelalderen? Båhuslen som del av et norsk nasjonalt fellesskap i middelalderen', in H Carlsson (ed), *Bohuslän som gränslandskap. Före och efter Roskildefreden* (2013) 11–22; E Opsahl, 'Foreign envoys and resident Norwegians in the Late Middle Ages – a cultural clash?' in S S Hamre (ed), *Foreigners and Outside Influences in Medieval Norway* (2017) 97–110; E Opsahl, 'Norwegian identity in the Late Middle Ages, Regnal or National?' (2017) 51 *Frümittelalterliche Studien* 449–460.

81 L-O Larsson, *Kalmarunionens tid. Från drottning Margareta till Kristian II* (1997).

82 *Samling af danske Kongers Haandfæstninger og andre lignende Acter* (1974) no 19.

83 Ø Rian, 'Why Did Norway Survive as a Kingdom?' (1996) 21 *Scandinavian Journal of History* 49–62; Ø Rian, 'Det norske riket i senmiddelalderen og tidlig ny tid', in *Fritt eller bundet? Det norske rikets selvstendighet gjennom 750 år* (2005) 22 Riksarkivarens skriftserie 19–27;

historian Erling Ladewig Petersen, no integration of Norway into Denmark as a province took place after 1537. Norway was still treated as a separate kingdom but was subject to the Danish Crown.[84] Christian III let himself be hailed as Norwegian king, represented by his son Fredrik (later Fredrik II), in Oslo in 1548. King Christian III instructed his son to promise at the ceremony in Oslo that they would both keep the Norwegians by "St Olaf's and the Kingdom of Norway's Law".[85] The Danish royal historiographer Johannes Pontanus' description of Norway in the first part of his unfinished Danish history from 1631 is characteristic. Here he writes that since Queen Margrethe's time, Norway had been linked to Denmark, but with its own laws and judiciary.[86] The Norwegian legal unity from 1274 was an act of politics and was still a political force 350 years later, contributing to the kingdom's unity.

G: THE CONGLOMERATE STATE

What came out of Christian III's political upheaval was not a Danish "national state". The Oldenburg state, or Denmark-Norway, became a typical European early modern conglomerate or composite state where, as mentioned, the monarch's rights and privileges were a fusion of different parts of the state's traditions, law, customs, and policy. A conglomerate state resulted from a historical process where one dynasty had achieved rule over different kingdoms, provinces and areas that together constituted a state. The state that the Oldenburg dynasty, which was founded by Christian I, reigned over consisted of two kingdoms, Denmark and Norway, the two dukedoms Schleswig and Holstein, and several "lands" or provinces like Gotland, Iceland, Faroe Islands and Greenland (the assertion of a claim to the last territory was essentially a pretence, because the geographic knowledge of Greenland's position had been lost during the late middle ages). One characteristic feature of the central government's domestic policy in such a state was that they were forced to adapt their administration to the provinces' political, cultural and social traditions with historical autonomy, like kingdoms, principalities, etc.[87]

E Opsahl, 'The Norwegian Kingdom in the Middle Ages' (2017) 22 *Quaestiones Medii Aevi Novae* 23–35.

84 E L Petersen, 'Norgesparagrafen i Christian III's håndfæstning 1536. Studier over det 16.århundredes fortolkning' (1973) 12 *Historisk Tidsskrift* 393–460 (Danish).

85 O A Johnsen (ed), *Aktstykker til de norske stændermøders historie 1548–1661*, vol 1 (1929) 12.

86 K Skovgaard-Petersen, *Historiography at the Court of Christian IV* (2002) 221.

87 E Opsahl, 'From state elite to regional elite. The political strategies and agency of the Norwegian nobility in the Oldenburg conglomerate state 1537–1661', in K Dørum, M Hallenberg and

When Norwegian independence and Royal Council disappeared after 1537, it is, of course, true that the Norwegians became subjected to the same authority as the Danish people, the crown of Denmark.[88] However, the kings continued to act as kings of two kingdoms, the two admittedly "being incorporated", and administrating two crowns. However, the political reservoir that the Norwegian kingdom had built up over the centuries as a political unit gave the Oldenburg monarchs a different foreign policy platform than if they had only been kings of Denmark. The kings based their dialogue with their Norwegian subjects on the rights of the Norwegian crown. King Fredrik II (1559–1588) proclaimed after the Nordic Seven Years' War (1563–1570) that the Swedish occupied territories such as Jemtland and Herjedalen were to be handed over to him and the Norwegian crown, according to the peace treaty.[89] Both King Fredrik III (1648–1665) and the viceroy in Norway, Hannibal Sehested, adopted the same agitative approach towards the inhabitants of the two Norwegian border areas, Idre and Serna (today Särna), and Swedish authorities, that the regions belonged to the Norwegian crown. The Swedes had occupied them during Torstensson War (in Norway called Hannibal's War after the viceroy Hannibal Sehested) of 1643–1645, and the Swedes refused to hand them over to Norway after the end of the war.[90] The king also pleaded the rights of the Norwegian crown to secure his interest in foreign policy, as Christian IV (1588–1648) did when he defended his control over Finnmark, the northernmost part of Norway.[91] In 1751, a treaty was entered, not between "Denmark" and Sweden, but between the king of Denmark and Norway and the king of Sweden. The treaty established the border between the kingdoms of Norway and Sweden. As part of the agreement, the Sami, who used both Norwegian and Swedish territory, were to choose whether they were "Norwegian" (not "Danish") or "Swedish subjects".[92]

Terminology and the Norwegians' demands towards the regime also point out that Norway was still a political, territorial unit within the conglomerate

K Katajala (eds), *Bringing the People back in. State Building from below in the Nordic Countries ca. 1500–1800* (2021) 183–198.

88 L Jespersen, 'The Constitutional and Administrative Situation' in L Jespersen (ed), *A Revolution from Above? The Power State of the 16th and 17th Century Scandinavia* (2000) 31–90.

89 C C A Lange (ed), *Norske Rigs-Registranter*, vol 1 (1861) 679.

90 See E Opsahl, '"Norge [. . .] thette rige som vort federne rige og land". Norsk identitet i Lydriketida (1537–1660)?' (2002) 81 *Historisk tidsskrift* 99–118 (Norwegian). Both areas remained Swedish despite Danish-Norwegians protests.

91 Bjørgo et al, *Selvstendighet og union* (n 6) 156–161.

92 *The Treaties of Norway 1661–1966*, 1, *1661–1944* (Oslo 1967) 8–22, especially 14; see also *Major Peter Schnitlers grenseeksaminasjonsprotokoller 1742–1745*, I–III (1929–1985).

state after 1537. Norwegians, first and foremost the nobility and increasingly the clergy and bourgeoisie, formed claims on behalf of the kingdom of Norway and the Norwegian society based on a view of a state community built on the union between Norway and Denmark, not that Norway was integrated into Denmark. From the Norwegian perspective, the kingdoms were incorporated.

Orkney and Shetland were subject to the Oldenburg monarch's Norwegian crown, heritage and rights. The demand in every Danish electoral charter after 1524, where the king was elected as monarch both over Denmark and Norway, to redeem Orkney and Shetland, was a logical result of this "incorporation" of the two kingdoms.[93] That Christian III already had this clause in his electoral charter from 1536 directly resulted from the same charter's announcement of the cessation of Norway's political independence.[94] But again, Christian III adopted a different stance towards the Norwegians. The king ordered his men, who were to secure control of Norway in 1537, to send out a proclamation that they were to post in central places in the "kingdom of Norway" to make known the reasons why the king had gone to war to secure dominion over Norway. The proclamation was to have apparent propagandistic features containing reasonably substantial distortions of the course of events, especially regarding the king's succession and path to the throne. The promise from the charter to turn Norway into a Danish province was not mentioned, nor was it discussed in other letters the king sent to his men in Norway in 1537. King Christian III presented himself as a rightful king of Norway, partly by right of inheritance and partly by the election to king in the other union kingdom, Denmark, and – according to what he claimed – subsequent acceptance and election in Norway.[95]

Nevertheless, no matter how much the Oldenburg dynasty played on Norwegian constitutional law and constitutional custom to legitimise the rule of Norway, it was ultimately political and military power that was behind the state upheaval in 1536–1537. Characteristically, however, the Oldenburg regime tried to attire the real power-political conditions in a juridically acceptable costume. Christian IV's Norwegian Code from 1604, a Danish translation and revision of Magnus Lawmender's Code of 1274, stated that Norway was a separate kingdom and the Oldenburg king was the Norwegian king. The law justified the Danish-Norwegian union with

93 *Danske Kongers Haandfæstninger*, nos 19, 22, 24, and 27 (n 82) Norwegian law was actually applied in Shetland and Orkney all the way to 1611; see D Braun's contribution.

94 *Danske Kongers Haandfæstninger* (n 82) 86.

95 C R Unger and H J Huitfeldt-Kaas (eds), *DN*, vol XII (1888) no 378.

Queen Margrethe's joint rule of the kingdoms and the Norwegian-Danish Act of Union from 1450. At the same time, the Code established Denmark's and the Danes' political precedence within the union: "And which lord and prince, Denmark's Council of the Realm, nobility, and estates, is elected king of Denmark, he shall also be king in Norway, and be hailed there as in Denmark".[96] This Danish precedence was a blatant violation of the Act of Union from 1450, to which the same law referred. Nevertheless, it was the power-based political reality within the union until the introduction of autocracy in 1660–1661 when the two kingdoms were formally equated under the autocratic king.[97]

H: CONCLUDING REMARKS

The embryo of the Norwegian kingdom goes back to the late-ninth and early-tenth centuries. Nevertheless, the Treaty of Perth initiated or was part of a decisive phase in what we can call state-building in Norway in the middle ages. In the decades that followed, from the end of the thirteenth century into the first half of the fourteenth century, the borders of the Norwegian kingdom and the Norwegian king's whole realm were more clearly delimited through demarcation of boundaries with neighbouring powers and through the introduction of unified legislation for the entire realm. This process created a political framework for Norwegian society; there was a Norwegian kingdom with its own laws. This framework became the primary platform for Norwegians through the centuries until today, whether Norway was the centre in a larger political community or a subordinate peripheral part of a conglomerate state. It has been claimed that it is almost insignificant whether Norway remained a separate kingdom after 1537 or not. Such a view neglects the realities that the sources from the period testify to, in my opinion. Furthermore, as Øystein Rian has rightly pointed out, in politics, concepts and symbols can become important realities when someone in a particular situation can fill them with content.[98] The law was a fundamental foundation for the coherence of this historic community. Even during the autocracy 1660–1814 when the centralisation and unification of the state were at its strongest, Norway got its lawbook, which replaced the old Code of 1274, Christian V's Norwegian Law, in 1687, four years after the

96 *Kong Christian den fjerdes Norske Lovbog af 1604* (1981) 22.

97 *Kong Christian den femtes Norske Lov 15de April 1687 med Kongeloven 1665* (1982) 286–295.

98 Rian, 'Why Did Norway Survive as a Kingdom?' (n 83) 62.

corresponding law for Denmark, Christian V's Danish Law.[99] Perhaps more than anything else, the idea that there was a distinctive Norwegian law sustained a separate Norwegian identity long after the eclipse and indeed destruction of the realm's medieval political institutions.

99 *Christian den Femte's Norske Lov*; see also *Forarbeiderne til Kong Christian den Femtes norske lov af 15 April 1687* (1887).

2 The Treaty of Perth: Union of the realm and the laws of the kingdom

Dauvit Broun[*]

A: INTRODUCTION

In a "final agreement" between King Magnus Håkonsson and Alexander III, concluded on 2 July 1266 at the Dominican house at Perth, the king of Norway ceded Man and the islands around Scotland's west coast to the king of Scots for a sum of money, while explicitly retaining Orkney and Shetland.[1] In the Chronicle of Man a scribe not long afterwards noted tersely that "the kingdom of Man and the Isles was transferred to Alexander king of Scots".[2] The last king of Man and the Isles, King Magnus, son of Ólaf, had

* Latin quotations from editions and manuscripts have been standardised with *e* for *æ*, *i* rather than *j*, *u* for *v*, and minimal punctuation. I am very grateful to Alice Taylor and Jo Tucker for reading a draft of this chapter and for their very helpful comments and corrections, and for the very helpful feedback and suggestions of the editors. All errors and oversights are my own.

1 See below, 72–3, for editions and copies of the text. For a recent commentary, see N H Reid, *Alexander III 1249–1286: First Among Equals* (2019) 191–197.

2 *Translatum est regnum Mannie et Insularum ad Alexandrum regem Scottorum*: London, British Library Cotton MS Julius A. VII, f.49v, available at *http://www.bl.uk/manuscripts/Viewer.aspx?ref=cotton_ms_julius_a_vii_f049v* (last accessed 8 August 2022). This sentence appears to have been added in a contemporary hand as part of a series of piecemeal entries relating to events in 1257, 1263, 1265, 1266 and 1274 added to what was then the last page of the Chronicle (but not the manuscript: the Chronicle was originally accompanied by an account of the bishops of Man and the Isles). The most recent edition is G Broderick (ed and tr), *Cronica Regum*

died eight months earlier. Alexander was not the new king of Man and the Isles, however; neither was he the kingdom's overlord, as the king of Norway had been. He was ruling the Isles as part of his own kingdom. This has been seen from a modern perspective as the moment when (to quote Keith Stringer), Alexander III "effectively secured Scotland's identity as a unitary state by bringing nearly all its inhabitants and territories under his sole and undisputed authority".[3] This paper will take a different approach and explore what the Treaty of Perth might have meant to the Scottish ruling elite at the time in terms of the kingdom's unity and identity. As such, the Treaty will be regarded first and foremost as a source; not for what actually happened in practice when Man and the Isles were incorporated into the Scottish kingdom, but for what was envisaged at the time. This complements Erik Opsahl's chapter not only by viewing the Treaty from the perspective of Scottish history, but by tackling the issue of the unity and identity of the realm according to what was imagined about the kingdom's past and its laws rather than its actual political and constitutional development.[4] This is partly a reflection of the disparity of material at a Scottish historian's disposal compared to their Norwegian counterpart. It is also possible because our understanding of the development of the Scottish state in this period has recently been transformed by Alice Taylor's seminal book.[5]

The discussion of the Treaty of Perth in this chapter will hinge on a particular passage relating to the observance of the laws and customs of the kingdom. This will lead ultimately to a consideration of the nature of the relationship between the kingdom's laws and medieval Scottish identity (particularly in the thirteenth century) – a topic discussed perceptively and authoritatively by Hector MacQueen over twenty-five years ago.[6] MacQueen was concerned to show that law was a core aspect of Scotland's identity as a territory and people, and was more than just a "defensive badge": for MacQueen this was exemplified when the Western Isles became part of the realm.[7] What follows is an attempt to take MacQueen's insights further

Mannie et Insularum: Chronicles of the Kings of Man and the Isles, 2nd edn (1995). Each page corresponds to a page in the manuscript, identified by its folio number, recto and verso.

3 K J Stringer, 'The emergence of a nation-state, 1100–1300', in J Wormald (ed), *Scotland: a History* (2005) 38–68, at 49–50.

4 For a reading of the treaty in relation to Scotland's constitutional development, see especially Reid, *Alexander III* (n 1) 197, 292–293.

5 A Taylor, *The Shape of the State in Medieval Scotland, 1124–1290* (2016).

6 H L MacQueen, '*Regiam Majestatem*, Scots law and national identity' (1995) 74 *Scottish Historical Review* 1–25.

7 MacQueen, '*Regiam Majestatem*' (n 6) 3–13, esp. 9–10, 13 (responding in particular to A Harding, '*Regiam Majestatem* among medieval lawbooks' (1984) 29 *Juridical Review*, new series, 97–111,

by delving deeper into patterns of thinking at the time about law and the kingdom's identity: as such it can best be seen as accompanying MacQueen's discussion by providing a different approach and ultimate destination. It will be suggested that a simple sense of the kingdom as a jurisdiction from its ancient beginnings, rather than Scottish common law as such, holds the key to understanding the relationship between law and identity. Seen in this light, the kingdom's laws, although more significant than a badge or symbol, were essentially an idea rather than a reality rooted in practice and procedure. As a result, it can be asked whether a basic sense of the kingdom as a jurisdiction could have arisen simply from a general experience of royal authority through judicial fora ranging from local baronial courts to kingdom-wide assemblies, and could have inspired attempts to provide "connected or structured accounts of the law"[8] and to increase the role of the king in law-making, rather than the other way round.[9] The paper will finish by considering briefly whether it would have been conceivable for a king of Scots in the thirteenth century to commission an authoritative written statement of the kingdom's law as King Magnus the Lawmender did in Norway in 1274.

Instead of setting the scene by describing the kingdom's political and institutional development, it will be more relevant to consider how the kingship was perceived by those at the heart of government, and potentially by the elite generally. The early part of Alexander III's reign (1249–1286) saw key innovations in developing a sense of the Scottish kingdom as an ancient independent realm whose authority touched the livelihoods of its inhabitants. In the 1250s there was an ambitious reform of the coinage, with mints established across the realm in a way that was not to be repeated for the rest of the middle ages.[10] By at least the 1230s Scotland had become integrated into a currency zone dominated by English coin: certainly English coin is prevalent in Scottish hoards and stray finds datable to the mid-thirteenth

who argued that *Regiam*, written in the second half of Robert I's reign (1306–1329), was a symbolic assertion of the kingdom's independence fuelled by the experience of Edward I's overlordship and conquest and the continuing threat from Edward II.

8 MacQueen, '*Regiam Majestatem*' (n 6) 2.

9 Contrast with S Reynolds, *Kingdoms and Communities in Western Europe 900–1300*, 2nd edn (1997) 261: "being under a single law meant being a people", and also MacQueen's citation of Reynolds on this same point (MacQueen, '*Regiam Majestatem*' (n 6) 2; note also 7 n 21).

10 Taylor, *The Shape of the State* (n 5) 390–394; for mints from c. 1136 to the reign of Mary I (1542–1567) see the table at I H Stewart, *The Scottish Coinage*, rev. edn with supplement (1967) 167. (An up-to-date discussion of the identification of locations is given in Taylor, *The Shape of the State* (n 5) 393. Sixteen mints have been identified for the type of penny introduced in 1250: it continued to be coined until 1280 (see *ibid.*, 391, Table 6.5).)

century.[11] If so, it may be guessed that the expansion of mints was not simply for economic or practical reasons, but represented a concerted attempt to increase the chances that the silver pennies in the pockets of the kingdom's inhabitants, wherever they may be, were more likely to bear the head of their king rather than that of a foreign ruler.[12] In the 1260s it is likely that the first full-scale narrative of the kingdom's history from its ancient origins was written, probably by Richard Vairement: he had been chancellor to Marie de Coucy, Alexander III's mother, and was a member of the royal chapel at St Andrews.[13] The most daring innovation was in Alexander III's inauguration itself in 1249. It has been suggested that the ceremony was adapted on that occasion to represent the seven-year-old Alexander as not only king by God alone – enthroned at a cross in the cemetery rather than on the moot hill – but also as the Lord's anointed, with all the assembled notables casting their cloaks at the boy-king's feet as if he were King Jehu in the Book of Kings.[14]

To some extent these innovations were but a passing phase. The number of mints was reduced for Alexander III's second coinage in 1280.[15] Vairement's history does not survive as such: it appears, however, to have been expanded into a history of the kingdom datable to between 1320 and (probably) the 1370s, which, although also largely lost, formed the basis of John of Fordun's history, datable to the mid-1380s.[16] The refashioning of the royal inaugura-

11 The evidence is assembled and discussed in M Allen, 'The first Sterling Area' (2017) 70 *Economic History Review* 79–100, at 84. It was presumably in recognition of this reality that the new Scottish coinage in the 1250s was based on an English design introduced a few years earlier. This suggests that English coinage was so prevalent that Scottish coinage had to look the same in order not to disturb establish patterns of currency usage in Scotland.

12 See also Taylor, *The Shape of the State* (n 5) 393, who suggests that this was only "a short-term measure to indicate the presence of the new young king in the further reaches of the kingdom rather than to establish new permanent mints in all places".

13 D Broun, *Scottish Independence and the Idea of Britain from the Picts to Alexander III* (2007) 252–260. For Richard Vairement, see D E R Watt, *A Biographical Dictionary of Scottish Graduates to A.D. 1410* (1977) 559–560; G W S Barrow, *The Kingdom of the Scots. Government, Church and Society from the Eleventh to the Fourteenth Century*, 2nd edn (2003) 192–193.

14 2 Kings 9: 12–13 (a reference I owe to Walter Ullmann); see also J Cooper, *Four Scottish Coronations* (1902) 9; and more fully Broun, *Scottish Independence* (n 13) 179–182.

15 Nine mints have been identified in Phase I: Taylor, *The Shape of the State* (n 5) 392, Table 6.5 and n 245. Even so, far more places were used than prior to the 1250s, as emphasised in *ibid.*, 394; note also the suggestion (*ibid.*, 393) that many mints in the 1250s may only have been intended to be temporary. The coinage of 1280 was also of a significantly higher quality and (in terms of monetary growth) has been described as "outstanding" (N Mayhew, 'Alexander III – a silver age? An essay in Scottish medieval economic history', in N Reid, *Scotland in the Reign of Alexander III 1249–1286* (1990) 53–73, at 63).

16 Broun, *Scottish Independence* (n 13), 215–229, 260–262. The dating to 1285 suggested there is flawed: see D Broun, 'A Scottish perspective on the emergence of medieval "national" history: histories of the Scottish kingdom in the mid-fourteenth century' (forthcoming).

tion ceremony was followed in 1251 by an unsuccessful request to the pope for coronation and anointment.[17] At the end of the decade Alexander III appears to have had to make do with papal recognition of the kingdom's independence on parchment only, without the enduring and unambiguous symbols of crown and unction[18]: the rite of coronation and anointment was not requested again until near the end of Robert I's reign, and was finally granted on 13 June 1329, six days after his death.[19] The ambition for their kingdom of those at the heart of Scottish kingship in the first decades of Alexander III's reign is notable, however.

There is no indication that Alexander III or those close to him had any plans to reform or renew the kingdom's laws. Alice Taylor refers to the "Alexandrian leap forward in the late 1220s–1250s", witnessed for example in the greater availability of royal written instructions in a legal context; she has also highlighted changes in record-keeping attributable to early in Alexander III's reign. By the 1250s and 1260s, however, these developments were largely responsive rather than proactive in nature.[20] She has also emphasised that, although these changes were cumulatively transformative, they had little "structural impact": in general, "the institutions of royal government developed with and alongside the jurisdictional powers that kings expected aristocrats to exercise in their own lands".[21] Although the Treaty of

17 A A M Duncan, *The Kingship of the Scots 842–1292: Succession and Independence* (2002) 151–152; M Bloch, 'An unknown testimony on the history of coronation in Scotland' (1925–1926) 23 *Scottish Historical Review* 105–106. On this and earlier requests, see also Broun, *Scottish Independence* (n 13) 15–18, 180–182, 203–204.

18 Unfortunately, the royal archive does not survive, but in an inventory of bulls and other documents kept in the treasury at Edinburgh in 1282 mentions a "bull of Innocent IV on the protection and confirmation of the king's and kingdom's rights and liberties" and a "similar bull of Alexander IV" (1254–1261, Innocent IV's successor) (*Item bulla Innocentii quarti de proteccione et confirmacione iurium et libertatum regis et regni. Item similis bulla Alexandri quarti*): T Thomson and C Innes (eds), *The Acts of the Parliaments of Scotland* [*APS*], vol. i *A.D. MCXXIV–A.D. MCCCCXXIII* (1844) 107. These could refer to a recognition of the kingdom's independence: certainly in 1251 Innocent IV was prepared on that basis to rebuff a request from Henry III of England to collect a papal levy in Scotland (see Broun, *Scottish Independence* (n 13) 182).

19 C Innes (ed), *Facsimiles of the National Manuscripts of Scotland*, 3 parts (1867–1871) ii, no.xxx; it is translated into English in Cooper, *Four Scottish Coronations* (n 14) 47–49. The only king of Scots not to be crowned and anointed thereafter was Edward Balliol in 1332: he recognised Edward III of England as overlord of Scotland, in opposition to Robert I's son, David II, who was crowned and anointed in 1331.

20 Taylor, *The Shape of the State* (n 5) chs 5 and 7.

21 Taylor, *The Shape of the State* (n 5) 436, 455. For another recent discussion, with a slightly different emphasis, see K J Stringer, 'Law, governance and jurisdiction', in K J Stringer and A Winchester (eds), *Northern England and Southern Scotland in the Central Middle Ages* (2017) 87–136.

Perth can be read in the context of a period of innovation, therefore, this was largely limited to the kingship's status expressed in symbols and imagined histories.[22]

Crown and unction, and the kingdom's ancient past are likely to have mattered not only to those at the heart of government but also to the kingdom's elite generally, especially as – to quote Alice Taylor – "aristocratic power . . . was explicitly built into the structures of royal government, itself growing through and with the power of aristocrats".[23] This would also have been reinforced by personal familiarity. The size of the ruling elite at its greatest extent can be gauged by the number who are named as acknowledging Alexander III's granddaughter, Margaret, as his heir in a document dated 5 February 1284.[24] Thirty-eight "barons of the Scottish kingdom" are listed, ranging geographically from Magnus, earl of Caithness and Orkney, and William, earl of Sutherland, in the north, to Aonghas mac Dòmhnaill, lord of Islay, and Alan mac Ruaidrí, lord of Garmoran, in the north-west, and Robert Bruce, lord of Annandale, and his son, Robert, earl of Carrick, in the south-west. A similar number of bishops and monastic leaders would bring the total to around eighty. All in all, this was not so large a group as to prevent a level of intimacy when a significant number gathered together on royal occasions – all the more so for those who attended regularly. Each would, in turn, have stood at the apex of followers, family and other relationships.

Intimacy can, of course, breed competition and rivalry rather than solidarity. This does not, however, diminish the potential for the ruling elite to have identified with the kingdom both individually – by seeing their own local power as manifestations of royal authority – and collectively, by gathering regularly to collaborate in governing the kingdom as a whole. A particularly poignant instance of identification with the kingship, seen

22 In the only discussion specifically of the law in Alexander III's reign, H L MacQueen, 'Scots law under Alexander III', in N H Reid, *Scotland in the Reign of Alexander III 1249–1286* (1990) 74–102, written when a key scholarly concern was the relationship between incoming and earlier ("Celtic") law, it is concluded (at 95) that "the process of eliminating these archaic features from the legal mainstream, as opposed to adapting and amending them, had barely begun under Alexander III".

23 Taylor, *The Shape of the State* (n 5) 446: she shows that, as far as the administration of justice was concerned, this interdependence was made explicit in Alexander II's legislation.

24 T Rymer (ed), *Fœdera, Conventiones, Literæ, et Cujuscunque Generis Acta Publica*, 20 vols (1704–1735) vol ii (1705) 266–267; Record Commission edition (1816–1869) vol i part 2 (1816) 638. It is 4/42/5 in Matthew Hammond's numbering system in the *People of Medieval Scotland 1093–1371* database [*PoMS*], available at *https://www.poms.ac.uk/record/source/4285/* (last accessed 12 July 2022). It survives as an original single sheet: Edinburgh, National Records of Scotland RH5/9.

through Norwegian eyes, is related in the fullest version of *Saga of Håkon Håkonsson*. There we are told that when Magnus Håkonsson was crowned in 1261, a Scottish knight who was present on his king's affairs "was so struck by the consecration that he sobbed".[25] It is explained that the knight was not accustomed to see Scottish kings crowned. The inference is that he wished they could be; as someone involved with royal business he may have been keenly aware that this had been denied by the pope.[26]

B: LAWS, CHARTERS AND THE TREATY OF PERTH

Any attempt to discuss the Scottish elite, ideas of kingship and the law in this period faces the fundamental challenge of having to work with only a limited and haphazard range of material on these topics.[27] There is a particularly sharp contrast between Scotland and Norway in medieval manuscripts of the kingdom's laws. Not only are those for Scotland more limited in scope and fewer in number, but they represent a confusing array of royal enactments, only some of which can be shown to be authentic legislation.[28] The earliest manuscript of this material is datable to 1267×1272, where the compilation is referred to not as the laws of a king, but *leges Scotie*, the "laws of Scotland".[29] In the fourteenth century this was refashioned and expanded into texts entitled the "laws of David I", the "laws of William I" or "the laws of Alexander II".[30] Alice Taylor's ground-breaking study of these texts in all their extant forms has shown how they represent a growing body of laws and

25 *Hónum fanzt svá mikit um vigsluna, at hann klökk*, Gudbrand Vigfusson (ed), *Hakonar Saga and a Fragment of Magnus Saga, Icelandic Sagas*, vol ii (1887) 319; translation (slightly adapted) from G W Dasent (tr), *The Saga of Hacon and a Fragment of the Saga of Magnus, Icelandic Sagas*, vol iv (1894) 331.

26 A fuller discussion of this passage is in Broun, *Scottish Independence* (n 13) 1.

27 It would be impossible, for example, to write a Scottish equivalent of Sverre Bagge's perceptive and detailed monographs on kingship, society and politics: S Bagge, *The Political Thought of the King's Mirror* (1987); S Bagge, *Society and Politics in Snorri Sturluson's Heimskringla* (1991); S Bagge, *From Gang Leader to the Lord's Anointed: Kingship in Sverris saga and Hákonar saga Hákonarsonar* (1996); S Bagge, *From Viking Stronghold to Christian Kingdom: State Formation in Norway, c. 900–1350* (2010).

28 A Taylor (ed and tr), *The Laws of Medieval Scotland. Legal Compilations from the Thirteenth and Fourteenth Centuries*, Stair Society vol 66 (2019) and the pioneering study of the oldest extant compilation in A Taylor, '*Leges Scocie* and the lawcodes of David I, William the Lion and Alexander II' (2009) 88 *Scottish Historical Review* 207–288.

29 Taylor (ed), *The Laws of Medieval Scotland* (n 28) 33–38.

30 Taylor (ed), *The Laws of Medieval Scotland* (n 28) 219–242, 281–356; and 484–613 for editions and translations of *Capitula Assisarum et Statutorum Domini Dauid Regis Scocie*, *Leges Willelmi Regis* and *Statuta Regis Alexandri*.

remedies enacted in royal assemblies from 1177 to 1248.[31] None of these compilations had the authority of King Magnus's lawcode, however. The first mention of authoritative texts of the kingdom's laws in 1426 names two other works, *Regiam Maiestatem* and *Quoniam Attachiamenta*: both have been dated to the first half of the fourteenth century and both claimed the authority of David I (1124–1153).[32] There was a central copy of "assises" and "statutes" by the end of the thirteenth century: in the inventory of the records handed over to John Balliol on his becoming king in 1292, there is a reference to two rolls of parchment that contained the "laws and assizes of the kingdom of Scotland, the laws and customs of the burghs of Scotland and some statutes enacted by kings of Scotland".[33] Unfortunately this, along with virtually all the other records mentioned in the inventory, has gone forever.[34]

The predominant material surviving from Scotland in this period is Latin charters: 3,422 survive that are datable to 1266 or earlier.[35] It has been noted, however, that although royal charters can provide evidence for gatherings of the ruling elite in the twelfth century, any relationship between charter-witnessing and royal assemblies ceases by the reign of Alexander III.[36] It has also been pointed out that detail on enactments at these assem-

31 Taylor (ed), *The Laws of Medieval Scotland* (n 28) esp. 221–242, 329–350, and the handy table at 330–331.

32 A R C Simpson and A L M Wilson, *Scottish Legal History, volume one 1000–1707* (2017) 60–64. T D Fergus (ed and tr), *Quoniam Attachiamenta*, Stair Society vol 44 (1996); T Thomson's edition of *Regiam* is in *APS*, i, 597–641; see also T M [Lord] Cooper, *Regiam Majestatem and Quoniam Attachiamenta based on the Text of Sir John Skene*, Stair Society vol 11 (1947). On *Regiam* see A Taylor, 'What does *Regiam Maiestatem* actually say (and what does it mean)?' in W Eves, J Hudson, I Ivarsen, and S White (eds), *Common Law, Civil Law and Colonial Law: Essays in Comparative Legal History from the 12th to the 20th Centuries* (2021) 47–85. For a new approach to editing the text taking account of all its versions, see J R Davies, A Taylor, P Caton, G Ferraro, G Noël, M Vieira, D Broun, 'A model of a dynamic edition of *Regiam maiestatem*', online at *The Community of the Realm in Scotland, 1249–1424: history, law and charters in a recreated kingdom*, available at *https://cotr.ac.uk* (last accessed 12 July 2022). Since going to press an edition of the earliest version of *Regiam* based on the earliest manuscripts has been published by J R Davies and A Taylor for the Stair Society.

33 "*de legibus et assisis regni Scotie, et legibus et consuetudinibus burgorum Scotie et quibusdam statutis editis per reges Scotie*": *APS*, i, 114–15. The "customs and laws of the burghs of Scotland" presumably refers to the compilation known to scholarship as the *Leges Burgorum*: Taylor (ed), *The Laws of Medieval Scotland* (n 28) 8; edited in *APS*, i, 329–56.

34 J M Thomson, *The Public Records of Scotland* (1922) 2–10, 15.

35 The figure is reached by searching "charters" under "Sources" in *PoMS*: this includes charters with date ranges that include 1266 and could therefore be later. For a discussion of the "documentary landscape" of this period see M Hammond, 'Introduction: the paradox of medieval Scotland, 1093–1286', in M Hammond (ed), *New Perspectives on Medieval Scotland 1093–1286* (2013) 1–52, at 14–30, and J Tucker, 'Survival and loss: working with documents from medieval Scotland' (forthcoming) for issues of survival.

36 M Hammond, 'Assemblies and the writing of administrative documents in the central medieval

blies (i.e. "assizes") are no longer found in charters during the reigns of Alexander II and Alexander III: the only source for these are the legal compilations that Alice Taylor has placed on a proper footing as sources for this period.[37] The infrastructure for using Scottish charters for research into the twelfth and thirteenth centuries, however, is highly developed, culminating in the *People of Medieval Scotland 1093–1371* [*PoMS*].[38] This has instrumental in a study of the development of regnal solidarity in Scotland from the perspective the elite's own charters rather than royal documents. This found that a key dynamic was "the standardisation of judicial power with the king as the legitimising point of reference" by 1200.[39]

For a scholar of thirteenth-century Scotland used to studying predominantly charters, it seems natural to consider the Treaty of Perth as a source for kingship, the unity of the realm and law. The text of the Treaty has been examined closely, most notably by Richard Lustig in an article published in 1979.[40] This paper focuses on one particularly striking statement which Hector MacQueen first drew attention to in 1995. In the text it is explained that:

kingdom of the Scots', in M Mostert and P S Barnwell (eds), *Medieval Legal Process: Physical, Spoken and Written Performance in the Middle Ages* (2011) 123–146.

37 Taylor (ed), *The Laws of Medieval Scotland* (n 28) 8; the texts for at least eleven statutes survive from Alexander II's reign (1214–1249): see *ibid.*, 342–346, and 572–591 for edition and translation. For potentially another statute, see below, n 53. The problems posed by previous editions are discussed in Taylor, *The Shape of the State* (n 5) 457–460; see also Taylor (ed), *The Laws of Medieval Scotland* (n 28) 15–18.

38 A Beam, D Broun, J Bradley, D Carpenter, J R Davies, K Dutton, N Evans, M Hammond, R Ó Maolalaigh, M Pasin, A Smith, *The People of Medieval Scotland 1093–1371*, 1st edn *1093–1286* (2010); 2nd edn *1093–1314* with S Ambler, A Giacometti, B Hartland, and K J Stringer (2012); 3rd edn including mapping and SNA functionality, with C Jackson and N Jakeman (2016); 4th edn *1093–1371*, with G Ferraro, E Hall and A Taylor (2019) available at *http://www.poms.ac.uk/* (last accessed 12 July 2022). It is important to stress that this is a database of what is stated in charters, not of charter texts themselves: as such, it hardly compares with the twenty-three-volume *Diplomatarium Norvegicum* and accompanying website (available at *https://www.dokpro.uio.no/dipl_norv/om_dn.html* (last accessed 12 July 2022): last updated on 3 March 1998 by Nina Kristiansen, and before that on 31 December 1997 by Christian-Emil Ore). For a critical discussion, see D Broun and J Tucker, 'The *People of Medieval Scotland* database as history', in J Nyhan, G Rockwell and S Sinclair (eds), *On Making in the Digital Humanities: John Bradley and the Scholarship of Digital Humanities Development* (in press). A research resource with digital images, transcriptions and translations of charters surviving as original single sheets up to 1250 is being expanded and developed: the first edition is S Brookes, D Broun, J R Davies, G Noël, P Stokes, A Taylor, J Tucker and T Webber, *Models of Authority: Scottish Charters and the Emergence of Government 1100–1250* (2017).

39 D Broun, 'Kingdom and identity. A Scottish perspective', in K J Stringer and A Winchester (eds), *Northern England and Southern Scotland in the Central Middle Ages* (2017) 31–85, at 74.

40 R I Lustig, 'The Treaty of Perth: a re-examination' (1979) 58 *Scottish Historical Review* 35–57.

> all the people of the said islands [ceded to the king of Scots] . . . both greater and lesser, shall be subject to the laws and customs of the kingdom of Scotland and be dealt with and judged according to them from now into the future.[41]

As Hector MacQueen has observed, "the extension of Scottish sovereignty carried with it the rule of Scottish law".[42] Unfortunately for historians it was not deemed necessary in the Treaty to explain what was meant by "the laws and customs of the kingdom". It is tempting, nevertheless, to gaze searchingly at the sentence for potential clues, however inconclusively. Presumably, if a text of the "laws and assizes of the kingdom" was kept in the royal archives, as in 1292, then the Scots who drafted the Treaty may have had this in mind; if so, it is possible that "customs" was understood to cover whatever was left unwritten.[43] The phrase "laws and customs", however, could be used quite naturally for a written collection of laws: it will be recalled that a copy of the "laws and customs of the burghs" was also kept in the royal archives in 1292.[44] It also has to be admitted that the phrase "laws and customs of the kingdom" could be used without having any texts in mind at all. If so, this could indicate an approach to law and the unity of the realm that would stand in sharp contrast to that of King Magnus the Lawmender. This will be explored in more detail in due course. A deeper question is whether a specific body of law was necessarily intended or not, and whether there was a distinct Scottish law at this time: we will return to this towards the end.

Unfortunately the original parchment of the Treaty no longer survives: the most recent edition is from copies of copies that were made when the text was repeated in subsequent treaties.[45] There is therefore no way to

41 "*Ita quod omnes homines dictarum insularum que prefato domino regi Scocie sunt concesse resignate et quiete clamate tam maiores quam minores subiaceant legibus et consuetudinibus regni Scocie et secundum eas ex nunc in posterum tractentur et iudicentur*": A A M Duncan (ed), *Regesta Regum Scottorum*, vol v, *The Acts of Robert I King of Scots 1306–1329* [*RRS*, v] (1988) no 24, at 308–309.

42 MacQueen, '*Regiam Majestatem*' (n 6) 10.

43 I am grateful to Alice Taylor for raising the issue of "custom" as unwritten law and alerting me to the statement in Isidore of Seville's *Etymologies* (V.3.2): "*Lex est constitutio scripta. Mos est uetustate probata consuetudo, siue lex non scripta. Nam lex a legendo uocata quia scripta est*". "Law is a written formulation. Custom is a usage demonstrated by old tradition, or unwritten law. For 'law' is so-called from 'reading', because it is written" (W M Lindsay (ed), *Etymologiarum sive Originum Isidori Hispalensis* (1911) book V available at *https://penelope.uchicago.edu/Thayer/L/Roman/Texts/Isidore/5*.html* (last accessed 12 July 2022)).

44 The text known to scholarship as *Leges Burgorum* is referred to as *Leges et consuetudines quatuor burgorum . . . constitue per DD regem Scocie* ("The laws and customs of the four burghs . . . established by David king of Scotland") in the earliest manuscript (datable to 1267×1272): Taylor (ed), *The Laws of Medieval Scotland* (n 29) 37.

45 *RRS*, v, no 24 (n 41), the renewal of treaty by Robert I and King Håkon Magnusson as part of the Treaty of Inverness, 29 October 1312. This is the earliest surviving text of the treaty of 1266.

resolve a potentially significant difference in word order in the key sentence on the laws and procedures to be applied in the Isles: rather than "be dealt with and judged" (*tractentur et iudicentur*, where, taken literally, *tractentur* may be read as referring to the process leading to judgment), as in copies kept in Copenhagen, the copy kept in Edinburgh has "judged and dealt with" (*iudicentur et tractentur*, where *tractentur* could be taken to refer to how those convicted were to be punished).[46] There is no way to tell which was the original reading; the only consolation is that, if the word order mattered, this was lost on at least one medieval scribe. It would not seem to be too rash, therefore, to take *tractentur* to refer to judicial procedures in general.

Although the sentence in the Treaty about the laws of the kingdom is not as detailed or unambiguous as might be hoped for, it is more than a bland statement: those who drafted it have gone to some effort to explain that Scottish laws and customs applied to everyone from now on. At first glance, this seems to be unproblematic. Nothing is said, however, about any distinct laws and practices in the Isles (which there probably were).[47] It might be inferred that, as far as the Treaty was concerned, it was expected that these would, in effect, be replaced by the laws and procedures of the Scottish kingdom. When considered more closely from a contemporary Scottish perspective, however, this creates a challenging conundrum. To begin with, it will become apparent that there was no expectation that the kingdom's laws and customs – in the fullest sense that was understood at the time – would be uniform throughout the realm. It will also become clear that, in this period, it would have been so remarkable for a kingdom to be subsumed in this way by another that this would have been unthinkable in 1266. On either count, there appear to be serious difficulties with reading the Treaty

46 The transcript in Edinburgh is National Records of Scotland PA5/4, ff.7r–8v, a copy of the renewal of the Treaty of Perth as part of the Treaty of Inverness (29 October 1312): see *RRS*, v, 312 (n 41) (under 'Source'). The transcripts kept in Copenhagen are of a ratification of the Treaties of Perth and Inverness on 29 July 1426: see *Diplomatarium Norvegicum*, viii, nos 9 and 276 (search *https://www.dokpro.uio.no/dipl_norv/diplom_field_eng.html* (last accessed 12 July 2022)). The variant readings are noted in *RRS*, v, 312 nn. *i* and *j* (n 41).

47 See Simpson and Wilson, *Scottish Legal History* (n 32) ch 5; J M Munro and R W Munro (eds), *Acts of the Lords of the Isles, 1336–1493*, Scottish History Society fourth series vol 22 (1986) xliv–xlv: see further, below, 75. J and R W Munro also note a reference by Donald Monro (writing in 1549) to the "laws of Renald McSomharkle" (Ragnall son of Somairle, king/lord of Argyll and the Isles, *floruit* 1164–1207, available at *https://www.poms.ac.uk/record/person/6562/* (last accessed 12 July 2022)); see also Simpson and Wilson, *Scottish Legal History* (n 32) 92–93. This identification of a major king in the (by then) remote past as lawmaker may be compared with Cinaed mac Ailpín in a Scottish context (discussed below, 87–89).

straightforwardly as a statement of the Scottish kingdom's legal unity. Each of the conundrum's two dimensions will be discussed in more detail. This will lead to a wider consideration of how the Isles were regarded from a Scottish point of view, focusing on ideas about the beginning of the Scottish kingdom that were current by the 1260s. This, in turn, will offer a fresh perspective on the even deeper question of the nature of the kingdom's laws in relation to the unity of the realm.

C: LEGAL DIVERSITY IN THE SCOTTISH KINGDOM

Let us turn, then, to the nature of legal diversity in the Scottish kingdom. It will be recalled that there were laws and assizes of the kingdom that were considered implicitly to apply to all its inhabitants.[48] Law and the administration of justice could, however, also take different forms from one major division of the kingdom to the next, even in those areas where royal government was most securely established. On 15 February 1244, for example, a statute intensifying the process of bringing those accused of murder, robbery, theft and homicide to trial was enacted by Alexander II.[49] Its terms only applied to Lothian – that is, to the kingdom south of the Forth. Alice Taylor, in her essential discussion of this legislation, notes that it could have been intended as a temporary measure.[50] The key figure in the provisions of 1244 was the justiciar of Lothian, an office that Alice Taylor has shown was established in the early 1220s along with the justiciar of "Scotland" (i.e. the kingdom north of the Firth of Forth).[51]

This division at the Firth of Forth had deep roots.[52] It was possible, for example, in the twelfth and possibly the early thirteenth centuries for laws to be made specifically for "Scotland", the region in the east between the Firth of Forth and the River Spey.[53] These laws were enacted *per omnes iudices*

48 See above, 70. On the broader issue of how extensively there was a "common law", see below, 92–93; Simpson and Wilson, *Scottish Legal History*, vol i (n 32) chs 2 and 3; and Simpson, 'Foreward' (cited in n 129, below).

49 Taylor (ed), *The Laws of Medieval Scotland* (n 28) 576–579 (for edition and translation), and 342–346 for its textual history, concluding tentatively (at 346) that it was one of a series of enactments "taken from a document (a short roll, a membrane) containing miscellaneous but authentic material from Alexander II's reign".

50 Taylor, *The Shape of the State* (n 5) 240–242.

51 Taylor, *The Shape of the State* (n 5) 211–229.

52 D Broun, 'Britain and the beginning of Scotland' (2015) 3 *Journal of the British Academy* 107–137 at 119–130.

53 Taylor (ed), *The Laws of Medieval Scotland* (n 28) 506–509, 608–609, for a potential example from 1221 (the *Law of Armies*); at 349–350, however, it is explained that it could be dated

Scocie ("by all the judges of 'Scotland'"), whose role was to "know the law".[54] This suggests that this region not only had specific laws made for it but also had a distinct tradition of legal knowledge embodied in its *iudices* (at least until the mid-thirteenth century, by which point they had ceased to have a special role in determining the law).[55] David I (1124–1153) decreed that *iudices* in "Scotland" were required to meet the king when he entered their province, and to remain with the king unless given permission to leave – a clear indication of their importance for administering justice in the region.[56] Judgments were also made specifically by "all the judges of Galloway" in the late twelfth and early thirteenth century.[57] There was one part of the kingdom where *iudices* were prominent long after the thirteenth century: the lordship of the Isles.[58] A hierarchy of *iudices* can be inferred from the appearance of an *archiiudex* ("chief judge") as a witness to a charter in 1485; a *iudex Insularum*, "judge of the Isles" in 1457 might be another title for this office.[59] It appears from this that the Isles had its own pattern of judicial administration that was distinct from the kingdom's courts and legal expertise at that time. It is tempting to see the *iudex* here as directly comparable to the Norwegian *lagmann*: there are, indeed, references in Gaelic to *lagmainn* of the Isles raiding Ireland in 962 and 974.[60]

to 1188. See also A Taylor, '*Leges Scocie and the lawcodes of David I William the Lion and Alexander II*' (2009) 88 *Scottish Historical Review* 207–288 at 234–266; A Taylor, 'Common burdens in the *regnum Scottorum*: the evidence of charter diplomatic', in D Broun (ed), *The Reality Behind Charter Diplomatic in Anglo-Norman Britain* (2011) 166–234 at 224–233, available at *https://paradox.poms.ac.uk/redist/pdf/chapter3.pdf* (last accessed 12 July 2022). On the *Law of Armies* see also D Broun, 'Statehood and lordship in 'Scotland' before the mid-twelfth century' (2015) 66 *Innes Review* 1–71, at 62–65 (with corrigendum on 64: *Innes Review* 67 (2016) 62).

54 Taylor (ed), *The Laws of Medieval Scotland* (n 28) 255–259.

55 Taylor (ed), *The Laws of Medieval Scotland* (n 28) 257–259; on *iudices* see also especially Simpson and Wilson, *Scottish Legal History* (n 32) 9–13. The pioneering study is G W S Barrow, *The Kingdom of the Scots*, 2nd edn (2003) ch 2 (originally published in 1966).

56 Taylor (ed), *The Laws of Medieval Scotland* (n 28) 257; 514–515 (but see 300–301 for why this is probably, but not certainly, David I's). For the *iudex* of a province, see also D Broun, 'Statehood and lordship' (n 53) 60–62, and 61 n 243 for six provinces whose *iudex* is named in a document (nine provinces can be identified by around 1150: *ibid*., 15 n 51).

57 Taylor (ed), *The Laws of Medieval Scotland* (n 28) 259; 420, 610.

58 Simpson and Wilson, *Scottish Legal History* (n 32) at 93–94; J W M Bannerman, *Kingship, Church and Culture: Collected Essays and Studies* (2016) 270–271.

59 Munro and Munro (eds), *Acts of the Lords of the Isles*, (n 47) xliv; no 119 (at 188); 205 (citing Edinburgh, National Library of Scotland Charter 16061).

60 A Woolf, *From Pictland to Alba: Scotland 789–1070* (2007) 212–213: see *http://research.ucc.ie/celt/document/G100005B* (last accessed 12 July 2022), '*Annals of the Four Masters*': *Annála Ríoghachta Éireann*' 960.14 and 972.13. I am grateful to Andrew Simpson for this reference. On distinctive aspects of law and legal procedure in the Lordship of the Isles and the Council of the Isles see Simpson and Wilson, *Scottish Legal History* (n 32) 91–94, 98. The earliest account of the Council of the Isles is in the same source in 1549, which refers to the laws of Ragnall, son

Galloway not only had its own "judges", but distinct "laws", too, especially in relation to judicial procedure. A striking aspect of the statute of 1244 is that Galloway was explicitly excluded because it had its own laws.[61] A feature of Galwegian law appears to have been the capacity of individual officers, on their own say-so, to bring people to trial.[62] The "community of Galloway" complained of this to Edward I sometime between 1300 and 1306.[63] Another reference to this practice is in the earldom of Carrick,

of Somairle: see n.47, above. There are no sources, however, that might show whether the lord of the Isles and his *iudices* in the later middle ages made decrees that might have paralleled the king of Scots and the *iudices* of "Scotland" centuries earlier.

61 "*preterquam in Galwydia que leges suas habet speciales*", "except in Galloway, which has its own special laws": Taylor (ed), *The Laws of Medieval Scotland* (n 28) 576–577 (there are minor variations between the witnesses: Taylor gives the oldest manuscript as the base text quoted here). See in general H L MacQueen, 'The laws of Galloway: a preliminary survey', in R D Oram and G P Stell (eds), *Galloway: Land and Lordship* (1991) 131–143.

62 W C Dickinson, 'Surdit de sergaunt' (1960) 39 *Scottish Historical Review* 170–175; G W S Barrow, *The Anglo-Norman Era in Scottish History* (1980) 160–161, shows that this practice occurred in Lennox (which was never part of Galloway); Taylor (ed), *The Laws of Medieval Scotland* (n 28) 305–306, shows that it continued into the fourteenth century. It has been suggested, first, that these officers are mentioned in charters of the earls of Carrick and Lennox in 1225 and 1227 releasing the tenants of Glasgow Cathedral from the requirement to provide accommodation to officials known as "kethres", and secondly, that "kethres" is the same word as "kadrez" used of divisions of Galloway (such as Carrick: see texts cited in n.64, below), suggesting that these officials operated in a designated area or "circuit", as in Wales: G W S Barrow, *Scotland and its Neighbours in the Middle Ages* (1992) 148. It is unlikely, however, that "kadrez" (which is also attested as "cadred") and "kethres" are the same word: see D Broun, 'The changing face of charter scholarship: a review article' (2001) 52 *Innes Review* 205–211, at 210. Perhaps "kardez" is a term for lordly power related to the word *cadredd* in Welsh, which can mean "splendour, strength" (as cited in *Geriadur Prifysgol Cymru*, available at *https://welsh-dictionary.ac.uk/gpc/gpc.html* (last accessed 12 July 2022)); "kethres" seems more likely to refer to a particular type of official, and may (given its appearance in Lennox as well as Carrick) be a Gaelic word, perhaps linked to *cethrae*, "cattle" (*Electronic Dictionary of the Irish Language* [eDIL], available at *http://www.dil.ie/8925* (last accessed 12 July 2022)) or livestock generally, e.g. perhaps as collectors of *calp*, the payment of livestock due to a lord in Galloway: see M Brown, *The Black Douglases. War and Lordship in Late Medieval Scotland, 1300–1455* (1998) 172. *Dictionary of the Older Scottish Tongue*, s.v. *calp*,[2] in *Dictionary of the Scots Language* (2004) (*https://dsl.ac.uk/entry/dost/calp* (last accessed 12 July 2022)) shows the prevalence of the term *calp* in Galloway and Carrick: it is explained there that the word was borrowed from Gaelic (see also eDIL s.v. *colp(th)ach*, "yearling heifer", *http://www.dil.ie* (last accessed 12 July 2022)). *Dictionary of the Older Scottish Tongue*, s.v. *calp*[1] shows that this was also levied in parts of the Highlands, but was only due on a tenant's death, rather than more regularly, as appears to have been the case in Carrick and Galloway.

63 J Bain (ed), *Calendar of Documents Relating to Scotland preserved in Her Majesty's Public Record Office, London*, vol ii, *A.D. 1272–1307* (1884) 500 (no 1874): for the date see *PoMS*, available at *https://www.poms.ac.uk/record/source/7755/* (last accessed 12 July 2022). Dickinson, 'Surdit de sergaunt' (n 62) 170–173; MacQueen, '*Regiam Majestatem*' (n 6) 5. The specific complaint was that this practice was being imposed on them by the "barons and great lords of the country" despite the fact that the community of Galloway were the king's tenants and had been released from this by Alexander III a year before his death (he died on the night of 19 March 1286). The practice had evidently continued for tenants of other lords who were, it seems,

which was originally within Galloway.[64] In a well-known charter of Robert and Margery, earl and countess of Carrick, in 1285, the monks of Melrose and their men were granted exemption from accusations by an individual officer[65]; the earl and countess instead allowed them to claim what is strikingly referred to as "English law" (*lex Anglicana*).[66] A specific ethnic context may be involved here: if the monks still regarded themselves as culturally English, it would have been useful to emphasise their difference from the local population in seeking exemption from Galwegian law.[67] Be this as it

encroaching on royal lands. As Dickinson points out, it appears that Alexander III's release was ineffective, at least in the long run.

64 Carrick was one of four divisions "of that part of Galloway" ("*de illa Galweia*") that David received renders of livestock and cheese from before he became king in 1124: see G W S Barrow (ed), *Regesta Regum Scottorum*, vol. i, *The Acts of Malcolm IV King of Scots 1153–1165* [*RRS*, i] (1960) no 131, at 194, and discussion at 39; G W S Barrow (ed), *The Charters of King David I: the Written Acts of David I King of Scots 1124–53 and of his Son Henry Earl of Northumberland 1139–52* (1999) no 57.

65 The original single sheet is Edinburgh, National Records of Scotland GD55/316: C Innes (ed), *Liber Sancte Marie de Melros*, Bannatyne Club vol 59(i) (1837) 277–278 (no 316). For brief discussions, see e.g. Dickinson, 'Surdit de sergaunt' (n 62) 72; Barrow, *The Anglo-Norman Era* (n 62) 119; MacQueen, 'Scots law' (n 22) 95. The charter is dated 1 June 1285: perhaps, therefore, the monks of Melrose were prompted by the king's release of his tenants from this practice in law enforcement that may have occurred shortly before (see above). Because this was evidently a special exemption for the benefit of Melrose by the earl and countess of Carrick it may be inferred that they were not following Alexander III's example and releasing all their tenants from this practice.

66 The fullest discussion is D Carpenter, 'Melrose abbey and English law (*lex anglicana*): attitudes to England in the period before the Wars of Independence', Feature of the Month for February 2010, available at *http://paradox.poms.ac.uk/feature/february10.html* (last accessed 12 July 2022), where it is cogently explained that this presumably refers ultimately to the provision in Magna Carta that no one should be brought to trial by a bailiff on the word of the bailiff alone, without witnesses. (This was also suggested by P Brand *apud* MacQueen, 'Scots law' (n 22) 102 n 124.) It became established practice instead in England to bring accusations before a jury in order to establish whether the case should proceed to a trial. This, as Alice Taylor has observed, was also the process in the Scottish kingdom that appears to have been in place for bringing cases to the justiciar, a process that she suggested the statute of 1244 sought to intensify by requiring every township to seek out anyone suspected of the most serious offences (apart from rape) in the previous fifteen months: Taylor, *The Shape of the State* (n 5) 241–242.

67 For the English identity of the monks of Melrose, see D Broun, 'Melrose abbey and its world', in D Broun and J Harrison, *The Chronicle of Melrose Abbey: a Stratigraphic Edition*, vol.i, *Introduction and Facsimile Edition* (2007) 1–12, at 10–12; D Broun, 'Becoming Scottish in the thirteenth century: the evidence of the Chronicle of Melrose', in B B Smith, S Taylor and G Williams (eds), *West over Sea: Studies in Scandinavian Sea-Borne Expansion and Settlement before 1300. A Festschrift in Honour of Dr Barbara E. Crawford* (2007) 19–32, at 20–25. It should have been made clearer there that, when we see in the Chronicle that monks of Melrose began (by around 1290 at the latest) to identify themselves as "Scottish", there is no indication that they would have seen this as conflicting with their English identity. Being Scottish (as argued in that piece) was about identifying with the Scottish king and kingdom, not with the other dimensions of being Scottish (such as the "Scottish language", i.e. Gaelic). The notion that being Scottish or English as mutually exclusive was a legacy of the Wars of Independence: even so, the

may the appeal to "English law" lends additional colour to the legal diversity that was accepted in the kingdom as a matter of course by its ruling elite.

It is only much later that we find a clear indication that a single law may have been expected to apply exclusively across the entire kingdom. In the parliament held in March 1426 it was enacted that all the king's subjects "should be governed only under the king's laws and statutes of the realm, and not under any particular laws or special privileges, nor by the laws of other countries or realms".[68] The "particular laws or special privileges" seem to have included not only the laws of Galloway but also the law of Clan Macduff, applying to the kin of the earl of Fife.[69] This can be inferred from an act of the royal council in November 1384 tightening up the administration of justice throughout the kingdom: it was acknowledged in this legislation that the support of the earl of Fife and lord of Galloway for these measures would not be to the future detriment of the law of Clan Macduff or law of Galloway, and that "other points of Galwegian law" (which were not specified) would be reserved to the lord of Galloway (*reseruatis sibi aliis punctis legis Galwidiensis*).[70] Whatever may have been intended in parliament in 1426, uniformity in the exercise of law and justice was not achieved in the fifteenth century. For example, the procedure for making arrests continued to be more arbitrary north of the Forth than south of the Forth until 1474, when it was enacted that the procedure south of the Forth should be used.[71] Uniformity was, at best, approached gradually, even in the kingdom's heartlands.

references to *Scoti Anglicati* in the fourteenth century shows that this was not a hard-and-fast distinction (see M H Brown, '*Scoti Anglicati*: Scots in Plantagenet allegiance', in A K and M A Penman (eds), *England and Scotland in the Fourteenth Century: New Perspectives* (2007) 94–115).

68 ". . . *all and sindry the kyngis legis of the realme of Scotland leyff and be governyt generally undir the kingis lawys and statutis of the realme and undir na particulare lawys na speciall privelegis na be na lawis of uthir cunttreys na realmys*": K M Brown, G H MacIntosh, A J Mann, P E Ritchie, R J Tanner (eds), with A Grosjean, A R MacDonald, K F McAlister, D J Patrick, L A M. Stewart et al, *The Records of the Parliaments of Scotland to 1707* (St Andrews, 2007) (RPS) available at *http://www.rps.ac.uk* [*RPS*] (last accessed 12 July 2022), 1426/6; MacQueen, '*Regiam Majestatem*' (n 6) 12–13.

69 MacQueen, '*Regiam Majestatem*' (n 6) 12; Simpson and Wilson, *Scottish Legal History* (n 32) 10–11.

70 *RPS*, 1384/11/12 and *RPS*, 1384/11/13.

71 *RPS*, 1474/5/7. A proposal to bring all the kingdom's laws together in a single authorised book, and destroy all others, was on parliament's agenda in 1469, but no enactment is recorded: *RPS*, 1469/34; Simpson and Wilson, *Scottish Legal History* (n 32) 64. On this and the more comprehensive parliamentary proposal in 1473 to produce a single authorised volume of the kingdom's laws, see Taylor (ed), *The Laws of Medieval Scotland* (n 28) 388–390.

In March 1504 another statement about the universal and exclusive application of the laws of the king and kingdom appears in an Act of Parliament, this time with the Isles mentioned in particular. It was insisted there that "all our sovereign lord's lieges who are under his authority, and in particular all the Isles, be governed by our sovereign lord's own laws and the common laws of the realm, and not by any other laws".[72] In an earlier draft it was specified that the act applied to "all our sovereign lord's lieges *both within Orkney, Shetland and the Isles and in other places* who are under his authority, and in particular all the Isles", but the passage in italics was removed[73]; it is clear, therefore, that "the Isles" referred to the Western Isles. On the face of it, then, this could be read as a tacit acknowledgement that there were "laws of the Isles".[74] The Act occurs, however, in the context of a campaign against rebels that was framed as an attempt to re-establish law and order to a region whose "people had almost become wild".[75] The Western Isles may have been singled out, therefore, simply because of the perceived extent of resistance there, bringing to mind the possibility of "other laws" because the laws of the king and kingdom were being denied. The expectation that only one law should apply throughout the kingdom was part of a specific attempt to assert royal authority in the Western Isles.

In the case of the Northern Isles, there can be no doubt that Norse law continued in practice.[76] This was acknowledged by the Scottish parliament in 1567, nearly a century after Orkney and Shetland had been placed under the control of kings of Scots: the question of the use of the common law of the realm was considered but it was concluded that "they ought to be subject to their own laws".[77] In 1611, however, the Privy Council, as part of its proceedings against the arbitrary rule of Patrick Stewart, earl of

72 *RPS*, 1504/3/45: "*. . . all oure soverane lordis liegis beand under his obesance, and in speciale all the Ilis, be reulit be oure soverane lordis aune lawis and the commoune lawis of the realme, ande be nain other lawis:*"

73 *RPS*, 1504/3/45, with additional draft text "*batht within Orknay, Scheteland and the Ilis and uther placis*" given in a popup before "*beand*".

74 MacQueen, '*Regiam Majestatem*' (n 6) 13, saw this as "directed against the recently supressed Lordship of the Isles"; see also Simpson and Wilson, *Scottish Legal History* (n 32) 98.

75 *RPS*, 1504/3/103: "*the pepill ar almaist gane wilde*". For the context, see S Boardman, *The Campbells 1250–1513* (2006) 317–321.

76 G Donaldson, 'Problems of sovereignty and law in Orkney and Shetland' in D Sellar, (ed), *Stair Miscellany II*, Stair Society vol 35 (1984) 13–40 at 25–36.

77 *RPS*, 1567/12/60: "*thai aucht to be subject to thair aune lawis*". See K Anderson, 'The Influence of Scots and Norse Law on Law and Governance in Orkney and Shetland 1450–1650', unpublished PhD thesis, University of Aberdeen (2015) 26; also 22, 24–25, and Donaldson, 'Problems of sovereignty and law' (n 76) 32–33, for the continued use of Norse law in the Northern Isles in the sixteenth century.

Orkney in the Northern Isles, revived the principle that all the kingdom's subjects should be governed only by its own laws, and condemned the way that those in authority had sometimes been "making choise sometimes of foreyne [foreign] lawis and sometimes of the proper lawis of this kingdome" according to what was to their advantage; it ordered as a consequence that the use of "foreign laws" should cease forthwith.[78] Although this marked the formal abolition of Norse law in the Northern Isles, it would seem that King Magnus's lawcode was still in use and may have lingered in local discourse for a while longer.[79]

This diversity and lack of legal unity can be understood in light of what Alice Taylor has revealed about the nature of royal authority and government in the thirteenth century, and how this continued through to the later middle ages.[80] Because royal jurisdiction worked through aristocratic power in medieval Scotland, there was no conceptual difficulty in acknowledging that some of the most powerful lords, such as the lord of Galloway and the earl of Fife, exercised their judicial authority in particular customary ways referred to as the laws of Galloway and the laws of Clan Macduff.[81] The continuation of Norse law under the auspices of the earl of Orkney fits into this paradigm. It will also be recalled that the earl of Carrick had authority over distinctive procedures of law enforcement identical with the laws of Galloway: given that Carrick was originally within Galloway, this may have been referred to as Galwegian law, too. Be this as it may, there would have been no problem, it would seem, in recognising in 1266 the same diversity of practice for the likes of the lord of Islay and lord of Garmoran within what had been the kingdom of Man and the Isles. When attempts to impose legal uniformity were made (as in 1611), it is notable that this occurred as part of an attack on a recalcitrant magnate's power and was targeted specifically at their territory, rather than across the kingdom as a whole. There is no indication that a similar context may have been a factor in 1266. The idea of mounting a fundamental challenge to the judicial aspects of lordship would, in any event, appear to have been unthinkable in the mid-thirteenth

78 D Masson (ed), *The Register of the Privy Council of Scotland*, vol ix, *A.D. 1610–1613* (1889) 181–182; for the context, see R S Barclay (ed), *The Court Books of Orkney and Shetland, 1614–1615*, Scottish History Society 4th series, vol 4 (1967) xix–xx.

79 For the Privy Council's abolition of Norse law, see, for example Barclay (ed), *The Court Books* (n 78) xix; Anderson, 'The Influence of Scots and Norse Law' (n 77) 26–27.

80 For the later middle ages, see A Grant, *Independence and Nationhood: Scotland 1306–1469* (1984) 147–162.

81 See above, 78.

century.[82] All in all, it is unlikely that the salient sentence on law in the Treaty should be read as a glimpse of what may have only been a short-lived aspiration to establish standard laws and customs throughout the realm – and potentially therefore another passing innovation in the way the Scottish kingship was conceptualised early in Alexander III's reign.

D: THE ISLES AS PART OF THE SCOTTISH REALM

If uniformity across the Scottish kingdom was hardly conceivable in 1266, however, it would appear nevertheless that the Isles were regarded as not only within the Scottish realm, but as no different from those areas where the laws and procedures of the kingdom prevailed exclusively. This leads at once to another dimension of the conundrum posed by a natural reading of this aspect of the Treaty: it was unprecedented in this period for a country or kingdom to be incorporated into another so that its own laws and customs would be replaced by those of the annexing kingdom, regardless of any marked disparity in their power.

It was not unusual, of course, for the same person to rule more than one country or kingdom. When that occurred each continued to have its own laws. This is exemplified particularly vividly in the case of Norway in the later middle ages, as shown by Erik Opsahl in his chapter. Another example in the twelfth and thirteenth centuries is the king of England, who was duke of Normandy and then count of Anjou, and later ruled Gascony. None of these territories were subjected to English law or incorporated into the government of England. They continued to function as independent entities.[83] Closer to home, the kingdom of Galloway was drawn in stages into becoming part of the Scottish kingdom, culminating in Alexander II's suppression of a revolt in 1235 against the division of the lordship among the heiresses of Alan, lord of Galloway and their husbands.[84] Galwegian law continued, however. An even more striking case is Scotland itself when arrangements were made in 1290 for the marriage of Margaret, daughter

82 See Simpson, 'Foreward', xxxv–xlvi (as cited in n 129, below) for a general and perceptive discussion of the issues and possibilities relating to the relationship between royal and baronial jurisdictions.

83 J L Patourel, 'The Plantagenet dominions' (1965) 50 *History* 289–308.

84 R Oram, *The Lordship of Galloway* (2000) 51–163. The latest reference to Galloway as a kingdom is in a lost charter of Fergus (lord of Galloway, d.1161) referring to himself as *rex Galwitensium* ("king of the Galwegians"): K J Stringer, 'Acts of lordship: the records of the lords of Galloway to 1234', in T Brotherstone and D Ditchburn (eds), *Freedom and Authority: Scotland c. 1050–c. 1650. Historical and Historiographical Essays Presented to Grant G. Simpson* (2000) 212 (no 1).

of King Eirik Magnusson of Norway and granddaughter of Alexander III, with Edward I's son and heir, the future Edward II. It was anticipated that as a result, Scotland and England would have the same monarch. The Scottish leaders at the time were anxious to secure from Edward a guarantee that Scotland would not be brought under English royal government. The result was a detailed series of written promises (*obligationes*) given by Edward I on 28 August 1290: this amounted to the first explicit recognition of Scottish independence by a king of England (albeit not yet as part of a formal treaty).[85] It began with a commitment that "the rights, laws, liberties and customs of the same realm of Scotland [were] to be preserved in every respect and in all time coming throughout the said realm and its borders, completely and without being impaired".[86]

The fate of the kingdom of Man and the Isles as envisaged in the Treaty of Perth appears, therefore, to have been unthinkable. In one key respect, however, nothing changed: ecclesiastically the former kingdom continued to be a bishopric under the authority of the archbishop of Trondheim. The bishopric itself became divided in the wake of the Great Schism when England and Scotland recognised different popes, with one bishop in the Isle of Man, which was now part of the kingdom of England, and another in the Western Isles, based at Snizort on Skye. The diocese's unity was never restored.[87] The bishopric of the Western Isles was only formally incorporated into the Scottish church, however, when an archdiocese of St Andrews was created in 1472, which included the Northern Isles too. This was the first occasion when the Scottish realm in its entirety formed a single ecclesi-

85 Duncan, *The Kingship of the Scots* (n 17) 185–194; W B Stevenson, 'The Treaty of Northampton (1290): a Scottish charter of liberties?' (2007) 86 *Scottish Historical Review* 1–15; MacQueen, '*Regiam Majestatem*' (n 6) 4. Duncan has shown that what was negotiated at Birgham on 14 July 1290 and agreed by Edward I at Northampton on 28 August 1290 was a stage in a process leading up to what would have been a marriage treaty involving King Eirik of Norway, Edward I and the Scottish government, rather than a formal treaty itself: the next stage – there was apparently an initial meeting between Anthony Bek, bishop of Durham, representing Edward I, and some Scottish magnates at Perth on 1 October (Duncan, *The Kingship of the Scots* (n 17) 194–195) – had barely begun when news of Margaret's death brought proceedings to an end.

86 "*quod iura leges, libertates et consuetudines cuiusdem regni Scotie in omnibus et per omnia per totum ipsum regnum et eius marchias integre et inuiolabiliter perpetuis temporibus obseruentur*": J Stevenson (ed), *Documents Illustrative of the History of Scotland 1286–1306*, 2 vols (1870) i, 164–173, at 165: translation from G W S Barrow, 'A kingdom in crisis: Scotland and the Maid of Norway' (1990) 69 *Scottish Historical Review* 120–141, 137–141, at 137.

87 D E R Watt, *Medieval Church Councils in Scotland* (2000) 128–129; see S E Thomas, 'Rival bishops, rival cathedrals: the election of Cormac, archdeacon of Sodor, as bishop in 1331' (2009) 60 *Innes Review* 145–163, for the emergence of Snizort as a cathedral and the pre-Schism roots of the division of the diocese between Man and the Western Isles.

astical province.[88] Uniformity in ecclesiastical laws and customs came later: in at least one aspect, relating to the regulation of wills, the Western Isles was only explicitly brought into conformity with the rest of the kingdom in 1552, in line with a similar statute for the diocese of Orkney in 1549.[89]

As far as the secular sphere is concerned, it should also be acknowledged that in Gaelic sources there was still a king of the Isles (*rí Innse Gall*) long after 1266. The most notable was Eoin Mac Dòmhnuill, who at his death in 1387 is referred to in the *Annals of Ulster* as "king of the Isles".[90] In Latin he bore the title *Dominus Insularum*: this was how he and his successors referred to themselves in Latin in their own documents.[91] This is comparable to Galloway, and also Argyll, where Gaelic *rí*, "king", was rendered *dominus*, "lord", in Scottish Latin: *rex* was reserved for *rex Scottorum*, "king of Scots".[92] It will be recalled that the lordship of the Isles in the fifteenth century appears to have had its own hierarchy of judicial professionals headed by a "chief judge" (*archiiudex*).[93]

The effectiveness or otherwise of the incorporation of the kingdom of Man and the Isles into the Scottish realm, however, is not the main point. The crux is what appears to have been envisaged in the Treaty in relation to secular authority and the kingdom's laws and customs. It is important to bear in mind, however, that the Treaty was between the king of Scots

88 Watt, *Medieval Church Councils* (n 87) 167. Galloway had been in the province of York; the last occasion, however, when a bishop of Galloway gave an oath of obedience to the archbishop of York was in 1355, after which, in practice, its bishops were part of the Scottish church. During the Great Schism rival bishops were appointed by the archbishop of York but had no power. See Watt, *Medieval Church Councils* (n 87) 127–128.

89 Watt, *Medieval Church Councils* (n 87) 136 n 92. J Robertson (ed), *Concilia Scotiae: Ecclesiae Scoticanae Statuta tam Provincialia quam Synodalia quae Supersunt, 1225–1559*, 2 vols (1866) ii, 130 (no. 243), and 112–13 (no. 213) for the 1549 statute; David Patrick (tr), *Statutes of the Scottish Church 1225–1559* (1907) 137 and 116. The delay in achieving uniformity may partly be a result of the failure to hold a council of the Scottish church for more than sixty years after the archbishopric of St Andrews was created: Watt, *Medieval Church Councils* (n 87) 137. I am very grateful to Joanna Tucker for alerting me to the question of the Isles in relation to the Scottish church and its potential implications for church law.

90 *Annals of Ulster* 1387.7, available at *https://celt.ucc.ie/published/G100001C/index.html* (last accessed 12 July 2022).

91 For example, Eoin is *Dominus Insularum* in his letter to Edward III of England on 21 September 1336 (Munro and Munro (eds), *Acts of the Lords of the Isles* (n 47) 3), and when a title is used by him and his successors, it is *Dominus Insularum* (and later additionally earl of Ross).

92 J W M Bannerman, *Kingship, Church and Culture: Collected Essays and Studies* (2016) 330–333, 386–387 (in papers published originally as 'The Lordship of the Isles', in K A Steer and J W M Bannerman, *Late Medieval Monumental Sculpture in the West Highlands* (1977) 201–213, and 'The Scots language and the kin-based society', in D S Thomson (ed), *Gaelic and Scots in Harmony. Proceedings of the Second International Conference on the Languages of Scotland, University of Glasgow 1988* (1990) 1–19.

93 See above, 75.

and the king of Norway, not the king of Scots and the king of Man and the Isles. Laws and procedures were conceived in relation to being a subject of the king of Scots rather than of the king of Norway, not with respect to the status of the Isles within the Scottish kingdom. When the Treaty went into detail it was to explain that those who wished to continue in the king of Norway's allegiance would be permitted to leave the Isles peaceably with their possessions; there was no need to mention the laws and customs of the Isles because this was not relevant to the question of allegiance to the king of Scots or king of Norway. The silence about any laws of the Isles leads to an intriguing question: given the reality of regional diversity within the Scottish realm, is it possible that "being subject to the laws and customs of the kingdom of Scotland" amounted to no more than that justice was to be administered in the name of the king of Scots? Far from replacing existing laws and customs with Scottish laws, it may have been assumed that these would continue – especially if abolishing them would have been unthinkable at this time.

There is, however, an additional factor that, from a Scottish perspective, would have made the acquisition of the Isles seem fundamentally different from one kingdom taking over and subsuming another. It can be shown that, in the eyes of the Scottish elite, the Western Isles may have been seen as historically an integral part of the kingdom. This was not based on how they were perceived geographically. In the Chronicle of Melrose, for example, in a passage relating to the negotiations leading up to the Treaty of Perth, the Western Isles are described graphically as "tiny islands lying around the full realm (*ampla regio*) of the Scots".[94] This placed them explicitly on the kingdom's periphery. By contrast Galloway, even as early as around 1220, was referred to in the Chronicle of Melrose, almost in passing, as part of "Scotland".[95] A different picture, however, is revealed according to contemporary ideas of the Scottish kingdom's history. From this vantage point the Isles were regarded as an ancient part of the realm.

94 J Stevenson (ed), *Chronica de Mailros, e Codice Unico in Bibliotheca Cottoniana Servato*, Bannatyne Club vol 52 (1835) 196; *http://www.bl.uk/manuscripts/Viewer.aspx?ref=cotton_ms_faustina_b_ix_f065v* (last accessed 12 July 2022); Broun, 'Becoming Scottish' (n 67) 30. This is in the annal for 1265, which is part of Stratum 38 (entered sometime after 14 April 1286 and probably before May 1291): D Broun, 'Charting the Chronicle's physical development', in D Broun and J Harrison, *The Chronicle of Melrose Abbey; a Stratigraphic Edition*, Scottish History Society sixth series, vol 1 (2007) 125–173, at 168–169.

95 Stevenson (ed), *Chronica de Mailros* (n 94) 125; *http://www.bl.uk/manuscripts/Viewer.aspx?ref=cotton_ms_faustina_b_ix_f033v* (last accessed 12 July 2022) (beginning of new section). This is part of Stratum 9 (annal for 1216 and first part of 1217, probably entered in 1218 or not long thereafter): Broun, 'Charting the Chronicle's physical development' (n 94) 134.

The first explicit hint of this primordial relationship between the Isles and the Scottish kingdom is in a king-list datable probably to 1124, in which nearly every Scottish king is said to have been buried on Iona.[96] The king-list itself only begins with Cinaed mac Ailpín (who died as "king of the Picts" in 858). It is stated, however, that Iona was also the burial place of Fergus and his brothers, sons of Erc, who are presented in genealogical material from the late tenth century onwards as the original royal ancestors who established the Scottish kingdom.[97] In the late twelfth century the Scottish king-list itself, headed by William the Lion (1165–1214), had been extended back to Fergus, son of Erc. It now began with a statement of the bounds of the original kingdom, imagined as extending from the mouth of the River Bann in northern Ireland to the mountains of Drumalban, and to *Innsi Gall*, i.e. the Isles in the west.[98] This was the first time that the kingdom's original territory had been envisaged in this way as the Isles and Argyll. Previously it had been identified (from at least the ninth century) as the landmass north of the Forth.[99]

Both ideas of the ancient kingdom – the Isles and Argyll in the west and the landmass north of the Forth – continued to be influential: they were ingeniously combined by Richard Vairement in the first full-scale narrative of Scottish history (referred to earlier), probably written in the 1260s.[100] In the process Vairement created an earlier sequence of kings in the west, beginning with another Fergus in 330 BC. It will be recalled, however, that Vairement's history does not survive; it may not, therefore, have been widely read. It can reveal how it was possible to think about the kingdom, but not necessarily how these ideas were expressed more widely.

96 This is part of the main thirteenth-century Scottish king-list: M O Anderson, *Kings and Kingship in Early Scotland*, 2nd edn (1980) 52–67, 264–291 (for edition of most witnesses of the text); D Broun, *The Irish Identity of the Kingdom of the Scots in the Twelfth and Thirteenth Centuries* (1999) 153–160.

97 The medieval texts of the genealogy are discussed in D Broun, 'The genealogy of the king of Scots as charter and panegyric', in J R Davies and S Bhattacharya (eds), *Copper, Parchment, and Stone: Studies in the Sources for Landholding and Lordship in Early Medieval Bengal and Medieval Scotland* (2019) 209–260, at 234–247 for the earliest extant version (datable to 995–997) and its revision possibly in either 997 or 1005. (The volume is available online at *https://www.poms.ac.uk/information/e-books/* (last accessed 12 July 2022).)

98 Broun, *The Irish Identity* (n 96) 146–53; Broun, *Scottish Independence* (n 13) 168–169. The context for this change in relation to ideas of kingdoms as peoples is discussed in D Broun, 'Ireland and the beginning of Scotland' (forthcoming).

99 D Broun, 'Rethinking Scottish origins', in S Boardman and S Foran (eds), *Barbour's Bruce and its Cultural Contexts: Politics, Chivalry and Literature in Late Medieval Scotland* (2015) 163–190, at 182–187; Broun, *Scottish Independence* (n 13) 54–61, 75–79.

100 Broun, *Scottish Independence* (n 13) 252–257.

The simpler form of a king-list is more likely to reflect the views of at least some of the elite.

An important innovation during Alexander II's reign (1214–1249) was the addition of a list of Pictish kings to the list extending back to Fergus, son of Erc.[101] This can be seen as a cruder attempt to show that the Isles and Argyll on the one hand and the mainland north of the Forth on the other were elements of the ancient kingdom. Because Cinaed mac Ailpín was portrayed as Fergus's descendant, and as destroyer of the Picts, however, a Scottish reader would naturally have identified with the Isles and Argyll. It is not so surprising, therefore, that the text came to be understood as presenting the kings from Fergus and the Pictish kings not as reigning in parallel in separate realms, but as a single sequence ruling a single kingdom beginning with Fergus and his successors followed by the Picts and then Cinaed mac Ailpin to the thirteenth century.[102] Both versions of the text that included Pictish kings circulated in Scotland throughout the remainder of the middle ages; texts of the list without Pictish kings or without Fergus and his successors appears to have continued to circulate only in England.[103] The next step, traceable to only one text of the king-list, was to revise the statement of the bounds of the original kingdom so that it was imagined that Fergus ruled an area equivalent to the later medieval kingdom: this was delineated as extending all the way from the Isles in the west to the Orkneys in the north and Stainmore (in Cumbria) in the south – a rather ambitious view of the Scottish realm.[104]

At the end of the day, the stipulation that the inhabitants of the Isles should be dealt with and judged according to the "laws and customs of the Scottish kingdom" can be understood in the context of the Treaty as implicitly embracing whatever laws and customs were current in the Isles: the only necessary change was that the administration of justice was now in the name of the king of Scots rather than the king of Norway. It is possible, however, that because the Isles were regarded as a primordial part of the Scottish kingdom itself, they were not seen in the same way as Galloway, as a distinct entity with its own laws and customs. Neither suggestion seems entirely satisfactory. This leads to a fundamental question: does Scottish law

101 Broun, *The Irish Identity* (n 96) 161–164; Broun, *Scottish Independence* (n 13) 245.

102 Broun, *The Irish Identity* (n 96), 106–109; Broun, *Scottish Independence* (n 13) 237–239.

103 Broun, *The Irish Identity* (n 96) 134–145 (where the "X-group" survive predominantly in Scottish contexts, and the "Y-group", which lack the Pictish king-list and (usually) the list from Fergus to Cinaed mac Ailpín's father, survive predominantly in England).

104 Broun, *Scottish Independence* (n 13) 166–170.

and jurisdiction necessarily mean a unitary power in deciding legal disputes, with judicial mechanisms to make this a reality, or could a simple idea of the king as ultimate authority over the Scots have been sufficient? If something like the latter is true, then this could help to reconcile the reality of legal diversity with the idea of the realm as a single jurisdiction that is glimpsed in the Treaty of Perth. This can be pursued by considering what part was played by the idea of "Scottish law" in contemporary views of the kingdom's remote past.

E: THE KINGDOM'S BEGINNINGS AND THE SCOTTISH LAW

Scottish origins were imagined as beginning initially with eponymous ancestors in biblical times and culminating in the "destruction" of the Picts by Cinaed mac Ailpín. Sometimes these founding figures were portrayed as establishing the laws of their people. Fordun's history of the Scots, for example, portrays "Gaythelos" (i.e. Gaedel, a Gaelic eponym for the Scots), a Greek prince, teaching his people to observe the law of the Greeks: this could readily have originated in Vairement's lost work.[105] This finishes by stating that "our Scots have prided themselves that they use these same laws to the present day".[106]

As far as ideas of law and the kingdom's beginnings in the early years of Alexander III's reign is concerned, the most significant surviving statement is a passage on Cinaed mac Ailpín in the Chronicle of Melrose, datable to sometime between 1246 and 1264. This was part of a campaign by a scribe who added a complete series of Scottish kings to the Chronicle's text from 731 (where this part of the Chronicle begins).[107] The scribe added a stanza

105 See above, 66, for Vairement. The initial sentence and final section of Fordun's book I ch 19 go together (linked by King Phroneus giving his law to the Greeks); this could have originated in Vairement's text if the intervening section was added by "proto-Fordun". See also next note.

106 W F Skene (ed), *Johannis de Fordun Chronica Gentis Scotorum* (1871), *The Historians of Scotland* vol 1, 18: "*usque hodie Scoti nostri eisdem legibus se usos gloriati sunt*". The way of referring to "our Scots" in the third person (*se usos gloriati sunt*) seems awkward and might perhaps reflect the perspective of a Frenchman like Vairement who had made Scotland his home.

107 Stratum 21, consisting of additions by Scribe 28 taken from a king-list beginning with Fergus and then a Latin verse king-list beginning with Cinaed mac Ailpín: the verse king-list is edited from the Chronicle of Melrose and two other manuscripts in W F Skene, *Chronicles of the Picts, Chronicles of the Scots* (1867) 177–182 (as 'The Metrical Chronicle, commonly called the Cronicon Elegiacum'), and discussed in D Broun, 'Contemporary perspectives on Alexander II's succession: the evidence of king-lists', in R D Oram (ed), *The Reign of Alexander II, 1214–1249* (2005) 79–98, at 84–88. Scribe 28's work is datable to between probably 2 November 1246 and probably mid-1265 (possibly before 1259); he was perhaps prompted to add this king-list

on Cinead from a king-list in elegiac verse where Cinaed is referred to as the "first to have ruled in Scotland (*Albania*)"; this prompted the scribe – who had added kings prior to Cinaed – to explain that Cinaed mac Ailpín "is called the first king not because he was, but because he was first to establish Scottish laws, which they call the laws of mac Ailpín".[108] It is tempting to try and see a connection here with a statement in a king-list chronicle (sometimes referred to as the 'Chronicle of the Kings of Alba') datable to the early 960s: it survives as part of a compilation of historical material found only in a mid-fourteenth-century manuscript.[109] We are told there that, in the time of Cinaed's brother and successor, Domnall ("king of Picts" 858–862), "the Gaels with their king made the rules and laws of the kingdom, of Aed mac Echdach, at Forteviot".[110] Aed mac Echdach died in 778 as king of Dál Riata (a Gaelic kingdom in the west); it has been suggested, therefore, that this event marked a renewal of the relationship between the king of the Picts and the king of Dál Riata that had originally been established a century or so earlier.[111] It is difficult, therefore, to see a meaningful connection with "the laws of mac Ailpín" in the thirteenth century. There are no grounds, therefore, for supposing that "the laws of mac Ailpín" relate to any event in the ninth century. No text purporting to be these laws was created in the middle ages either (in contrast to the so-called laws of Mael Coluim mac Cinaeda, who reigned 1005–1034, dated to the fourteenth century).[112] It was left to the

material by the burial of Alexander II in Melrose Abbey in July 1249: Broun, 'Charting the Chronicle's physical development' (n 94) 149–151. Most of the text of this stratum is published separately in Stevenson (ed), *Chronica de Mailros* (n 94), 223–229 under the title 'Chronicon Rythmicum' (omitting the verse on William the Lion added to the annal for 1214, which is also overlooked in the edition of the annal for 1214 itself at *ibid*., 114: it can be seen in the top margin of f.30v: *http://www.bl.uk/manuscripts/Viewer.aspx?ref=cotton_ms_faustina_b_ix_f030v* (last accessed 12 July 2022)).

108 "*Iste uocatus est rex primus non quia fuit set quia primus leges Scoticanas instituit quas uocant leges Mac Alpin*", London, British Library Cotton MS Faustina B. IX f.5r, addition to inner margin, see *http://www.bl.uk/manuscripts/Viewer.aspx?ref=cotton_ms_faustina_b_ix_f005r* (last accessed 12 July 2022); Stevenson (ed), *Chronica de Mailros* (n 94) 224; MacQueen, '*Regiam Majestatem*' (n 6) 7.

109 Anderson, *Kings and Kingship in Early Scotland* (n 96) 249–253; B T Hudson, 'The Scottish Chronicle' (1998) 77 *Scottish Historical Review* 129–161; D N Dumville, 'The Chronicle of the Kings of Alba', in S Taylor (ed), *Kings, Clerics and Chronicles in Scotland, 500–1297* (2000) 73–86; A Woolf, *From Pictland to Alba, 789–1070* (2007) 88–93. (The dating is explained in an unpublished study of the text.)

110 "*iura ac legis regni Edi filii Ecdach fecerunt Goedeli cum rege suo i Fochiurthabaicth*", Hudson, 'The Scottish Chronicle' (n 109) 148.

111 Woolf, *From Pictland to Alba* (n. 109) 105–106.

112 A A M Duncan, 'The Laws of Malcolm MacKenneth', in A Grant and K J Stringer (eds), *Medieval Scotland: Crown, Lordship and Community. Essays Presented to G. W. S. Barrow* (1993) 239–273; MacQueen, '*Regiam Majestatem*' (n 6) 11–12.

humanist art of Hector Boece, renown for spinning narratives from the most meagre material, to bring the laws of Cinaed mac Ailpín fully to life in his vivid rewriting of the kingdom's history published in 1527.[113] Cinaed's law-making prior to Boece was not solely the idea of a Melrose scribe, however. A similar statement about the laws of mac Ailpín is also found in Fordun's history and could therefore have potentially been in Vairement's work.[114] The idea of Cinaed as "first" king establishing laws named after him may also have appeared in the original text of the elegiac verse king-list itself that was composed a generation or two before it was copied by the Melrose scribe.[115]

If we are to look for an equivalent of King Magnus Håkonsson the "Lawmender" in mid-thirteenth-century Scotland, therefore, it is not a king who actually commissioned an authoritative written statement of the kingdom's laws, but the reimagining of Cinaed mac Ailpín as the king who established what the Melrose scribe referred to as *leges Scoticana*, "Scottish laws". It was not until the reign of Robert I (1306–1329) that legal compilations were presented as if they were the laws of an individual king. The most extensive texts of the kingdom's laws in the middle ages were written at this time: all were attributed to David I (1124–1153).[116] This was the first occasion when a king's image as a founding figure was expressed principally in terms of law-making: in the case of Cinaed mac Ailpín, law-making was a corollary of the older image of him as "first king". The earliest association of the kingdom's laws specifically with David I is in Edward I's commission

113 H Boece, *Scotorum Historiae a Prima Gentis Originis* ([1527]) ff.ccvii^{r}–ccviii^{r}. (I am grateful to Alice Taylor and Gilbert Márkus for alerting me to this.) Boece does not refer to the "laws of mac Ailpín" as such, however; it is conceivable that he was prompted to list the laws simply by Cinaed's role as a founding figure. On Boece and his history see U Hogg and M MacGregor, 'Historiography in Highlands and Lowlands', in N Royan (ed), *The International Companion to Scottish Literature 1400–1650* (2018) 100–123 at 107–109.

114 Skene (ed), *Johannis de Fordun* (n 106) 151: "*iura uero que leges Macalpine dicuntur componens obseruari statuit quarum hactenus quedam restant ac inter populos cursum habent*", "[Cinaed mac Ailpín], moreover, putting together the corpus of laws which are called the laws of mac Ailpín, ordained that they be observed, of which some remain and are in use among the people"; MacQueen, '*Regiam Majestatem*' (n 6) 7.

115 It has been suggested that the poem may have been composed for the funeral of King William I on 10 December 1214: Broun, 'Contemporary perspectives' (n 107) 85–86. The verse king-list was incorporated into Andrew of Wyntoun's *Original Chronicle* (in Scots verse) composed initially sometime between 1408 and 1424 (Broun, *The Irish Identity* (n 96) 96 n 40). Wyntoun did not use the Chronicle of Melrose as a source. When Wyntoun observes that Cinaed "made laws that were afterwards called the laws of mac Ailpín", therefore, he may have been repeating a comment found in his text of the verse king-list: F J Amours (ed), *The Original Chronicle of Andrew of Wyntoun*, Scottish Text Society, 6 vols (1903–1914) iv, 174, 175.

116 *Regiam Maiestatem* and *Quoniam Attachiamenta*, Simpson and Wilson, *Scottish Legal History* (n 32) 60–62, and above, 70, and below, 93. On *Regiam* and David I, see esp. Taylor, 'What does *Regiam Maiestatem* actually say' (n 32) 51–56, 63–71.

of legal reform in 1305 during his second period of governing Scotland.[117] This view of David I may have been only a recent development: it is striking how little of the legislation originating in thirteenth-century compilations refer to David I.[118] Although David I was already a point of reference for legal innovations in charters of his grandson William I (1165–1214),[119] there is no indication that a collection of David I's enactments was made during or shortly after his reign: Alice Taylor has identified only a single potential example in extant compilations – a decree that applied only to one of the "countries" in his realm, not the kingdom as a whole.[120]

Regnal solidarity and ambitions to enhance the kingdom's status were, no doubt, to some extent shaped by a shared experience of royal judicial authority by the Scottish elite.[121] A fundamental degree of diversity, however, was inherent in a realm where royal authority was manifest through aristocratic power. As Alice Taylor has observed;

> The common law of the land did not mean that all people interacted with the same judicial institutions in the same way, but that, regardless of jurisdiction, the common law or the law of the kingdom was supposed to be upheld.[122]

There was no expectation that there should be a single legal system, as it were, across the kingdom in the here-and-now. It was, it seems, sufficient to imagine the kingdom as a uniform society when it first began in ancient times.

All in all, taking a broad view of the issue of law and the unity of the realm, it is possible to discern a progression in the way the kingdom was imagined between the twelfth and fourteenth centuries.[123] In David I's reign "Scotland" as a kingdom was conceptualised not as the territory ruled by the king, but as the landmass north of the Firth of Forth, even though the realm in reality comprised many "countries" north and south of the Forth. By the beginning of the thirteenth century it was possible to regard the kingdom as a whole as the point of reference for defining landholding and lordship[124]:

117 E L G Stones (ed and tr), *Anglo-Scottish Relations 1174–1328: Some Select Documents* (1970) no 33, 241–259, at 250–251; MacQueen, *'Regiam Majestatem'* (n 6) 8.

118 See above, 69–70, and 75, for a rare example.

119 Taylor, *The Shape of the State* (n 5) 180–187.

120 Taylor (ed), *The Laws of Medieval Scotland* (n 28) 300–301.

121 See above, 65.

122 Taylor, *The Shape of the State* (n 5) 347; see also Simpson and Wilson, *Scottish Legal History* (n 32) 47–55.

123 Broun, 'Kingdom and identity' (n 39) 32–39; Broun, 'Rethinking Scottish origins' (n 99) 165–188.

124 Broun, 'Kingdom and identity' (n 39) 63–74.

this allowed it to be conceptualised as a single country north and south of the Forth embracing all the territory under the king's authority. In the fourteenth century this sense of the kingdom as a jurisdiction had developed into an expectation that the kingdom's laws could be "gathered together in an analytical or systematic way" (to quote Hector MacQueen on *Regiam*) – an expectation that was acted on by at least some legal scholars at the time, but never fully achieved.[125] The addition of lawmaker to Cinaed mac Ailpín's profile as the "first king" can be seen in this context as a reflection of the thirteenth century idea of the kingdom as primarily a jurisdiction, but without any expectation that its laws would or could be stated in a fresh authoritative text commissioned by the king.

It is notable that the Melrose scribe saw Cinaed not simply as a king who made laws (which on its own would not have been remarkable), but as establishing *leges Scoticana*, "Scottish laws". This phrase is reminiscent of "English law" or "Galwegian law". The scribe, however, was engaged in a careful campaign to establish the kingship's history throughout the centuries covered in the Chronicle of Melrose up to their own times. In this context, therefore, the intention was not to define these laws with a particular ethnic group: it was Cinaed's role as "first king" of the current kingdom of the Scots that triggered the idea of "Scottish laws" in the scribe's mind. There is no reason to doubt, therefore, that the scribe was imagining the moment when the laws and customs of the kingdom were first established. On the face of it this might be compared with the way other distinctive and long-established features of the social landscape (such as army service and horizontal mills) could be described as "Scottish", too.[126] If so, however, "Scottish" here was

125 MacQueen, '*Regiam Majestatem*' (n 6) 3; on *Regiam* as an unfinished work, see now Taylor, 'What does *Regiam Maiestatem* actually say' (n 32) 61–63. On *Regiam* and its counterpart (as it were) for baronial courts, *Quoniam Attachiamenta*, see Simpson and Wilson, *Scottish Legal History* (n 32) 60–62, and above, 70.

126 It has been suggested that whenever language, roads, mills, measures, land units and common obligations are referred to as "Scottish" in this period, this was "to distinguish anything recognized to belong to the older order before the advent of French and English speech and customs" (Barrow, *The Anglo-Norman Era* (n 62) 161–162); see also the discussion of "Scottish" mills and roads in A P Morgan, 'Ethnonyms in the Place-names of Scotland and the Border Counties of England', unpublished PhD thesis, University of St Andrews (2013) 186–187, 197–198, where it is suggested that this may have referred to the older horizontal type of mill (in contrast to vertical mills) and to traditional routeways. There is a tendency to see this use of "Scottish" as negative (and even as medieval instances of the "Scottish cringe": *ibid*., 198), but a modern view of "progress" should best be avoided: it seems more likely, on the face of it, that in the middle ages it is more likely to have been positive to view anything as "traditional" and "old", because this would have endowed it with authority as something established by long usage.

not referring to actual older laws but to the kingdom's laws as a whole as an idea that was as old as the kingdom itself.

F: A SCOTTISH PERSPECTIVE ON LAW AND REGNAL UNITY

This could offer a way to address a final fundamental conundrum faced by legal historians in particular. It has been suggested that, despite Alice Taylor's ground-breaking study of the development of the kingdom's laws in the thirteenth century, "We seem further from understanding how medieval Scots could have believed that they had a common law of their own than we were (or thought we were) a few years ago".[127] The issue is not only that Scotland lacked a central court, but that it is unclear how a body of common law could have developed in the absence of forms of action that might have generated decisions that passed into law. This is not to deny that there was legislation that applied to all the kingdom's inhabitants, or procedures that were generally available, or references to particular customs as "common law" [128] An element of regional diversity, moreover, is not the key problem. The issue, from the perspective of legal history, is how to envisage "Scottish law" as a body of judicial practice with its own identity separate from the laws of other kingdoms. An answer has been sought by considering whether there were legal remedies that were available to all the kingdom's inhabitants, and were used frequently by them, in baronial as much as royal courts. This has become a richly contested topic, with a wide divergence of perspectives fashioned cogently from the limited evidence.[129]

It is possible to step back from this, however, and offer a different kind of answer. In considering how medieval Scots could have believed there was "Scottish law" it is not necessary to suppose that there was a distinct and

127 J D Ford, 'Review of Taylor, *The Shape of the State in Medieval Scotland 1124–1290*' (2017) 80 *Modern Law Review* 555–559, at 558.

128 See above, 69–70, and Taylor, *The Shape of the State* (n 5) ch 5 ('The Development of a Common Law, 1230–1290'): note the reference (*ibid*., 266) to *ius commune*, "common law", in a charter of Alexander III on 21 July 1264 affirming the right of monks of Melrose to get pasture overnight for their animals drawing carts on journeys through the country: Innes (ed), *Liber Sancte Marie de Melros* (n 65), i, 273 (no. 309); *PoMS* Hammond number 1/8/49.

129 For a perceptive analysis of points under discussion see A R C Simpson, 'Foreward: common law and feudal society in scholarship since 1993', in H L MacQueen, *Common Law and Feudal Society in Medieval Scotland*, Edinburgh Classics Edition (2016) xxix–lxi, at xxxv–xlvi. The key work, apart from Taylor, *The Shape of the State* (n 5), Taylor (ed), *The Laws of Medieval Scotland* (n 28) and MacQueen, *Common Law and Feudal Society* (originally published in 1993) is D Carpenter, 'Scottish royal government in the thirteenth century from an English perspective', in M Hammond (ed), *New Perspectives on Medieval Scotland 1093–1286* (2013) 117–159.

internally coherent body of common law or, minimally, a shared repertoire of generally available remedies. It is sufficient simply to think like the scribe in the Chronicle of Melrose who explained that Cinaed mac Ailpín was "first king" because he established "Scottish laws". From the perspective of the thirteenth century, the belief in "Scottish laws" or the common law of the realm was simply a function of being a kingdom with royal authority embodied in a network of courts. It rested not on an actual body of law, but on an assumption that the kingdom was a distinct jurisdiction, and that it must have been so from the beginning (whenever this was imagined to have been). This was made easier by the fact that the laws of the Scottish kingdom, if they were regarded as an integrated body of laws rather than a piecemeal collection of royal enactments, were at root an idea rather than a reality: they existed, like those of Cinaed mac Ailpín, primarily in the mind rather than in practice. They are, nonetheless, a potent indication of patterns of thinking about law and the kingdom that were part of the social reality of the Scottish ruling elite in the mid-thirteenth century.

It was only later, when it was considered desirable in the early fourteenth century to provide a systematic written account of the kingdom's laws, that it may have begun to be assumed that there was a body of laws of a kind that legal historians today might recognise. Even so, when an attempt was eventually made in *Regiam* to create a Scottish lawbook, it was (as Alice Taylor has shown) written self-consciously as an account of old laws rather than current practice: she has argued, indeed, that it was a calculated attempt to appropriate *Glanvill*, the earliest account of English common law, as originally Scottish.[130] What made this material Scottish was that it was imagined as established by David I.[131] The essential ingredient was a sense that the kingdom's laws – however diverse or patchy that may have been in reality – was grounded in long-established experience.[132]

The comparison with Norway prompts a final question: could patterns of thinking in Scotland have supported the idea of a king of Scots in the present, rather than in the past, establishing the kingdom's laws? Certainly, in reality, this could not have been achieved, as Magnus did, through engaging with

130 Taylor, 'What does *Regiam Maiestatem* actually say' (n 32) 155–171.

131 Taylor, 'What does *Regiam Maiestatem* actually say' (n 32) 163–171.

132 This bears a clear resemblance to the insights about *Regiam* in Harding, '*Regiam Majestatem* among medieval lawbooks' (n 7): a key difference, however, is that here the primary idea of the kingdom as a jurisdiction is understood as already well-established in the mid-thirteenth century, rather than simply a response to the challenge posed by Edward I and Edward II. See also comments on Harding's ideas in MacQueen, '*Regiam Majestatem*' (n 6) 3–8.

provincial assemblies: by the thirteenth century these had either evolved into sheriff courts or been eclipsed by them.[133] Alice Taylor has shown how baronial courts became regularised and established from the 1170s and 1180s as the prevailing judicial fora in the kingdom.[134] The sheriff court was comprised of barons or their representatives; when laws were enacted by the king it was through assemblies of the greatest secular and ecclesiastical barons in the Scottish realm. An authoritative statement of the kingdom's laws would only have been conceivable, therefore, through the active involvement and self-interest of the ruling elite. It was through possessing these courts that they formed a kingdom-wide elite exercising royal authority in local society. There is no indication in the thirteenth century that they (or anyone else) felt that a text defining the kingdom's laws was necessary. As far as the ruling elite were concerned enhancing the kingdom's status was best achieved through symbols and imagined histories, leaving the day-to-day reality of the kingdom's laws largely in their hands. This was, after all, a fundamental dimension of their local power.

At the end of the day, if we wish to understand the relationship between the king's law and the union of the realm in a Scottish context, the most fruitful approach is to focus not so much on law as it was practiced at the time, or Acts of Parliament seeking to change current realities, but on statements about the kingdom's beginnings. By the mid-thirteenth century a founding figure like Cinaed mac Ailpín or perhaps Gaedel Glas could be imagined as establishing or initiating Scottish law; in this we can recognise the force of the idea of the kingdom as a single jurisdiction distinct from other kingdoms and peoples, regardless of legal diversity within the realm and the dependence of royal authority on local judicial power.

133 On the nine provinces in "Scotland" (north of the Forth and south of the Spey) in the reign of David I see Broun, 'Statehood and lordship' (n 53) 15 n 51; three became sheriffdoms: Angus (also known as Forfarshire), Fife (with Cupar as its caput) and the Mearns (known as Kincardineshire).

134 Taylor, *The Shape of the State* (n 5) esp. 157–164.

3 Law and Administrative Change in Norway, Twelfth–Fourteenth Centuries

Jørn Øyrehagen Sunde[*]

A: REGULARISATION AND LEGAL PLURALITY

The history of law and administrative change in Norway during the central middle ages is, as in Scotland, a history of growing regularisation of royal justice and of legal plurality, both in terms of legal institutions and legal rules. Regularisation and legal plurality do, at first glance, appear to be opposing forces on the battlefield for legal unification. However, that hostility only really emerged in the seventeenth century, and crystallised in the eighteenth century. In the central middle ages, their relationship was far more complex. In short, the level of state formation made it possible for regularisation to

[*] This article was written whilst the author was a partner in the project *Social governance through legislation* at the Centre for Advanced Study in Oslo.

happen alongside toleration of a certain degree of legal plurality. This pluralistic tolerant regulation was at the core of medieval politics in Norway in the second half of the thirteenth and first half of the fourteenth century.

The most important event in Norwegian medieval legal history is the making of the Code of the Norwegian Realm in 1274. However, the regulation of law started in the second half of the twelfth century and the emerging legal order would not finally take its full shape before the first half of the fourteenth century. We are hence talking of a process that took at least 200 years, with roots stretching further back and consequences reaching further ahead in time. The process is to some extent paralleled in Scotland and Norway, taking place over the same time period and also the same time span. This is, however, a process that is taking place all over Western Europe at this time. The uniqueness lies rather in how the relationship between regulation and pluralism was settled in different parts of Christendom. A comparison between Scotland and Norway is of great interest. On one hand, the two realms had a comparable population size and economy and parallels in terms of the history of political unification. On the other hand, the Scottish feudal aristocracy, and hence military and administrative organisation, the number and, to an extent, the size of towns, and not least the vastness of the Norwegian realm, are important differences between the Scottish and Norwegian realms. In short: the similarities make a comparison possible and the differences make it interesting.

B: THE REGULATION OF LAW THROUGH LEGISLATION

(1) The legal provinces

Present-day Norway was the core of the medieval Norwegian realm. This realm also included the Isle of Man and the Hebrides until the Treaty of Perth in 1263, Orkney and Shetland until at least the mortgage in 1468 and 1469, Jemtland and Herjedalen at the border with Sweden until 1645, Baahuslen – also at the border with Sweden – until 1658, and the Faroe Islands, Greenland and Iceland until 1814. The Isle of Man, the Hebrides, Orkney, Shetland, the Faroe Islands, Greenland and Iceland were under the rule of the Norwegian king, but not a part of the kingdom, which was mainland Norway. Mainland Norway was, in the first half of the eleventh century, split into four legal provinces, each with an assembly (*þing*) where several hundred representatives from the entire province met once a year around midsummer. The system of compensation for travel costs indicates that even these provincial assemblies were not for aristocrats alone, but for a broader segment of the population.[1]

We do not know the age of the legal provinces. According to the saga tradition, King Håkon I the Good supposedly made the law for the Gulathing province in western Norway and the Frostathing province in the middle of the tenth century,[2] while King Olaf II the Holy supposedly gave the law for the Borgarthing province around the Oslo fjord and the Eidsivathing province in the interior of the south eastern part of Norway in the early eleventh century.[3] Kings would definitely have had a great interest in these legal provinces, since they could be considered communication centres suited for governance purposes. It is only at this level that there is any regulation initiated by central government before the thirteenth century. Beyond this upper level of social governance, there was a multitude of assemblies that made and applied legal norms in a certain geographical area from the toon (i.e. the individual farming community) to the region. Their origin and organisation, and the norms they applied are basically unknown, even if reconstruction has been attempted based on the little evidence we have.[4]

What we do know is that it was only after several centuries that a Norwegian king, Magnus VI the Lawmender, first managed to unify law between the four legal provinces in 1274. We do not know the law made and applied before the first surviving manuscript fragments of the Gulathing Law from the late-twelfth century. From the middle of the thirteenth century we have a complete version of both the Gulathing and Frostathing Laws, while most of the Borgarthing and Eidsivathing Laws are lost; only the Christian laws are preserved. Comparing the Gulathing and Frostathing Laws, we see that they represented independent and different legal traditions. For example, the Gulathing Law appears more archaic, more influenced by aristocratic interests and more concerned with trade, while the Frostathing Law is more updated with learned law, more influenced by the archiepiscopal see situated in the province, and more concerned with legal procedure. However, it is when we compare the Christian laws of the four provincial Laws that we are confronted with the legal plurality of the time. Christian laws were the canon law adapted at the provincial assemblies, at times seemingly even in

1 See K Helle, *Gulating og Gulatingslova* (2001) 68–69.

2 Helle, *Gulating* (n 1) 30–31, J R Hagland, and J Sandnes, 'Innleiing' (1994) in J R Hagland and J Sandnes (eds), *Frostatingslova*, x.

3 K Robberstad, *Rettssoga I* (1976) 139 and 141.

4 See J Ø Sunde, *Speculum legale – Rettsspegelen: Ein introduksjon til den norske rettskulturen si historie i eit europeisk perspektiv* (2005) 83–85.

conflict with canon law, like the rule in the Boargarthing Christian law on the locals' right to employ and control priests. Even when the archiepiscopal see was established in Nidaros in 1152 or 1153, a unification of the rules on, for instance, baptism was not achieved before the 1260s.[5]

Unification, even at a most basic level, was impossible because of the lack of a central authority that could challenge the authority and autonomy of the legal provinces. This was also the case in relation to questions of law that naturally should have been unified. In the above example, we have seen how even law originating in canon law varied from secular province to province in Norway until the second half of the thirteenth century, even though it was slowly unified from the middle of the twelfth century. The same applies for royal legislation on the defence of the realm. According to the sagas, the first legislation on the defence of the realm was passed on Gulathing by King Håkon I the Good in the middle of the tenth century.[6] We have no reliable sources on the content of this alleged legislation. However, in the manuscript with the complete Gulathing Law from the middle of the thirteenth century, we have an interesting statement made by the nameless scribe. After having recorded the laws on the defence of the realm, he adds:

> Now we have committed to writing (our laws concerning) the defence of the country, but we do not know whether the statement is right or wrong. But if it is wrong, we shall follow the legal regulations about our defence duties which we have had before and which Atle explained to the men in Gulen, unless the king wants to grant us other plans and we all agree to them.[7]

From this statement we can learn that the king was, even as late as the mid-thirteenth century, not regarded as having sole charge of legal regulation of the defence of the realm – which was clearly his responsibility – but had to cooperate with the provincial assembly.[8] No wonder the regulations on defence of the realm in the Gulathing and the Frostathing Laws are not unified – each issue had to be negotiated separately with each assembly. Secondly, we also learn that the spoken word has authority over the written word – the scribe does not operate with rules about which manuscripts have authority over others in the case of differences in content, but claims

5 T Landro, *Kristenrett og kyrkjerett – Borgartingskristenrett i eit komparativt perspektiv* (2010) 187–202.

6 Helle, *Gulating* (n 1) 32.

7 E Simensen (ed), *The Older Gulathing Law* (2021) 209.

8 For Scotland, see A Taylor, *The Shape of the State in Medieval Scotland 1124–1290* (2016) 102–113.

that that which can be remembered of what Atle, a high ranking aristocrat, explained around 1040 is most authoritative.[9] The unification of law was hence a question of the authority of different kinds of communication technology as much as of politics and culture until the second half of the thirteenth century.

(2) St Olaf's law

The Code of 1274 was neither the beginning nor the end of a tradition of legislation in medieval Norway. Rather, it was a peak in a long tradition. The Code itself makes four references[10] to the laws of St Olaf (*logum hinns hælga olafs konungs*).[11] King Olaf II Haraldsson, later called the Holy and regarded a saint, reigned as Norwegian king from 1015–1028, and was killed in 1030 during an attempt to regain the throne. It is easy to dismiss these references as purely rhetorical, since Olaf II in general came to be regarded as the source of all things good. Furthermore, it can be hard to say what was the work of Olaf II, or rather – as we shall see – the work of his English-born bishop Grimkjell, or later added in his name. However, it is thought certain that the saintly king was in charge of a program of legislative activity; and this was sufficiently extensive to be subsequently regarded as being of at least some significance.[12] This is important for the royal legislative activity more than a hundred years later.

In the turbulent years of the Norwegian civil wars, starting with the death of King Sigurd I the Crusader in 1130 and ending with the death of Earl Skule in 1240, an important event was the coronation of the infant Magnus V in Bergen in 1163 or 1164. Magnus was not by law an heir to the throne – he was son of the daughter of Sigurd I, and only sons – born within or outside wedlock – could be elected king of Norway. However, after thirty-one years of strife between different pretenders to the throne, Magnus' father, Erling Skakke, made a deal with the church. Erling Skakke, also a former crusader, had married Kristin, the daughter – and only legitimate child – of Sigurd I. Magnus was hence the legitimate son of a legitimate daughter; his father was a powerful magnate willing to give the church a major say in the election of

9 Helle, *Gulating* (n 1) 21 and 39, see also Simensen (ed), *The Older Gulathing Law* (n 7) 209 n 55; M T Clanchy, *From Memory to Written Record – England 1066–1307* (2013) 295–300.

10 The Code of the Norwegian Realm II-3, 8, 11 and 12.

11 M Rindal and B D Spørck (eds), *Kong Magnus Håkonsson Lagabøtes landslov – Norrøn tekst med fullstendig variantapparat: del I* (2018) 173.

12 See Helle, *Gulating* (n 1) 18 and 49.

future kings, and to acknowledge St Olaf as the *rex perpetuus* of Norway, to whom future Norwegian kings would be vassals. Subsequently, Erling Skakke and then Magnus V were killed in 1179 and 1184 respectively by King Sverre Sigurdsson, who at best was the illegitimate son of King Sigurd II Munn, and in all likelihood just a gifted opportunist. On the other hand, the descendants of Sverre Sigurdsson would to a large extent take over the St Olaf rhetoric to legitimise their right to the throne and, additionally, to legitimise their right to legislate.

When crowned in Bergen in 1163/1164, Magnus V – or rather his father and Archbishop Øystein Erlingsson – issued new legislation. This was not done at the Gulathing assembly north of Bergen, but at the parliament in Bergen that elected Magnus as king. Probably in order to legitimate this breach of tradition, surpassing Gulathing, the new legislation was presented as changes in the existing legislation ascribed to St Olaf. This was done by noting in the text what was legislated by Olaf II and what had been changed, added or even deleted by Magnus V.[13] There also circulated manuscripts that ascribed legislation only to St Olaf[14] and this might have given rise to the idea of a St Olaf's law.

We can hence only know with certainty that the alleged legislation of Olaf II dates back to before the legislation of Magnus V was added, so that ascribing it to St Olaf did not appear as an obvious fraud. There are two other factors that are more important than the age of the content ascribed to St Olaf. First, is seems undisputed that a meeting was held at Moster on the island of Bømlo, south of Bergen, in the early 1020s.[15] This is referred to once in the Frostathing Law[16] and four times in three different chapters in the Gulathing Law:

> The next thing is that we shall maintain all those churches and observe those decrees about Christianity which the Holy Olaf and Bishop Grimkjell laid down at the Moster assembly.[17]

> Now the next thing is that our bishop shall govern the churches as the Holy Olaf promised Bishop Grimkjell at the Moster assembly and we agreed to later. Our bishop must now appoint to all churches such priests as are capable of giving proper services to people. We should provide them with such

13 Helle, *Gulating* (n 1): 17–20. See also E Simensen, 'Translator's Introduction', in E Simensen (ed), *The Older Gulathing Law* (2021) 10.

14 K Robberstad, 'Innleidning', in K Robberstad (ed), *Gulatingslovi* (1952) 9 (C).

15 Helle, *Gulating* (n 1) 177. See also Landro, *Kristenrett og kyrkjerett* (n 5) 191.

16 Frostating Law III-1.

17 Simensen (ed), *The Older Gulathing Law*, (n 7) 23-24 (ch 10).

maintenance as the Holy Olaf and Bishop Grimkjell laid down at the Moster assembly.[18]

These are the days which Saint Olaf and Bishop Grimkjell laid down at the Moster assembly, thereby declaring a preceding fast and holiness from the preceding nones, they are to be observed just as Sundays.[19]

Moster was in the Gulathing province, but a couple of days' journey by boat from where the assembly met up until about 1300. That the meeting was held at Moster and not at the proper meeting place for Gulathing seems to be because it was a meeting for magnates from the entire realm and not only from the province. It might hence be that the legal historian Absalon Taranger was right when claiming that this was the first Norwegian parliament held, and the first attempt to do politics and legislate independently of the legal provinces.[20] What might support this view is that at the meeting it was decided how many representatives should meet at the Gulathing assembly every year.[21] This part of the alleged legislation of Olaf II has not been disputed either. By deciding the number of representatives delegated to the assembly at Gulathing, the meeting at Moster displays a greater authority than that of the provincial assembly. The next time a decision is made on the issue is at the meeting for magnates of the entire Norwegian realm in Bergen when Magnus V was crowned in 1163/1164. It hence seems that the establishment of an organ for regulating the law of the realm was attempted in the early 1020s. With Olaf II chased from the Norwegian kingdom in 1028, and eventually with his death at the battle of Stikklestad in 1030, no new attempts to legislate at a meeting of the realm were made before the meeting in Bergen about 140 years later. However, Magnus V died at the battle of Fimmreite in 1184 and the meeting of the realm in 1163/1164 was the only one held during his reign to pass legislation. On the third occasion that a meeting of the realm was held for this purpose, it was convened by Håkon IV in 1260.[22]

Unlike Olaf II and Magnus V, Håkon IV's right to reign as Norwegian king was not at all disputed at the time of the meeting of the realm in 1260; the rival to the throne – Earl Skule – was killed on the king's order in 1240.

18 Simensen (ed), *The Older Gulathing Law* (n 7) 25 (ch 15).

19 Simensen (ed), *The Older Gulathing Law* (n 7) 26 (ch 17).

20 A Taranger, *Udsigt over den norske rets historie: II, 1: Statsrettens historie (indtil 1319)* (1904) 204.

21 The Older Gulathing Law, ch 2.

22 K Helle, *Konge og gode menn. I norsk riksstyring ca. 1150–1319* (1972) 114–156. Helle also includes a church meeting in Trondheim in 1152 or 1153. However, it was not initiated by a king and hence it is not included here.

There is also no evidence that the royal legislation of 1260 for the entire Norwegian realm was disputed either. However, the meetings in the early 1020s and in 1163/1164 were also successful when it came to regulation by law, even though they politically did not ensure the king's continued rule in the long run. Even though we do not know how much Olaf II actually legislated, some legislation was passed, like the one on the number of representatives at the Gulathing assembly. Whether Olaf II passed more extensive legislation or not, Knut Helle claims that the legislation ascribed to him was influential and had some regulatory effect.[23] This established St Olaf as a legislator. Magnus V could hence legislate under the pretence of only mending the legislation of his processor St Olaf and by this strengthen a tradition of legislation for the entire realm.

It is to this legislative tradition that Håkon IV refers in the introduction to his New Law of 1260, when he states that St Olaf's law should be unaltered ("*at løg hins Helga ólafs konungs sandi eftir þvi sem hann hafði skipct*").[24] The same reference to St Olaf's law ("*at log hins Helga Olafs konungs standa epter þui sem hann skipaðe*")[25] was made in a revision of what we would today call criminal law, written between 1258 and 1263.[26] It is this tradition that is referred to in Håkon IV's saga from the 1260s, when the lawman Gunnar Grotbak in 1223 speaks of the lawbook made by St Olaf that was for all the kingdom ("*þat laugbok ens Helga Olafs konungs er eptir hans skipan uar gor um allan Noreg*").[27] It is this legislative tradition to which Magnus the Lawmender refers four times in the Code of 1274. It does not, however, end there, and in later legislation this legitimation would almost take the shape of an ideology. In the preamble of a decree in 1302 by Håkon V, on a daughter's right to inherit the throne in a situation when he only had two daughters and no sons, the following statement was made:

> Sumt man fylgia lagum kirkunnar oc keisarens, en uera skildi rikinu til mykils haska, oc allu folkenu til mykilla unada er Þat byggia. Nu saker Þess at uer iat-

23 Helle, *Gulating* (n 1) 178–180.

24 P A Munch and R Kryser (eds), *Norges gamle Love indtil 1387: første bind* (1846) 16 (henceforth NgL vol I).

25 P A Munch and R Keyser (eds), NgL, vol I (n 24) 266.

26 Archbishop Einar participated in the revision of the law and he held the office between 1258 and 1263.

27 M Mundt (ed), *Hákonar saga Hákonarsonar* (1977) 55. See also 54 *(laugum hins helga Olaf konungs)* and 104 *(laug ins Helga Olafs konungs)*. Be aware of J Knirk, *Hákonar saga Hákonarsonar – Etter Sth.8 fol.,AM 325 VIII,4° og AM 304,4°* (1982).

tadom gudi i vigslu vara, at uer skuldum Þau logh halda oc haldazt leta sem hin helgi Olafr konongr hof oc hans retter eftir komandar hafa sidan til sett og samtyct.[28]

Some follow the laws of the Church and some of the Emperor, and it shall have caused confusion and been harmful for the inhabitants. Now, since we have promised God at our coronation, that we shall keep, and see to the keeping of the laws of St Olaf, later acknowledged and followed by his rightful heirs.[29]

In the preamble, Håkon V does not use the tradition of Olaf II as the original and ultimate legislator to legitimise his own legislation – after the Code of 1274 there could be no question of the Norwegian king's right to legislate. The reference to St Olaf's law is, instead, a justification for the superiority of the king's legislation, in terms of content, consequences and legitimacy, over both Roman law and canon law.

Let me recapitulate. Olaf II held a meeting at Moster in 1022, and must have passed some legislation, even if the extent and content of the legislation might be disputed. This event made it possible for Magnus V to legislate in the same fields of law in which Olaf II had allegedly legislated. This, coupled with the circulation of manuscripts with the alleged legislation of Olaf II, made it plausible to speak of a St Olaf's Law at least from the 1260s. St Olaf's law was a law for the realm, different from the provincial laws. The idea of the legislation of Olaf II was hence a handy instrument for justifying royal legislation replacing the laws of the provinces.

(3) The Code of the Norwegian Realm of 1274

With the Code of 1274, Norwegian law was unified. To achieve this, the legal provinces had to be made to submit to royal legislation for the entire realm. The idea of St Olaf's law was a rhetorical instrument in this process. However, it was no game changer but was only one of several factors working together without there being a master plan behind them. The end result was regulation that would last the rest of the middle ages.

The New Law of Håkon IV is dated to 1260 because the Icelandic annals record a meeting of the realm that year at Frostathing,[30] one of the old legal provinces. It has been suggested that the content of the New Law was not new at all, but a decree composed of different pieces of legislation from 1240

28 P A Munch and R Keyser (eds), *Norges gamle Love indtil 1387: Tredie bind* (1849) 45 (henceforth NgL vol III).

29 Translation by the author.

30 Helle, *Konge og gode menn* (n 22) 153.

to 1260.[31] One guess is as good as any other in this matter. The main point is that the legislation appears to be aimed at the entire realm, even though it was only preserved as a kind of preface to a manuscript of the Frostathing Law dating back to around 1260, lost in 1728.[32] At the same time, or shortly thereafter, the king, the archbishop, bishops, barons ("*lendra manna*"),[33] the lawmen ("*logmanna*") and other wise men ("*annarra hina vitrastu manna i landino*") were gathered to revise what we today would call the criminal law. We have the revision preserved in the Icelandic Code Jarnsiða from 1271[34] and partly in the Code of 1274. The underlying purpose of the revision seems to be the same as in the New Law – to reduce the use of vengeance as an instrument for conflict resolution, which was still a legal phenomenon attested in the Gulathing and the Frostathing Laws as they are recorded in complete manuscripts from around 1260.[35]

Because the New Law and the revision have an overlapping purpose, they were presumably made at different times as steps in the same process towards abolishing vengeance, which was finally done in the Code of 1274.[36] The revision cannot have been made later than the spring of 1263, since Håkon IV and Archbishop Einar participated, and they both died that year, Håkon IV in Kirkwall in the Orkneys after the campaign against Scotland. The revision of what we would today call criminal law might not have been an isolated legislative effort. The reason for this statement is that according to *Annales regii*, King Magnus VI presented a new law code for Gulathing in 1267, one for Borgarthing and Eidsivathing in 1268, and one for Frostathing in 1269.[37] It might be that the revised law had been intended from its inception to be a part of this code of law. The problem is that the four codes of law have been lost. Anna Horn has recently argued that they were not, as stated in previous research, four different codes of law, but one code of law for the entire realm. She further claims that Jarnsiða for Iceland from 1271 was not an Icelandic code at all, but simply an attempted introduction of the Norwegian Code

31 Hagland and Sandnes, 'Innleiing' (n 2) xxxi.

32 Hagland and Sandnes, 'Innleiing' (n 2) xxxiii.

33 It is first in 1277 that the "lendra manna" are called "barons", but the term is still best translated into "baron" before 1277.

34 Munch and Keyser (eds), NgL, vol I (n 24) 266–273 (chs 20–41).

35 J Ø Sunde, 'Daughters of God and counsellors of the judges of men – a study in changes in the legal culture in the Norwegian realm in the High Middle Ages', in S Brink and L Collionson (eds), *New Approaches to Early Law in Scandinavia* (2014) 131–183 at 143 and 143.

36 The Code of 1274 IV-17.

37 G Storm (ed), 'Annales regii', in *Islandske Annaler indtil 1578* (1888) 137–138.

of 1267 for Iceland as well.[38] If she is right, the revised criminal law we find in Jarnsiða, and later in the Code of 1274, was an important part of a legislative project aiming at unifying law in the entire Norwegian realm, taking place in the 1260s when St Olaf's law became a part of the political and legal rhetoric.

The legislative project 1267–1271 was not a success. There are two reasons for this. First, the code presented at Frostathing was rejected since it regulated all fields of law, including what until then had been regarded a part of Christian law – the canon law adopted at the provincial assemblies. Norwegian kings had traditionally been involved in the making of Christian law. This was allegedly true of Olaf II, was definitely true of Magnus V, and was also true of Håkon IV in the 1250s.[39] However, each of these kings legislated in the field of Christian laws together with a bishop (Olaf II) or archbishop (Magnus V and Håkon IV). Magnus VI had included Christian law in his code after – allegedly – consulting with the bishop of Oslo,[40] but without the participation of the archbishop, and this was why the code was rejected. By this, the legislative project could be regarded as stranded in Norway, since the unification of law only included three of four legal provinces.

However, this is not quite true. All that was rejected was the part on the Christian laws. They had to be exempted from all the codes and instead the archbishop would unify this law for the entire realm. This is what Archbishop Jon the Red did in the 1270s and by this finally ended the tradition of each legal province having their own Christian laws. We might take Jarnsiða as evidence that this was now the strategy, since it is a code with no Christian laws. It was still rejected at Alþingi on Iceland. Due to the reactions to the code introduced ten years later in 1281, it has been assumed that Jarnsiða was shaped too much by Norwegian law. It might be that behind this rhetoric in 1281 we find a slightly different reality: that the codes of law in 1271 and 1281 contained too much new law and it is this new law that is associated with Norwegian law. Be that as it may, according to the *Annales regii*, only bits and pieces was accepted by the Alþingi in 1271 and 1272, before the

38 A Horn, 'Fra landskapslov til landslov: En studie av tekstorganiseringen i norrøne middelalderlover', in A C Horn and K A Seip (eds), *Lov og lovgivning i middelalderen – Nye studier av Magnus Lagabøtes landslov* (2020) 99–132.

39 B D Spørck, 'Etterord', in B D Spørck (ed), *Nyere norske kristenretter (ca. 1260–1273)* (2009) 158. See also A I Riisøy and B D Spørck, 'Datering av nyere Borgartings kristenretter' (1999) 12 *Collegium Medievale*.

40 Helle, *Konge og gode menn* (n 22) 41.

entire code of law was taken on by the Icelanders in 1273 with the promise that they would soon get a new code.[41]

A revised code of law was presented at Frostathing in 1274,[42] at Gulathing in 1275, at Borgarthing and Eidsivathing in 1276, and the Icelandic code – later named Jónsbók – was presented at Alþingi in 1281. This code had no Christian laws. Its acceptance went unnoticed in the Icelandic annals.[43] The reason is probably that it was not a completely new code but the old one with the adjustments demanded at Frostathing in 1269, with an improved structure of the code, of each of the nine books of the code and of the different chapters in each of the books, as suggested by Anna Horn, but with a larger degree of harmonisation. The code of 1274 was hence simply promulgated, as stated in the epilogue.[44] This was no royal coup in respect of the legislative powers of the provincial assemblies – they had approved the first code and the new code was just an improvement. However, it was a new legislative Act, performed without the consent of the assemblies. Later royal decrees made to fill loopholes in the Code of 1274, or to change it, were also issued by promulgation alone. Law was unified, and it would stay unified because the legislative powers of the assemblies were transferred to the king by the events in 1267–1271 and 1274–1276. The efforts of Olaf II to subdue the four provincial assemblies were accomplished almost exactly 250 years later without a master plan but as a result of a series of interacting factors.

However, here we have to make a halt. It is stated that a code of law was presented, first at Gulathing in 1267, then at Borgarthing and Eidsivathing in 1268 and finally at Frostathing in 1269. It is further stated that the revised code was presented at Frostathing in 1274, Gulathing in 1275 and Borgarthing and Eidsivathing in 1276. It hence seems that the provincial assemblies were still of importance. The preserved manuscripts of the Code of 1274 also address one of the four assemblies in the prologue, as the recipient of the lawbook. However, the law is the same whichever assembly is being formally addressed. Not in a single preserved medieval diploma is the

41 G Storm, 'Annales regii' (n 37) 138–139. See also G Storm (ed), 'Henrik Høyers Annaler' i *Islandske Annaler indtil 1578* (1888) 68 and G Stefánsson and M Stefánsson (eds), *Biskop Arnes saga* (2007) 34 and 36.

42 S Imsen, 'Magnus Håkonsson Lagabøtes landslov. Loven som samlet Norge og nordmennene, og som formet de norrøne landene vest i havet' in *Strinda, den gang da – Årbok for Strinda historielag* (2021) 52–73, and G Storm (ed), 'Gottskalks Annaler', in *Islandske Annaler indtil 1578* (1888) 332.

43 G Storm, 'Annales regii' (n 37) 139–140.

44 M Rindal and B D Spørck (eds), *Kong Magnus Håkonsson Lagabøtes landslov – Norrøn tekst med fullstendig variantapparat, del II.* (2018) 1005.

law of Gulathing, Borgarthing or Eidsivathing mentioned even once, and only one manuscript speaks of the Frostathing Law. Instead, references are made to the law of the land (*landzlogh*).[45] For instance, in 1293 the abbot in Munkeliv Abbey in Bergen declared that a piece of land was bought according to the correct law of the land ("*køyptom þessa iordh eftir rettom landz loghum*").[46] Especially interesting is the statement of four witnesses to a payment in 1403, declaring that the payment was made according to the law of the land and the right Frostathing Law ("*þetta gort medh landz loghom oc rættom Frostatings loghom*").[47] This is the only known time the law of one of the legal provinces is mentioned, and in a way that has to be read as indicating that the law of the land was also the established law of Frostathing. A little later, in 1424, twelve men made a statement where they spoke of the Code of 1274 as a Norwegian lawbook ("*konungsins loghbook j Norghe*"), underlining the political as well as the legal unification the Code of 1274 had achieved.[48]

(4) Local adjustment through legislation

It seems that the idea of one law for the entire country was established fairly quickly, despite the Code of 1274 being a mixture of old and new law. Brage Hatløy has studied Book VIII, which contains rules mainly relating to contract and trade and found that: 25 per cent of the rules in the Code were taken from the Gulathing and Frostathing Law without changes; 15 per cent were take from the same laws with minor changes; 37.5 per cent were taken from the Gulathing and Frostathing Law with major changes; and 22.5 per cent were completely new laws.[49] Since the Borgarthing and Eidsivathing Law is not preserved, it might be hypothesised that the Code of 1274 did not contain any new law at all. This argument can only be advanced tentatively, since much of the new law together with the major changes can be fitted into a political program for the Code. However, from the perspective of the king's subjects in each of the legal provinces, all law adopted from one of the three other provinces would be new law to them. Hence, the amount of new law

45 C C A Lange and C A Unger (eds), *Diplomatarium norvegicum*, vol IV (1858) no 90 (henceforth DN).

46 C A Unger and H J Huitfeldt-Kaas (eds), *DN*, vol XII (1888) no 17.

47 C C A Lange and C A Unger (eds), *DN*, vol II (1852) no 574.

48 C C A Lange and C A Unger (eds), *DN*, vol I (1849) no 697; See also C A Unger and H J Huitfeldt-Kaas (eds), *DN*, vol VI (1864) no 529.

49 B T Hatløy, *Kontinuitet og endring i formuesretten i Magnus Lagabøters Landslov – Lovgjevingsomsyn, lovgjevingsteknikk og rettsleg innhald* (2021) 93.

in the Code of 1274 was more then 22.5 per cent even if not a single rule was made from scratch. Why was there no shock of the new in 1267–1269 on the Norwegian mainland?

Before we attempt to answer this crucial question, we have to make a detour to Iceland. As we have seen, Jarnsiða was not well received in 1271 and it was not until 1273 that all of it was taken as Icelandic law at Alþingi. This is recorded both in the *Annales regii* and the saga of Bishop Arne, but they do not inform us of the reason for the resistance. The saga of Bishop Arne claims that there was also resistance when Jónsbók was introduced to Alþingi in 1281, and that this was partly due to differences between new and old law.[50] It is interesting that in the saga the knight Lodin Lepp argues on behalf of the king that Alþingi does not have the right to discuss the content of the Code, because only the king could make law. This was the ideology established in 1274. In the end, the Icelandic Code is accepted by all but nine of the men present at the assembly.[51] However, Lodin Lepp also promised that the king would look into some of the matters discussed. In 1294, 1305 and 1314 royal decrees were issued that altered or added to the Icelandic Code of 1281.[52] This was not only a response to the protests in 1281 but seems to have been the general policy after the failure with Jarnsiða in 1271.

Jónsbók was far more influenced by Icelandic law than Jarnsiða had been. Furthermore, Iceland was not the only part of the territories ruled by the Norwegian king that got concessions after the legislative project ended with the death of King Magnus VI in 1280. In 1298 Duke Håkon, who reigned from 1299 as Håkon V, drafted a decree for the Faroe Islands later known as the Sheep Letter (*Sauðabrefit*).[53] A law tailored for the specific conditions at the Faroe Islands had already been requested in 1271,[54] along with a request for the islands to receive the new law for the Gulathing province from 1267.[55] We can imagine that the living conditions in Iceland and the Faroe Islands were so obviously different that a policy of deviating from the unifying Code of 1274 appeared less of a problem. However, it might be that the desire for unification was less strong than we can imagine today. At least, the same Duke Håkon issued decrees for the regions of Hedmark, Toten,

50 Stefánsson and Stefánsson (eds), *Biskop Arnes saga* (n 41) 80.

51 Stefánsson and Stefánsson (eds), *Biskop Arnes saga* (n 41) 87.

52 G Storm (ed), *Norges gamle Love indtil* 1387, *Fierde Bind* (1885) 341–347 (henceforth NgL vol IV). See also 347–348 and 349–353.

53 Munch and Keyser (eds), NgL, vol II (n 28) 33–40.

54 J Agerholt, 'Sauebrevet 1298: En undersøkelse i norrøn diplomatikk' (1959) vol 74 *Arkiv for nordisk filologi*, 236–263 at 260–262.

55 Storm (ed), NgL, vol IV (n 52) 353–354.

Hadeland and Ringerike and Haalogaland in 1293, 1297, 1298 and 1313, which also appear as local adjustments of law after the Code of 1274 was issued. For instance, the right to kill horse thieves seems like an old custom that is reintroduced after vengeance was prohibited by the Code of 1274.[56]

This means that after using legislation to create legal unity in the Norwegian realm, Norwegian kings used the same regulatory technique to make local and regional law, and by this method harmed the legal unity they had achieved. This seemingly illogical policy is still logical because legal unity is of little worth if the laws are not heeded. The adjustments must have been seen as necessary concessions to avoid any challenge being made to the authority of the laws because they appeared of little relevance to the subjects. The policy of Magnus VI, and his sons Eirik II and Håkon V, therefore seems not to have been to force the Code of 1274 and legal unity on the subjects, but rather to try to lure them into accepting it. Much like Lodin Lepp at Alþingi in 1281: take a firm stand before you negotiate. This can also be said to be the core of the system for applying the Code of 1274.

C: THE REGULATION OF LAW THROUGH APPLICATION

(1) The lawmen

The authority of the Code of 1274 can be seen from six diplomas from the fifteenth century, which speak of being summoned to meet before the chancellor, the lawman or the jury and the lawbook.[57] It is almost as if the lawbook is a relic next to a source of information about what the law actually is. In a critical political situation in 1449, the knight Eirik Sæmundsson even spoke of what St Olaf's law and our *holy* lawbook proved ("*sancti Olafs konungx lag oc waar helaga lagbook wtskyrir*").[58] The relationship between the Code of 1274 and the mythical legislation of St Olaf would, of course, add authority to the decrees of the lawbook. However, its authority was

56 Keyser and Munch (eds), NgL, vol III (n 28) 19–23 ('Hertug Haakon Magnussøns store Retterbod for Hedemarken og Thoten'), 27–30 ('Hertug Haakon Magnussøns store Retterbod for Ringerike og Hadeland') and 106–108 ('Kong Haakon Magnussøns Retterbod for Haalogaland om Søgsmaal i Fisketiden, om Tiender og om Finnerne').

57 C C A Lange and C A Unger (eds), *DN*, vol III (1855) no 790, no 929; C A Unger and H J Huitfeldt-Kaas (eds), *DN*, vol VIII (1874) no 334, no 421; C A Unger and H J Huitfeldt-Kaas (eds), *DN*, vol X (1880) no 170; C A Unger and H J Huitfeldt-Kaas (eds), *DN*, vol XIII (1891) 86 (no 112).

58 Unger and Huitfeldt (eds), DN, vol X (n 10) no 201 [emphasis added].

probably due to the system for application of the law established within the code, which made plurality within unity possible.

Prior to the late-twelfth century, we do not have any reliable information on legal professionals in Norway, defined in this context as individuals who dedicate a significant amount of time to law and legal questions. Torleiv Spake is supposed to have assisted both the Icelanders when they got a common law in 930 and also Håkon I when he revised the Gulathing Law a little later[59]; we have seen that Bishop Grimkjell seems from the Gulathing and Frostathing Laws to have been the mastermind behind the legislation passed by Olaf II in the early 1020s; we have already become acquainted with Atle who formulated and explained, around 1040, the law of defence allegedly made by Håkon I around 950. But these are isolated individuals and we do not know if they actually participated in the application of the law at the assemblies. However, the Irish *Annals of the Four Masters – Annála Ríoghachta Éireann* – from 969 speak of the lawmen from the islands (*Lagmannaibh na n-Innsedh*).[60] There is no reason to believe that it was only in the Hebrides, in the Norse cultural sphere, that there were lawmen at this time. This follows not least because we know of lawmen also from Iceland, and later from Norwegian sources. The problem is that the sagas of Norwegian kings are mainly concerned with politics and not law at the assemblies, and hence they rarely report the events at the assemblies – unlike the Icelandic sagas.

It is first in *Håkon Håkonssons saga* that we get some knowledge of the lawmen, and that is only because they – according to the saga – gathered in Bergen in 1223 with magnates of the realm to decide who had the better right to the throne, Håkon IV or Earl Skule. It is an interesting but failed effort to settle such a power conflict with law; as we have seen, Earl Skule was eventually killed on the order of Håkon IV in 1240 after an unsuccessful rebellion during which Skule swore on the relics of Olaf II to keep his law as king of Norway.[61] The lawmen do not appear much in the saga as legal professionals. What is more striking is that they appear to be commoners. The exception is that the lawman Bjarne Mårdsson from Haalogaland in Frostathing was an aristocrat and a legal specialist.[62] In Sverres saga,

59 Robberstad, *Rettssoga I* (n 3) 140.

60 A Wolf, *From Pictland to Alba 789–1070* (2007) 212; J O'Donovan (ed), *Annals of the Kingdom of Ireland, by the Four Masters, from the earliest period to the year 1616*, vol 1 (1856) 698–699.

61 A Holtsmark (ed), *Håkon Håkonssons saga* (1964) 172.

62 Helle, *Gulating* (n 1) 17 and Simensen (ed), *The Older Gulathing Law* (n 7) 211–219 (chs 316–319).

Dagfinn Bonde and Grunnar Grjonbak, on the other hand, definitely appear more as military leaders than professional lawyers.[63] However, we cannot deduce from this that the lawmen had not appeared differently at an earlier period. The reason is that King Sverre succeeded to the throne after a civil war where he defeated the representatives of an old and established power. He was also the first to appoint lawmen at the assemblies from the 1180s, an authority the assemblies themselves must have exercised previously. It is therefore just as likely that the lawmen had been more of an aristocratic and professional group before King Sverre appointed his own unprofessional followers as lawmen. It might follow that a more professionalised legal system than that which we meet in *Håkon Håkonssons saga* was an aspect of the Norwegian assemblies, as it was at Alþingi at Iceland. It should also be noticed that when the criminal law was revised between 1258 and 1263, the participating lawmen were called learned (*lærðra logmanna*)[64] and it might be that the unusual situation created by the political takeover by King Sverre had finally normalised. An indication of this is that the first extensive legal practice we have documented after the promulgation of the Code of 1274 is performed in Aga by the lawman Sigrud Brynjulfsson, a knight administering justice in his manor in Hardanger in Gulathing.[65]

The lawmen became royal officials from the end of Sverre's reign, and both he and his political opponents appointed lawmen. One of the earliest disputes that we know a lagmann helped to resolve was related to the Hovedøya Abbey near Oslo. In a diploma from 1207–1217, King Filipus refers to Simon lawman (*Simun logh maðr*) who had clarified the law on the issue.[66] This was the task of the lawmen – to declare what the law was. Judging was the privilege of the assemblies. This changed slightly in the New Law of Håkon IV, probably enacted in 1260. According to this law reform, lawmen were given the role as sole judge in cases where one of the parties chose to take the case to the lawman rather than an assembly.[67] It does not seem like much of a revolution, but it was. The New Law of 1260 appears at the same time that the making of the Code of 1274 is likely to have commenced. This happened after a large number of persons from the Norwegian

63 D Gundersen (ed), *Sverres saga* (1996) 197–198 and 234.
64 Keyser and Munch (eds), NgL, vol I (n 24) 266.
65 J Ø Sunde, 'Lagmannen og Landslova – Lagmannen i norsk mellomalderrettshistorie frå slutten av 1100-talet til 1400', in A C Horn and K A Seip (eds), *Lov og lovgivning i middelalderen – Nye studier av Magnus Lagabøtes landslov* (2020) 169–174.
66 Lange and Unger (eds), DN, vol II (n 57) no 3.
67 Sunde, 'Daughters of God' (n 35) 144.

court had been in Castille and witnessed the making of *Las Siete Partidas*, when the Norwegian princess Kristina married Prince Filipe in 1258.[68] That means that Håkon IV had already made a move, in 1260, towards control of both the making and the application of law. Magnus VI took a much larger step forward towards controlling the application of the law with the Code of 1274, when the lawman became the very backbone of the court system.

(2) The assemblies

The public assemblies had a court function but cannot be characterised as courts. This is because they were more political institutions that made decisions, sometimes in cases of conflict of law, but also in relation to a wider variety of matters. With the Code of 1274, they became less politicised institutions and more characterisable as courts, since resolving conflicts had become their dominant task. This is in itself a quite surprising choice made by Magnus VI. Why did he not just erase the assemblies as judicial organs as he did with the *domr*? It is actually the *domr*, and not the assemblies, that appear as the main conflict resolving organ in the Gulathing and Frostathing Law. The *domr* was an ad hoc body appointed by the parties in a conflict to resolve that very specific conflict. Each party appointed an equal number of members of the body and its decision had to be unanimous. In cases of disagreement, the case would be taken to an assembly to be decided.[69] Executing the decision of the *domr* seems to have given royal power a role to play in the legal system at an early period; this was achieved through the legislation of Magnus V in 1163/1164.[70] However, in 1274 the *domr* would appear as a problem rather than an opportunity in the eyes of the Norwegian king. The reason is its unruly character – an ad hoc body appointed by the parties will pop up and disappear beyond royal control. This was partly also the case with local assemblies, since they met both regularly and on demand. The provincial assemblies, on the other hand, met regularly. They were therefore perfect to use as a basic structure in the system for applying law, since the regularity enabled the presence of royal officials.

This is probably one of the reasons why the assemblies were not ignored in the Code of 1274, but rather turned into royal organs for conflict resolution. We can speculate as to whether or not another reason for this lay in the

68 Sunde, 'Daughters of God' (n 35) 132–134.
69 Sunde, 'Daughters of God' (n 35) 143 and 148–149.
70 Sunde, *Speculum legale* (n 4) 73–74.

failed attempts of Olaf II and Magnus V to create legislatory meetings of the realm above the provincial assemblies. There are several reasons why they met rebellion and subsequently death, in 1030 and 1184, but we can speculate that one reason may have been that both tried to get around the provincial assemblies and the power structures they represented by legislating at a meeting of the realm. When Håkon IV possibly passed his New Law at a meeting of the realm in 1260, it was a meeting held at Nidaros; but this was followed by subsequent presentation of new legislation at Frostathing.[71] We cannot know if this was a deliberate choice. However, he was the grandson of King Sverre, and the way in which he – according to the saga – addresses his grandfather's loyal men Dagfinn Bonde and Grunnar Grjonbak as commoners in 1223 might indicate an awareness of the anti-aristocratic policy that had brought his family to power.

The regularity of the meetings of the provincial assemblies in particular, and their long-established legitimacy, were probably reasons why they were placed at the heart of the royal justice system in 1274. Yet another reason was that they were well-established centres for communication. With no feudal estates and few and small towns, the assemblies on different levels had no real competition from other structures of political or social communication. However, making the assemblies the core of the royal justice system must have felt a bit like opening Pandora's Box: the assemblies were in the habit of making and applying law according to their liking and why would they not hold on to their habit and apply the Code of 1274 as they pleased? When choosing between carrot and stick, Magnus VI chose the carrot and the Code of 1274 gave the assemblies leeway when applying law in six different ways.

(3) The tolerance for legal plurality in the application of law

First, the Code of 1274 operated with the power of judging split in two parts: the law was decided by the lawman and the facts decided by six or twelve men. This was really an unexplained precondition in the Code. The lawman was to deliver his *orskurð*, which literally means that he was to carve out the relevant law from the corpus of law and is a direct translation of *decisio*.[72] The six or twelve men would then decide if the relevant law should be applied in the specific case. This seems like a fairly straightforward process

71 Helle, *Konge og gode menn* (n 22) 158.
72 Robberstad, *Rettssoga I* (n 3) 147.

but could be rather complicated in practice. This can be illustrated if we turn to VIII-2, 3, 4 and 5 in the Code on repayment of debt.[73] According to the Code VIII-2, 3 and 4 debts should be repaid. However, if the debtor was poor and had been victim of a fire or shipwrecking, the debt should be repaid when God made him able, according to VIII-5. The lawman would hence inform the six or twelve men on this and they would then discuss if VIII-2, 3 or 4 was to be applied or if the debtor was poor and VIII-5 was to be applied instead. If the six or twelve men decided that the debtor was poor, the lawman had to decide if a fire or shipwrecking had taken place. If the financial difficulty of the debtor was due to a landslide, for instance, legal practice seems to indicate that the lawman had to decide if that was an analogy for a fire or shipwrecking. After this back and forth between the lawman and the six or twelve men, the case was decided by proposing a decision to the public assembly, who had the final say and had to approve. This arrangement meant that the king, through his – at the absolute most – sixteen lawmen,[74] had some control of how the law was read and interpreted and hence control of the unity of law, while the local or regional community had some control of how it was applied and hence the real-life consequences of the legislation in society. In this way, Magnus VI invited the local or regional community into the decision-making process but kept control of the content of the law. The end result was a mix of unity of law and plurality in application that was in the interest of both parties.

Secondly, in several parts of the Code of 1274, a third level in the decision-making process is present. Let us turn to III-2 in the Code of 1274 for an example. This provision is concerned with the situation in which one of the warships each municipality was obliged to muster had aged and no longer could be used. Then a new ship had to be built. It could be built anywhere but damage to fields was to be compensated after the assessment of wise and equitable (*skynsamir* and *skilrikir*) men.[75] That means that after the lawman had decided that III-2 was applicable, and the six or twelve men had decided that damage was done, the actual assessment of damage done was done by a group of locals called *nefnd*. The widespread use of *nefnd* is well docu-

73 I use the same numbers for books and chapter in the Code of 1274 that is used in the translation of A. Taranger, *Kong Magnus Lagabøters Landslova* (1915).

74 Sunde, 'Lagmannen og Landslova' (n 65) 197–198. Compare with Taylor, *The Shape of the State* (n 8) 417–434.

75 E Hertzberg, 'Glossarium' in G Storm and E Hertzberg (eds), *Norges gamle love indtil 1387, Femte Bind* (1895) 569 and 589.

mented by Steinar Imsen[76] and this meant that the local community was heavily involved in the actual decision-making in case of legal conflicts. The reference to *skynsamir menn* and *skilrikr menn* is made a total of eighty-one times in the Code of the Norwegian Realm, in sixty-seven different chapters of the Code, in various contexts, but all have to do, in one way or another, with conflict resolution.[77] To the local community, this participation in the legal process must have been attractive because it signalled actual power to influence the outcome of the case. Again, we see that the end result was a mix of unity of law and plurality of application that benefitted both the king and local communities.

Thirdly, the Code of 1274 I-11 stated that the six or twelve men deciding the case were bound to apply the law found relevant by the lawman. The only way to ignore the opinion of the lawman was to write to the king and ask him to investigate what was the correct law in the case, since the king was above the law.[78] This could be seen as a way to empower the lawman at the expense of the six or twelve men. However, it was just as much an instrument to control the lawmen. This rule must be seen in relation to I-12, which says that anyone who does not enjoy justice at the local assembly or through the lawman, shall appeal the case to the provincial assembly and have it decided there. This became the legal foundation of a tradition of communication between local communities and the king.[79] This policy had several purposes and facets. However, the loyalty of royal officers was key in the system of applying law set up in the Code of 1274. Their job was to secure legal unity, while local and regional participants in the court would cause legal plurality in practice. This was a fine-tuned system that could easily turn into anarchy if the royal officers brought in legal plurality through too much corruption or other actions motivated by self-interest.

Fourthly, the Code of 1274 I-4 stated that the gaps in the law were to be filled by the judges. In this context, the judges were the six or twelve men together with the lawman. The Code of 1274 is split into nine books,

76 S Imsen, *Norsk bondekommunalisme fra Magnus Lagabøte til Kristian Kvart; Del 1 Middelalderen* (1990) and S Imsen, *Norsk bondekommunalisme fra Magnus Lagabøte til Kristian Kvart; Del 2: Lydriketiden* (1994).

77 See Sunde 'Daughters of God' (n 35) 157–158.

78 J Ø Sunde, 'Norwegian Constitutionalism and the Code of 1274' in J Ø Sunde (ed), *Constitutionalism Before 1789 – Constitutional Arrangements from the High Middle Ages to the French Revolution* (2014) 165–185.

79 M Njåstad 'Tinget – lokalt og sentralt styre i krisetid i senmiddelalderen», in J Ø Sunde and B T Hatløy (eds), *Eidsivating – tingtradisjonen gjennom 1000 år* (2022).

containing altogether about 220 chapters,[80] which can again be said to have all-in-all about 1,000 legal rules. That was not impressive, even in the middle ages. If we compare the Code of 1274 with the Gulathing or the Frostathing Law, the latter contain a greater wealth of rules and words. If we compare with the canon law or Roman law corpus at the time, the Code of 1274 is even less impressive. As Eirik II observed in 1280 – or rather as his council observed, since he was only twelve years old – it could not be expected that such a small lawbook (*litil bok*) could contain all the legal rules for which there was a need.[81] Magnus VI's expectation that there would be loopholes in the law is readily intelligible. They would then be filled locally. However, this could only be done without further ado if the lawman and the six or twelve men all agreed. If they did not, the opinion of the lawman would prevail, even if he was the only person to hold that opinion. Only the king could change the lawman's *orskurð* according to I-11 in the Code of 1274. Such a system could only operate smoothly locally if both parties would compromise. Again, we see how Magnus VI invited the local or regional community into the decision-making process, but kept control, and by this balanced legal unity and legal plurality.

Fifthly, the Code of IV-18 operated with a duty for the judges to not apply the law when it was too strict or too lenient. This radical demand to apply equity might at first glance appear to be the ultimate resignation of the legal unity created by one common code of law. However, the letter of the law could only be abandoned after certain types of arguments had been considered. There was a lengthy description in the Code of the intellectual process to be undertaken prior to abandoning its provisions; this was to be read aloud before a judgment was passed in all major cases.[82] However, we must presume that the rule for filling loopholes in the law still applied – that all judges had to agree and if they did not the opinion of the lawman would prevail unless the king decided differently. It is likely, but not certain, that this rule was applied in a case in 1329. The servant Olaf had led his mistress on horseback over a river. What then happened is unknown but his mistress died and her two sons asked for damages. According to IV-14 in the Code, they were entitled to half of the normal damages for causing death if it was

80 The exact number will vary somewhat from manuscript to manuscript.

81 Munch and R Keyser (eds), NgL, vol III (n 28) 4.

82 See J Ø Sunde, 'The Virtues Building Jerusalem: The Four Daughters of God and Their Long Journey to Norwegian Law in the Thirteenth Century', in K B Aavitsland and L M Bonde (eds), *Tracing the Jerusalem code: Volume 1: The holy city Christian cultures in medieval Scandinavia (ca. 1100–1536)* (2021) 515–519.

a regular accident, and one quarter damage if the accident occurred when doing something useful. The lawman Bård Petersson and nine other men, among them the experienced lawman and knight Hauk Erlendsson, still concluded that Olaf was not to pay any compensation since he was not to blame.[83] There seems to be no other reason why the judges should abandon law but that it appeared too strict.

Sixthly, the Code of 1274 did not attempt to regulate certain issues, and thus the Code gave room for local customs and the self-regulation of different groups in society. One field of law that was to a large extent left to local regulation was the use of natural resources like timber, water, stone, tidal fishery, etc. In VII-30 it is once mentioned that a toon or neighbourhood meeting (*granna stæfna*) should be held in the spring to decide if the fences between the fields were sufficiently strong. We know that in the early twentieth century such neighbourhood meetings applied a whole series of norms and were crucial instruments for conflict resolution in local communities.[84] We also find traces of neighbourhood courts in the towns, even if this is virtually unstudied.[85] The Code of 1274 did not interfere in their doings except by providing a general and important framework for their operation.

We see from the legislation of Eirik II from 1295 and Magnus VII from 1320 that this kind of tolerance was problematic. In 1295, it was decreed that both Norwegians and foreigners (*"bedi indlendzskum og utlendzskum"*) in Bergen should not form associations or groups (*"samheldi . . . samlaup"*) and make laws or rules (*"lagh ædr settningar"*), since this was the task for the king and his good men (*"konungr með goðra manna raade"*).[86] This has been understood in relation to the abolition of a number of guilds in Bergen in the same law.[87] However, in a piece of legislation promulgated by Magnus VII in 1320, restating former legislation for Bergen, almost exactly the same wording was used to state that if a group (*"samhælldi"*) of Norwegians and foreigners (*"inlændzskom ok utlændzskom"*) wanted to make rules (*"logh æða sætningar"*) for their group, these rules should be

83 Lange and Unger (eds), DN, vol III (n 57) no 153.

84 See B Seland, 'Grannmøter og gardsfutverv – Formalisert styre i mangebølte tun' (1996) 75 *Historisk tidsskrift* 303–324; K Østberg, *Norsk bonderet, 5. bind: Sedvaner i granneforhold* (1928) and H O Opedal, 'Makter og menneske – folkeminne ifrå Hardanger', vol VIII (1954) no 73 *Norsk folkeminnelag*.

85 See the State Archive in Bergen, Norway, The Archive for Sorenskriveren i Nordhordland, Court record (tingbok) 1796–1802 I.A.48, 118b. See also Y Nielsen (ed), *Vedtægter og Dokumenter fra det hansiatiske Kontor i Bergen og dettes enkelte Gaarde* (1892).

86 Keyser and Munch (eds), NgL, vol III (n 28) 24–25.

87 A Taranger, *Udsigt over den norske rets historie I: Indledning – Rettskildernes historie* (1935) 91.

approved by the king's sheriff, the lawman and twelve from the town council (*"sysslumaðr, logmaðer, ok tolf raðsmenn"*).[88] It is hard to know if there was a shift in policy or not between 1295 and 1320, or if there was a consistent practice despite the less consistent wording in the legislation. However, the royal decree of 1320 might still be said to display the essence of the balance between control and plurality in the royal policy in the second half of the thirteenth and the first half of the fourteenth century: there was no royal control without some tolerance for plurality.

(4) The regulation of plurality

According to IV-18 in the Code, the judges could alter the prescribed law in a specific case if the application of it generated an unfair result. As we have seen, a deviation of the law in the Code of 1274 had to be justified with a certain set of arguments according to IV-14. In this way, the king still maintained some control even when ordering the judges not to follow black letter law. What made this control mechanism more than law in books was that it was decided at a meeting the king held with the barons (*"lenðom monnum"*), the legal advisers at court (*"stallarum"*), the lawmen (*"logmonnum"*) and the sheriffs (*"syslumonnum"*) in the eastern part of the Norwegian mainland in 1273,[89] that in all major cases the date, the name of the judges, the name of the parties, and what was decided (*"huar ðømt var"*) was to be recorded. Furthermore, the record had to specify what was to be paid, the reason for the reduction of fines and the deadline for the payment.[90] This was all to be written in the king's book (*brefabok konongs*).[91] No such overview is preserved, if it ever existed. However, it might be that judgments like the one concerning Olaf in 1329 were written down for this reason. Olaf was a servant and probably had insufficient financial means to pay for a written judgment. There was no property involved in the judgment and hence no one else would have had any interest in paying for it to be recorded. The fact that a judgment concerning a servant was committed to writing and then preserved must be attributed to pure chance, or to the fact that the decision was ground-breaking and therefore of future interest.

88 Keyser and Munch (eds), NgL, vol I (n 24) 149–150.

89 S Imsen (ed), *Hirdskråen. Hirdloven til Norges konge og hans håndgangne menn. Etter Am 322 fol.* (2000) 132–133.

90 Imsen, *Hirdskråen* (n 89) 140–141.

91 Compare with Taylor, *The Shape of the State* (n 8) 401–407.

The decision from 1273 was, later that decade, put into chapter 31 of the regulation Magnus VI made for his vassals. This regulation (*Hirðskrá*) we find written in the same manuscript as the Code of 1274, with other legal sources of particular interest. Some of these sources are judgments. The most common are the judgments made by the king and good men. Håkon V's decision from 1318 on legitimisation of children born outside wedlock is preserved today in thirty-eight manuscripts,[92] his decision on taxes is found in seven manuscripts,[93] while Queen Margrethe I (1388–1412) passed a decision preserved in twenty-seven manuscripts.[94] It should be noted that when Håkon VI gave a decision on the inheritance rights of illegitimate children in 1375 it provided expressly that it should be written into the lawbook because it changed what was law (*setiett þenna vorn vrskvrd j logbok til rettabota*).[95] The decision was made in a case from Iceland and the lawbook referred to must be the Icelandic Code of 1281. However, since the decision must also have been regarded as relevant in Norway, it is found in eight manuscripts containing the Code of 1274.[96] In these manuscripts, we also find decisions passed by lawmen. An example is a judgment by four lawmen on the streets of Bergen from 1310, a decision by a lawman in 1375 and another by a lawman from 1408.[97] By treating judgments as a legal source, some of the variations in the application of the law would have been evened out. However, variations must have been much, much more extensive than any such practice could accommodate. More important, in all probability, was the fact that the practice signalled the king's desire for legal unity.

(5) Royal involvement in the legal order

No instrument equivalent to the Scottish brieve or the English writ was used in Norway to achieve legal unity. However, the king was definitely involved in the legal system, mainly in three different ways.

First, the king was considered the superior judge, according to the Code of 1274, since he was above the law. This statement is founded on the

92 Storm (ed), NgL, vol IV (n 52) 393, 396, 412, 419, 429, 436, 438, 443, 456, 472, 481, 494, 519, 533, 537, 558, 560, 573, 598, 600, 648, 649, 649, 658, 670, 674, 702, 705, 710, 712, 716, 726, 733, 736, 752, 761, 777 and 788.

93 Storm (ed), NgL, vol IV (n 52) 459, 481, 591, 595, 661, 668 and 675.

94 Storm (ed), NgL, vol IV (n 52) 396, 412, 419, 433, 443, 451, 460, 472, 494, 497, 558, 575, 578, 590, 611, 661, 680, 689, 710, 713, 716, 726, 729, 736, 752, 754 and 789.

95 H Magerøy (ed), *DN*, vol XXI (1976) no 153.

96 Storm (ed), NgL, vol IV (n 52) 396, 419, 436, 442, 472, 659, 713 og 788.

97 Storm (ed), NgL, vol IV (n 52) 517 (and maybe 518), 529 and 659 and 523.

princeps legibus solutus est ideology. This meant that conflicts could in the end be resolved by the king. In doubtful cases like the decision on illegitimacy in the Icelandic case from 1375, it meant that the king not only could finally settle the case but also immediately turn the decision into law, which would contribute to the unity of the law. However, there are few such cases.

Secondly, and much more importantly, the king was guarantor of the peace that followed from a judgment, because he made refusal to comply with the decision the equivalent of a breach of the king's peace (*bref brot*). At times, this must have been needed for the cessation of conflict. An example could be a case from Eidsivathing in 1270, 1308 and 1317. In 1270, Magnus VI ordered a group of men to settle a conflict between a priest and his neighbours in Vågå in the north of Gudbrandsdalen. However, the same conflict was taken to the lawman in Eidsivathing in 1308, who cited the judgment from 1270 and confirmed it.[98] In 1317, Håkon V confirmed the lawman's decision and reminded that parties that a breach of the judgment would incur a fine.[99]

Thirdly, the king could take the initiative to have a conflict resolved after one of the parties had asked the king for assistance. These tended not to be cases where very valuable property was at stake. Most often, this happened in conflicts concerning ecclesiastical properties. The conflict above, where Magnus VI appointed a group for men to solve a conflict in Vågå concerning a small piece of land in 1270, is representative. There are several other examples, but not many. There are also examples when the king ordered a case settled without ecclesiastical property being at stake. For instance, in 1322 the regime of Magnus VII ordered the lawman in Gulathing to settle a conflict regarding two boat houses in Hardanger. It is important to note that in such cases the king did not give an order on what was to be observed and applied in the actual case. Instead, the lawman was ordered to judge according to law so he had a clean conscience before God and the king (*þu seer at loglegr er eptir þui sæm þu vilt suara firir gudi ok oss*) and the king – without conditions – promised to confirm the judgment with his own seal, noting there would be a fine for breaching it (*þui at ver vilium þan orskurd stadfæsta med varo brefue ok jnsigli*), just as if the decision had been passed by the king himself.[100] It follows that the king did not create law with his *bref* (letter), but confirmed the authority of the Code of 1274.

98 Magerøy (ed), DN, vol XXI (n 95) no 8.
99 Magerøy (ed), DN, vol XXI (n 95) no 19.
100 Lange and Unger (eds), DN, vol I (n 48) no 166.

D: CONCLUDING REMARKS

Norwegian law went through extensive changes during the twelfth and especially the thirteenth centuries, culminating with the promulgation of the Code of 1274. The essence of these changes was a regularisation of law. However, this did not exclude legal plurality. Rather, the Code of 1274 tried to balance the desire for a centrally governed and unified law with a decentralised application of law and regional and local legal plurality. This was a policy of necessity since the very limited size of royal administration made a very high degree of regularisation impossible. However, it was also – consciously or unconsciously – a smart policy. The flexibility of the Code of 1274 made it easier for the popular assemblies to embrace the Code, since there was always a legitimate escape route if the Code was too strict or too lenient. Despite the reduction in the power and influence of the assemblies, they retained their role as centres for the application of law. This is the backdrop for the Code of 1274 being widespread within the Norwegian realm, with an average of one copy per 1,060 inhabitants around 1350.[101] Hence, the policy regarding the Code made the policy in the Code more influential.

This policy continued after the Code of 1274 was issued, for instance by issuing royal decrees with law adjusted to different localities like Iceland, the Faroe Islands and regions of the Norwegian mainland. At the same time, the king seems to have refrained from seeking to influence individual cases and instead insisted on royal legislation being applied. Pursuing too strict a policy on regularisation might not have had the same success.

101 There are preserved thirty-five complete manuscripts and fifty manuscript fragments of the Code of 1274 from before 1350; Rindal and Spørck, *Kong Magnus Håkonsson Lagabøtes landslov: del I* (n 11) 50. It is assumed that 90 per cent of medieval manuscripts are lost. Let us imagine that in this case 80 per cent are lost. In 1350 there were about 450,000 inhabitants in Norway, meaning that there would have been one copy per 1,059 inhabitants in Norway at that time.

4 Law and Administrative Change in Scotland, Twelfth–Fourteenth Centuries

Alice Taylor°

A: INTRODUCTION

The history of law and administrative change in Scotland during the central middle ages has, by and large, been understood as a narrative of state formation along what might well be called "the English model". That is, a single authority (in this case, the king) assumes basic responsibility for and thus capacity to control the mechanisms for dispute settlement that otherwise would have occurred through other means, invoking other forms of power and authority to do so.[1] Institutional development is a necessary corollary of

° *Acknowledgements*: I am grateful to the editors for their detailed and helpful comments on an earlier draft of this chapter, to the workshop participants for their comments on its first presentation in Aga and to Joanna Tucker and Dauvit Broun for their encouragement about the scope of the piece.

1 Approaches to medieval statehood are summarised in S Reynolds, 'The Historiography of the Medieval State', in M Bentley (ed), *Companion to Historiography* (1997) 117–138; and see

this process: a more standardised system of courts develops in the process of realising and enforcing this responsibility. In central medieval Scotland, the royal judicial system – as opposed to the law upheld and developed within its courts – has (again by and large) traditionally been limited to considering the justice offered in local sheriffdom courts, the touring "ayre" of the justiciar, and the burgh courts, whose profits were collected by the chamberlain in his ayre.[2] These courts and ayres were introduced and developed over the thirteenth century and, for civil pleas, offered litigants the opportunity to initiate their claims in courts by purchasing a "brieve" (Latin: *breve*, a short formulaic command) from the royal chapel that would then be sent to the official presiding over the court instructing them to open the case on the points and articles of the particular claim as set out in the brieve. Over twenty-five years ago, Hector MacQueen described this development as the "growing regularisation of royal justice".[3] In this short paper, I will briefly summarise what can be known about law and administration in the medieval kingdom of the Scots. This complicates – even if does not completely challenge – the narrative of the regularisation of justice over the twelfth and thirteenth centuries and raises some issues, particularly about the trajectory of fourteenth-century legal development, which require further discussion and consideration.

B: THE "ENGLISH MODEL", THE SCOTTISH COMMON LAW AND NORWEGIAN COMPARISONS

Two things are meant by the rather provocative phrase "English model". First is the long-standing preoccupation of Anglophone historians and historians of England to examine state formation as a process realised through institutional development and bureaucratisation.[4] This is not the case

the still important comments in T Reuter, 'All Quiet on the Western Front? The Emergence of Pre-modern forms of statehood in the central Middle Ages', in T Reuter, *Medieval Polities and Modern Mentalities*, J L Nelson (ed) (2006) 432–458. This 'institutional' model of state formation was neatly summed up by J R Strayer, *On the Medieval Origins of the Modern State*, with a foreword by C Tilly and W C Jordan (2016, first published 1970); for the (problematic) influence of ideas about the origins of the modern state on our understanding of twelfth century European politics more broadly, see A Taylor, 'The problem of politics in twelfth-century Europe' (forthcoming).

2 G W S Barrow, 'The Justiciar', in G W S Barrow, *The Kingdom of the Scots: Government, Church and Society from the Eleventh to the Fourteenth Century*, 2nd edn (2003) 68–111.

3 H L MacQueen, *Common Law and Feudal Society in Medieval Scotland* (2016) 248.

4 This is critiqued in N Vincent, 'Royal Diplomatic and the Shape of the Medieval English State, 1066–1300', in A Taylor (ed), *Identifying Governmental Forms in Europe, c. 1100–c. 1300* (forthcoming).

everywhere: historians of the twelfth- and thirteenth-century kingdom of León-Castile, for example, have been much more willing to treat the creation of a more monolithic cultural memory about the history, family and lineage of the kings and queens of León-Castile as a fundamental part of state formation than, traditionally, historians of England have been.[5] Second is the preoccupation in England with the English common law and its origins and formation, often (but not always) treated as a separate field of enquiry from administration.[6] This preoccupation has, until recently, led to the relative neglect of, for example, the complex role civil and canon law played, formally and informally, in the English common law that has long been seen as isolated and insulated from either tradition, as opposed to its (much later) Scottish counterpart.[7]

Why historians of central medieval Scotland have, until relatively recently, followed a similar (although not in any way identical) path is both easy and difficult to understand. It is easy to understand because much of Scotland's medieval administrative and judicial institutions *as well as* its new legal procedures of the thirteenth century were borrowings and adaptations from those developed earlier in England (the importance of "borrowing" is something Scottish historiography shares with its Norwegian counterpart).[8] While the English common law was motored by an increasingly unmanageable number of returnable writs (short, formulaic letters addressed to royal court holders, ordering them to initiate some legal procedure and return the results to the chancery), the medieval Scottish common law, it has been

5 See, among many, M C Puerta, 'La impaginatio en los documentos de Alfonso VII, expresión simbólica del poder real', in M E Martín and V García (eds), *Impaginatio en las inscripciones medievales* (2012) 135–153; A Rodríguez, 'La preciosa transmisión. Memoria y curia regia en Castilla en la primera mitad del siglo XIII', in P Martínez and A Rodríguez (eds), *La construcción medieval de la memoria regia* (2011) 293–322; F Arias Guillén, '*Algun fecho señalado que sea a honra del rey*: royal privileges and the construction of royal memory in Castile (c. 1158–1350)' (2019) 11 *Journal of Medieval Iberian Studies* 40–58.

6 Historians who work on Exchequer and some chancery records – asking essentially questions of finance and administration – do not often work on plea rolls and records of King's Bench. The ERC-funded project *Common Law, Civil Law, Customary Law: Consonance, Divergence and Transformation in Western Europe from the late eleventh to the thirteenth centuries* is opening up new questions about English law's 'separate' legal development, https://clicme.wp.st-andrews.ac.uk/ (last accessed 14 July 2022).

7 A major new reassessment of the relationship between Roman, canon and common law can be found in T J MacSweeney, *Priests of the Law: Roman law and the Making of the Common Law's First Professional*, (2019). For the idea of Scots law as a "mixed" tradition, see W D H Sellar, 'Scots law: mixed from the very beginning? A tale of two receptions' (2000) 3 *Edinburgh Law Review* 3–18.

8 MacQueen, *Common Law* (n 3); S Bagge, *From Viking Stronghold to Christian Kingdom: State Formation in Norway, c. 900–1350* (2010).

argued, was powered by pleadable *brieves*, of which there were far fewer varieties than in England, but which nonetheless did the same basic thing. Both returnable writs and pleadable brieves were documents purchased from the royal "chancery" by a would-be litigant, were addressed to a royal official, instructing them to initiate a process of adversarial litigation. We first have evidence of returnable writs from England in the 1170s and 1180s, whereas in Scotland, the first clear evidence of "pleadable brieves" is not until 1230.[9] It is on the basis of these pleadable brieves – documents issued in the name of the king, initiating litigation in a standard form – that a Scottish common law (characterised as a "legal transplant", on the English model) was thought to have developed.[10] Like their English counterparts, the "justices" – Scottish justiciars – went on "ayres", journeys around local sheriffdoms where they heard the cases that had come to their jurisdiction since the last visit. Although the remit of the Scottish common law was less complex and its cases less categorised, real divergence from the English common law only began to happen in the later middle ages, when royal legislation, enacted in the Scottish Parliament, began to play a larger role in law's scope than in England, while the judgments of the irregular sessions of the King's Council over the fifteenth century acted as umbrella court for many of the cases brought into courts by brieve (although with some important limitations). An even more important development occurred in the sixteenth century, which saw the final demise of the brieve system – although now it is understood to have survived well into the fifteenth century[11] – when court procedure and judicial authority were transformed and formalised by the establishment of a central court, the College of Justice, in 1532.[12] In "the session", the Lords of Session frequently made recourse to the authority of the *utrumque ius*, the civil law tradition based on the Roman and canon law studied, circulated and used in schools and courts across Europe, both in addition to and as a reworking of the authority that the old Scottish common

9 This is the introduction of dissasine, seemingly by statute, see *Statuta Regis Alexandri*, c. 7, in A Taylor (ed), *The Laws of Medieval Scotland: Legal Compilations from the Thirteenth and Fourteenth Centuries*, Stair Society vol 66 (2019) 586–587.

10 MacQueen, *Common Law* (n 3) passim. For the genealogy of the idea of legal transplants, see, for example, J W Cairns, 'Watson, Walton, and the history of legal transplants' (2013) 41 *Georgia Journal of International and Comparative Law* 637–696.

11 This finding – established by Hector MacQueen – was of immense importance and raised several key questions for the development of Scottish land law, in particular how and why the Session acquired jurisdiction over fee and heritage. See the summary in A R C Simpson, 'Foreword: Common Law and Feudal Society in Scholarship since 1993', in MacQueen, *Common Law* (n 3), xlvi–li.

12 A M Godfrey, *Civil Justice in Renaissance Scotland: The Origins of a Central Court* (2009).

law had to offer.[13] It therefore seems clear why the "origins" of Scots law as a self-conscious, separate body of law with its own procedures, are increasingly placed in the sixteenth century.[14]

Yet even for the central middle ages, however – the period when influence from England was at its height – the unacknowledged dominance of the English model is also difficult to understand. The administrative and judicial institutions of Scotland in the central middle ages were very different to those of England. While both English royal justices and Scottish royal justiciars went on *itineres* ("eyres" and "ayres") respectively, the way in which they held their courts differed, as did the pleas that belonged to their respective jurisdictions.[15] Royal courts were not so pervasive either. Whereas in England there was a much clearer *jurisdictional* separation between royal courts and "liberties" – courts that operated outside the king's purview – in Scotland, this formal separation produced a far more enmeshed system than in England.[16] From 1230, statutes made it clear how procedure was to work in aristocratic courts as well as royal courts, and how baronies were integrated into the functioning of those royal courts.[17] Indeed, in the early fourteenth century, aristocratic jurisdiction further cemented its position as one of the types of law courts in the Scottish kingdom with the emergence of "regality" jurisdiction, which explicitly granted to regality-

13 For a broad consideration of the plurality of positions, see A R C Simpson, 'Legislation and Authority in early-modern Scotland', in M Godfrey (ed), *Law and Authority in British Legal History, 1200–1900* (2016) 85–119. For the view that the Court of Session was a *ius commune* court, see G Dolezalek, 'The Court of Session as a *Ius Commune Court*, witnessed by "Sinclair's *Practicks*", 1540–1549', in H L MacQueen (ed), *Miscellany Four by Various Authors*, Stair Society vol 49 (2002) 51–84.

14 For the developing position that the late seventeenth century saw the 'origins' of Scots law as an autonomous system, see the analyses and comments in C Kidd, *Subverting Scotland's Past: Scottish Whig Historians and the Creation of an Anglo-British Identity, 1689–c. 1830* (1993) 144–165, at particularly 148–151; H L MacQueen, '*Regiam Majestatem*, Scots law and national identity' (1995) 74 *Scottish Historical Review* 1–25. A R C Simpson and A L M Wilson, *Scottish Legal History, volume one 1000–1707* (2017) ch 7 at 130–152.

15 For a comparison between royal justices in England and the Scottish justiciar, see D Carpenter, 'Scottish royal government in the thirteenth century from an English perspective', in M Hammond (ed), *New Perspectives on Medieval Scotland, 1093–1286* (2013) 117–160; and the subsequent study of the justiciar in Scotland in A Taylor, *The Shape of the State in Medieval Scotland, 1124–1290* (2016) 210–244.

16 See the collection of essays in M Prestwich (ed), *Liberties and Identities in the Medieval British Isles* (2008); and, most recently, K J Stringer, *The King of Scots, the Liberty of Penrith and the Making of Britain, 1237–1296* (2019) 135 *Cumberland and Westmorland Antiquarian and Archaeological Society*.

17 The version of the 1230 statutes survive in *Statuta Regis Alexandri*, cc. 4–7, edited in Taylor (ed), *Laws* (n 9) 580–587.

holders the right to hear the pleas of the crown.[18] Ecclesiastical courts also seem to have had jurisdiction over a much wider area of law in Scotland than they did in England by the early fourteenth century.[19] Indeed, many of the major narratives of *law* (whether criminal or civil) between the two polities diverge quite significantly. Why did the English writ system multiply whereas the Scottish brieve system remained so limited in their forms of action? Differing population levels provide one answer, but hardly a sufficient enough one to explain the extent of the disparity. Crime also prompts similar types of question. For example, although Paul Hyams has shown that "feud-like" dispute settlement continued to drive litigation in twelfth and thirteenth-century England, in Scotland, compensation for homicide was still a formal part of the legal order in the early fourteenth century, *despite* some sources treating it *quasi crimen fuit*.[20] The evidence is slight but suggestive. It does not seem that crime was defined and delineated by its formal punishment in Scotland as it was in England, creating a rather legally murky world in which lawyers often do not like to tread.

As we move into the later middle ages, the "English model" becomes far less instructive; indeed, it arguably ceases to be relevant. Indeed, Lord Cooper (Thomas Mackay Cooper, First Baron of Culross, 1892–1955), whose work on the history of Scots law did much to maintain it as a dynamic subject of enquiry in the first half of the twentieth century, characterised the period from "the death of Bruce [that is, Robert I "the Bruce", or Robert de Brus, king of Scots, 1306–29]" to perhaps as late as the mid-seventeenth century as the "dark age" of Scottish legal history.[21] For Cooper, although there were some bright sparks of legal light, the problem obstructing legal development was caused by the lack of a "powerful and skilled" central court, and the absence of a permanent, self-reproducing group of professional lawyers expert in Scotland's law. Those who exercised "judicial function" in late medieval Scotland could, he acknowledged, have been "accomplished

18 The standout study here is A Grant, 'Franchises North of the Border: Baronies and Regalities in Medieval Scotland', in M Prestwich (ed), *Liberties and Identities* (2008) 155–199.

19 J R Davies (ed) with A Taylor, *Regiam Majestatem from the earliest manuscripts; with an Introduction by Alice Taylor*, Stair Society vol 68 (2022) c. 2. Unlike in England, there was no *utrum* procedure known to have developed in Scotland, for which see Taylor, *Shape of the State* (n 15) 342–343.

20 *Quoniam Attachiamenta* again is clear that homicide was treated as a felony, T D Fergus (ed and trans), *Quoniam Attachiamenta*, Stair Society vol 44 (1996) c. 16 at 158–159; P R Hyams, *Rancor and Reconciliation in Medieval England* (2003).

21 Lord Cooper of Culross, 'The Dark Age of Scottish Legal History, 1350–1650', in idem, *Selected Papers, 1922–1954* (1957) 219–236. For Cooper, see H L MacQueen, 'Legal Nationalism: Lord Cooper, Legal History and Comparative Law' (2005) 9 *Edinburgh Law Review* 395–406.

civilians and canonists", but the majority were not. Most, he thought, were "capable of dispensing rough justice, but quite incapable (especially in the absence of reports) of making any coherent contribution to the orderly exposition and development of Common Law".[22]

Much of the edifice of Cooper's "Dark Age" has been chipped away by more recent work. As stated above, Hector MacQueen has shown that, far from declining into obsolescence, much of the brieve system and its accompanying pleading survived well into the fifteenth century – and, in the case of the brieve of right, well into the sixteenth.[23] Alexander Grant has shown that "regality" jurisdiction did not occur in a weakening of the royal judicial system but instead constituted a key part of royal government.[24] Arbitration was a significant part of legal process well beyond ecclesiastical courts.[25] Criminal law, as upheld in royal and baronial courts, and as recorded in the earliest surviving justice ayre roll from the very late fifteenth century, co-existed with forms of arbitration, compensation, as well as still supporting vengeance and feud in some respects.[26] However, there are still, as we shall see, substantial questions to be asked of law and administration in the fourteenth century. This period is far less well documented than the fifteenth, and appears, despite the "Second War of Independence" wreaking havoc, to have been particularly important for forming the position that Scots law was an autonomous body of *learning*, made up of authoritative legal texts, to which the knowledge not only of Roman and canon law could be applied, but also texts of the English common law. In this way, the "English model" was still important to Scottish jurists but as a "body of learning" that could aid the interpretation and understanding of Scots law, not as a collection of importable actions. A full study of the "laws of the realm" in later middle ages remains a desideratum; this chapter does, however, lay out a few future lines of enquiry.[27]

As a final note, the Norwegian kingdom seems to offer far fewer parallels to Scotland than England does.[28] There were no pleadable brieves that brought cases into court pushing the development of law. Unlike in

22 Cooper, 'Dark Age' (n 21) 227.

23 MacQueen, *Common Law* (n 3) 19–26, 153–162 (on dissasine); 177–183 (on mortancestry); 200–210 (on right).

24 Grant, 'Franchises' (n 18).

25 A M Godfrey, 'Arbitration in the *Ius Commune* and Scots law' (2004) 2 *Roman Legal Tradition* 122–135.

26 J W Armstrong, 'The Justice Ayre in the Border Sheriffdoms, 1493–1498' (2013) 92 *Scottish Historical Review* 1–37.

27 To be explored more fully in A Taylor, *The laws of the realm in later medieval Scotland, 1291–1549: Culture, Practice, Expertise* (forthcoming).

28 See above, pp. 95–121.

Scotland, the king himself was not, for most of the period, an active – as opposed to primarily symbolic – legislator: Magnus VI's Code of 1274 is the clearest example of a shift into this role that is only evident shortly before its promulgation. Instead, the judgment of the public assembly of each of the four major provinces of the Norwegian kingdom was the source of judgment and while lawmen existed – as they did in Scotland – their role was not to pronounce judgment but to proclaim what the law was – to know the law so that the case could be judged correctly by the assembly. In addition, the kingdom of Norway famously contained no "feudal" aristocracy, that is, a group of predominantly male elites who traditionally held their lands in return for some sort of service to the king and who held jurisdiction over their lands to greater and lesser extent. From the twelfth century onwards (although later in the twelfth century than has traditionally been thought), many of Scotland's elites held such jurisdiction, giving them the power to hold courts and the authority to judge over cases concerning life and limb. Yet, as this paper will show, there are, if not similarities, similar *echoes* heard in Scotland and Norway that raise real questions about why different medieval polities developed such different institutional apparatuses for maintaining law and order.

C: PROBLEMS WITH THE SOURCE MATERIAL

Before starting, however, I should explain the nature of the surviving evidence for Scotland in this period. In short, there is hardly any. We know that there were central royal archives kept in Edinburgh that contained records of the royal courts of sheriff and justiciar but these do not survive, having been taken on the orders of Edward I when he assumed the title "superior lord of the kingdom of the Scots" in 1291 and perishing on their return journey up the North Sea nearly 400 years later.[29] These would have contained not only records of judgments and punishments laid down in the cases heard within these courts, but also key information about process: about recognitions (a panel of men that returned a verdict about a case raised between two parties) and inquests (a panel of men that returned a verdict on a single

29 Inventories survive listing the contents of the treasury at Edinburgh castle from 1282 (Edinburgh, National Records of Scotland, RH5/8), 1291 (London, The National Archives, E39/3/53,/54), 1292 (NRS, SP 13/1) and 1296 (TNA, E101/331/5), for which see T Thomson and C Innes (eds), *The Acts of the Parliaments of Scotland* [*APS*], vol i *A.D. MCXXIV–A.D. MCCCCXXIII* (Edinburgh, 1844) 107–118 [red foliation].

question put to them, often by a single party).[30] But all these records are lost, meaning we have also lost key information about court process until the very late thirteenth and fourteenth centuries (the earliest surviving burgh records is from the burgh court of Aberdeen of 1317, and it is the sole survivor of almost the whole fourteenth century).[31] Our only sense of their operation comes from chance documents recorded by third parties and kept in some form in their archives (a good example of this is the perambulation records that survive in one of Arbroath Abbey's cartularies).[32] We also know that the royal archives contained rolls of the "assizes", that is, laws, enacted by kings.[33] If there ever was a live written legal culture surrounding the expertise of originally Gaelic-speaking "lawmen" (*iudices*, explained below), this does not survive in any form that allows us to speculate any further beyond tentatively positing the existence of such a tradition in the first place.[34]

What we have, therefore, to track law and administrative change is, first, mostly chance survivals of documentary material in the records of third party institutions, particularly the cartularies of monastic and regular houses.[35] These sometimes contain references that allow us to track changing institutional form, and even the odd full case.[36] But we have to acknowledge that the amount of case material we have is small. The *People of Medieval Scotland* (PoMS) database, for example, contains just 245 documents categorised as "agreements" and a mere 127 documents categorised as "settlements" out of over 10,000 currently entered in the database, and Cooper's *Select cases from the thirteenth century* is not such a small selection of the surviving cases as the slender size of the volume might suggest.[37] Indeed, quite a lot of these cases – particularly those with the most detail – tell us

30 The form these rolls might have taken are being examined by D Broun and J Tucker, 'The earliest central judicial records' (forthcoming). For a general study, see Taylor, *Shape of the State* (n 15) 399–417.

31 Aberdeen City archives, CA/5/6, with a new translation in A R C Simpson and J W Armstrong, 'The Roll of the Burgh Courts of Aberdeen, August–October 1317', in A M Godfrey (ed), *Miscellany VIII by Various Authors*, Stair Society vol 67 (2020) 57–93.

32 This is the *Registrum Vetus*, compiled in the early fourteenth century, perhaps at the behest of Bernard, abbot of Arbroath; National Library of Scotland, Advocates MS 34.4.2.

33 *APS*, i, 113–117, at 116–117.

34 For this tradition, see Taylor, *Shape of the State* (n 15) 123–132.

35 For a study of the manuscript context of some of Scotland's earliest cartularies, see J Tucker, *Reading and Shaping Medieval Cartularies: Multi-Scribe Manuscripts and their Patterns of Growth. A Study of the earliest cartularies of Glasgow Cathedral and Lindores Abbey* (2020).

36 Many of the most prominent cases are discussed in MacQueen, *Common Law* (n 3) with full references, and Taylor, *Shape of the State* (n 15) ch 5.

37 Figures generated from the faceted search in the *People of Medieval Scotland 1093–1371* database [*PoMS*], for which see *https://poms.ac.uk/search* (last accessed 14 July 2022). T M Cooper, *Select Scottish Cases of the Thirteenth Century* (1944).

about cases heard in front of papal judges delegate or attached in some way to an ecclesiastical court – which are important fora, but not the only ones.[38]

By contrast, most of the prescriptive law survives in manuscripts that were compiled long after their supposed date of compilation. Indeed, we are only just getting to grips with what legal material has survived, what authority it has and how it can be used.[39] We have one short twenty-one-chapter compilation, *Leges Scocie*, which survives in a single manuscript dating from 1267–1272 and contains statute material and prescriptive content dating mostly from the later twelfth and early thirteenth century (the reign of William the Lion, 1165–1214)[40]; one "miscellaneous" compilation, known as the Ayr Miscellany (because of the by-name of its sole manuscript witness), which seems to predate the 1320s[41]; and three further compilations that are attributed to kings of the twelfth and thirteenth centuries (David I, William the Lion, Alexander II) but which were all compiled during the fourteenth century and contain not much material that can be dated securely to those kings' reigns.[42] Andrew Simpson's chapter acknowledges that the *Leges Burgorum*, which, although it proclaims itself to be compiled by David I (1124–1153), seems to be a much later collection (its earliest manuscript witness is incomplete and dates to 1267–1272) that had undergone stages of revision even by the early fourteenth century. Certainly, *clear* references to the idea of the "laws and assizes of the burghs" do not survive until the beginning of the thirteenth century.[43] While this material is rich and still relatively untapped, even with it, it must be acknowledged that we examine Scottish legal and administrative development as through a crack in the door: if we press our eye firmly to it, we can make out quite a lot of what we see, but there is much in the room we can never see, for the angle of sight is so acute our range is very limited.

38 For a full study of these cases, see P C Ferguson, *Medieval Papal Representatives in Scotland: Legates, Nuncios and Judges-Delegate, 1125–1286*, Stair Society vol 45 (1997); for an example of a particularly full case, heard at an ecclesiastical synod held at Perth in 1206, see J Stuart (ed), *The Miscellany of the Spalding Club Volume 5*, Spalding Club vol 23 (1852) 209–213.

39 Taylor (ed), *Laws* (n 9) where introductions to all these compilations bar the burgh laws can be found.

40 This is the Berne manuscript: National Records of Scotland (hereafter NRS), PA5/1.

41 This is the Ayr manuscript: NRS, PA5/2.

42 All of these texts have been analysed, edited and translated in Taylor (ed), *Laws* (n 9) and all citations to them are from these editions. *Leges Scocie* = *LS*; *Leges inter Brettos et Scotos* = *LBS*; *Capitula Assisarum et Statutorum Domini Dauid Regis Scotie* = *CD*; *Leges Willelmi Regis* = *LW*; *Statuta Regis Alexandri* = *SA*; note that the Ayr miscellany referenced below is also edited in this volume.

43 Taylor (ed), *Laws* (n 9) 7–8.

Problems continue once one enters the fourteenth century, although current research is opening up some previously overgrown avenues. One legal manuscript, known as the Ayr manuscript, seems to have been compiled late in the reign of Robert I (1306–1329), and contains several texts that show the king and his counsellors to be preoccupied with law reform during his turbulent reign, particularly after 1314.[44] The parliamentary record for the fourteenth century as a whole is much richer than for the later thirteenth, although we still have very few pieces of *legislation* that survive from it.[45] Since the 1960s, *Regiam maiestatem*, Scotland's earliest surviving procedural and jurisprudential tractate, has been dated to the early fourteenth century but, given the complexities of its manuscript tradition, it has not been possible to develop a position on *why* its compilation was started until extremely recently.[46] Indeed, it was even thought that it exerted no influence in fourteenth-century Scotland: its earliest surviving manuscript survives only from the late fourteenth century and its earliest surviving external citation is not until 1426.[47] *Regiam* is difficult in another way: it is not finished and therefore one cannot be entirely sure whether the precise content of the earliest known version would have been retained had the tractate itself been fully realised. *Quoniam Attachiamenta* seems to have been the counterpoint (contemporary or later) to *Regiam*, as the core of it describes procedure in lords' courts, with, it seems, an aim of covering similar subjects as *Regiam* had done for royal courts (such as, for example, how to ensure that a summons would be made lawfully).[48] However, *Quoniam* had much material

44 NRS, PA5/2, described in Taylor (ed), *Laws* (n 9) 39–48.

45 The parliamentary register does not survive until 1466. Surviving parliamentary legislation issued before 1466 has been edited in K M Brown, G H MacIntosh, A J Mann, P E Ritchie and R J Tanner (eds), with A Grosjean, A R MacDonald, K F McAlister, D J Patrick, L A M Stewart et al, *The Records of the Parliaments of Scotland to 1707* (St Andrews, 2007) available at *http://www.rps.ac.uk* [*RPS*] (last accessed 14 July 2022) from eleven late medieval manuscripts, none of which have official status. For this see 'Note on the Sources for the Parliaments of Scotland, 1424–1466', available online at *https://www.rps.ac.uk/static/notesonsources.html* (last accessed 14 July 2022). For the *RPS* team, see the full list of acknowledgements here: *https://www.rps.ac.uk/static/acknowledgements.html* (last accessed 14 July 2022). There are a number of parliament rolls that survive from the very late thirteenth and fourteenth century but not in a continuous series, see NRS, PA1/1-7, while some legislation from 1357 onwards was transcribed in the 'Black Book' (NRS, PA5/4).

46 See the summary in A Taylor, 'What does *Regiam Maiestatem* actually say (and what does it mean)?', in W Eves, J Hudson, I Ivarsen and S White (eds), *Common Law, Civil Law and Colonial Law: Essays in Comparative Legal History from the Twelfth to the Twentieth Century* (2021) 47–82, and A Taylor, 'Introduction', in Davies (ed) with Taylor, *Regiam Majestatem* (n 19) 1–168.

47 *RPS*, 1426/13.

48 Fergus (ed and trs), *Quoniam Attachiamenta* (n 20).

added to it by the time of its first manuscript witness, making it difficult to know what was the "original" aim of *Quoniam* and what accrued later, although *Quoniam* did contain some (slightly altered) chapters from the pre-existing Ayr Miscellany.[49] Regardless, understanding this corpus of law allows us to ask different questions of law and legal expertise in the fourteenth century than we can in the twelfth and thirteenth. There is therefore a disjuncture in this paper between its "high middle ages" section and its fourteenth-century section. As detailed below, much of this later medieval material is comparatively understudied, particularly in the fourteenth century, so much of what follows about the period must be taken as tentative and preliminary.

D: THE REGULARISATION OF JUSTICE

The "regularisation of justice" narrative is important for Scotland but it makes more sense for the thirteenth century, particularly from 1230 onwards, rather than the twelfth. It is quite clear that Scottish kings were increasingly enforcing their authority by the collection of revenue and the dispensing of justice through representatives and institutions (denoting concrete organisational forms) from the late twelfth century onwards.[50] While the earliest known sheriffs in Scotland (known by the Latin *vicecomes*) appear in the reign of David I (1124–1153), there was no standard expectation that they would hold their own courts until the 1180s.[51] An itinerant financial audit, whereby the king's auditors brought sheriffs from particular regions to account for what they owed, was probably introduced at around the same time; the earliest date for its operation in some form is the 1190s/1200s.[52] Unlike in England, however, this audit (not yet called the Exchequer) was not fixed in one place – it moved around the kingdom, although it is unclear whether it did so separately from the person of the king.[53] Nor were all sheriffs called to account every year: the audit was regionalised and calculated according to accounting terms (each calendar year contained, it seemed two, ending at Martinmas and Easter).[54] As a result, by 1263–1266 (the date of

49 See the summary in Fergus (ed and tr), *Quoniam* (n 20) 51–52.
50 What follows summarises the evidence, literature and conclusions in Taylor, *Shape of the State* (n 15) and cites some of the basic evidence.
51 *LS*, c. 14 (n 42); Taylor, *Shape of the State* (n 15) 205–210.
52 Taylor, *Shape of the State* (n 15) 361–362.
53 Taylor, *Shape of the State* (n 15) 358–361.
54 Taylor, *Shape of the State* (n 15) 357–358.

the earliest surviving accounts) some sheriffs accounted for two, three, four terms at a time, sometimes even more.

The administration of law and justice tells a rather similar story. "Central" judicial offices seem to have been introduced in Scotland south of the Firth of Forth in the 1140s, and a major figure, known as the "justice" first appears north of the Forth from the 1160s onwards.[55] But these justices were only "central" in the sense that they were clearly responsive to and worked under the central authority in the kingdom, the king, not in the sense that they exercised jurisdiction over the whole kingdom from the "centre". Indeed, although the role of these justices is difficult to pin down at first, it seems that their activities were first confined to the region south of the Firth of Forth (but excluding Galloway).[56] Their authority clearly intensified in that area over the next few decades but it is only during the 1180s that they were expected to hold irregular judicial assemblies that all the religious and secular elites of the kingdom were supposed to attend.[57]

There thus was a change from the composition of the "justice" court, visible in the 1180s as an irregular, high-status affair, whose jurisdiction was not formally regionalised, to the "justiciar's court", whose jurisdiction spread over a large region (Scotland north of the Forth and Lothian) and who conducted "ayres" around those regions, travelling from sheriffdom to sheriffdom (or, in Latin, *de ballia ad balliam*).[58] Probably now as late as the 1220s, the justice (now known as the justiciar) started to hold an ayre and presided over the cases that pertained to him. In 1230, an assembly of Alexander II introduced procedures for the recovery of land following unlawful dispossession ("dissasine").[59] These cases were initiated by documents known as brieves, obtained from the king's writing office: a would-be litigant could purchase a brieve to bring against a person who they claimed had dissaised them of their land. By 1253, again inspired by the English possessory assize, we know that mortancestor, a remedy for the recovery of inheritance, had been introduced and, probably around the same time, remedies for *right* in land had been introduced.[60] Looking at later fourteenth-century formular-

55 Taylor, *Shape of the State* (n 15) 216–233.

56 Taylor, *Shape of the State* (n 15) 224–225.

57 *LS*, c. 14 (n 42).

58 Taylor, *Shape of the State* (n 15) 234–244.

59 *SA*, c. 7 (n 42); MacQueen, *Common Law* (n 3) 143–144; for the 1230 legislation as a whole, see Taylor, *Shape of the State* (n 15) 271–293.

60 C J Neville and G G Simpson (eds), *Regesta Regum Scotorum*, vol iv (part 1): *The Acts of Alexander III, 1249–1286* [*RRS*, iv, 1] (2013) no 18; see also C N Innes (ed), *Registrum de Dunfermelyn*, Bannatyne Club vol 72 (1842) no 83; MacQueen, *Common Law* (n 3) 169–170.

ies, the wording of these brieves followed their English exemplar, even if the court and official to which they were addressed was different. In short, these reforms introduced a system of adversarial pleading and legal procedure that took cases into royal courts. By the 1260s, a chamberlain's ayre had developed, overseeing legal procedure in the burghs; by 1314, at the very latest, a text entitled *De articulis inquirendis in burgo in itinere Camerarie secundum usus Scocie* ("The Articles to be enquired into in the burgh on the Chamberlain's ayre, following the custom of Scotland") had been drawn out which seem, again as Simpson has shown, *in places* follow attested court procedure in Aberdeen in 1317.[61]

By the early fourteenth century, we know that there was clear thinking about the scope and use of the brieves. Dissasine touched freehold alone; mortancestor, fief and freehold; right, freehold, fief and *right* – and, therefore, if someone lost land through either possessory assize, they could recover it through a claim of right.[62] By this point, pleadable brieves *seem* to have been used to such an extent that there developed rules about what should or should not be in the brieve to ensure their validity (in the case of dissasine: the standardised name of the land in question was required, which must have caused problems, as well as the names of man and wife when land was claimed in the name of one's wife).[63] Other (non-pleadable) brieves, such as perambulation, had been developed to such an extent by the early fourteenth centuries that provisions were written down that stated exactly what needed to be in the brieve of perambulation in order for the procedure not to be quashed, annulled or disallowed.[64] These sorts of "little rules" dot the early fourteenth-century compilation known as the Ayr Miscellany in particular: one chapter, for example, states that if anyone names a warrantor for the land claimed in a case of mortancestor, they had to name the warrantor and their province so that it was easy to produce them and the case could proceed efficiently.[65] These warranty procedures regarding claims to chattels or moveables – which were first developed in response to allegations of theft – were probably honed through trial and error, with many defenders trying to buy time by vouching warrantors without their sure name or location.[66]

61 NRS, PA5/2, fo. 15v–18v; described in Taylor (ed), *Laws* (n 9) 44–45; see below, Simpson's chapter, 181–208.
62 Ayr Miscellany, c. 33 (n 42).
63 Ayr Miscellany, c. 5 (n 42).
64 Ayr Miscellany, c. 4 (n 42).
65 Ayr Miscellany, c. 11 (n 42).
66 For the earliest evidence for detailed procedure on warrantors in accusations of theft, see *LS*, cc. 1, 11 (n 42); see also Fergus (ed), *Quoniam* (n 20) c. 8.

One final point is worth raising here before I go on to mention the "problems" with the singularity of this narrative of development. The absence of a central court separate from Parliament or the King's Council before the sixteenth century is frequently remarked upon.[67] What this means for legal expertise and legal training for the earlier period, particularly the thirteenth and fourteenth centuries, has not, however, been worked out fully.[68] In England, Paul Brand has argued that the presence of permanent royal courts in London and Westminster meant that a separate training school developed in the thirteenth century long before it was ever formalised as the Inns of Court. According to Brand, this allowed for the development of expertise in the English common law to develop along separate intellectual trajectories from the law studied in England's universities (essentially civil and canon).[69] This is an interesting argument, particularly here for the questions it poses for Scotland. Scotland's immediate legal model in the 1180s and the 1230s was England: the justice courts, then the ayres, then the brieve system all derived from England, which by this point was developing a focal point for the training of individuals to practise effectively within that system.[70] The absence of any similar focal point in Scotland must have made a difference but it was not necessarily a difference that resulted in a *lack* of expertise. The later thirteenth-century material found in the Ayr Miscellany is soaked through with Roman legal terminology and, indeed, cases involving laymen, heard in lay and ecclesiastical courts alike, could be framed in the terms and use the arguments of Roman and canon law.[71] Court procedure is one of the main topics of the Ayr Miscellany; its long "second" chapter begins with an account of how to plead on a brieve of right in a burgh court, how the defender should deny the claim, when they should submit their exceptions and when a view of land should be held. Procedural knowledge clearly disseminated, as Andrew Simpson shows in his chapter, to the practice of the burgh court of Aberdeen in 1317. Although equivalents to the Inns of Court in later medieval Scotland did not develop, there nonetheless were opportu-

67 See the important account of this change in A M Godfrey, *Civil Justice in Renaissance Scotland: the Origins of a Central Court* (2009).

68 See, however, for Scotland, MacQueen, *Common Law* (n 3) 74–84; A R C Simpson, 'Men of Law in the Aberdeen Council Register? A Preliminary Study, ca. 1450–ca. 1460' (2019) *Juridical Review* 136–159.

69 P Brand, 'Legal Education in England before the Inns of Court', in J A Bush and A Wijffels (eds), *Learning the Law: Teaching and the Transmission of Law in England, 1150–1900* (1999) 51–84.

70 For Scotland's dependence on English remedies, see the pertinent conclusions of MacQueen, *Common Law* (n 3) 264–266. For legal expertise in later medieval Scotland, see the important comments in MacQueen, *Common Law* (n 3) ch 3, and now Simpson, 'Men of Law' (n 68).

71 Discussed briefly in Taylor (ed), *Laws* (n 9) 272.

nities for a vernacular sort of expertise to develop around common law procedure. Moreover, the "common law", as we will see, was not the only form of expertise. *Regiam Maiestatem* itself contains cross-references to up-to-date commentaries on canon law (as well as citing the *Institutes*, *Codex* and *Digest*) that may well have been inserted by the original compiler.[72] What the absence of any "home" university (although many churchmen did train abroad) or alternative centre of legal training may have done is promote a certain flexibility of the legal register that worked across jurisdictions rather than within them.

Yet, as stated above, for all its merits, this narrative needs to be fleshed out and complicated in three main ways. First, it is a narrative that only holds for the period immediately before and following 1230; it cannot be held up as a twelfth-century phenomenon, as we shall see. Secondly, there are both important continuities with this more dynamic twelfth century that complicates the form of the thirteenth century narrative based on the regularisation of justice through a network of primarily royal courts. Thirdly, there remains much more to be said on the subjects of legal expertise, knowledge and practice beyond that attested by the enduring brieve system over the fourteenth century. What follows takes these points in turn.

E: THE DIVERSITY OF TWELFTH CENTURY LAW AND ADMINISTRATION

The gifting and granting of large territorialised jurisdictions to secular aristocrats, conveyed by charter, used to be seen as a practice, even a policy, of David I (1124–1153), which was continued by his grandsons.[73] This, however, has come under some challenge. First, it is becoming apparent that when charters were used by David to give land to his followers, it was more on the beneficiary's insistence than the king's policy: Matthew Hammond has shown that kings did not routinely grant land by charter to their lay

72 J R Davies, 'References to Roman and canon law in Regiam Majestatem', The COTR (Community of the Realm) blog, August 2019, *The Community of the Realm in Scotland, 1249–1424: History law and Charters in a Recreated Kingdom*, available at: *http://www.cotr.ac.uk/blog/regiam1* (last accessed 9 August 2022); Taylor, 'What does *Regiam Maiestatem* actually say?' (n 46); Taylor, 'Introduction' (n 46) 82–84, 92–100.

73 G W S Barrow, *The Anglo-Norman Era in Scottish History* (1980), among many of his publications on the subject. See also one of his early essays, reprinted in G W S Barrow, 'Scotland's "Norman" Families', in *idem*, *The Kingdom of the Scots: Government, Church and Society from the Eleventh to the Fourteenth Centuries*, 2nd edn (2003) 279–295.

followers until the 1160s/1170s.[74] Secondly, when these charters were used – as famously survives for the case of the gift of Annandale to Robert de Brus – their formulae and wording were often vague, framed in personal terms, and did not specify any formal jurisdictional privileges.[75] Any "early" examples of grants of jurisdiction – whereby land was given with sake, soke, toll, team and infangentheof, gallows and pit – have, on closer examination, been found to be spurious or later confections: perhaps the most famous example here is David's supposed grant not only of the hereditary stewardship to Walter fitz Alan but also large tracts of land in Ayrshire and Renfrewshire (in the south-west of the kingdom) with major jurisdictional privileges.[76] Both charters – one original, one surviving only as a copy – here are of later date than their supposed issue by David I's grandson, Mael Coluim, probably in 1161.[77] Jurisdictional formulae appear regularly in royal charters giving and confirming land to secular elites only from the 1170s and 1180s onwards.[78] The understanding that elites would hold singular authority over their land and have the singular right to hold their own court (and could pass this authority on to their heirs) seems to have gradually developed over the twelfth century and appears only regularly in charters from the century's last three decades.

If territorialised aristocratic jurisdiction was not an expected or regular part of the legal landscape of the Scottish kingdom, particularly north of the Firth of Forth, until the 1170s, then what was it replacing? We know that there is a superficial similarity with the Norwegian kingdom with the existence of provincial assemblies to which cases were brought and judgments were made. The kingdom of the Scots north of the Firth of Forth – Scotland "proper", as it is called, because only this region was called *Scotia* well into the thirteenth century – was divided into provinces in both historical-

74 M Hammond, 'The Adoption and Routinization of Scottish Royal Charter Production to Lay Beneficiaries, 1124–1195' (2014) 36 *Anglo-Norman Studies* 91–115.

75 For the most recent reassessment of this charter (which I find convincing), see D Broun, 'Southern Scotland as part of the Scottish Kingdom: the evidence of the earliest charters', in N McGuigan and A Woolf (eds), *The Battle of Carham: A Thousand Years on* (2018) 33–49.

76 G W S Barrow (ed), *Regesta Regum Scottorum* vol. i, *The Acts of Malcolm IV King of Scots 1153–1165* [*RRS*, i] (1960), nos 183–184.

77 For the argument that both charters are spurious, see A Taylor, 'A re-examination of Mael Coluim IV's charters to Walter, son of Alan, in 1161' (forthcoming). This paper was written after the publication of *Shape of the State* and so I could not incorporate its conclusions to the relevant passages of my book.

78 Taylor, *Shape of the State* (n 15) 159–161. See, more generally, the implications of this in A Taylor, 'Formalising aristocratic power in royal *acta* in late twelfth- and early thirteenth-century France and Scotland' (2018) 28 *Transactions of the Royal Historical Society* (sixth series) 33–64.

legendary material and legal chapters (although how exactly the provinces were divided and what they were called varied).[79] It seems that by the reign of David I it was expected that every province would have at least one *iudex* – a "judge" – and the one full case report that survives reports three judges all present at an assembly of the province of Fife and Fothrif.[80] Unlike in the Norwegian provincial assembly, however, these *iudices* seem to have been judges, in that they did determine the case (it was determined, said the Loch Leven record, by their sentence and the oaths of the perambulators of the land).[81] The extent of their expertise may well have been to know, among other questions, the limits of the compensation owed for various insults and injuries according to status and may well partly survive in written form in the chapters now known as *Leges inter Brettos et Scotos*.[82] These judges did not disappear over the thirteenth century; there are many attested by name and title in the surviving charter record, although such individuals may have acted at more local levels than they did in the twelfth century.[83] Their expertise was incorporated into the newer arrangements for perambulation in the thirteenth century and any default from them resulted in the annulment of the perambulation itself.[84]

The one account of a provincial assembly in action comes from early in the reign of David I and involved a local lord and knight, Robert of Burgundy (presumably a French-speaker), against a local monastic cell (of *Celi Dé*) at Loch Leven.[85] The case turned on some land that both parties claimed was their own and the judges found, perhaps unsurprisingly, for the *Celi Dé* (unsurprising, given which of the parties preserved the record). More interesting, however, for this purpose, is who attended. The king summoned the assembly but did not attend. The *mormaer*, the titular leader of the province turned up and so too did heads of local kin-groups as well as

79 For these provinces, see D Broun, 'Statehood and lordship in 'Scotland' before the mid-twelfth century' (2015) 66 *Innes Review* 1–71. For a historico-legendary description of Scotland in *De Situ Albanie* as divided into seven provinces (in three different ways), edited in D Howlett, *Caledonian Craftsmanship: The Scottish Latin Tradition* (2000) 29–39; for further provincial divisions in the legal material, see *LS*, c. 16 (n 42) and *SA*, c. 14 (n 42).

80 *CD*, c. 28 (n 42); A C Lawrie (ed), *Early Scottish Charters Prior to A.D. 1153* (1905) no 80.

81 "*Sed iste Dufgal primo pronunciavit sententiam pro monachis id est Keledeis et contra protervitatem et calumpniam Roberti Burgonensis quia alii judices detulerunt Dufgal propter sui senectutem et iuris peritiam. Et ita fuit decisum istud negotium sententionaliter et per juramentum.*"

82 *Leges inter Brettos et Scotos* is discussed, edited and translated in Taylor (ed), *Laws* (n 9) 243–263, 427–443.

83 For a list, see G W S Barrow, 'The *judex*', in G W S Barrow, *The Kingdom of the Scots: Government, Church and Society from the Eleventh to the Fourteenth Century* (n 2) 57–67.

84 Ayr Miscellany, c. 4 (n 42).

85 Lawrie (ed), *Early Scottish Charters* (n 80) no 80.

the leaders of the army of the bishop of St Andrews.[86] The interesting point here is the depiction of the assembly *not* as an amorphous "community" but as a community divided into elite figures and their retinues. The dense competition for power and status within this hierarchically organised province, therefore, might well go a long way to explaining how simple it was, in this area at least, to overlap territorial jurisdictions on to the defined retinues we glimpse in this particular case.

Finally, it is worth thinking about the role of the king as legislator. Jørn Øyrehagen Sunde has stressed the symbolic role of the king-as-legislator within the Norwegian kingdom, which was, in practice, cemented by the Code of 1274.[87] In Scotland, there is little clear evidence for the king-as-legislator before the mid-twelfth century:[88] there are references to "assizes" (statutes) of David in charters of William the Lion in particular, while *Leges Scocie* is itself in part a record of royal legislation made with the consent of the great men of the kingdom in 1177, 1180, 1184 and 1197.[89] However, the clear role for the king as legislator may have been developing, rather than constant, over the twelfth century.[90] Many of David's "assizes" referenced in William's charters are more often *claims* to antiquity than they are uncomplicated references to past legislative activity.[91] Moreover, even as the king did become more prominent as a *legislator* (there is a very interesting reference to Mael Coluim IV making law for the *patria* in the 1160s), he did not do so alone.[92] *Iudices* continued to make law and act as legislators – and not just give judgments – into the thirteenth century. A judgment passed in 1210 against Gillescop Mac Aedacán, who had probably plotted against King William, was laid down at Edinburgh "by the judges of Galloway and

86 "*[Rex] convocavit hominium multitudinem in unum locum, scilicet, Constantinum, comitem de Fyf, virum discretum et facundum, cum satrapys et satellitibus et exercitu de Fyf, et Macbeath thcynetum de Falleland, et primicerios et duces et lumnarcas exercitus Episcopi et Soen, ducem* [gap in MS] *cum familia sua. Et tunc temporis fuerunt duces exercitus episcopi Budadh et Slogadadh. Et hi omnes sunt testes hujus altercationis et dissentionis.*"

87 See above/below, pp. 95–121.

88 Although see Dauvit Broun's point above, where he notes that the idea of Cinead mac Ailpín as responsible for establishing Scottish laws is first attested in the late twelfth/early thirteenth century; see above, pp. 87–92.

89 G W S Barrow (ed) with collaboration from W W Scott, *Regesta Regum Scottorum, vol ii: the Acts of William I King of Scots 1165–1214* [*RRS*, ii] (1971) nos 281, 469, 475.

90 It is of interest that the reference to the making or giving of the laws of the kingdom at Forteviot in the reign of Domnall mac Aílpin (d.862), includes the king and the people doing the action; see the text in B Hudson, "The 'Scottish Chronicle'" (1998) 77 *Scottish Historical Review* 129–161 at 148.

91 See, for example, *RRS*, ii, no 281 (n 89), discussed in Taylor, *Shape of the State* (n 15) 63–64.

92 *RRS*, i, no 233 (n 76).

of Scotland".[93] The judges of Galloway again *made law* at Dumfries by enacting that anyone who breached the peace of the king had to pay 240 cows and three geldings to the king.[94] In (probably) 1221, the judges of Scotland laid down the fines to be raised on those who had failed to serve in the king's common army.[95] Well into the thirteenth century, then, *iudices* were still making law, albeit under the king's authority. Why kings continued to need *iudices* to act in a law-making capacity is an interesting question: there are certainly indications that kings made efforts to tie the authority of the judge – both as legal expert and *as* judge – more firmly to their own over the twelfth century.[96] Certainly, *iudex*-authority was limited: there is no evidence, for example, of its operation within Lothian as there is north of the Forth. It may be, as a parallel system of courts and legal authority (sheriffs and justiciars) developed first in Lothian and then north of the Firth of Forth by the 1180s, that kings no longer needed *iudices* to make law over issues that had previously constituted the *iudex*'s sole expertise. Certainly, in perambulation, by the late 1190s, a *iudex*'s role in conducting the perambulation was conducted under the supervision of the justiciar and according to a royal "assize" (which does not survive).[97] Seen in this light, therefore, the authority of the *iudex* was not so much replaced as gradually reduced in geographic and jurisdictional scope: it was still in use, even by the end of the thirteenth century, but no longer occupying a role as lawmaker and judge on a wide scale.[98]

F: COMMUNITY, STATUS AND DENIAL: THIRTEENTH-CENTURY LEGAL MATERIAL RE-EXAMINED

It is therefore clear that a more "regularised" system of royal justice not only developed later than has perhaps previously been acknowledged but did so alongside and necessarily effected a parallel set of expertise and legal culture based on notions of honour, injury and status, and centred on the legal expert known as the *iudex*. How, then, does its existence affect the

93 *LS*, c.19 (n 42) for discussion, see Taylor (ed), *Laws* 225–227 (n 9).

94 *LS*, c.18 (n 42).

95 *SA*, c.26 (n 42). Its date is discussed in Taylor (ed), *Laws* 349–350 (n 9).

96 Taylor, *Shape of the State* (n 15) 130–132; Taylor (ed), *Laws* (n 9) 253–259.

97 For this case, see D Broun, 'The King's *brithem* (Gaelic for "Judge") and the Recording of Dispute-Resolutions' (2010) *PoMS Feature of the Month, no. 11* available at *https://paradox.poms.ac.uk/feature/april10.html* (last accessed 9 August 2022).

98 For the growth of the office of *iusticia*, and how it might have interacted with the role *iudices* could play north of the Firth of Forth, see Taylor, *Shape of the State* (n 15) 218–233.

view of that more regularised system? First, there are questions we need to ask of its regularity. Did, for example, most "litigants" (and it is probably overly formalised to call them this) make regular recourse to an adversarial system, even if they did have their disputes heard and concluded in royal courts? This may seem like a surprising position to take as pleadable brieves are predominant in the (admittedly sparse) parliamentary legislation of the fourteenth century when this kind of material mentions brieves.[99] But the thirteenth-century evidence does present a more complex picture. For example, disputes over *ius* – over right in land – were not only initiated through a brieve of right in a sheriff's court, but were also pursued by the purchase of a brieve of inquest, in which the questions asked in the brieve were not articulating a claim against another person but, instead, asked factual, descriptive questions of who held the right in the land.[100] The substance of a claim of mortancestor, itself a possessory assize to determine rightful inheritance, could just as well be – and, indeed, was – settled by an inquest that asked the very same question of the very same body, the visnet, a set of twelve elected "good and trustworthy men" of the local area (known as the *patria*) – although the recorded number did often differ.[101] But the question asked by the brieve of inquest was the same as that asked of the visnet in an assize of mortancestor: was this individual or group the nearest heir of X, and had X died vested and saised in the land in question? The brieve of inquest therefore covered every question asked in the pleadable brieves of dissasine, mortancestor and right.

Why might disputants have used a brieve of inquest as opposed to a pleadable brieve? In cases of "mortancestor" or right, it is probable that brieves of inquest were quicker and thus offered speedier resolution than their pleadable counterparts. All the surviving brieves of inquest and their returns from Alexander III's reign (that is, 1249–1286) were resolved within four months.[102] By contrast, the little we know about the process of litigation on a brieve of right tells us that these cases could be slow and costly, allow-

99 This is particularly the case for the brieve formulae attached to Fergus (ed), *Quoniam* (n 20) cc. 36–42, and those cited in the important parliamentary legislation of 1318: *RPS* 1318/15, /21, /25 (actually referring to mortancestor), /27.

100 For this interpretation of the role of the inquest in thirteenth-century legal (as opposed to administrative) procedure, see Taylor, *Shape of the State* (n 15) 323–332. For an example, see *RRS*, iv, 1, no. 32 (n 60).

101 See, for example, the case of the five daughters of Simon, doorkeeper of Montrose, who procured a brieve of inquest to determine whether they were his "legitimate and nearest heir"; *RRS*, iv, 1, no 36 (n 60) (NRS, RH5/23); Taylor, *Shape of the State* (n 15) 332–333.

102 Taylor, *Shape of the State* (n 15) 324–325.

ing up to four lawful essoins (excuses for non-appearance in court) and then, if a warrantor was called, the process began again.[103] Even once litigation began, "exceptions" to the brieve (regardless of whether the case was about right or possessory) could also mean that a case was thrown out before the question was ever put to the assize. It is also possible that recourse to the brieve of right outside the burghs was limited to those who held directly from the king: if this was the case, then it would make sense that most disputants would pursue "right" through an inquest, rather than through a pleadable brieve.[104] But, in a case of unlawful dissasine and mortancestor, no essoins were allowed, so dissasine cases in England were much swifter, partly explaining their popularity there.[105] But, again, Scotland is different. Here, there seem to have been a large financial consequence to both raising a wrongful claim of dissasine and being found to have wrongly dissaised another – £10 for so doing.[106] Why the government introduced this remedy and then effectively hamstrung its popularity by imposing such large fines is an important question.[107] But, at this point, again it is clear why, if someone wanted to pursue a dissasine-like claim, the brieve of inquest might have seemed like the safer choice, particularly to begin with.

It is thus possible that an adversarial system of litigation initiated through pleadable brieves did not constitute the whole of the Scottish "common law", at least for much of the thirteenth century. Instead, the inquest may well have held the more prominent position – making cases more about truth than law – as suggested by the frequency of formulae for brieves initiating inquests into a diverse set of issues in the so-called "Ayr formulary", which survives in an early fourteenth-century legal manuscript and states that it lists the brieves sent from the royal "chancery" (*cancellaria*).[108]

103 According to the procedure described in *Regiam Maiestatem*, *Regiam*, cc. 6–10 (from the forthcoming edition based on the two earliest manuscripts; Davies (ed) with Taylor, *Regiam Majestatem* (n 19)). The limit of four essoins is confirmed in Ayr Miscellany, c. 2 (n 42) on the brieve of right in the burgh.

104 For this line of argument, see Taylor, *Shape of the State* (n 15) 315–318, now supplemented by the analysis of the passage in *Regiam* in Taylor (ed), *Laws* (n 9) 275–280; D A Carpenter, 'Scottish royal government in the thirteenth century from an English perspective', in Matthew Hammond (ed), *New Perspectives on Medieval Scotland, 1093–1286* (2013) 117–159, at 142–143; for an alternative position, arguing that a brieve of right existed in a different form and was addressed to the court-holder, see MacQueen, *Common Law* (n 3) 193–194.

105 See also MacQueen, *Common Law* (n 3) 258.

106 *SA*, c. 7 (n 42) discussed in Taylor, *Shape of the State* (n 15) 285–293; building on Carpenter, 'Scottish royal government' (n 104) 147–149.

107 My preliminary attempt to answer this is in Taylor, *Shape of the State* (n 15) 295–297.

108 This survives in a single manuscript copy in the Ayr manuscript (Edinburgh, NRS, PA5/2, ff. 18v–30r, described in Taylor (ed), *Laws* (n 9) 39–48. The whole formulary is edited in

Brieves of inquests merely instructed the sheriff to hold an inquest to determine the truth of a particular matter (was X vested and saised in dower land at the church door? Was Y the nearest heir or Z?). The sheriff did this by summoning the good men of the country; they determined on oath among themselves what they knew and the sheriff sent the answer back to the king who would act on the basis of the visnet's verdict. There was, thus, no formal process of judgment, there was only a "matter of fact" (although how "facts" or "truth" was isolated from their context necessarily depended on the existence of legal rules).

Secondly, the mode of proof. The changing method of proof and its socio-legal consequences has received very little attention from medieval legal historians of Scotland but, when it has, the focus has often been on the origins of the jury trial in Scotland. The narrative is similar to that elsewhere in Europe: as a consequence of the banning of clerical participation in the ordeals of iron and water by the Fourth Lateran Council in 1215, secular governments had to develop other ways of determining proof.[109] In Scotland, the ordeals of iron and water may have been formally abandoned by royal legislation enacted in 1230, even if they continued more informally thereafter.[110] But the general solution is that this led to more assize-based modes of proof in both criminal accusations and civil litigations – a question was put to a panel of men who produced a verdict.[111] The problem here is not just that it ignores the continuing prominence afforded to trial by battle in the legal material (for both criminal and civil accusations, although burgesses were exempt, as were women and clerics) but that it ignores the formal space given to compurgation within both the "criminal" sphere and also accusations of wrong or injury.[112] The abandonment of compurgation, or the "oath of denial" as Tom Lambert has recently described it, is a neglected

A A M Duncan (ed), *Scottish Formularies*, Stair Society vol 58 (2011) 3–36, and discussed in Taylor, *Shape of the State* (n 15) 301–307. Over twenty chapters are missing owing to the loss of two bifolia from the gathering.

109 R Bartlett, *Trial by Fire and Water: the Medieval Judicial Ordeal* (1986).

110 SA, c. 6 (n 42); for comment see H L MacQueen, 'Canon law, custom and legislation: Law in the Reign of Alexander II', in R D Oram (ed), *The Reign of Alexander II, 1214–1249* (2005) 221–251, at 240–241; Taylor, *Shape of the State* (n 15) 280–284.

111 I D Willock, *The Origins and Development of the Jury in Scotland*, Stair Society vol 23 (1966) 26–28.

112 *Quoniam Attachiamenta* confirms that a defendant in a case of theft has the option of trial by battle or to go to the assize if they deny the theft (Fergus (ed), *Quoniam* (n 20) c. 10). Ayr Miscellany c. 35 (n 42) said that the defendant had first to choose their mode of defence – either assize or battle. There were rules on who could have champions – although said rules also said that really lords should provide champions for their men, because "*corpus tenentis et omnia bona sua de iure esse debent in protectione et defencione domini sui*" (*CD*, c. 42 (n 42)).

but extremely significant change in legal procedure that occurred at some point in the twelfth century in England.[113] Lambert's basic point is that the oath of denial allowed for someone accused of something by someone else to defend themselves and effectively throw off an accusation: he suggests it is an important change in law when the basic idea that someone accused or challenged could throw off the accusation by having enough people swear to his innocence was abandoned. Although accounts have dealt with the decline of compurgation, it is mostly as a law-and-rationality account – that compurgation is an unfactual and irrational mode of proof, allowing people with power, status and authority to throw off accusations easily, and far more difficult, if not impossible, for the friendless and less powerful to do the same.

What happens with the oath of denial in Scotland is again another place where Scottish practice diverges from English. Compurgation remained a form of proof; formal denial remained part of the law, although it is unclear until when it did so. A chapter from the Ayr Miscellany shows that the oath of denial was still an option in small plaints – only if the defendant failed to turn up when they should have done was the option of the oath of denial removed (equally, the converse held true as well: if the pursuer didn't turn up, they effectively confirmed the denial).[114] The Ayr Miscellany also tells us that denial was an option in cases of non-manifest theft where the accuser had not produced any proof.[115] *Quoniam Attachiamenta*, an interesting text from, probably, the first half of the fourteenth century, confirms that oaths of denial still ran in lords' courts for any trespass, and against the king (just that the numbers were more: the accused needed twelve to deny something against his lord and twenty-four against the king).[116] The number of twenty-four in the king's court appears again in the assizes attributed to David I, but compiled in the reign of Robert I, probably after 1318, if not 1324, which stated that anyone appealed of a felony or of a case of life and limb could deny it with the oath of twenty-four trustworthy men of the sheriffdom where the delict was said to have occurred.[117] *CD* gives us more references to the oath of denial: anyone appealed of theft in the king's court or anyone else's court could choose battle or the oath of denial as a mode of proof,

113 T Lambert, *Law and Order in Anglo-Saxon England* (2017) 255–260.

114 Ayr Miscellany, c. 2 (n 42).

115 Ayr Miscellany, c. 6 (n 42).

116 *Quoniam* makes the caveat that oaths of denial did not hold against documents (Fergus (ed), *Quoniam* (n 20) c. 16).

117 *CD*, c. 20 (n 42).

suggesting it remained an active form of proof at the beginning of the fourteenth century.[118]

So this small selection of material (all concerned with legal procedure outside the burghs) suggests that the oath of denial was still a regular option for those accused of injury, trespass and theft. In non-royal courts, the most regular number required to deny an accusation was twelve; in royal courts it seemed to have been twenty-four. It is unclear whether women had recourse to the oath (and would not have been oath-takers). But what does this mean? First, it complicates our understanding of what happened to proof in this period, particularly in the "criminal" sphere (and that sphere is loosely bounded)[119]: it was not the case that the assize became the evermore accepted mode of proof.[120] Trial by battle, as far as our formal evidence goes, seems to have thrived and the option of the oath of denial remained even in the early fourteenth century. The appearance of this option in cases of wrong, injury and trespass, which in this period were very widely defined, also may suggest that compurgation/the oath of denial spread further than we might think into the "civil" world.[121]

We should see the use of the brieve of inquest in dispute settlement and the continued survival of the oath of denial (both outside the burghs) as similar products of the more limited way in which royal justice in Scotland inserted itself into communal practice. At the level of their basic functioning, neither inquests nor oaths of denial need any form of state *intervention*. They may need some form of *authority* to work, but that authority can work at any level: at the level of the family (if it's big enough), and certainly at the level of the village or small-town community. It is no surprise that compurgation, the oath of denial, is present in earliest medieval legal material, in which the mechanisms for enforcing law and order were located in the community rather than relying on any centrally located structure of enforcement.[122] The settlement of questions about right or possession by local inquest, and not

118 *CD*, c. 3 (n 42).

119 For this see W D H Sellar, 'Forethocht felony, malice aforethought and the classification of homicide', in W M Gordon and T D Fergus (eds), *Legal History in the Making* (1991) 43–59.

120 MacQueen, 'Canon law, custom and legislation' (n 110) 240; G Neilson, *Trial by Combat* (1890) 78–79, 93–96, 113–116, 144–146.

121 A Harding, 'Rights, wrongs and remedies in late medieval English and Scots law', in H L MacQueen (ed), *Stair Society Miscellany Four by Various Authors*, Stair Society vol 49 (2002) 1–8; H L MacQueen, 'Some notes on wrang and unlaw', in Hector MacQueen (ed), *Stair Society Miscellany Five by Various Authors*, Stair Society vol 52 (2005) 13–26.

122 For this basic position, see A Taylor, '*Lex Scripta* and the Problem of Enforcement: Anglo-Saxon, Welsh and Scottish Law Compared', in J Scheele and F Pirie (eds), *Legalism: Community and Justice* (2014) 47–75.

by adversarial system of pleading, also shows an embeddedness of law and law enforcement in the local community rather than in the court per se. The same also may explain why compensation for homicide (and the concordant ideas of honour, shame and slighted status that "allowing" the homicide of a kin-member entailed) remained into the fourteenth century; this communal emphasis too may help to explain the use of arbitration in the late middle ages as a form of dispute settlement, which, as Mark Godfrey has recently argued, ran parallel to, and did not contradict, the *assythment* ("compensations") payments taken as part of the justice of the feud.[123]

G: FOURTEENTH-CENTURY QUESTIONS AND POSSIBILITIES

There is very little space here to consider how this dynamic between local and central, between law and community, developed over the fourteenth century. Instead, I will outline two potential avenues for future research. The first concerns the role of statute law; the second, the development of a self-described body of texts that made up the "auld lawes" of the kingdom. To take statute law first, by the early seventeenth century one crucial perceived difference between the English and the Scottish systems was that the king exercised much greater authority over law-making in Parliament than his counterpart in England did.[124] Given that, in the early seventeenth century, James VI and I was considering a legal union between Scotland and England, the question had considerable contemporary political significance.[125] It was shown above how the role of the king as legislator developed over the later twelfth century, seemingly displacing the older authority of the *iudex* as *the* pronouncer of law. Over the thirteenth century, the sparse evidence we have reveals the king-in-assembly, establishing law (*statuere*) on matters such as agrarian policy, lawful and unlawful possession, theft and robbery and indictments ("dittays") on the justiciar's ayre.[126] It is clear that a

123 For the reference to *cró* and *enach* in the late thirteenth/early fourteenth century, see Ayr Miscellany, c. 31 (n 42); Davies (ed) with Taylor, *Regiam Majestatem* (n 19) c. 44; Duncan (ed), *Scottish Formularies* (n 108) A76; entry in 'Portuum' in the Bute manuscript (NLS, MS 21246, fo. 72v). For the integration of the justice of the feud with other legal processes, see A M Godfrey, 'Rethinking the Justice of the Feud in Sixteenth-Century Scotland', in S Boardman and J Goodare (eds), *Kings, Lords and Men: Essays in Honour of Jenny Wormald* (2014) 136–154.

124 See B P Levack, *The Formation of the British State: England, Scotland and the Union, 1603–1707* (1987) 68–101; see also J Goodare, *The Government of Scotland, 1560–1625* (2004) 70–86.

125 For a summary, see Simpson and Wilson, *Scottish Legal History* (n 14) 247–249.

126 For these, see *SA*, c. 1 (?1214); *SA*, c. 2 (1244); *SA*, c. 3 (1248); *SA*, cc. 4–7 (all 1230) (n 42). For the 'original' source behind these statutes, see Taylor (ed), *Laws* (n 9) 342–347.

roll of *statutes*, probably issued in royal *colloquia* attended by the great ecclesiastical monastic and lay lords of the realm, was kept in the royal archive in Edinburgh castle by 1292.[127] We have many references to the *parliamenta* held by King John Balliol (1292–1296), and, even, rolls of Parliament surviving from 1293.[128] Under Robert I, parliamentary activity and legislation became a key part of his kingship from 1306, in many ways culminating in a piece of legislation issued at a parliament held on 3–5 December 1318 at Scone at a moment of intense political tension for Robert himself.[129]

The wider political context for the issue of the 1318 legislation has been considered by others.[130] However, it is worth considering the legislation that was issued by the king in this parliament in more detail for the shift it seems to have attempted to engender in the dynamic between local community and legal procedure outlined above, and the growing role played by the king's courts in upholding law.[131] The legislation is categorised as a collection of *statutes* (*statuta*) and was addressed *to courtholders* – justiciars, sheriffs, grieve and bailies, and other *fideles* of the kingdom. It was explicitly intended for wide circulation to ensure broad-base knowledge of its contents, with court-holders, including "earls, barons and all others who have courts" being commanded to read and proclaim the statutes to their courts, or wherever there was a "congregation of people".[132] The aim of the statutes was to "honour God and the Holy Mother Church, for the improvement (*emendatio*) of his land, the protection (*tuitio*) of his people, and for the maintenance and affirmation of the peace".[133] The first two clauses promised protection for the church and common justice for all, according to ancient law and liberties. The rest of the legislation is more specific, covering homicide and other crimes, including robbery and theft; essonzies (lawful excuses for non-appearance in courts); poinding (seizure for debt); court procedure;

127 *APS*, i, 116–117.

128 *RPS*, 1293/2, 1293/8; NRS, PA1/1, PA1/2, PA1/3.

129 For a broad study, see M Penman, '"The king wishes and commands"? Reassessing political assembly in Scotland', in M Damen, J Haemers and A Mann (eds), *Political Representation: Communities, Ideas and Institutions in Europe (c. 1200–c. 1690)* (2018) 123–141.

130 T M Cooper, 'The First Law Reform (Miscellaneous Provisions) Act' in T M Cooper, *Selected Papers, 1922–1954: The Right Honourable Lord Cooper of Culross, Lord Justice-General and Lord President of the Court of Session, 1947–1954* (1957) 88–93. For the importance of the 1318 legislation for dissasine and mortancestor, see MacQueen, *Common Law* (n 3) 105–111, 146–153, 177–178; for a wider study, see M Penman, *Robert the Bruce: King of the Scots* (2014) 190–199.

131 This will be explored in more detail in Taylor, *Laws of the Realm* (forthcoming). The text of the 1318 legislation is easily accessible in the *RPS* edition.

132 *RPS*, 1318/1.

133 *RPS*, 1318/2.

and several political provisions, such as banning anyone from spreading "rumours" or "conspiring" that would divide the king from his people.

Although it is beyond the scope of this chapter, it is important to note that the 1318 legislation was not only extremely widely circulated, it also acted as a legislative model well into the fifteenth century (O'Brien, for example, has shown the lexical and structural similarities between the 1318 legislation and James I's 1426 legislation issued at Perth).[134] More pertinent here, however, is the changes the legislation attempted to bring about, which were numerous. Particularly instructive here is the banning of payments of *redemptio* for the crime of theft, in which a convicted thief could redeem their life by paying a "thief's *wergeld*", rather than face judgment (unless, of course, the court-holder had the specific *libertas* of so doing, granted by the king).[135] In addition, the legislation prescribed that no "magnate or noble" could pursue a dispute with another save "according to the laws of the land"; if they did otherwise, it would constitute a breach of the king's peace for breaking his statute.[136] In addition, the statute also laid down the rule that no one could be ejected from their tenement without the king's brieve, extended the application of the brieve of dissasine and ruled against the pre-existing privilege of lords to bar people from entering their land if they were pursuing thieves.[137] The 1318 legislation seemed to be aiming to remove a level of jurisdictional and judicial flexibility that had previously characterised the legal sphere. This does not mean that the oath of denial, or the brieve of inquest, disappeared; indeed, as stated above, the oath of denial retained prominence as a mode of proof in the contemporary "Assizes of David".[138] But the broad aim of the legislation was to bring more cases into royal courts, bound by tighter, adversarial procedure, and to centralise dispute settlement more broadly. Although the 1318 legislation did not, ultimately, succeed in establishing this more centralised procedure, its programme was part of a wider contemporary political rhetoric that aimed to formalise the relationship between the king and his law to associate far strongly the

134 I E O'Brien, 'The Scottish Parliament in the Fifteenth and Sixteenth Centuries' (1980) PhD Thesis, University of Glasgow, 4–7. There is much more to be said here on the effect of the 1318 legislation. It seems to have either set, or been an early example, of a legislative "style", which can be identified in the surviving statutes of David II, as well as some fabricated ancient statutes, such as the "laws of William the Lion", found in Edinburgh, NLS 16497, fos. 209v–210r, published as 'An anachronistic law of William the Lion', in Taylor (ed), *Laws* (n 9) 565–569.

135 *RPS*, 1318/11; cf. earlier provisions in *LS*, c.10 and *SA*, c.21 (n 42).

136 *RPS*, 1318/22.

137 *RPS*, 1318/9, /15, /27.

138 See H McKechnie, *Judicial Process Upon Brieves,1219–1532* (1956) 6–7 and 10–11.

sources of Scots law with the king's authority. *Regiam maiestatem*, which probably began to be compiled before the issue of the 1318 legislation, stressed the king's royal *maiestas* – his majesty, denoting his legal and political autonomy.[139] Although aristocratic jurisdiction continued to be a key part of the legal landscape of the Scottish kingdom, a new term came to be used to describe it – *regalitas*.[140] Although in practice this further decentralised the courts of medieval Scotland, in theory it further associated the highest jurisdictional privileges in the land with *royal* authority. The use of parliament to enact statute law as a vehicle within which an ideology of royal authority could be developed is first clearly attested in the 1318 legislation and had a substantial history beyond it, which requires further elucidation.

What, then, of legal knowledge? Andrew Simpson has most recently addressed the question of what kind of expertise local "men of law" in the mid-fifteenth-century Aberdeen burgh court might have had. Noting that, even within those substantial court registers, it is very difficult to identify who was understood to be knowledgeable in the law, there were, he showed, nonetheless a few men who can be identified as commonly chosen representatives for litigants in the burgh court.[141] Crucially, these men *seem* to have shared some "common assumptions" about the law they were applying and upholding. Hector MacQueen has recently reassessed the role played by magnates as the kingdom's justiciars during the later middle ages.[142] Having nobles fulfil this function had been commonplace since the emergence of the office in the late twelfth century. MacQueen has argued that although we cannot know whether these individuals received legal training (and, if so, what kind), we must assume that they were, to paraphrase, deemed fit for the task.[143] However, the absence of opportunity through training and study to practise (in both senses of the word) in the Scottish common law should, perhaps, not be confused with the extent of the diffusion of knowledge of the learned law more broadly and its influence on the interpretation of the authority of Scots law itself. Recent work on the Bute manuscript – containing one of the two earliest surviving manuscripts

139 Davies (ed) with Taylor, *Regiam Majestatem* (n 19) 198–199.

140 See Grant, 'Franchises' (n 18).

141 Simpson, 'Men of Law' (n 68); A R C Simpson, 'Andrew Alanson: Man of law in the Aberdeen Council Register, c.1440–1475?', in J W Armstrong and E Frankot (eds), *Cultures of Law in Urban Northern Europe: Scotland and its Neighbours, c .1350–c. 1650* (2020) 247–266.

142 H L MacQueen, 'Tame Magnates? The Justiciars of Later Medieval Scotland', in S Boardman and J Goodare (eds), *Kings, Lords and Men in Scotland and Britain 1300–1625: Essays in Honour of Jenny Wormald* (2014) 93–120.

143 MacQueen, 'Justiciars' (n 142) 117.

of *Regiam Maiestatem* and a copy of the earliest surviving version of the text – has shown that its text of *Regiam* contains a gloss, written out by the main scribe, which aided interpretation and understanding of *Regiam*'s provisions.[144] Drawing on history, encyclopaedias, texts of the English common law, as well as Roman and canon law, this gloss provided depth and nuance to some of *Regiam*'s more confused passages.[145] For example, in a passage on legitimacy, *Regiam* had stated that all children born before their parents' marriage were illegitimate.[146] This was in contravention to canon law, which had stated that all children whose parents had subsequently married (unless one of the parties was already married at the time of birth) would be considered legitimate *per subsequens matrimonium*. The gloss in the Bute manuscript refers the reader to this passage in the *Liber Extra* and the Roman law *Institutes*.[147] This gloss seems not to have originated with the Bute manuscript; it seems already to have been attached to *Regiam* itself, suggesting that contextualising *Regiam* within the *utrumque ius* and the English common law had already become commonplace.

There is not enough surviving fourteenth-century evidence to warrant confidence in when and why this gloss was produced – let alone in what circles. Yet not only did glossed copies of *Regiam* continue to circulate in the fifteenth century (which no longer survive) but the glossed *Regiam* could also be used as the model for later glosses and commentaries on the text.[148] In addition, much of the gloss made it back into the main text of later fifteenth-century copies of *Regiam*, sometimes explicitly as chapters entitled "Gloss", at other times silently.[149] But the importance of this observation is that, contrary to the state of historical knowledge ten years ago, we now know that *Regiam* was packed with Roman and canon law long before the Lords of Session began to apply "Bartolist" reasoning to the authority of different legal traditions from the 1530s onwards.[150]

The only reason to think that the "glossed" *Regiam* was completed in a relatively early stage of *Regiam*'s circulation is that the main text of *Regiam*

144 Edinburgh, National Library of Scotland, MS 21246, fully described in Taylor (ed), *Laws* 49–60 (n 9) and with a focus on *Regiam* in Taylor, 'Introduction' (n 46) 27–36.

145 Taylor, 'Introduction' (n 46) 32–35, 56–60.

146 Davis (ed) with Taylor, *Regiam maiestatem* (n 19) c. 81.

147 Davis (ed) with Taylor, *Regiam maiestatem* (n 19) 302, note 1; 303, note a.

148 Taylor, 'Introduction' (n 46) 59–60.

149 Taylor, 'Introduction' (n 46) 60.

150 Simpson and Wilson, *Scottish Legal History* (n 14) 144–149, see also the later conceptualisation of "the local laws of the realm as a body of learning", in *ibid.*, 172–191; and, more specifically, A R C Simpson, 'Legislation and authority in early-modern Scotland', in M Godfrey (ed), *Law and Authority in British Legal History, 1200–1900* (2016) 85–119.

had already undergone a revision by the end of the fourteenth century.[151] This revision jettisoned the gloss – and indeed the internal citations to Roman and canon law in the main text – and added a few more chapters, reorganising some of *Regiam*'s least well-organised sections. Both the glossed *Regiam* and the revised *Regiam* survive in separate manuscripts that date from shortly after 1389; they were therefore circulating at the same time. As the revised *Regiam* was a later text than that in the glossed *Regiam*, it seems logical to suggest that the glossed *Regiam* predated the revision.[152] Certainly, the revised *Regiam* seemed to circulate in a slightly different way. The revised *Regiam* seems to have first circulated *in a book* that had a clear order and contained what seem to have been accepted as the authoritative texts of Scots law (as an aside, one of these authoritative texts was the 1318 legislation, known by then as *Statuta Roberti Regis*).[153] In this "second" version, *Regiam* circulated in a small book, clearly designed for practical use, accompanied by the texts of *Quoniam Attachiamenta*, the *Assisa Regis David*, the *Leges Burgorum*, the *Statuta Roberti Regis*, among others. This book ended up being displaced by another authoritative arrangement of Scots law, probably by the mid-fifteenth century, and certainly was not the only "book of Scots law" to be in circulation in the later middle ages.[154] More work needs to be done but the possibility must be acknowledged that, by the end of the fourteenth century, an idea of the existence of a *book of law* for the kingdom of the Scots seems to have taken hold.

H: CONCLUDING REMARKS

How then does all this help us understand law and administrative change in Scotland between the twelfth and fourteenth centuries? For a start, it is clear that a narrative based on the "English model" does not capture the complexity and fluidity of legal practice in this period, even if its broad-brush strokes are useful. It is important to know that sheriff courts first developed properly from the 1160s, were instituted in the 1180s and the justiciars began going on ayres probably in the 1220s. It is important to know that dissasine procedure was introduced in 1230 and mortancestor by 1253 and this introduced a new way of conducting disputes whose legitimacy

151 This is found in the newly "discovered" manuscript of medieval Scots law in Harvard Law School, MS 164, described in Taylor, 'Introduction' (n 46) 142–161.

152 Taylor, 'Introduction' (n 46) 151–157.

153 Taylor, 'Introduction' (n 46) 157–165.

154 For a preliminary study into groups of manuscripts, see Taylor (ed), *Laws* (n 9) ch 10.

was displayed through accordance with a regularised court procedure.[155] The development of pleadable brieves to run in sheriff, justiciar and burgh courts is indeed part of this narrative, and some of the most obvious substantive law comes from the admittedly scarce writing about these subjects. It is true to say that royal justice did become *more regularised* over the period as a whole, as MacQueen put it.[156]

But there are two issues here. The first concerns how such an understanding misrepresents the twelfth-century kingdom, particularly the kingdom north of the Firth of Forth, and particularly until the 1160s–1180s. The second concerns the extent to which these changes – again, outside the burgh – resulted in royal judicial procedures becoming the primary means of justice requires some rethinking, which was in some way mimicked and upheld in aristocratic courts. The continued importance of *iudices* – judges – at a local level speaks to their long-standing role as legal expert, which sat alongside the new jurisdictions of the twelfth century, the bailie, sheriff and justiciar. We have glimpses that even their expertise in compensation and status might not have been entirely obsolete even by the early fourteenth century – who would know how much should be paid to a victim's family on the death of their kin? Who would know how much a man's life-value, his *cró*, was if he was run over by a horse whose rider was not looking where he was going? The "old" twelfth-century world was still working through the thirteenth – even the fourteenth (although this has less been the focus here) and this may help us understand what look like legal oddities in a more regularised system of royal justice. Although inquests were, like dissasine or mortancestor cases, initiated by brieve, their functioning differed: representatives from the community told the truth, they did not (at least formally) apply, dispute or widen the limits of the law. How these representatives came to this decision must have been based on a variety of forces – knowledge of "the law", of course, but also reputation, connection, power and status, the exact same forces that allowed an individual to successfully or unsuccessfully obtain the oath-helpers required to deny a formal accusation of theft. The new royal judicial and administrative system of the thirteenth century, of course, offered new avenues of status and reward for local trustworthy men – by serving on royal assizes, by being representatives from the barony, by being a grieve or estate manager. But these new statuses and roles had also to be worked out locally, they were subject to acceptance

155 Ayr Miscellany, c. 2 (n 42).
156 MacQueen, *Common Law* (n 3) 247–248.

from below as much as conferment from above.

I have written at length about the institutional "limits" of the structures of Scottish government that developed from the late twelfth century onwards. By "limits", I meant how "decentred" Scottish "central" institutions were: the financial chamber remained itinerant and regional, there developed no central court separate from the king in parliament or *in colloquio* and statute law incorporated non-royal jurisdiction actively into its content.[157] We should perhaps see procedural innovation in the same light. A Scottish common law based on pleadable brieves did develop over the thirteenth century *but* those pleadable brieves, particularly outside the burgh, may well have been "last resort" solutions. They take space in parliamentary legislation of the fourteenth and fifteenth centuries precisely because there was *more law* and more procedure in them that could be the subject of such legislation; they were also, by then, a key part of the Scottish common law. But they should not overshadow other forms of legal practice taking place within the same courts. The use of the fact-finding inquest to resolve disputes as well as the prominence of the oath of denial shows use that, while royal authority may have inserted itself far more into local practice, the justice it offered responded to and supported the informal but equally powerful moral order in the local community.

Over the fourteenth century, however, we do seem to witness a change, the extent of which needs further exploration and research. The extent to which Robert's legislative programmes and political theories cast a long symbolic (if not institutional) shadow over the *concept* of the law of the realm of Scotland itself needs further examination; the extent to which he might allow formal decentralisation of his jurisdiction seemed to be under threat, although not realised practically (indeed, decentralisation actually accelerated through the very same creation of regality jurisdiction). Knowledge of Roman and canon law seems to have been more widely diffused and applied to the content of *Regiam maiestatem*. We now know that *Regiam maiestatem* had been significantly revised during the fourteenth century, which reflects a level of legal knowledge and engagement that, ten years ago, scholarship could not have contemplated. Indeed, it may be that the idea of Scots law as made up of a series of authoritative texts to form a legal tradition itself developed over the fourteenth century. In short, far from being a "dark age" of Scottish legal history, we now know there are many more areas of enquiry upon which light may be shone.

157 Taylor, *Shape of the State* (n 15) 438–450.

5 Urban Legal Procedure in Fourteenth Century Norway

*Miriam Jensen Tveit**

A: INTRODUCTION

An unprecedented endeavour of legal reform in the 1260s and 1270s resulted in the promulgation of a code of law for Norway in 1274: the Code of the Norwegian Realm, by King Magnus "the Lawmender" Hákonarson (1263–1280).[1] Often regarded as an afterthought was the equally unique codification of urban law that was promulgated two years later, in 1276.[2] This codex appears to have been initially constructed for Norway's largest town and most important export hub, Bergen. However, through processes that are obscure to us, versions of the urban codex were adapted for three other important towns within a few decades: the metropolitan

* The article was written while the author was a partner in the project *Social governance through legislation* at the Centre for Advanced Study in Oslo.

1 The Norwegian Code can be found in M Rindal and B D Spørck, *Kong Magnus Håkonsson Lagabøtes landslov, Norrøn tekst med fullstendig variantsapparat*, 2 vols (2018) (henceforth ML). Also in R Keyser and P A Munch (eds), *Norges gamle Love indtil 1387: Andet Bind* (1848) 7–178 (henceforth NgL vol II).

2 Found in Keyser and Munch (eds), NgL vol II (n 1) 185–290.

Niðaros[3] and the royal seats of Oslo and Tunsberg.[4] Although the patterns of organisation in these towns do not contradict regulations of the new urban laws the question remains whether they also implemented the codex into their legal procedures. This article analyses the urban legal procedure in the three towns in cases where the town citizens were involved to better understand how law worked after the promulgation of the Code of the Towns of 1276 (the urban code).

The structure of the article is formed of three sections. First, the concept of Norwegian urban law will be explained. Secondly, urban law will be located in terms of the question of "law in the books" versus "law in action". The final part considers procedures in the towns of Niðaros, Oslo and Tunsberg from case studies that serve to illuminate this in terms of space of urban law, transaction, torts, urban women as litigants and finally trade related cases. The description of legal procedure that we can obtain from the surviving documents disclose that cases and their documentation were drawn up much in accordance with the Code of the Towns. More precisely, the procedure in practice rarely went against the procedure given by the urban code. Urban legal procedure was still performed in a rational way, a way that took into consideration the experiences of the towns in question, their institutional structures and the requirements of the urban legal subjects.

B: NORWEGIAN URBAN LAW

Urban settlements comprised a minor part of Norwegian society, compared to other regions of medieval Europe. At the beginning of the fourteenth century the kingdom is thought to have included fifteen, mostly small, towns within the mainland of the realm.[5] What has been defined as a "town" by contemporary observers and modern scholars in thirteenth and fourteenth century Norway would not meet traditional structural criteria of popula-

3 On town names: the medieval towns are spelled in many different ways. I use the generic forms Bergen, Niðaros, Oslo and Tunsberg.

4 Keyser and Munch (eds), NgL vol II (n 1) 182–184, and ex. 185 n 4, 187 n 8; G A Blom, 'Magnus Lagabøters bylov og Trondheim, med en innledning om Bergen bylovs overføring til rikets øvrige kjøpsteder' (1974) vol 9 no 2 in *Trondhjemske samlinger* 99–145 at 104–106; K Helle and A Nedkvitne, 'Norge. Sentrumsdannelser og byutvikling i norsk middelalder', in G Blom (ed), *Urbaniseringsprosessen i Norden Del 1: Middelaldersteder* (1977) 189–278, at 264. See the versions for unspecified towns in Keyser and Munch (eds), NgL vol II (n 1) 182–183.

5 The Norwegian realm consisted at 1300 of dependencies, or colonised 'taxlands': Greenland, Iceland, The Faroes, Orkney and Shetland in the west, and the Jemtland region in the east. Three of the fifteen towns were in the landscape of Bohus in Modern Sweden.

tion size and density, or functional criteria of – for instance – specialised crafts. Historiography of Norwegian urbanisation in the middle ages has tended to understand urbanisation in the specific context of this region's topography and economic conditions.[6] Nevertheless, Niðaros, Tunsberg and Oslo were considered prominent towns in the kingdom in terms of trade and central functions of administration. Furthermore, with respect to size, the estimated population of Oslo was around 2,000 inhabitants in the early fourteenth century; there were maybe 500 more in Nidaros and 500 fewer in Tunsberg.[7] In comparison, Bergen was the largest town in Norway and in Scandinavia, with an estimated number of around 7,000 inhabitants.[8] The scholarship invested into medieval urban history in Norway has been substantial. However, the study of urban law per se has been lacking, even if the Code of the Towns and other urban laws are frequently cited as points of reference to explain urban development.[9] How the law worked within, or indeed beyond, the frame of urban jurisdiction has yet to be examined closely.

For a kingdom especially lacking in urban culture, the Norwegian codification of town laws stands out as a *magnum opus*. Even so, only a part of the contents was novel legislation. Some of the rules were lifted from an older town law, called *Bjarkeyjarréttr*,[10] but the law text itself corresponds with the Code of the Realm in structure, form and content.[11] Both of the new codes were divided into ten books, *balkr*, modelled after earlier laws. Only one book in the Code of the Towns was entirely unique. This was the *Bøarskipings balkr*, the "Book of town regulations", which was placed where the Code of the Realm included two books regarding rural, agricultural property; one on landed ownership and one on tenancy.[12] Moreover, several

6 For a review of this discussion, see M Tveit, 'Urban law in Norwegian market towns: legal culture in a long fourteenth century' in J W Armstrong and E Frankot (eds), *Cultures of Law in Urban Northern Europe: Scotland and its Neighbours c. 1350–c. 1650* (2021) 105–122 at 106–108.

7 K Helle, F-E Eliassen, J E Myhre and O S Stugu, *Norsk byhistorie: Urbanisering gjennom 1300 år* (2006) 110 (henceforth Helle et al, *Norsk byhistorie*). Helle estimated that 5 per cent of the Norwegian population were town dwellers: *ibid.*, 229.

8 K Helle, *Bergen bys historie bd. 1: Kongssete og kjøpstad: fra opphavet til 1536* (1982) 488–489.

9 Helle and Nedkvitne, 'Norge' (n 4) 236–247.

10 R Keyser and P A Munch (eds), *Norges gamle Love indtil 1387: Første Bind* (1846) 303 (henceforth NgL vol I).

11 See Keyser and Munch (eds), NgL vol II (n 1) 190 ff, for instance I-4, about proceeding witnesses from the Code of the Norweigan Realm (henceforth the Code of 1274) 1274 on assemblies is not included in the Code of the Towns of 1276. Some chapters are redacted to town courts, such as Code of 1274 I-5 on which court the *gialdkyri* (town sheriff) had.

12 Regarding odal law in book VI and land rent in book VII in the Code of 1274.

copies of the town law had attached to them an older, revised, law of sea merchants, called *Farmannalog*.[13] The similarity of the codes for country and town made copying similar paragraphs superfluous. There exists only one full version of the urban code from the middle ages, a Bergen version.[14] In the others, manuscripts were abbreviated where the two codes coincided, inserting only the section title or the first words, followed by "et cetera".[15] In other sections, only the terminology of the courts was changed, for instance in the first chapter after the prologue, where *giælkyri eða sýslumaðr* ("town sheriff or [district] sheriff") replaced *lenðrmaðr eða sýslu maðr*, ("king's vassal or sheriff").[16] These versions also belong to a corpus of law including the Code of the Realm, and a user could consult the Code of the Realm in the abbreviated cases.

The *Bjarkeyjarréttr* may have been written down in the twelfth century.[17] Extant manuscripts of the old town laws, *Bjarkeyjarréttr*, are attributed to the town of Niðaros, but it is assumed that Bergen, Oslo and Tunsberg had similar versions.[18] This old town law also included a merchant's law, the *Farmannalog*, which claimed validity in other markets and fishing stations, as well as in commercial traveling.[19] Where the urban code of 1276 shares much of its contents with old law, there is reason to believe that the urban legal culture already encompassed some of the principles and procedures in them.

13 In some MS, the *Farmannalog* precedes the town laws or is separated from them. Three of the MS included in the corpus of versions of the *Code of the Towns* consist only of the *Farmannalog*. G Storm (ed), *Norges gamle Love indtil 1387: Fjerde Bind* (1885) 184 (henceforth NgL vol IV).

14 Anna Catharina Horn sees similarities in structure between the Code of 1276 and Járnsiða, the failed Code for Iceland of 1271: A C Horn 'Fra landskapslov til landslov. En studie i tekstorganiseringen i norrøne middelalderlover', in A C Horn and K A Seip (eds), *Lov og lovgivning i middelalderen: Nye studier av Magnus Lagabøtes landslov* (2020) 131.

15 See examples of this in the Book of human inviolability (*Mannhælgarbolkr*) ch 1, in NgL vol II (n 1) 210 n 5–15.

16 Book about Attending Assemblies, ch 1, in NgL vol II (n 1) 187 versus 10–11.

17 J R Hagland and J Sandnes, *Bjarkøyretten: Niðaros eldste bylov* (1997) XI.

18 Bergen, at least, would have had town regulations, also hinted at in the provincial law of Gulaþing, the provincial jurisdiction surrounding Bergen. Helle et al, *Norsk byhistorie* (n 7) 66. Sources mention old town laws of Tunsberg, O A Johnsen, *Tønsbergs historie: bind 1 Middelalderen* (1929) 334. It is assumed that Oslo would have had a similar town regulation: A Nedkvitne and P Norseng, *Middelalderbyen ved Bjørvika: Oslo 1000–1536* (2000) 236.

19 *Bjarkeyjarréttr* no 42, Keyser and Munch (eds), NgL vol I (n 10) 312–313; Code of the Towns, *Farmannalog*, ch 19.3, NgL vol II (n 1) 284; N Bjørgo, 'Vågastemna i mellomalderen' in S Imsen and G Sandvik (eds), *Hamarspor–Eit festskrift til Lars Hamre 1912–1982* (1982) 48–60 at 50; Hagland and Sandnes, *Bjarkøyretten* (n 17) xx–xxxxviii; G Dahlbäck, 'Svensk stadslagstiftning under medeltiden', in A Dybdahl and J Sandnes (eds), *Nordiske middelalderlover: Tekst og kontekst: rapport fra seminar ved Senter for middelalderstudier 29.–30. Nov. 1996* (1997) 103–115 at 109–111.

The urban law code of 1276 was consciously constructed and published as part of a process of legal reform – albeit that the prologue was mostly copied from the Code of the Realm and does not explain the process of making the law. The prologue even included a description of those parts of the national code that were excluded from the urban version. The *Bjarkeyjarréttr* for Niðaros, on the other hand, is comparable with the compilation of burgh laws in the Scottish *Leges Burgorum*.[20] However, in the same way that the text known as the *Leges Burgorum* was sometimes treated as providing a national framework for the Scottish burghs, the urban law code became a general law for Norwegian towns during the fourteenth century. Specific town privileges had not, as far as we know, been commonplace in Norwegian towns prior to the Code of the Towns of 1276; rather, the towns received specific privileges granting burghers exclusive rights to trade and craft during the fourteenth century.[21] When the Code of the Towns of 1276 was issued for Bergen it was a set of general privileges for the town consolidating existing town law for the urban inhabitants.

Medieval copies of the new town law survive in eight fragments and twenty-three manuscripts. The manuscripts are classified into five variants, according to the town to which they are adapted: Bergen; Niðaros; Tunsberg; and Oslo, with the fifth being a generic version. Only one manuscript survives that presents a true generic version of urban law while three others are inconsistent in their dedication or in mentioning specific town characteristics such as streets or churches.[22] Most surviving copies of the new urban code are Bergen versions. Apart from two master manuscripts, most extant copies of the Code of the Towns omit repeating identical rules from the Code of the Realm. The two Oslo manuscripts only include the books' town regulations, purchase and contracts and the opening sections from the Code of the Realm book of tenancy, as well as theft.[23] Two manuscripts survive of a consistent Tunsberg version.[24] Writing the history of Tønsberg, Oscar Albert Johnsen suggested that the new code and an old, lost, town law existed side

20 H L MacQueen and W J Windram, 'Laws and Courts in the Burghs', in M Lynch, M Spearman and G Stell (eds), *The Scottish Medieval Town* (1988) 208–227; A R C Simpson and A L M Wilson, *Scottish Legal History Volume One: 1000–1707* (2017) 61.

21 Oslo: R Keyser and P A Munch, *Norges gamle Love indtil 1387: Tredie Bind* (1849) no 78 (henceforth NgL vol III) nos 78 and 94 (Tunsberg). G A Blom, *Kongemakt og privilegier i Norge inntil 1387* (1967) 205–225.

22 *Codex Arnamagnanus* (AM) 31 8vo, 105r–116v; Keyser and Munch (eds), NgL vol II (n 1) 184; Storm (ed), NgL vol IV (n 13) 482, 559–560, 607–608. AM 64 4to and AM 307 fol. inconsistently reference both Bergen and Tunsberg.

23 Storm (ed), NgL vol IV (n 13) 485.

24 One of them called the *Codex Tunsbergensis*, see Storm (ed), NgL vol IV (n 13) 425–434.

by side for several decades, because an amendment from 1316 refers to foreign wintering in accordance with *Biarkræyar rettar*, and the new code does not contain such a regulation.[25] However, the only two Niðaros manuscripts date from the sixteenth century, suggesting that earlier copies are lost and that the law was and had been in use for some time.[26]

The Code of the Realm claimed to be valid throughout the provinces, replacing the old provincial laws in each of the four provincial assemblies. The process of diffusion and adaptation of the Code of the Towns to Bergen is less clear. Even if the prologue was mostly duplicated from the Code of the Realm, it included a greeting from King Magnus to "Bishop Askatin [of Bergen], abbots and sheriffs and councilmen, and all those of God's and his friends in Bergen that see or hear this letter".[27] Such a greeting, if it had accompanied any of the adapted versions, was not integrated in the surviving copies, as they opened with a common greeting of "peace and blessings" (*Friðr ok blæzan*).[28] We do not know if the Code of the Towns of 1276 was made valid for Niðaros, Oslo and Tunsberg by royal sanction or, if so, when. A general amendment from King Hákon V on 14 November 1316 for the town of Bergen was issued for the towns of Tunsberg and Oslo the next day.[29] The swift and obviously planned, extension of the decree may be based on precedent from the extension of jurisdiction of the Code of the Towns sometime between 1276 and 1316. Any royal agency in the diffusion of the urban code is not mentioned in the sources but it is likely that that was the case, given the high degree of involvement we see from the king in regulating the towns in the decades following 1276. Still, the idea of this law extending to other towns may not have materialised until after it was published.

Source material for urban case law is richer, albeit random. No town registers survive from medieval Norway. There are no systematised records from which to draw conclusions; instead, one must rely on single documents for an understanding of the workings of urban law.[30] There is a rise in sur-

25 Johnsen, *Tønsbergs historie: bind 1* (n 18) 343; Hákon Mangússon's amendment from 1316: Keyser and Munch (eds), NgL vol III (n 21), 118–120. The term *Biarkræyar rettar* was used on the new as well as old town law. One MS uses the term *bokinn*, the book, instead of *Biarkræyar rettar*, see *ibid.*, n 8.

26 AM Gks 3262 and AM 97 4to, both dated to the 1570s.

27 "*sender Askatíní biscupi abotum oc syslu monnum ok raðs monnum. oc ollum oðrum guðs vínum oc sínum þæim sem þætta bref sea eða høyra i biorgwin*"; Keyser and Munch (eds), NgL vol II (n 1) 185.

28 Keyser and Munch (eds), NgL vol II (n 1) 185.

29 Keyser and Munch (eds), NgL vol III (n 21) 121–124 (Bergen) and 124–128 (Tunsberg and Oslo).

30 Many of the known written documents relating to Norway in the middle ages were transcribed

viving documents postdating 1300, which is certainly a result of the Code of the Realm itself, as with it came a demand for written documentation of transactions.[31] The material that could be termed "case law" is not abundant enough to permit any general conclusions regarding the procedures used in towns. Predominantly, the documents are witness letters that include some dispositive elements and therefore would not be simply *notitia*, but would still not fit the definition of a *charta*. Lars Hamre has suggested these witness letters represent a domestic development, although a parallel could be sought in Dauvit Broun's description of *nota* in Anglo-Norman Britain.[32] As such, the description of legal procedure that can be extrapolated is limited and a study of legal procedure in Norwegian towns can therefore only be cursory. The possibility of deriving a pattern of procedure from the material is restricted, but examples will testify as to how they stand apart from law, and thus a conclusion can be drawn as to how legal practice pertained to the word of law. The documents that do survive consist, to a large degree, of cases related to property transactions in the form of sale, inheritance, exchange or privileges connected with them.[33] Compared to Scottish and English records that experienced a vernacularisation from Latin mainly in the fifteenth century, Norwegian domestic records were commonly constructed in Old Norse from the late twelfth century, although foreign correspondence and canon law related documents were in Latin.[34]

The non-royal charters and witness letters were commonly constructed with a list of witnesses in the protocol. The location of the hearing was given in the protocol of the witness letters, while the place of writing was in the end of the charters, as *escatol*. Few non-royal documents include an *arenga*, with motivation or legal basis for the case.

and published in the volumes of the continuing collection *Diplomatarium Norvegicum*, the first volume of which was published in 1847 and now numbers twenty-three volumes: *Diplomatarium Norvegicum, Oldbreve til Kundskab om Norges indre og ydre Forhold, Sprog, Slægter, Sæder, Lovgivning og Rettergang i Middelalderen*, vols 1–23 (1847–2011) (henceforth DN).

31 The Code of 1274 *Um skilorð i quenna giptingum Capitulus*.

32 L Hamre, *Innføring i diplomatikk*, 2nd edn (2004) 63; D Broun, 'The presence of witnesses and the writing of charters', in D Broun (ed), *The Reality behind Charter Diplomatic in Anglo-Norman Britain* (2011) 235–290 at 266–267.

33 G A Blom, *Urbaniseringsprosessen i Norden: del 2: De anlagte steder på 1600–1700 tallet* (1977).

34 A D Havinga, 'Vernacularisation of the Aberdeen Council Registers (1398–1511), in J W Armstrong and E Frankot (eds), *Cultures of Law in Urban Northern Europe: Scotland and its Neighbours c. 1350–c. 1650* (2021) 80–102; A L Knudsen, 'Latin and the Vernacular in Medieval Legal Documents: The Case of Denmark', in M W McHaffie, J Benham and H Vogt (eds), *Law and Language in the Middle Ages* (2018) 107–127.

C: LAW AND PRACTICE

It is generally difficult to identify references to law in the material of Norwegian case law. Most charters, letters and diplomas postdate 1300, which makes it challenging to compare the situation before the promulgation of the codes in the 1270s. Nevertheless, it is reasonable to assume that when legislators like Magnus VI made law, they did so with a view to having some effect on legal practice on the ground – even if all they wanted to achieve was consolidation of existing practice. Without going into a lengthy discussion of whether law derives from customs or vice versa, the relationship between law and practice is of interest here. In the Code of the Realm, Magnus the Lawmender included a paraphrase of the grandiose sentence from Justinian's enterprise of collecting Roman law in the 530s, much copied by aspiring royal legislators throughout the early middle ages: of "amending all earlier laws by adding that which is lacking and eliminating that which is superfluous".[35] The medieval author of law would portray themselves to be amending custom, although only introducing what the royal apparatus thought to be better solutions.[36]

Grethe Authén Blom asserted in 1974 that the main towns of Niðaros, Tunsberg and Oslo had "developed sufficient administrative power by the 1270s and thus were able to enforce the new Town Law".[37] Few legal historians take such a positivistic view today regarding the functionality of written law and a more updated view is that the distribution of medieval law tended to be based on its practicality rather than on the assumptions of jurisdiction. A study of the law in these three towns must take as its point of departure that having a (royally sanctioned) law carried a certain legitimacy for the town, including both its burghers and its council, and that this was welcomed by the urban administrations and counted more than the actual letters of the law or the system in place that enforced the rules.

The documents recording urban legal practice rarely or never cited law. This is not unusual in a European context, in which charters contain varying

35 Justinian, 'De Conception Digestorum' 7, in A Watson (ed), *The Digest of Justinian*, vol 1 (1998 [1985]). The Code of 1274 Prologus, in NgL vol II (n 1) 7–8.

36 For instance seen in how agency of lawmaking was portrayed in the *Regiam maiestatem*, see A Taylor, 'What Does *Regiam maiestatem* Actually Say (and What Does it Mean)?', in W Eves, J Hudson, I Ivarsen and S White (eds), *Common Law, Civil Law, and Colonial Law: Essays in Comparative Legal History from the Twelfth to the Twentieth Centuries* (2021) 47–85, at 64 and n 65.

37 Blom, 'Magnus Lagabøters bylov og Trondheim' (n 4) 102.

degrees of evidence concerning the citation of law in court.[38] Paul Hyams argues that the lack of references to law in Anglo-Saxon documents indicate there is much more to the legal process than the texts of law tell us.[39]

The basis for the legal procedures of the small towns of Norway is difficult to pinpoint. The diplomas rarely go into detail about procedure but what can be said is that the procedures described do not oppose the Code of the Realm, nor its urban equivalent, the Code of the Towns. Law and practice in the early middle ages are rarely completely conflicting. From this fact, one could argue that the written laws followed the normative standards of practice in society, or that settlements followed the normative standards of law, or a combination of both. A recent study of the legal culture in Norway's small medieval towns demonstrated that even if legal practice was centralised to urban courts, the procedures found in diplomas from the small towns could not be distinguished from legal activity outside the towns.[40] The situation would have been similar in the main towns, as the urban legal boundaries were porous and many rural cases were brought to the towns for processing there.

D: PROCEDURE IN NIÐAROS, OSLO AND TUNSBERG

The Code of the Towns gave an account of the institutions that were expected to deal with legal matters; but things were different in practice. The Code of the Towns was based on an understanding that law would be conducted at or by the town assembly, the *mót*, both at regular intervals and ad hoc. The *mót* was the equivalent of the rural assembly, the *þing*, which was the backbone of the legal system. The urban code presumed that the town assembly would take place annually in January, with twelve council men as well as twelve men from each farthing of the town (riding in Tunsberg).[41] The town meetings were presided over by the sheriff (*sýslumaðr*), the town sheriff (*gialdker*) and the *logmaðr*. The town sheriff was given a prominent position in procedural descriptions in the Code of the Towns, but the role seems to have

38 P Wormald, *The Making of English Law: King Alfred to the Twelfth Century: Volume 1: Legislation and its Limits* (2001) 479–480; M A Kelleher, 'Boundaries of Law: Code and Custom in the Legal Practice of Early Medieval Catalonia' (1999) vol 30 issue 1 *Comitatus: A Journal of Medieval and Renaissance Studies*.

39 P Hyams, *Rancor and Reconciliation in Medieval England* (2003) 87.

40 Tveit, 'Urban Law in Norwegian Market Towns' (n 6) 111–118.

41 *Code of the Towns* I-1-6. See in *Kulturhistorisk Leksikon for Nordisk Middelalder*, vol 17 (1972) 10–11.

lost its function during the fourteenth century.[42] The urban code prescribed an urban *logmaðr*, in addition to those on the provincial assembly.

In reality, the *mót* had outplayed its role during the thirteenth century while the town council grew in importance. The *mót* rarely acted as the legal body in the sources, although it was probably used as a medium for communication of information and for common tasks. However, as Nedkvitne and Norseng point out, in letters and amendments the king always addressed the "town men", i.e. those whom the *mót* represented, and never the council.[43] This would have been a rhetorical act towards the united citizens, tying the town directly to the king while also implying a sense of independence of the town jurisdiction from the countryside.

The town council numbered twelve members, probably as the equivalent of the full jury that the Code of the Realm established. This was later increased in most towns: in the fifteenth century in Bergen to twenty-four men and in Tunsberg to fourteen.[44] Council men were often witnesses in all types of cases, together with a legal official, usually the *logmaðr*. The Code of the Towns, like the Code of the Realm, made the king the high judge and his law was given through his appointed judge, the *logmaðr*. Tunsberg had the same *logmaðr* as the province, while Niðaros at least had its own urban *logmaðr*.[45]

The town meeting lost its status as court of law in the decades following the publication of the law and, in the extant sources from the towns, many cases went before the *logmaðr*. Nedkvitne and Norseng suggest that if the *logmaðr* ultimately had the final word in legal matters, people would take their case directly to their chair rather than via the council.[46] However, the law text made the *logmaðr* the first instance in procedures within urban boundaries, and they were to advise the jury of the *mót*.[47] This was different from the procedure of the countryside as it was described in the Code of the Realm, where the opinion of the *logmaðr* was binding unless overruled by the king.[48] In practice, the council men would join the *logmaðr* as jurors.

42 Johnsen, *Tønsbergs historie: bind 1* (n 18) 346. See also amendment from 1320.

43 Nedkvitne and Norseng, *Middelalderbyen* (n 18) 251.

44 C R Unger and H J Huitfeldt-Kaas (eds), DN, vol X (1880) no 188; Johnsen, *Tønsbergs historie: bind 1* (n 18) 345. The Tunsberg versions operate with twelve council members, six *håndgangne* men and six town house owners: Keyser and Munch (eds), NgL vol II (n 1) 188 n 9.

45 J Ø Sunde, 'Lagmannen og Landslova. Lagmannen i norsk mellomalderrettshistorie frå 1100-talet til 1400', in A C Horn and K Seip (eds), *Lov og lovgivning i middelalderen. Nye studier av Magnus Lagabøtes landslov* (2020) 207.

46 Helle and Nedkvitne, 'Norge' (n 4) 243 and 268.

47 The Code of the Towns of 1276 I-3, VI-6 and VII-5, 6, 15.

48 The Code of 1274 I-4.

There would have been a high number of private settlements and there were legal channels available to parties seeking contract or settlement, such as legal arbitration and agreement with witnesses.[49] There were also alternatives to judicial solutions that would not be recorded, including out-of-court settlement that were considered legal, or vengeance, which was illegal at this point.[50]

Even if the law was applied by the institutions differently from the manner anticipated in the law text, research has revealed that town development happened in accordance with the Code of the Towns. Crafts involving ovens and the use of fire were ordered to the outskirts of towns and in Niðaros smithies ceased to be located in the city centre in the late thirteenth century.[51] In Bergen, the German guilds incorporated the regulations for house owners when they expanded into town houses previously owned by Norwegian burghers.[52] Exporting from Tunsberg was done according to the revised law in the early fourteenth century.[53] The town planning to some degree followed the new law decree of twelve ells (approximately six and a half metres) for the broad street (*strete*) and eight ells (approximately four metres) for the other streets (*almenning*).[54] The urban landscapes seem to match the legal map and in this context it is of interest to look more closely at the encounters between the citizens and the law.

E: URBAN SPACES FOR THE ADMINISTRATION OF JUSTICE

It was a practice in other European towns for legal business between citizens to be conducted in locations, private or public, that we today would consider informal. As demonstrated by Edda Frankot, transactions in Aberdeen or Kampen taking place outside the court did not diminish their legally binding

49 W I Miller, 'Reviewed Work(s): Disputes and Settlements: Law and Human Relations in the West by John Bossy' (1986) 30 no 3 *The American Journal of Legal History* 266–268; Maurizio Lupoi warns at viewing arbitration as a medieval replacement system to courts, M Lupoi, *The Origins of the European Legal Order* (2000) 29.

50 Rights to take vengeance on a perpetrator was abolished with the Code of 1274 and the Code of the Towns of 1276 IV-21, except where the king's official neglected the responsibility of taking action.

51 A Christoffersen, *I kongers kaupang og bispers by: arkeologi forteller byhisotire* (1992) 65 and 111–112.

52 K Wiberg, *Hanseaterne og Bergen– Forholdet mellom de kontorske og det bergenske bysamfund* HMS 6, Bergen (1932) 24–29, 44–53; K Helle, *Bergen bys historie bind 1* (1982) 220 and 738–744.

53 Johnsen, *Tønsbergs historie: bind 1* (n 18) 307.

54 The Code of the Towns of 1276 VI-4. Johnsen, *Tønsbergs historie bind 1* (n 18) 444; Nedkvitne and Norseng, *Middelalderbyen* (n 18) 89.

nature.[55] The actors and witnesses created a space of law among themselves. While the material from Flemish towns includes taverns as institutionalised legal spaces, as well as private houses with serving privileges, the cases from Norway were often heard inside or outside private houses.[56] Legal space would be created where the parties made their agreement. In the charters from Norwegian towns, the place of the agreement was often described in the document. The multiple places that could form a legal space means that the notion of a difference between public and private does not apply and we should rather understand these places as what Shannon McSheffrey calls "social space".[57] The place can appear coincidental, although there often is a significance to the location, when it was relevant to the case, to the witness or either of the parties.

The idea of out-of-court places as spaces of law was also sanctioned in the Code of the Towns, which located oath swearing by the church portal, and would have the town sheriff, *logmaðr* or council performing inspections in matters regarding security and trade.[58] Hence, only a portion of the surviving material that illuminates the legal situation in Norwegian towns can be said to document cases presented in places specifically designated for legal business. Unlike the small towns, Niðaros, Oslo and Tunsberg undoubtedly had a *rathaus* where the town council met.[59] The town *mót* in Tunsberg took place in a hall belonging to the guild of St Olaf.[60] The place and space of legal transaction was still most often outwith the places designated for legal affairs. The street, churches, houses and rooms in a house all occur in records. Much of the material relates to legal business taking place in the office of the person of authority overseeing the agreement, in the street or in private houses. The streets act as legal spaces in witness letters from Oslo. The *lǫgmaðr* in Oslo himself confirmed in 1310, "I was in the street in front of the gate to the smith's quarter" (*"ek var viðr a strætenu firir garðliðinu a Smiz garðe"*) in Oslo to witness the payment of a rural property.[61] To confirm the sale of three parts of a cellar in Oslo 1353, two witnesses met with the

55 E Frankot, 'Legal Business Outside the Courts. Private and Public Houses as Spaces of Law in the Fifteenth Century', in J W Armstrong and E Frankot (eds), *Cultures of Law in Urban Northern Europe: Scotland and its Neighbours c. 1350–c. 1650* (2021) 173–191.

56 Frankot, 'Legal Business' (n 55) 179–80.

57 S McSheffrey, 'Place, space, and situation: Public and private in the making of marriage in late-medieval London' (2004) 79 *Speculum* 960–990 at 973.

58 The Code of the Towns of 1276 VI-19 (inspection of ovens), VII-22 (on searching ships), VII-28 (inspection of measuring devices).

59 M Tveit, 'Urban law in Norwegian market towns' (n 6) 112–113.

60 Keyser and Munch (eds), NgL vol II (n 1) 187 n 14 and 188 n 18.

61 Chr C A Lange and C R Unger (eds), DN, vol III (1855) no 87.

two parties in "the street outside the Valter quarter" ("*a stræteno vti firir Va*(l)*taragarde*"), an aristocratic town quarter if we are to judge by later owners.[62] In Tunsberg, two councilmen witnessed in 1400 the rental agreement between the old *logmaðr* and the new in the street by *Matrauden*, a building that hosted a number of cases during the fourteenth century.[63] The evidence from Niðaros does not include private houses as locations comprising a legal space but the letters predominantly recorded transactions taking place in the church or on ecclesiastical property.

F: TRANSFERS OF URBAN LAND AND BUILDINGS

Town planning would invoke town regulations, and the Code of the Towns contains tools for urban governance in developing the town. Little is known about Norwegian urban planning in the middle ages, but charters provide evidence for the distribution of plots of land by the king. It would seem that the king maintained overlordship of urban ground, as he exercised rights of pre-emption in respect of all town land and claimed ownership to the commons within the urban boundaries. House owners need not have been the owners of the ground.[64]

A string of charters following a transaction of a plot in Tunsberg, in 1343, illustrates how each different document formed part of the procedure, protecting the seller from breach of contract.[65] The seller, Einar, acknowledged having sold the plot to Thord in February and, in July, one document states two witnesses confirmed that Einar had received full payment, while in another *notitia* from the same day four witnesses confirmed that Einar's wife agreed to the sale. In a fourth *notitia*, from earlier that month, the same two witnesses who had confirmed the payment swore that Einar had offered the property to another man, Rolf, but that he declined due to lack of money to buy it.[66] There is nothing remarkable about this deal, which is

62 Chr C A Lange and C R Unger (eds), DN, vol II (1852) no 322, 1353; 1399: Chr C A Lange and C R Unger (eds), DN, vol IV (1858) no 693, *mer vaarom j Valtærgarde j [Oslo soom ok høyrdom a* [at] *þæssir godir men giærdo þettæ skipte siin j millom.*

63 C R Unger and H J Huitfeldt-Kaas (eds), DN, vol XI (1878) no 99. From year 1336, C R Unger and H J Huitfeldt-Kaas (eds), DN, vol XI (1884) no 20; 1369, Unger and Huitfeldt-Kaas (eds), DN, vol XI, no 59; 1376, C R Unger and Huitfeldt-Kaas (eds), DN, vol VIII (1874) no 198; 1382, Chr C A Lande and C R Unger (eds), DN, vol V (1861) no 316; 1392, Unger and Huitfeldt-Kaas (eds), DN, vol XI, no 85; 1395, Lange and Unger (eds), DN, vol IV (n 62) no 644 and Lange and Unger (eds), DN, vol II (n 62) no 52.

64 Helle et al, *Norsk Byhistorie* (n 7) 103–104.

65 Unger and Huitfeldt-Kaas (eds), DN, vol XI (n 63) no 30–33.

66 Unger and Huitfeldt-Kaas (eds), DN, vol XI (n 63) no 32.

a straightforward sale of town land, though the level of information given to us is rare. Nevertheless, in the context of urban law there are several aspects of the sale worth examining. First, it is one of few urban cases where we have subsequent letters describing stages in a transaction, with the declaration first and a receipt and approval for the payment later, together with confirmation of offering the land to another. The Code of the Towns would have the seller offer a town property first to the king at the *mót*, and second to his neighbour in the same town quarter, before selling it openly.[67] There is no trail of evidence that house owners gave the king first refusal, but the abovementioned Rolf, who did not have the money, may have been this neighbour. Secondly, the detail of the documentation is unusual, with a description of position of the plot within the street structure of the town and the status of the property. Further, the example shed light on how a spouse became involved in the sale of urban property. The codes maintained the *félag*, an institution of joint ownership in a marriage.[68] Possibly, Einar and his wife had *félag*, which demanded that each partner needed the spouse's approval for changes in their own property.

The number of witnesses was not regulated in law, but the procedure seems from the witness letters to have been fairly standardised. Two witnesses confirmed a private transaction, while three or six witnessed donations to the church. In Anglo-Norman charters, Dauvit Broun suggests that the scribe did not always know how many witnesses there would be before they began the letter.[69] Norwegian witness letters and charters open with the number of witnesses already in the protocol of the document. The social standing of the witness is not always given, but in the surviving material they were often among the elite, as were the parties themselves.

Legal officials acted as subsitutes for the private witnesses when the transaction included dispositive elements. Such a case can be illustrated with the documents relating to the possession of half a town quarter, the northern part of *Jonsgaard* in Tunsberg in the late fourteenth century. A charter from 1397 states that a couple, Sigrid and Þorer, were to keep their houses in *Jonsgaard* if, within a year, they made a pilgrimage to Aachen and to Niðaros on behalf of the soul of one Ivar Lodvikson.[70] If not, the

67 The Code of the Towns of 1276 VI-5.

68 L I Hansen, 'The Field of Property Devolution in Norway During the Late Middle Ages: Inheritance Settlements, Marriage Contracts and Legal Disputes' in K Esmark, L Hermannson, H J Orning and H Vogt, *Disputing Strategies in Medieval Scandinavia* (2013) 247–277.

69 D Broun, 'The presence of witnesses (n 32) 235–290.

70 Unger and Huitfeldt-Kaas (eds), DN, vol XI (n 63) no 92.

other parties to the agreement, Simon and his daughters, would receive a proportion of the house equal to what the trips would have cost. Ivar, who also had been in financial dealings with the king, had bought the northern part of *Jonsgaard* in 1378.[71] In a charter from 1384, an earlier agreement of pilgrimage to Aachen had been made for Sigrid's first husband, Strange.[72] In this charter, two women, Ingeborg and Ivar's widow, Sunniva, acted on behalf of Sunniva and Ivar's son Lodvik. We do not know Ivar's relationship with Sigrid, but we learn that he had paid her dowry of sixty marks as well as promising a half cloth to the church of St Mary in Tunsberg, both valuables that formed part of the agreement. Based on this charter, a deed was issued by the *logmaðr* and the town council of Tunsberg.[73] The procedure, status of witnesses and values involved in the case of northern *Jonsgaard* suggest the parties were wealthy burghers. Both charters were witnessed by six men, one cleric and five laymen, while the original sale to Ivar in 1378 was witnessed by as many as eight, one of them a knight. In the last charter where two pilgrimages were pledged, the *logmaðr* and five secular squires were present with a canon from the church of St Laurentius in Tunsberg. The involvement of clergy was most likely due to this sacral part of the agreement. The witnesses had seen the parties shake hands (*handerbande*) and attested to a legally binding agreement.

The text from 1397 probably echoed a provision in the law text when stating that in case of failure to make a pilgrimage, the couple would owe their counterpart Simon and his daughters "as much as six or twelve men judge or assess him for the two mentioned pilgrimages" ("*swa mykit som sæx ædher tolf men dømde æder mææte honum firir þææр twææг oftnempdar pelagrims reisur*").[74] The Code of the Realm and the Code of the Towns give variations of six- or twelve-man juries.[75] The primary Tunsberg manuscript variation also includes a variation in the number of men summoned to the *mót*, with six house owners, and six henchmen.[76]

The background for the conflict over this property, and Simon's claim against Sigrid and Þorer, is obscure to us. The agreement that the couple

71 C R Unger and H J Huitfeldt-Kaas (eds), DN, vol VI (1864) no 297, Unger and Huitfeldt-Kaas (eds), DN, vol XI (n 63) no 64.

72 Unger and Huitfeldt-Kaas (eds), DN, vol XI (n 63) no 70.

73 Chr C A Lange and C R Unger (eds), DN, vol I (1849) no 489 and 490.

74 Unger and Huitfeldt-Kaas (eds), DN, vol XI (n 63) no 92 and 81.

75 The Code of 1274 IV-15: *lagadom*, variations between six and twelve; The Code of the Towns of 1276 VII-12.

76 The *Codex Tunsbergensis* also divides the town into ridings, not farthings: Keyser and Munch (eds), NgL vol II (n 1) 188 n 9 and 189 n 27.

would be allowed to keep the house on certain conditions was obviously a repetition of an earlier pledge, as the charter states that they would keep and have unchanged what had been decided, after they had produced evidence and witnesses. It could be that Strange never managed to go through with his one journey before he died, given that Sigrid and her new husband had two pilgrimages imposed on them thirteen years later.

Transactions could be made without exchange of money. Privileges and exemptions could be used as currency (see below), as religious acts, in the shape of pilgrimages. A pilgrim voyage was a costly activity, undertaken by those with means. The two trips therefore had value in economic as well as religious terms. Niðaros, with its cult of St Olaf, had long been a popular destination of the faithful, and Aachen had become a popular pilgrimage destination from the mid-fourteenth century.[77] The family of Ivar Lodvikson must have been among the new urban elite in Tunsberg. The urban legal system acknowledged the value of the participation of religious men in cases between town people. However, we do not know if anyone ever carried out the task of praying for Ivar's soul in either place. Nevertheless, the extended network connected with *Jonsgaard* continued their pious work, as the daughter of Strange, the failed first pilgrim, kept a part of the house and subsequently donated its income to St Mary's.[78]

G: FIRE HAZARDS AND TOWN PLANNING

Fire was naturally a concern in the towns, which contained mainly wooden structures, and fire safety was part of the substantive laws as well as the procedural law in the Code of the Towns. The concern was real, as Norwegian towns saw devastating fires in the middle ages.[79] Law demanded that all crafts using ovens or fire be situated on the outskirts of the town. As we have seen, archaeology confirms that they were already there, or established on the fringe of the town, after the promulgation of the urban code.

Procedure dictated that the officials inspect new ovens and there do survive exceptional grants allowing new ovens to be built in town centres.

77 B L Chunko, 'Aachen', in L J Taylor, L A Craig, J B Friedman, K Gower, T Izbicki and R Tekippe (eds), *Encyclopedia of Medieval Pilgrimage* (2010) 2.

78 Unger and Huitfeldt-Kaas (eds), DN, vol XI (n 63) no 186: In 1447, a *notitia* describes a part of the property that "Margarete Strangedatter gave many years ago to the priests table of St. Mary's".

79 For instance, the fire of Oslo in 1137, 1159, 1254 and 1352; Bergen 1198 and 1248; Nedkvitne and Norseng, *Middelalderbyen* (n 18) 80, 90 and 102. Workshops of metallurgy and smithies are often found outside the town centre, *ibid*., 93.

This suggests that the building of ovens was monitored by town authorities. A royal permit was given to Arnald the baker and his wife Magdalena in October 1372 to construct an oven on a plot of land in Spaken, next to the bishop's house in Oslo.[80] The location placed the bakery in the middle of the town, not on the outskirts.[81] Later that month, "Thord *bonde*", a Swedish nobleman in the king's circle,[82] and his sister attested that they, on the king's request, had given a plot to the pair where they had already raised a house.[83] The urban ground was by default royal land and the king's to distribute. Thus, Thord and his sister may have been the privileged landholders only by royal favour. His byname furthermore referred to the term for freeholders of land. Thirteen years later, Magdalena, now a widow, again received land from Thord in the same area, Spaken.[84] We do not learn whether she was given more land because she continued or expanded her business as a widow, but later documents prove she protected her rights to the place. Her letters of confirmation would have become relevant in 1405 when, in March, her rights were renewed by the Kalmar Union King Erik and in June, she was involved in a dispute with her neighbour.[85] King Erik's letter further mentions an earlier (lost) confirmation from King Olaf (1380–1386), probably at the same time and for the same reason that Thord had again given her land. Thus, Magdalena's family had received three royal sanctions for the use of Spaken in Oslo. The dispute may have been a reason behind her obtaining a renewal of her rights at this point, as Magdalena had claimed her neighbour Vidar Reidarsson had raised a house too close to her own.[86] The question seems to have been whether Vidar had violated building regulations, and thus would have to demolish his – probably newly built – house. The Code of the Towns stated that already existing houses should stand, but new houses should be built in accordance with the council of the *logmaðr*, and in the Oslo version, also the *syslumadr*.[87] Houses that had been constructed without regard to these rules should be demolished by the town men, if not the owner.

80 C R Unger and H J Huitfeldt-Kaas (eds), DN, vol X (1880) no 73.

81 Nedkvitne and Norseng, *Middelalderbyen* (n 18) 269, suggest that exemptions were given to ovens in stone-built houses.

82 F L F Wernstedt, *Äldre svenska frälsesläkter: ättartavlor*, bind 1(1957).

83 Unger and Huitfeldt-Kaas (eds), DN, vol XI (n 63) no 46. Wrongly dated to 1356, see G Pettersen and K Sprauten (eds), *Regesta Norvegica*, vol VII (1998) no 139.

84 Lange and Unger (eds), DN, vol II (n 62) no 489.

85 Denmark, Norway and Sweden entered into the Kalmar union in 1397. A personal union between Norway and Sweden had been established in 1319.

86 Lange and Unger (eds), DN, vol IV (n 62) no 751.

87 The Code of the Towns of 1276 VI-4: Keyser and Munch (eds), NgL vol II (n 1) 243.

Furthermore, the Code's book of town regulations dealt with how "land captures house and house [captures] land".[88] This concerned cases when a house was built on someone else's land, or when a house had stood unchallenged on the same spot for more than twenty years. Both the principle of house becoming subsumed to land and the time prescription were basic principles of Roman law, although according to Roman law, land could never accede to a house.[89] In Norwegian urban law it was the rule that in case of a house built on another's land, the landowner would take surety (*taksette*) from the housebuilder and the *logmaðr* with the town sheriff and council men should conduct an inspection, while the claimant would produce two witnesses that the land was theirs. In the case between Magdalena and Vidar, the question was not if his house was on her land, but whether it was too close to her house, a problem regarding which there were no specific regulations in the town laws.

To find a solution to the conflict, the *logmaðr* and five town men, among them two knights, heard the case on site. The case has been interpreted as *sáttmál* – that is, arbitration outside the legal system, not involving the court.[90] However, in the document, the tribunal demanded that the parties hold their judgment as legally binding. Magdalena's royal letters would have served as witnesses if needed. The decision was that Vidar's house would stand, although he would make amends. Vidar had to design his drip rail (*dælor*) in such a manner that her house was untouched by drops from it, and further pay Magdalena twelve marks, which she, according to the document, "had earned in plenty" ("*þet hafuer hon wpboret til nøgio*").[91] Seeing that the town laws were informed by Roman law, it is interesting that in Roman law, "the right to discharge eavesdrip on to a neighbour's roof or vacant ground or the right to prevent such discharge" was listed among the urban praedial servitudes.[92] In Norwegian urban law, it seems, the right of preventing discharge had precedence. According to the codes, a six-man jury would be put into an arbitration tribunal to find a solution in cases of pre-emption, involuntary or voluntary damages, or to act as jury in case of theft within the town.[93] As such, the six-man jury was attached to serious

88 The Code of the Towns of 1276 VI-6: Keyser and Munch (eds), NgL vol II (n 1) 244.

89 WW Buckland, *A Text-Book of Roman Law from Augustus to Justinian*, 3rd edn, rev. Peter Stein (1963) 208–215.

90 Nedkvitne and Norseng, *Middelalderbyen* (n 18) 243.

91 Lange and Unger (eds), DN, vol IV (n 62) 751.

92 *Digesta* 8.2.2; Watson (ed), *The Digest of Justinian*, vol I (n 35) 252. See Buckland, *A Text-Book of Roman Law* (n 89) 264.

93 For example, theft: the Code of the Towns of 1276 VI-13; compensation for homicide: the Code

cases of damage, while crimes of violence or adultery demanded a twelve-man jury. The number of guards appointed for night watch within a town was also six.[94] The number must have carried a semiotic meaning of justice and peace.

The rather high price of the compensation awarded to Magdalena suggests that the law saw the inconvenience caused to her by the neighbouring house as substantial.[95] They nevertheless considered this inconvenience to be resolvable, compared to the dramatic step of requiring Vidar to move his house. Between the royal favours and high-status men hearing the case, it is clear that Magdalena's family had some status and standing. The cases of the bakery's land may therefore not represent most craftsmen's dealings with the law. It would nevertheless seem that a concern for sound justice was at the root of the solution reached in this case; and the procedures used in the resolution of the dispute were in accordance with the Code of the Towns.

H: WOMEN'S LEGAL STANDING IN URBAN LAW

In Magdalena's case, we see a female litigant, and a successful one at that. It is not rare to find women among the parties in the surviving letters of urban or rural law. From the earlier provincial laws, women held increased inheritance rights according to the Code of the Realm and were given rights as legal actors with the Code of the Towns: they could act in court when unmarried or with their husbands' consent if married.[96] In a case from Oslo dated 1345, a woman named Gyrid was being hindered in enjoying her dowry, which would form part of her inheritance, of two farmsteads east of the town.[97] Two clergymen had for some time possessed the land in question and enjoyed its surplus, although the letter does not reveal how this situation came about. The Archbishop Pål of Niðaros presided over the case

of 1274 IV-12; harmful animals: the Code of 1274 IV-22; odal land: the Code of 1274 VI-8; involuntary damages: the Code of 1274 VII-58; and voluntary damages: the Code of 1274 VIII-27. See discussion on the six- and twelve-man juries in J Ø Sunde, 'Daughters of god and counsellors of the judges of men: changes in the legal culture of the Norwegian realm in the high middle ages', in S Brink and L Collinson (eds), *New Approaches to Early Law in Scandinavia* (2014) 131–183, at 146–147.

94 The Code of the Towns of 1276 VI-3.

95 For an overview of the concept of mark, see H Bjørkvik, 'Mark – Noreg', in *Kulturhistorisk Leksikon for Nordisk Middelalder fra vikingtid til reformasjonstid*, vol 11: *Luft-motståndsrätt*. (1966) 430–431 and N L Rasmusson, 'Mark penning – Norge', in *Kulturhistorisk Leksikon*, vol 11 (1966) 439–440.

96 The Code of the Towns of 1276 VII-26.

97 Lange and Unger (eds), DN, vol I (n 73) no 292 (1345).

that took place in the bishop's residence in Oslo during one of his visits to the town. The case was therefore principally run before an ecclesiastical court. Gyrid produced witnesses and a written contract proving that her father had granted her the properties as dowry and the outcome was that she resumed the right to access at least one of the properties.

In the charter for the case, the archbishop seemed most annoyed with one of the two litigants, represented by proxy. His representative makes a very bad impression, leaving the court with "wailing and complaints" and not producing any "legal protection" ("*laga værndum*"), probably meaning documentation of the claim to the property.[98] It may be that this behaviour turned the case in favour of Gyrid as the litigant in question was deprived of the property on the spot, while the other was given time to prove his argument of rightful possession. However, Gyrid's claim had a basis in law. The book of inheritance in the urban code stated that those who interfered with the property claims of the rightful heir should be summoned to the *mót* by the litigant and charged with unlawful possession, although this section is not part of the surviving Oslo versions.[99] As such, there was legal authority in the secular law for Gyrid to take her case there. Gyrid had, according to the charter, approached Archbishop Pål insistently before he yielded to hear the case. As Grethe Authén Blom suggests, she could have tried to bring the case before a secular court already.[100] The defendants were clergy and would possibly maintain the right to be tried before a canonical court. The church further claimed jurisdiction over marital transactions, but this had been a topic of conflict between state and church in the process of the legal reform.[101] Possibly, the secular court would stay clear of what was within the jurisdiction of the Church. Nevertheless, the case is one of many indicators that jurisdictions were overlapping or intertwined between the law of the country and the town, as well as between secular and canon law.[102]

Archbishop Pål was legally trained in Paris, Orleans and Avignon, and he was probably the most knowledgeable man of law in the kingdom at this time.[103] The conclusion that he reached was based on the written document, as well as the misconduct of the defendant. Written contracts for purchases

98 Lange and Unger (eds), DN, vol I (n 73) no 292.

99 The Code of the Towns of 1276 V-17.

100 G A Blom, 'Loven og livet' (1991) 104 *Tidsskrift for Rettsvitenskap* 543–569.

101 S Bagge, 'Kristens jurisdiksjon i kristenrettssaker før 1277' (1981) Nr 2 bind 60 *Historisk Tidsskrift* 133–159; J Ø Sunde, *Speculum Legale – Rettsspegelen. Ein introduksjon til den norske rettskulturen si historie i eit europeisk perspektiv* (2005) 127–135.

102 The Code of the Towns of 1276 VII-26.

103 Blom, 'Loven og livet' (n 100).

over a certain value and gifts in the marriage agreements were introduced with the Code of the Realm and Code of the Towns.[104] The fact that it weighed so heavily in favour of Gyrid may be due to the secular law but also to the archbishop's own legal understanding.

Gyrid herself was aware of the legal status of written contracts and readily produced one in court. Women were given greater rights with the new urban code than they held according to the Code of the Realm, which again had increased women's rights to inheritance and consent from the old provincial laws. The town law gave women the right to make purchases, while for property they needed a pass from their husband or (probably male) heir, a privilege not granted to their rural sisters.[105] In the countryside, women had access to the assembly, according to the Code of the Realm, a right that Else Mundal has deduced must also have been granted to female urban estate owners regarding the *mót*.[106] The Code of the Towns also gave women the right to stand surety for someone.[107] Gyrid's dowry was nevertheless not an example of equal rights, but a case of possession. Even if she represented the landowning elite, her understanding of law indicates that the new procedures from the codes were accessible knowledge in Norwegian society.

I: TRADE, CRAFT AND THE HARBOUR

The urban code incorporated some particularly urban topics in the Norwegian context, relating to the crafts performed and trade. According to the Code of the Towns, the only criterion for practising a craft or trade was to pay the urban tax and, in the Bergen versions, to perform the trade at the allotted location within the town boundaries.[108] The only craft that managed to establish a guild that required training was that of the shoemakers in Oslo.[109] They were situated in *Myklagard* from 1304.[110] This craft, along

104 The Code of 1274 VIII-11 and The Code of the Towns of 1276 VII-17.

105 The Code of the Towns of 1276 VII-6. A rural woman could make low value purchases depending on marital and social status and a husband could overturn any of his wife's transaction within a month: the Code of 1274 VIII-21.

106 E Mundal, 'Kva hadde kvinnene på tinget å gjere. Kvinneroller på tinget etter norske landskapslover og Landslova', in A C Horn and K A Seip (eds), *Lov og lovgivning i middelalderen: Nye studier av Magnus Lagabøtes landslov*, 238–239.

107 The Code of the Towns of 1276 VII-26.

108 The Code of the Towns of 1276 III-8 and VI-8,

109 C R Unger and H J Huitfeldt-Kaas (eds), DN, vol VII (1869) no 267. On shoemakers in Oslo: Lange and Unger (eds), DN, vol II (n 62) no 74, 350, Keyser and Munch (eds), NgL, vol III (note 21) no 86; *NgL, Anden Række*, bind 1 no 201,

110 Lange and Unger (eds), DN, vol II (n 62) no 74; Unger and Huitfeldt-Kaas (eds), DN, vol VI

with those requiring ovens, was allotted to the fringe of the town, according to law. The regulation of shoemakers was repeated in King Hákon's amendment to Niðaros from 1313.[111] Landlords would be fined for housing shoemakers in their town houses. King Magnus VII repeated their compulsory location in Myklagard in 1352, after having learned that some town men housed shoemakers.[112] It was a reminder of the order given by King Hákon in an earlier *mót* (*bønom mote*) and added that the king himself could make exceptions. King Hákon VI addressed the craft in Niðaros in 1370, ensuring them continued privileges.[113] The royal fisc gave the shoemakers of Niðaros a receipt in 1371 for 10 shilling *grot*, a Flemish currency that suggests international trade, which they owed the king.[114] This would exempt them from other taxes, possibly also the abovementioned urban tax due to the town sheriff. The shoemakers in Tunsberg were situated in a separate complex, the *Sudergarthen* in the western end of the town complex.[115] We learn this from the donation letter from 1395, where the woman Birgitta gave the "shoemaker-house" to St Mary's of Oslo, the royal chapel, along with 100 marks. The substantial gift suggest that the Tunsberg guild must have been of some size and standing. Queen Margrethe could advise her protégé Erik of Pommern that he should annually tax 100 pairs of boots and 200 pairs of shoes from shoemakers in both Tunsberg and Oslo, before his visit sometime after 1404.[116]

The foundation of Norwegian medieval towns, and their main activities, have often been connected to trade and export.[117] Even if modern research ties the towns' functions to administration, and especially law, the position of the towns almost exclusively along coastal trade routes reveals their role as hubs for the exchange of goods. A number of charters relate to the harbour, trade policies or foreign merchants in the towns. Trade was otherwise heavily regulated in the many amendments following the Code of the Towns. We do not find a large number of cases involving trade or traders per se, although there is a substantial number of letters discussing the rights of domestic

(n 71) no 208, Keyser and Munch (eds), NgL, vol III (n 21) nr 86; Blom, *Kongemakt og privilegier* (n 21) 38, 49, 192, 196–198.

111 Keyser and Munch (eds), NgL, vol III (n 21) no 36b.

112 Unger and Huitfeldt-Kaas (eds), DN, vol VI (n 71) no 208.

113 Keyser and Munch (eds), NgL, vol III (n 21) 188.

114 Chr C A Lange and C R Unger (eds), DN, vol V (1861) no 264; E Kroman, *Oversigt over møntthistorien med særligt Hensyn til regneenhederne* (1964) 3–4.

115 Lange and Unger (eds), DN, vol IV (n 62) no 649. J Wienberg, *Arkeologiske rapporter fra Tønsberg 9: Grund og gård i Tønsberg* (1992) 5.

116 Unger and Huitfeldt-Kaas (eds), DN, vol XI (n 63) no 110, 100.

117 Helle et al, *Norsk byhistorie* (n 7) 80.

versus foreign traders. Foreigners were present in most Norwegian towns south of Bergen, and possibly also in those further north, but in 1294 foreign traders were banned from venturing further north than Bergen without a special permit.[118] German and Flemish merchants in particular prospered in Bergen, Tunsberg and Oslo, as in other Northern European towns.[119] However, German traders, even if they became burghers, never acted as witnesses or jurymen in letters from Oslo before the end of the fourteenth century, and then only very rarely.[120]

The balancing act that the royal administration performed between foreign policy and domestic interests regarding the privileges of foreign merchants will not be treated here, other than when foreign town dwellers encountered the law.[121] However, there are few documents pertaining to cases involving individual merchants or conflicts of trade. From Niðaros, it was only when the interest of the archbishopric was affected that surviving documents were produced. In 1340, two Icelandic merchants complained about the taxes they had to pay and the ecclesiastical court decided that Norwegian merchants traveling to Iceland would pay their tithe in cod, cod liver oil and sulphur, in addition to wadmal, the Icelandic currency.[122] The merchants that sailed to Greenland also had to pay their tithe in Niðaros, according to a letter from the archbishop to the bishop of Bergen in 1325.[123]

The harbour was a crucial point of a town's structure and this is reflected in the Code of the Towns. In the book of town regulations, several chapters are directly or indirectly part of easing the harbour activity of stowage.[124] The town men were obliged to come "when the horn sounds" to help pull a docking ship on pain of a fine, meaning that the town was expected to have a system of summoning its citizens by noise and a system of allocating ships in the harbour for efficiency and protection to both ship and town.[125] There is little reflection of these duties in the surviving material – not surprisingly, as breach of these substantial laws would probably not produce a record or the record would not be worth saving – but we see that the procedure was

118 Lange and Unger (eds), DN, vol V (n 114) no 23.
119 Helle et al, *Norsk byhistorie* (n 7) 80–86.
120 Nedkvitne and Norseng, *Middelalderbyen* (n 18) 366 table. See, for instance Lange and Unger (eds), DN, vol IV (n 62) no 298 and 301.
121 For this, consult, for instance: J Wubs-Mrozewicz, *Traders, ties and tensions: the interactions of Lübeckers, Overijsslers and Hollanders in Late Medieval Bergen* (2008).
122 Lange and Unger (eds), DN, vol I (n 73) no 235.
123 Unger and Huitfeldt-Kaas (eds), DN, vol VII (n 109) no 104.
124 The Code of the Towns of 1276 VI-16, 17 and 18.
125 The Code of the Towns of 1276 VI-15.

operating in the way in which groups were given exemption from the duty. German merchants were, after making a request, exempt from many of the duties of Norwegian towns in 1278, among them *"sint liberi a tractione nauium"*, while Norwegians were obliged to help them if they experienced distress at sea.[126] This has been understood as a reaction to the Code of 1276.[127]

As an amendment to the agreement of 1277 between state and church on the new law, the servants and smith of the archbishop were excused from the duty of pulling ships (here: *skiffdrattum*) in Niðaros.[128] As part of a donation by King Hákon V to the church of St Mary in Oslo in 1318, the tenant of a property in Bergen were exempt from a number of duties, among them pulling ships.[129] The clergy in St Stephanus' hospital, on the outskirts of Tunsberg, were exempt from *skiffdrattum* as part of renewed privileges given to them by King Magnus VII (1319–1355) in 1320.[130] The friars at Lyse cloister in Bergen and their associates were exempted from pulling ships in Bergen by King Magnus in 1344. The long-standing tradition of relieving clergy from pulling ships suggests that this duty was actually exacted in the harbour towns and also that it was considered hard labour that could be traded as a privilege. A number of valid exemptions from this duty were already integrated into the urban law, which were applicable to those performing sacraments in church, those undergoing treatment and those caring for sick relatives.[131] In a negative sense, the existence of such a privilege in the decades from the promulgation of the law until the mid-fourteenth century suggests the duty of ship pulling existed in the same form as it was described in the law for other urban citizens. We do not find ship pulling connected with the countryside; it was a purely urban legal phenomenon.

Another perspective on the legal significance of the harbour can be found in property transactions. Harbour warehouses were valued properties, entered as part of inheritances, or as objects of sale in themselves, and were valued among the urban church as it was deeply involved in trade. Margareta Halvardsdatter gave a warehouse in Oslo as part of a gift of land

126 Lange and Unger (eds), DN, vol V (n 114) no 10.

127 N Bjørgo and S Bagge (eds), *Regesta Norvegica*, vol. II (1978) no 201, p. 96 n 2.

128 *Diplomatarium Islandicum. Íslenzkt fornbréfasafn*, vol II (1893) 151–152. The agreement, 'Sættargerð Magnúsar konungs lagabætis og Jóns erkibiskups rauða', from 1277, can be found at 139–147.

129 Lange and Unger (eds), DN, vol II (n 62) no 133.

130 Lange and Unger (eds), DN, vol II (n 62) no 139. For position, see J Wienberg, *Arkeologiske rapporter fra Tønsberg 9: Grund og gård i Tønsberg* (1992) 5.

131 The Code of the Towns of 1276 VI-17.

and movables to Asleif Gudbrandssön in 1362.[132] This was one of two large donations, the second to several churches. Both transactions took place in the church of St Halvard in Oslo and they were witnessed by the bishop of Oslo and two others. The transaction was sealed by Margareta and Asleif shaking hands.[133] Botholf, on behalf of Þorgrim, shook hands with the priest Þorer in the sale of an Oslo harbour warehouse in 1364.[134] The transaction took place in a private town house with two witnesses. This was in the same area that a warehouse was sold in 1409 for 7.5 *lest* of salt, paid in full, according to the unwitnessed receipt.[135] An urban harbour warehouse was also part of a donation from the bishop of Oslo to the altar of St Edmund in 1389, where in addition five witnesses confirmed the gift.[136] Overall, it seems that in documenting transactions of property, the church included more witnesses than other institutions and individuals.

J: CONCLUDING REMARKS

These examples from urban law can only provide glimpses into the procedures that were applied in Niðaros, Oslo and Tunsberg in the century following the promulgation of an urban code in Norway. There are certain procedural patterns to be found in the examples, but when considering how the procedures compare with the law, one quickly realises that the parallels are commonplace and can perhaps even be described as ubiquitous. The parties met with witnesses in a location; agreement was reached, alone, or through the use of arbitration or a jury, depending on the case type. There were rituals to perform, such as taking each other's hand in agreement, and then a notary wrote while witnesses confirmed the transaction with their names alone or with seals. If nothing else, these procedures pertained to urban law and to procedures elsewhere in urban medieval Europe.

There are however some conclusions to draw from the material that are worth emphasising. First, the different types of cases illustrate that the legal processes in the towns happened to a large degree outwith the places

132 Lange and Unger (eds), DN, vol IV (n 62) no 432 and 433.

133 "*heldo handum saman*", "held their hands together": Lange and Unger (eds), DN, vol IV (n 62) no 432.

134 Lange and Unger (eds), DN, vol V (n 114) no 251.

135 Lange and Unger (eds), DN, vol II (n 62) no 609. *Lest* was a measure of volume, counted in a certain number of barrels.

136 Unger and Huitfeldt-Kaas (eds), DN, vol IV (n 62) no 565 and 567. In 1413, Oslo Cathedral secured a plot for a warehouse in the 'bishop's kay', Unger and Huitfeldt-Kaas (eds), DN, vol IV (n 62) no 793.

designated for legal affairs. What constituted legal space in the execution of urban law was much more related to either party than the institutionalised law, and social spaces performed as legal spaces.

Secondly, the parties appear knowledgeable when seeking their rights. However, this only follows from a consideration of the registered cases and the many undocumented disputes may have been completely different. The sources are biased as most of the cases represent the elite owners of property, by all accounts a more educated section of the population. Nevertheless, the town dwellers sought to use correct procedure in order to secure their assets. A female litigant presented an understanding of her legal rights and actively sought them, which indicates that the new procedures from the codes were known and understood in Norwegian urban society.

Thirdly, examples suggest that the procedural steps surrounding property transactions were executed with a fixed number of witnesses and according to a fixed procedure, much in accordance with law. The evidence demonstrates that the numbers of witnesses, arbitrators or jurors were not coincidental but rather followed a formula that was either already part of the legal culture or, alternatively, introduced the new codes. The numeral correspondence suggests more than a legal cultural congruence between law and practice and represents literal knowledge of law in addition to the traditions of legal culture. The relevance of the numbers could be studied further, but in procedure, legal practice mirrored the laws. Furthermore, these number formulae are present in cases of both canon and secular law, although the exact number of witnesses appear to be higher in the cases where the church was involved. Many of the cases reveal that jurisdictions were overlapping or intertwined between the law of the country and the town, as well as between secular and canon law. The – admittedly random – examples from canon law in Niðaros, Oslo and Tunsberg appear to be more in dialogue with the king's laws than the conflicts regarding jurisdiction in the wake of Magnus' codes would suggest. Urban legal procedure, it seems, was performed on the basis of law; but it also took into account the case in question, together with local custom.

6 Urban Legal Procedure in Fourteenth Century Scotland: A fresh look at the 1317 court roll of Aberdeen

Andrew R C Simpson°

A: INTRODUCTION

In 1317, a court of the burgh of Aberdeen had regard to what it called the *leges burgorum Scocie* – the laws of the burghs of Scotland – in determining the outcome of a particular legal process. The *leges* were used in part to identify the procedures that had to be followed when transferring claims to lands within the burgh from one person to another.[1] Yet what did the court

° This article was written whilst I was a partner in the project *Social Governance through legislation* at the Centre for Advanced Studies at the Norwegian Academy of Science and Letters in Oslo; it is based on a paper given at a seminar at Lagmannsstova at Aga, the Hardangerfjord, on 20 August 2019. I am very grateful to Hector MacQueen, Alice Taylor and Eddie Simpson for their comments, and to Tom Green for his assistance in helping me to find a missing reference. Any errors remain my own.

1 See A R C Simpson and J W Armstrong 'The Roll of the Burgh Courts of Aberdeen, August–October 1317' in A M Godfrey (ed), *Stair Society Miscellany Eight by Various Authors*, Stair Society vol 67 (2020) 57–93 at 74–75, 76–77; the text of the 1317 court roll (Aberdeen City Archives (ACA) Ref 5/6) is discussed in more detail below.

mean when it referred to the *leges burgorum Scocie*? In essence, that is the central question that will be considered throughout this chapter.

Those familiar with the history of the laws of the medieval Scottish kingdom might quite reasonably assume that when the court considered the *leges burgorum Scocie*, it was in fact referring to a text that survives in several manuscript witnesses dateable to the late-thirteenth and fourteenth centuries.[2] The earliest manuscript witness bar one to the surviving text – the Ayr MS, dateable to 1323–1346 – refers to it as the "*captiula legis burgorum Scocie*" (i.e. the chapters of the law of the burghs of Scotland),[3] whilst what may be the next earliest witness – the Bute MS, dateable to the final years of the fourteenth century – labels a Scots translation of it the "*leges burgorum Scocie facte apud nouvm castrum super Tynam per Dauid regem Scotorum illustrisimum*" (i.e. the laws of the burghs of Scotland made at Newcastle upon Tyne by David, most illustrious king of the Scots).[4] This text may itself

2 For what seem to be the earliest four surviving witnesses to this text, see National Records of Scotland (NRS) Ref PA5/1 ff. 62r–63v (the text in the Berne MS); NRS Ref PA5/2 ff. 49v–67v (the text in the Ayr MS); National Library of Scotland (NLS) MS 21246 ff. 153v–162v (the text in the Bute MS) and Harvard Law Library, MS 164 ff. 63r–76r (the text in the Harvard MS). For the texts in the Berne MS, the Ayr MS and the Bute MS, see A Taylor, *The Laws of Medieval Scotland: Legal Compilations from the thirteenth and fourteenth centuries* (2019) 37–38; 48; 59. For the Harvard MS, see A Taylor, 'Introduction', in J R Davies with A Taylor (eds), *Regiam Majestatem: The earliest known version* (2022) 142–165. I am very grateful to Professor Taylor for sharing with me an advance draft of this text. The Berne MS, the Ayr MS and the Harvard MS are available online (see *http://stairsociety.org/resources/manuscripts/the_berne_manuscript/*, *http://stairsociety.org/resources/manuscripts/the_ayr_manuscript/* and *https://iiif.lib.harvard.edu/manifests/view/drs:466199984$1i* (all last accessed 15 July 2022). Note that at the time of writing, the version of the Ayr MS that appears on the Stair Society website does not display folios 52v–53r; where one would expect to find ff. 52v–53r, one in fact finds a duplicated version of ff. 54v–55r. I am very grateful to Simon Johnson of the National Records of Scotland for his help in locating alternative images of the relevant folios, without which it would have been impossible to complete this article. Editions of the text of the *Leges quatuor burgorum/Leges burgorum Scocie* can be found in T Thomson and C Innes (eds), *The Acts of the Parliaments of Scotland* [*APS*], vol i *A.D. MCXXIV–A.D. MCCCCXXIII* (1844) (hereafter *APS*, i) 327–356 and in C Innes (ed), *Ancient Laws and Customs of the Burghs of Scotland Vol I AD 1124–1424* (1868) 3–58. A satisfactory modern edition has yet to be produced. For modern studies of the *Leges burgorum Scocie*, see H L MacQueen and W J Windram, 'Laws and Courts in the Burghs' in M Lynch, M Spearman and G Stell (eds), *The Scottish Medieval Town* (1988) 208–227; A Taylor, *The Shape of the State in Medieval Scotland 1124–1290* (2016) 260; see also the discussion in J Kopaczyk, *The Legal Language of Scottish Burghs: Standardisation and Lexical Bundles 1380–1560* (2013) 123–126.

3 See NRS Ref PA5/2 f. 153v; Taylor, *Laws of Medieval Scotland* (n 2) 48; the date of the Ayr MS is discussed in Taylor, *Laws of Medieval Scotland* (n 2) 39–41. Taylor points out that Ayr MS was "orginally made out of two separate units", the larger of which was "a coherent volume" that may be dateable to 1323–1329, albeit that the *terminus ante quem* of 1329 is less secure than the *terminus post quem* of 1323. The text known as the *capitula legis burgorum* is to be found in the volume and may possibly be dateable to 1323–1329.

4 See NLS MS 21246 f. 153v; Taylor, *Laws of Medieval Scotland* (n 2) 59; the date of this section

have owed something – or nothing, or a great deal, it is impossible to know for certain – to lost texts of burgh laws once contained in two rolls in the Scottish royal treasury in Edinburgh Castle in 1292. The rolls were labelled "*de legibus assisis regni Scocie et de legibus et consuetudinibus Burgorum Scocie et de quibusdam statutis editis per reges Scocie*" (i.e. concerning the laws and assizes of the kingdom of Scotland and concerning the laws and customs of the burghs of Scotland and concerning certain statutes brought forth by the kings of Scotland).[5] Of course, anyone assuming that the court of the burgh of Aberdeen must have had the text attested in the Ayr MS and the Bute MS in mind when it referred to the *leges burgorum Scocie* might pause to reflect on the fact that the earliest witness to that text is labelled rather differently. The Berne MS, dateable to 1267–1272, does *not* refer to it as the *leges burgorum Scocie* or as the *leges et consuetudines burgorum Scocie*; rather, it refers to it as the "*Leges et consuetudines quatuor burgorum scilicet Edinburg Rokisburg Berewic Striueling constitute per dominum DD* [i.e. David] *regem Scocie*" (i.e. the laws and customs of the four burghs, that is to say Edinburgh, Roxburgh, Berwick [and] Stirling, made by David, the lord king of Scots).[6] This title continued to be used in the fourteenth century; the Harvard MS, which can probably be dated to the closing years of the century, refers to the text as follows: "*Iste sunt leges et consuetudines quatuor burgorum Scocie videlicet Berwyk Roxburgh Edynburgh et Strivelyne facte et confirmate per recolendissime memorie dominum regem David primum ipsius nominis Scocie*" (i.e. these are the laws and customs of the four burghs, that is to say Berwick, Roxburgh, Edinburgh and Stirling, made and confirmed by the lord king David of Scotland, first of his name,

of the Bute MS is discussed in Taylor, *Laws of Medieval Scotland* (n 2) 49–52. Only the title is in Latin; the rest of the text is in Scots – see Taylor, *Laws of Medieval Scotland* (n 2) 59. At present, it is difficult to be certain whether the witness to the text found in the Bute MS or that found in the Harvard MS is older; as is noted in Taylor, 'Introduction' (n 2) both manuscripts have a *terminus post quem* of 1389. On the (generally spurious) attribution of medieval Scottish legal texts to David I, see, for example, A Taylor, 'The Assizes of David, King of Scots, 1124–1153' (2012) 91 *Scottish Historical Review* 197–238 at 225–235; H L MacQueen, *Common Law and Feudal Society: Classic Edition* (2016) 86–89; H L MacQueen, '*Regiam Majestatem*, Scots Law, and National Identity' (1995) 74 *Scottish Historical Review* 1–25 at 7–8. Taylor cautions against taking the attribution of the *Leges quatuor burgorum* to David I at face value; see Taylor, *Shape of the State* (n 2) 260.

5 *APS*, i (n 2) 114–115, discussed in the MacQueen and Windram, 'Laws and Courts in the Burghs' (n 2) 213. For a discussion of the archive preserved in the Scottish royal treasury at this time, see Taylor, *Shape of the State* (n 2) 399–417.

6 See NRS Ref PA5/1 f. 62r; Taylor, *Laws of Medieval Scotland* (n 2) 37; the date of the Berne MS is discussed in Taylor, *Laws of Medieval Scotland* (n 2) 33–34.

of most celebrated memory).[7] In addition to this point about the labelling of the text, over twenty years ago, MacQueen and Windram demonstrated that there was a distinction between the laws of the burghs of Scotland as they were understood and applied by medieval Scots at any given time and the provisions found in the surviving text known as the *Leges burgorum Scocie*.[8] As they pointed out, "[p]resent knowledge does not allow us to date many of the laws, whether from the point of view of establishing their introduction or their obsolescence".[9] They argued convincingly that more secure evidence for what constituted the laws of the burghs of the realm at any particular period is to be found in other sources that can be securely dated, such as royal charters granting privileges to particular towns and indeed the court records of 1317 mentioned above.[10]

Nevertheless, it remains possible that the burgh court of Aberdeen did have in mind a version of the text witnessed in the Berne MS, the Ayr MS, the Bute MS and the Harvard MS when it referred to the *leges burgorum Scocie* in 1317. The first aim of this paper is to consider this possibility.[11] It will do so by comparing the references to the *leges burgorum Scocie* in the Aberdeen court records of 1317 with the textual *Leges burgorum Scocie*, as attested in the thirteenth and fourteenth century witnesses thereto found in the Berne MS, the Ayr MS, the Bute MS and the Harvard MS.[12] It will be argued that there is evidently a link between the *leges burgorum Scocie* referenced in the roll of the Aberdeen burgh courts of 1317, on the one hand, and the text of burgh laws to be found in the Berne MS, the Ayr MS, the Bute MS and the Harvard MS, on the other.[13] However, it will also be argued that the nature of that link requires – and merits – further exploration. To explain, the *leges burgorum Scocie* referenced in Aberdeen in 1317 were used to articulate the correct procedure for transferring lands within a

7 See Harvard Law Library, MS 164 f. 63r. On the date of the Harvard MS, see Taylor, 'Introduction' (n 2); the *terminus post quem* of the manuscript is 1389 (see Harvard Law Library, MS 164 f. 74v).
8 MacQueen and Windram, 'Laws and Courts in the Burghs' (n 2).
9 MacQueen and Windram, 'Laws and Courts in the Burghs' (n 2) 222.
10 MacQueen and Windram, 'Laws and Courts in the Burghs' (n 2) for example at 211.
11 MacQueen and Windram, 'Laws and Courts in the Burghs' (n 2) considers the 1317 court records at 216 and 218, but they do not directly discuss what the specific references to *leges burgorum Scocie* in the records might have meant in Aberdeen in 1317.
12 It is important to emphasise that no attempt has been made here to consider later manuscript witnesses to the *Leges Burgorum*, and that a satisfactory modern edition of the text has yet to be produced.
13 A similar point is made about the laws of the burghs of Scotland more generally and the texts of the *Leges burgorum Scocie* in MacQueen and Windram, 'Laws and Courts in the Burghs' (n 2) for example at 216 and 221.

burgh. The procedures attested in the court roll are similar in many regards to the procedures outlined in the texts of the *Leges burgorum Scocie*, and indeed in another contemporary source, the so-called Ayr Miscellany[14]; but they are also quite different in some important respects. In other words, the procedures had some things in common, but not everything. Nevertheless, both proclaimed themselves to be the procedures laid down in the commonly applicable laws of the burghs of Scotland.

Explaining this phenomenon will be the second aim of this chapter. It will be suggested that both the *leges burgorum Scocie* as they were understood in the courts of Aberdeen and also the texts labelled the *Leges burgorum Scocie* are best viewed as witnesses of a common law of the burghs of Scotland that fundamentally existed elsewhere – and not in some official text held in the royal treasury in Edinburgh. The argument will be that the common laws of the burghs of Scotland in a real sense existed in the minds of a small group of royal administrators and clerks, headed up by a royal official known as the chamberlain, who supervised the administration of justice within the burghs by proceeding round the country on a progress known as an "ayre".[15] If correct, this way of thinking about what was meant by the common *leges burgorum Scocie* may shed light on the nature of the common law of the medieval Scottish realm more generally. The question of whether or not there really was a medieval Scottish common law, in the sense of a law commonly applicable to all subjects of the king, has attracted considerable discussion of late.[16] It is hoped that this chapter will provide a fresh perspective on how the evidence of the burgh laws might, in time, contribute to the discourse.

These last points explain the link between this chapter and the chapter of Miriam Tveit in the present volume.[17] Prima facie, there are curious

14 See Taylor, *Laws of Medieval Scotland* (n 2) 445–481, 265–280. I am grateful to Professor Alice Taylor for drawing the importance of this source to my attention.

15 On the chamberlain and his ayre, see Taylor, *Shape of the State* (n 2) 244–262.

16 For secondary literature on the nature of the medieval Scottish common law, see MacQueen, *Common Law and Feudal Society* (n 4); Taylor, *Shape of the State* (n 2) particularly at 114–75, 265–348; D Carpenter, 'Scottish Royal Government in the Thirteenth Century from an English Perspective' in M Hammond (ed), *New Perspectives on Medieval Scotland, 1093–1286* (2013) 117–159; for introductions to the topic, see A R C Simpson and A L M Wilson, *Scottish Legal History Volume One: 1000–1707* (2017) 1–66; A R C Simpson, 'The Scottish Common Law: Origins and Development, c. 1124–c. 1500' in H Pihlajamäki, M D Dubber and M Godfrey (eds), *The Oxford Handbook of European Legal History* (2018) 450–473.

17 See M Tveit, 'Urban Legal Procedure in Fourteenth Century Norway' (above 155–180). See also M Tveit, 'Urban law in Norwegian market towns' in E Frankot and J Armstrong (eds), *Cultures of Law in Urban Northern Europe: Scotland and its Neighbours c. 1350–c. 1650* (2021) 105–122.

parallels between the *Leges burgorum Scocie* and the Norwegian Code of the Towns. Both texts purported to express laws commonly applicable to all burghs throughout particular territorial realms but both also seem to have owed much to earlier texts that were conceptualised as having a more limited scope, as the laws of particular towns. So, the surviving text of the *Leges burgorum Scocie* owed much to the *Leges quatuor burgorum* apparently applicable in Edinburgh, Roxburgh, Berwick and Stirling, whilst the Norwegian Code of the Towns owed much to the *Bærkoyar rettr* apparently applicable in Niðaros. Norwegian historians have explained when and why this development happened in Norway, with reference to the efforts of Magnus VI as a lawmaker. The explanation for why an apparently similar development occurred in Scotland must await further study. Yet Tveit also demonstrates that Norwegian historians are interested in the question of how the Code of the Towns came to be applied and followed in practice across Norwegian urban centres. It is just possible that the attempt to explain how legal practice in Scotland – or at least in Aberdeen – came to be linked with the ideas found in the textual *Leges burgorum Scocie* may shed some light on this discussion. The point will be considered in more detail in the conclusion.

B: BURGHS, BURGESSES AND THEIR COURTS

Before considering the references to the *leges burgorum Scocie* in the court records of the burgh of Aberdeen, it is worth explaining what is meant by certain terms such as burghs and burgesses, and something should be said about their courts generally. Some brief remarks will then be made about the nature of the surviving evidence of the work of the burgh courts of Aberdeen in 1317. The evidence to be surveyed here will also serve to introduce the idea that there is some sort of link between the provisions of the textual *Leges burgorum Scocie*, on the one hand, and the customs actually observed in the burgh courts of Aberdeen in 1317, on the other.

A burgh was essentially a town that had received a range of privileges from the king of Scots, including trading and jurisdictional privileges.[18] The merchants and craftsmen who held and exercised those privileges were known as the "burgesses". Those burgesses were entitled to admit others to

18 For discussion, see W C Dickinson, *Early Records of the Burgh of Aberdeen 1317, 1398–1407* (1957) particularly at xxiv–xl; MacQueen and Windram, 'Laws and Courts in the Burghs' (n 2) 208–209.

their privileged community.[19] They elected from amongst themselves the town councillors and the officers who governed the burgh. The most important burgh officers were the bailies and the alderman, or provost.[20]

Amongst the burgh's jurisdictional privileges was the right to hold courts.[21] Croft Dickinson emphasises the centrality of the burgh courts to the community of the burgh as follows[22]:

> This court . . . is of the very essence of the burgh. The burgh, created by "act" of the king, is embodied in its court; and the "head court" of the burgh, the assembly of all the burgesses, declares the burgh's "customs" which are agreed by all and to which all are subject . . . So, just as the court of the baron bound together the lands of the barony, or the court of the sheriff bound together the lands of the sheriffdom, in a like way the court of the burgh bound together the burgesses, the men of the "lands" of the burgh.

Scottish medieval burghs did not simply operate one court; there were, in fact, several burgh *courts*. The passage just quoted from Croft Dickinson mentions the head court of the burgh, the *curia capitalis*. This is attested in the textual *Leges quatuor burgorum* and the *Leges bugorum Scocie*; one chapter made reference variously to the "*placita principalia*" (in the Berne MS and the Harvard MS), the "*placita capitalia*" (in the Ayr MS) and the "principale mutys" (in the Bute MS) that took place each year, one after Michealmas, one after Christmas and one after Pasch. All burgesses were required to attend these head courts unless they had some lawful excuse; and those who failed to attend had to pay fines, which varied depending on whether they lived within the burgh (four pence) or outwith the burgh (eight shillings).[23] The fragmentary evidence of the Aberdeen burgh court records of 1317 (which only covers the months August, September and October of that year) reveals that a *curia capitalis* was indeed held on the Monday immediately after Michaelmas; and the names of those who remained outwith the burgh were duly listed, presumably with a view to their being

19 Dickinson, *Early Records* (n 18) xxiv–xl, lii–liii.

20 Dickinson, *Early Records* (n 18) lxxvii–xc.

21 See Dickinson, *Early Records* (n 18) cix–cxl; MacQueen and Windram, 'Laws and Courts' (n 2); see also the brief discussion in Simpson and Armstrong, 'The Roll of the Burgh Courts of Aberdeen' (n 1) 63–66.

22 Dickinson, *Early Records* (n 18) xl.

23 NRS PA5/1 f. 63r (c. 33 in the numbering given in Taylor, *Laws of Medieval Scotland* (n 2) 37–38, which is adopted hereafter – the chapters are not numbered in the manuscript); NRS PA5/2 ff. 56v–57r (c. 40); NLS MS 21246 f. 158v (c. 56); Harvard Law Library, MS 164 ff. 66r–66v (c. 43); *APS*, i (n 2) 340; Innes, *Ancient Laws and Customs* (n 2) 19; see also Dickinson, *Early Records* (n 18) cxvii–cxviii.

fined.[24] In addition to the head courts there were other burgh courts that sat throughout the year; according to one text in the *Leges burgorum Scocie*, courts were supposed to be held to deal with matters concerned both with lands and also with moveable property *a quindenda in quindendam* – which meant, in practice, once a fortnight. The judges presiding in these courts were not permitted to delay giving justice to one who sought it beyond the fifteen day period unless there was "debility" of court or necessary "counsel" was lacking.[25] The court records from Aberdeen in 1317 indicate that this practice of holding fortnightly courts was broadly followed in Aberdeen[26] – and on one occasion, the bailies presiding over the court deferred judgment on a particular matter until the next "quindene" – i.e. for a fortnight – "*propter debilitatem curie*".[27]

One other court is mentioned in the court records of 1317 – the chamberlain's court.[28] The chamberlain was a royal officer who had a range of responsibilities; one of their roles was to oversee the administration of justice in the royal burghs, which they were supposed to do by progressing around the burghs on their ayre every year.[29] The work of the chamberlain is described in the near-contemporary text labelled *De articulis inquerendis in burgo in itinere camerarii secundum usum Scocie*.[30] It is preserved in the Ayr MS, which, as will be recalled, can be dated to 1323–1346; internal evidence reveals that the text itself – at least, in the form in which it survives – was composed after 1314.[31] It will be argued that the role of the chamberlain and their clerks in maintaining a common law of the burghs in Scotland may

24 Simpson and Armstrong, 'The Roll of the Burgh Courts of Aberdeen' (n 1) 86–93.

25 Dickinson, *Early Records* (n 18) cxx–cxxi; MacQueen, *Common Law and Feudal Society* (n 4) 79–80; NRS PA5/1 f. 63v (c. 40); NRS PA5/2 f. 58r (c. 47); NLS MS 21246 f. 158v (c. 59); Harvard Law Library, MS 164 f. 66v (c. 50); *APS*, i (n 2) 342; Innes, *Ancient Laws and Customs* (n 2) 28.

26 Simpson and Armstrong, 'The Roll of the Burgh Courts of Aberdeen' (n 1) 70–93; Dickinson, *Early Records* (n 18) cxx–cxxi.

27 Simpson and Armstrong, 'The Roll of the Burgh Courts of Aberdeen' (n 1) 82–83. On debility of court, see Dickinson, *Early Records* (n 18) cxxii. There were additional sittings of *curiae* in Aberdeen too. Perhaps this was because there was too much business to be dealt with by the fortnightly meetings of the burgh *curia*; Croft Dickinson certainly thought that the later distinction between the *curia legalis tenta per ballivos* and the *curia tenta per ballivos* owed its origins to this issue, with the *curia legalis* being the fortnightly court referred to in the text of the *Leges burgorum Scocie*, and the *curia tenta per ballivos* being additional courts set up to deal with the pressure of business. For these points, see Simpson and Armstrong, 'The Roll of the Burgh Courts of Aberdeen' (n 1) 92–93; Dickinson, *Early Records* (n 18) cxxi.

28 Simpson and Armstrong, 'The Roll of the Burgh Courts of Aberdeen' (n 1) 84–87.

29 On the chamberlain and his role, see Taylor, *Shape of the State* (n 2) 259–262.

30 *APS* (n 2) i.680–3; see PA5/2 ff. 15v–18v; see also Dickinson, *Early Records* (n 18) cxvi n 5.

31 For the text and its date, see Taylor, *Shape of the State* (n 2) 259–260.

have been significant; but this point is best considered later in the present chapter.

The fact that a senior royal officer supervised the administration of justice in the burgh courts is a reminder of the fact that those courts were ultimately answerable to the king. Croft Dickinson emphasised that the courts were royal courts; indeed, the officers who were appointed to preside over them were the king's officers, a point mentioned in a document sewn into the court records of Aberdeen in 1317, which was addressed from the king "*prepositis et ballivis burgi de Abirden, fidelibus suis*".[32] Different titles are given to these officers at different points, including *ballivi* and *prepositi*; in the late-thirteenth century at least the terms were probably still synonymous.[33] While these individuals were royal servants they were chosen by elections from amongst the burgesses at one of the head courts, a process attested in the textual *Leges burgorum Scocie*.[34] There also seems to have been a recognised head of the community in Aberdeen by 1281 – the "*aldirmannus*" or alderman; later this figure would also be known as the *prepositus*.[35]

If the *prepositi* and the *ballivi* of Aberdeen and other burghs in Scotland had to answer for their activities in administering justice to the chamberlain, they were also answerable to the royal administration in another way. The document mentioned above that was sewn into the court records of Aberdeen in 1317 was a brieve, a standardised royal writ directing the burgh officers to do justice in a particular case.[36] In this instance, the brieve was a brieve of right, which instructed the officers of the town to determine whether or not the purchasers of the brieve were being unjustly deforced of lands within the burgh; the officers were to do right to the parties according to their findings.[37] While the evidence is limited, the court records of 1317 do reveal that the burgesses and those who pleaded in the burgh courts had

32 See Dickinson, *Early Records* (n 18) lxxxi–lxxxii; Simpson and Armstrong, 'The Roll of the Burgh Courts of Aberdeen' (n 1) 67, 78–79.

33 See the discussion in Simpson and Armstrong, 'The Roll of the Burgh Courts of Aberdeen' (n 1) 67 n 56, considering the earlier views of Croft Dickinson on the subject, as expressed in Dickinson, *Early Records* (n 18) cii n 11 and cxv.

34 Dickinson, *Early Records* (n 18) lxxx; see NRS Ref PA5/2 f. 62r (c. 72); NLS MS 21246 ff. 160r–160v (c. 79); Harvard Law Library, MS 164 ff. 68v–69r (c. 74); Innes, *Ancient Laws and Customs* (n 2) 34–35; *APS*, i (n 2) 347.

35 Dickinson, *Early Records* (n 18) cii–ciii n 11.

36 Simpson and Armstrong, 'The Roll of the Burgh Courts of Aberdeen' (n 1) 78–79; on brieves, see MacQueen, *Common Law and Feudal Society* (n 4) 105–135; several of MacQueen's central arguments – at least as regards the state of the law in the thirteenth century – are challenged by Taylor in her study of the brieves; see Taylor, *Shape of the State* (n 2) 266–348.

37 On the brieve of right, see the (differing) analyses in MacQueen, *Common Law and Feudal Society* (n 4) 188–214 and Taylor, *Shape of the State* (n 2) 315–318.

some familiarity with the brieves more generally. There is reference to a brieve of attorney at one point[38]; at another, as MacQueen has discussed in more detail, there is a reference to a technical rule of pleading to the effect that a man should not have to answer for his heritage unless he was brought into court by means of "a letter [i.e. brieve] of the chapel of the lord king".[39] Although no reference was made in the court records to the textual *Leges burgorum Scocie* (or the *Leges quatuor burgorum*), it has been pointed out in the past that here the litigant was relying on a rule also attested in these texts.[40] In essence, the rule was that if a man was challenged in respect of his lands or tenements within a burgh, then he did not have to answer the claim without the king's letters (i.e. without a brieve) unless he freely wished it.[41] The intriguing fact that those who pleaded in the burgh courts of Aberdeen were familiar with such a technical rule of pleading, which is also attested in the *Leges quatuor burgorum* and the *Leges burgorum Scocie*, will be considered in more detail shortly. For now, what matters is to emphasise the inter-connectedness of the king's justice and the justice administered in the burgh courts – a point forcefully made by MacQueen and Windram.[42]

In the course of explaining what was meant by terms like burgh, burgesses and burgh courts in Scotland during the early-fourteenth century, it has been seen that there were several links between the customs observed in the burgh courts of Aberdeen in 1317, on the one hand, and the provisions of the textual *Leges burgorum Scocie*. This serves to contextualise the explicit references to the "*leges burgorum Scocie*" in the records of the burgh courts that survive from 1317. Before considering those references, it is worth saying something about the court records themselves. The records survive in a single parchment roll of four membranes sewn together, which is preserved in Aberdeen City and Aberdeenshire Archives.[43] The roll seems

38 Simpson and Armstrong, 'The Roll of the Burgh Courts of Aberdeen' (n 1) 74–75.

39 Simpson and Armstrong, 'The Roll of the Burgh Courts of Aberdeen' (n 1) 76–77; MacQueen, *Common Law and Feudal Society* (n 4) 105–106, 189 and 197.

40 MacQueen, *Common Law and Feudal Society* (n 4) 105–106, 189 and 197.

41 MacQueen, *Common Law and Feudal Society* (n 4) 105; NRS Ref PA5/1 f. 63v (c. 36); NRS Ref PA5/2 f. 57v (c. 43); NLS MS 21246 f. 156r (c. 19); Harvard Law Library, MS 164 f. 66r (c. 46); Innes, *Ancient Laws and Customs* (n 2) 21; *APS*, i (n 2) 341.

42 MacQueen and Windram, 'Laws and Courts in the Burghs' (n 2).

43 ACA/5/6; for a description of the roll, see Dickinson, *Early Records* (n 18) vii. The roll was transcribed by Dr Margaret Moore and published by Professor William Croft Dickinson in 1957 in his edition of the early burgh records of Aberdeen (see Dickinson, *Early Records* (n 18) ix). Together with Dr Jackson Armstrong, I subsequently translated that transcription and it is that transcription and translation that is used here (Simpson and Armstrong, 'The Roll of the Burgh Courts of Aberdeen' (n 1) 70–93). The Dr Moore's transcription has not been checked against the original (which seems in places to have deteriorated since she worked on it); however, Dr

to be a selective record of proceedings before the burgh courts of Aberdeen; while it discusses some of the matters discussed in the *curia capitalis* of October 1317 and lists those who were absent from the head court, it does not record the election of the bailies. It is primarily concerned with disputes over lands within the burgh and other matters,[44] including pleas of wrang and unlaw.[45] While the record is selective, and while it only covers the period August to October 1317, it seems to be the only surviving example of a burgh court roll from the fourteenth century.[46] It therefore provides important – albeit limited – evidence concerning what the term *leges burgorum Scocie* was understood to mean in the practice of one Scottish burgh. It is to this evidence that this essay will now turn, bearing in mind the point that has already been established here. That is to say, there was evidently *some* link between the customs applied in the burgh of Aberdeen, on the one hand, and the textual *Leges quatuor burgorum* and the *Leges burgorum Scocie* considered above. Yet the precise nature of that link is not yet clear.

C: THE *LEGES BURGORUM SCOCIE* IN THE ROLL OF THE ABERDEEN BURGH COURTS (1317)

The references to the *leges burogum Scocie* in the roll of the burgh courts of Aberdeen can be found in a record of proceedings that had commenced in 1316 and they were concluded on or shortly before 8 August 1317.[47] It is helpful to provide some background information about those proceedings before considering their reliance on the laws of the burghs. The proceedings were brought by a seventeen-year-old woman named Ada. She had been born in 1299 into an influential Aberdonian family.[48] Her maternal grandfather, Malcolm of Balgownie, had held the office of alderman for a time during the 1280s. Malcolm had one son, Duncan, and also a daughter who married a man named Roger of Hauwood; they were Ada's parents.[49]

Armstrong and I have, at the time of writing, secured funding to have the roll digitised and it is hoped that it will shortly be made available publicly online. In this regard, the help of Phil Astley, the City Archivist, is gratefully acknowledged.

44 These matters are discussed in Simpson and Armstrong, 'The Roll of the Burgh Courts of Aberdeen' (n 1) 65–66.

45 See H L MacQueen, 'Some Notes on Wrang and Unlaw' in H L MacQueen (ed), *Stair Society Miscellany Five by Various Authors*, Stair Society vol 52 (2006) 13–26.

46 This point is discussed in more detail in Simpson and Armstrong, 'The Roll of the Burgh Courts of Aberdeen' (n 1) 57–58.

47 Simpson and Armstrong, 'The Roll of the Burgh Courts of Aberdeen' (n 1) 70–77.

48 Simpson and Armstrong, 'The Roll of the Burgh Courts of Aberdeen' (n 1) 74–75.

49 Simpson and Armstrong, 'The Roll of the Burgh Courts of Aberdeen' (n 1) 70–73; for Malcolm

Ada was personally present in court, as was the other party to the proceedings, of whom more will be said shortly. Ada began by explaining that her family had fallen on difficult times. Her father, Roger, had borrowed money from one Roginald of Buchan. Roger's father-in-law, Malcolm of Balgownie, had stood as security or "pledge" that Roginald would receive repayment of the debt in full. In order to underwrite the whole transaction, Malcolm transferred a property of his to Roginald, to be held by Roginald in security until the debt was repaid. The property – a tenement – was in the Gallowgate, an area on the northern side of the burgh. Once the debt was repaid, the creditor, Roginald, would have been required to return it to Malcolm of Balgownie.[50] This much of the legal position of the parties is clear from the 1317 court roll itself.[51] The texts of the *Leges burgorum Scocie* also attest to a procedure to be used for lands set "*in vadimonio*", whereby an individual might transfer lands within the burgh to another in security for a debt. If there was no fixed term to the arrangement, then the lands could be redeemed by the debtor at any point. If there was a fixed term, and that term expired without satisfaction of the debt, then after a year – i.e. after three head courts of the burgh had met – the lands could be sold for satisfaction of the debt, with any surplus from the sale being returned to the debtor.[52] However, it is impossible to know whether or not the court's understanding of the law governing the use of land in security for debt was informed by the

of Balgownie (sometimes spelt Polgoueny, or in some other variant way) see C Innes (ed), *Registrum Episcopatus Aberdonensis: Ecclesie Cathedralis Aberdonensis Regesta Que Extant in Unum Collecta*, Spalding Club vols 13–14 (1845) vol 13, 35, 37; vol 14, 279, 281; A F Munro, *Memorials of the Aldermen, Provosts, and Lord Provosts of Aberdeen 1272*–1893 (1897) 2–3; see also A Beam, D Broun, J Bradley, D Carpenter, J R Davies, K Dutton, N Evans, M Hammond, R Ó Maolalaigh, M Pasin, A Smith, *The People of Medieval Scotland 1093–1371*, 1st edn *1093–1286* (2010); 2nd edn *1093–1314* with S Ambler, A Giacometti, B Hartland, and K J Stringer (2012); 3rd edn including mapping and SNA functionality, with C Jackson and N Jakeman (2016); 4th edn *1093–1371*, with G Ferraro, E Hall and A Taylor (2019): available at *http://www.poms.ac.uk/* [*PoMS*] (last accessed 15 July 2022), 'Malcolm of Balgownie, Burgess of Aberdeen', *PoMS* no 3199, available at *https://www.poms.ac.uk/record/person/3199/* (last accessed 15 July 2022); *PoMS*, 'Malcolm De Pelgon, Alderman of Aberdeen', *PoMs* no 15265, available at *https://www.poms.ac.uk/record/person/15265/* (last accessed 15 July 2022). I am grateful to a member of the audience at a talk given on 20th November 2017 to celebrate the 700th anniversary of the creation of the roll of the burgh courts who first pointed out to me the link between "Polgoueny" and "Balgownie". It seems likely that the "Duncan Mersar" mentioned alongside Malcolm of Balgownie in Innes, *Registrum Episcopatus Aberdonensis* at 35–36 can be identified with his son Duncan mentioned in the court roll of 1317.

50 Simpson and Armstrong, 'Roll of the Burgh Courts of Aberdeen' (n 1) 70–71.

51 Simpson and Armstrong, 'Roll of the Burgh Courts of Aberdeen' (n 1) 70–77.

52 NRS Ref PA5/2 f. 63v (c. 81); NLS MS 21246 f. 156v (c.22); Harvard Law Library, MS 164 f. 69v (c. 52); *APS*, i (n 2) 349; Innes, *Ancient Laws and Customs* (n 2) 39. The reading of the Scots text given by Innes and in *APS* makes less apparent sense than the reading preserved in the Bute MS.

texts of the burgh laws; all that can be said is that the rules observed in the burgh seem to have been consistent with the provisions found in those texts.

It seems that Ada's father never managed to repay his debt and her grandfather, Malcolm, died waiting for him to do so; and so Roginald retained the tenement. Malcolm's son, Duncan, together with his impecunious brother-in-law Roger of Hauwood and his young niece, Ada, left Aberdeen.[53] Whether this relocation was something to do with the events that followed is unclear. Those familiar with the early 1300s will be conscious that the period was one of great political turbulence. A succession crisis over the Scottish throne had invited English interference and, ultimately, invasion. This was combined with what was effectively a civil war amongst different claimants to the throne and their supporters. One of those claimants is remembered to history as Robert the Bruce; he was crowned as King Robert I in 1306. Some of his most powerful rivals were the Comyn earls of Buchan, immediately to the north of Aberdeen. Robert I defeated the Comyns in battle in 1308 and after that many Comyn lands were forfeited.[54]

This probably explains what happened next. Roginald of Buchan, still holding the tenement in the Gallowgate in security for the debt owed to him, was forfeited for his rebellion against Robert I – perhaps he had been an adherent of the Comyns. The tenement was then re-granted by the king to one of his own adherents, a clergyman called William of Lindsay. Of course, William of Lindsay only held the lands on the basis that Roginald of Buchan had held them – i.e. effectively in security for the debt owed to him by Roger of Hauwood. The difficulty was that Roginald of Buchan then did what many others did once it was clear that Robert I was winning the war. Roginald entered into the peace of Robert I and was restored to his former lands and privileges[55]; Robert I was keen to bring his former enemies back into the fold, so to speak.[56] This policy caused legal difficulties, as some of Robert I's loyal adherents now found themselves facing challenges to their land holdings from his former enemies.[57] In this instance, William of Lindsay decided

53 Simpson and Armstrong, 'Roll of the Burgh Courts of Aberdeen' (n 1) 70–73.

54 For introductions to the complex history of the period, see M Brown, *The Wars of Scotland 1214–1371* (2004) 155–231; see also G W S Barrow, *Robert Bruce*, 4th edn (2005). For the defeat of the Comyns in 1308, and forfeitures at this time, see Brown, *Wars of Scotland* 204; Barrow, *Robert Bruce* 227–228, 351–380 (particularly at 353–354, 362–363); MacQueen, *Common Law and Feudal Society* (n 4) 106–107.

55 Simpson and Armstrong, 'Roll of the Burgh Courts of Aberdeen' (n 1) 70–73.

56 See the discussion in Barrow, *Robert Bruce* (n 54) 351–380, 388–389.

57 See MacQueen, *Common Law and Feudal Society* (n 4) 106–107, 146–153, 177–178; for a comment, see also Taylor, *Shape of the State* (n 2) 346.

to pay the money owed to Roginald of Buchan; in exchange, Roginald conveyed the tenement to William of Lindsay. It seems that Roginald could only convey the tenement on the basis on which he had held it – i.e. in security for a debt owed to him. Consequently, if Malcolm of Balgownie's family were to be able to pay off the debt – now to William – then they would have been able to recover the property in question.[58]

Malcolm's son Duncan apparently showed no interest in recovering his father's land in the Gallowgate; but when he died his niece, Ada, hoped to bring the family's claim to the attention of the man now holding the tenement – William of Lindsay.[59] Something more now should be said about this individual. Lindsay was the son of Sir Alexander Lindsay, a knight from Ayrshire. The elder Lindsay had been a prominent Bruce supporter from the outset, having apparently been art and part in the murder of Robert's principal rival for the throne, the Red Comyn. One of Sir Alexander's younger sons, William, became a clergyman and was Rector of Ayr. Perhaps as early as October 1309, and certainly by 1313, he held the position of the king's chamberlain.[60] The chamberlain oversaw the collection of royal revenues, both from the burghs and from landward areas and, as was mentioned above, he also had responsibility for overseeing the governance of the burghs and the administration of justice there. It will be recalled that the chamberlain discharged these duties by travelling round the burghs on his "ayre".[61]

It follows that Ada was engaged in legal proceedings with the man who was, in a very real sense, trusted by the king to administer justice in the burghs across the kingdom. Yet it is probably wrong to characterise the proceedings as particularly adversarial. Ada was asserting her family's right against the man currently holding the tenement in the Gallowgate; but she did not have the funds required to pay off her father's debt. The 1317 roll states that William, moved by compassion on Ada's poverty, resolved to buy out her claim, and that Ada agreed to this. The transaction would

58 Simpson and Armstrong, 'Roll of the Burgh Courts of Aberdeen' (n 1) 70–73.

59 Simpson and Armstrong, 'Roll of the Burgh Courts of Aberdeen' (n 1) 70–73.

60 For these details, see D E R Watt, *A Biographical Dictionary of Scottish Graduates to AD 1410* (1977) 355–356; A A M Duncan (ed), *Regesta Regum Scottorum, vol v, The Acts of Robert I King of Scots 1306–1329* [*RRS*, v] (1988) [*RRS* v] 111, 206; Barrow, *Robert Bruce* (n 54) 204, 208, 240, 363; S Cameron, 'Lindsay family of Barnweill, Crawford, and Glenesk (per c. 1250–c.1400), nobility' (2004) *Oxford Dictionary of National Biography*, available at *https://www.oxforddnb.com/view/10.1093/ref:odnb/9780198614128.001.0001/odnb-9780198614128-e-54260* (last accessed 15 July 2022). See also PoMS, 'William Lindsay, Chamberlain', PoMS no 16466, available at *https://www.poms.ac.uk/record/person/16466/* (last accessed 15 July 2022).

61 On the chamberlain, see Taylor, *Shape of the State* (n 2) 259–262.

also have benefitted William by giving him virtually unchallengeable title.[62]

It was at this point that the clerk recording proceedings first made reference to *leges burgorum Scocie*. It had to be established that Ada was of sufficient age to transfer her claim to the lands in question. Accordingly, "good and sufficient . . . leading men" of the burgh community were appointed to form an assize to establish her true age.[63] Assizers were in principle supposed to decide such questions of fact with reference to their own knowledge,[64] and it seems that this was lacking, because the good and sufficient men had to ask an older woman – Ada's wet-nurse – to join their ranks. Duly assisted by someone who actually knew something about the date of Ada's birth, the assizers were able to swear that Ada had attained the age of fifteen on the feast day of St Martin 1314. Therefore, "*secundum leges burgorum Scocie, perfecte fuit etatis convencionandi contractus, inpignorandi, vendendi et alienandi terras et possessiones quascunque*" – i.e. "following the laws of the burghs of Scotland, she was of perfect age for the purposes of making contracts, pledging, selling and alienating lands and possessions whatsoever".[65] This is curious. As has been observed, there are many points of crossover between the customs observed in the burgh courts of Aberdeen and the textual *Leges burgorum Scocie*. One might therefore reasonably expect that this rule – which is attributed directly to the *leges burgorum Scocie* – would be attested in the text; but it would seem that it is not. Nothing has been found in the witnesses to the text considered here to indicate that there was a rule that the heiress of a burgess attained majority at fifteen. Nor has any such rule been found in the texts surveyed by Taylor in her *Laws of Medieval Scotland*,[66] or indeed in the edition of the earliest text of the early-fourteenth-century Scottish lawbook *Regiam Majestatem* that Davies and Taylor have recently published with the Stair Society.[67] The text of *Regiam* (as Davies and Taylor give it) is that heirs of burgesses "are said to have age when they know how to distinguish between coins

62 Simpson and Armstrong, 'Roll of the Burgh Courts of Aberdeen' (n 1) 72–73.

63 Simpson and Armstrong, 'Roll of the Burgh Courts of Aberdeen' (n 1) 72–75.

64 MacQueen, *Common Law and Feudal Society* (n 4) 79–80; 257.

65 Simpson and Armstrong, 'Roll of the Burgh Courts of Aberdeen' (n 1) 72–75.

66 Taylor, *Laws of Medieval Scotland* (n 2).

67 Davies with Taylor (eds), *Regiam Majestatem*. On the date and origins of *Regiam*, see A Taylor, 'What Does *Regiam maiestatem* Actually Say (and What Does it Mean)?' in W Eves, J Hudson, I Ivarsen and S B White (eds), *Common Law, Civil Law, Colonial Law: Essays in Comparative Legal History from the Twelfth to the Twentieth Centuries* (2021) 47–85.

and measure cloth and exercise their father's other business".[68] Casting the net slightly more widely, Bateson's edition of the English borough customs, which were printed by the Selden Society in 1904 and 1906, reveals that customs varied in the English boroughs as regards when the heir of a burgess reached majority.[69] In Shrewsbury, it was found in 1339–1340 that "whoever is of the age of fifteen, and knows how to measure yards of cloth and knows a good penny from a bad, is of age to give and alienate his land by his deed";[70] that this is close to the rule in *Regiam* is unsurprising, given the English origins of the passage in question.[71] Yet in other boroughs the age of majority seems to have been different.[72] Regardless, for present purposes what matters is that the rule attributed to the "laws of the burghs of Scotland" does not seem to be attested in the textual *Leges burgorum Scocie*.

Having established that Ada was indeed of age to transfer her claim in the lands to William of Lindsay *secundum leges burgorum Scocie* – whatever that meant – the clerk of the burgh court then noted that Ada had,

> offered the said land [for sale] in full court of the burgh of Aberdeen at three head courts of the burgh according to use and wont and through the laws of the burghs of Scotland [*rite et secundum leges burgorum Scocie*], to the closest of her kin of her blood, who might wish to buy the lands for the same, or for a similar, sum of money to pay off the debt for her.[73]

68 Davies with Taylor, *Regiam Majestatem* II c.69. Later manuscripts seem to have inserted a provision that one would be held to be of age if one met these criteria and one had reached the age of fourteen; see John Skene (ed), *Regiam Majestatem* . . . (Edinburgh 1609) 54–55, II.41.5; see also *APS*, i (n 2) 616, II.35; T M Cooper, *Regiam Majestatem and Quoniam Attachiamenta*, Stair Society vol 11 (1947) 151–152, II.41.5. It is worth noting that Davies with Taylor (eds), *Regiam Majestatem* II (c. 68) mention that the heir of a *sokeman* attained majority at fifteen. This is intriguing, because in England burgage tenure was classified as a form of soccage, at least at a later period, as was known in early modern Scotland. Consider John Skene, *De Verborum Significatione* 1597 s.v. 'SOKMANRIA' and Leslie Dodd (tr and ed), *Jus Feudale Tribus Libris Comprehensum by Thomas Craig of Riccarton Book I*, Stair Society vol 64 (2017) 293, I.11.19; see also J H Baker, *An Introduction to English Legal History*, 5th edn (2019) 245 and 266. This raises the intriguing possibility that someone clever who was present in the burgh court in Aberdeen classified Scottish burgage tenure as a species of soccage, and that *that* was why the age of majority was set at fifteen. This chapter is not going to venture down that particular rabbit hole, but perhaps the point should be investigated elsewhere; even if the inquiry were to be found to be illuminating, it would not affect the basic point made here about the nature of the link between the *leges burgorum Scocie* and the textual *Leges burgorum Scocie*.

69 Mary Bateson, *Borough Customs*, Selden Society vols 18, 21 (1904–1906) vol ii 157–160.

70 Bateson, *Borough Customs* (n 69) vol ii 158–159.

71 Davies with Taylor (eds), *Regiam Majestatem* II c.69; on the link with the English text *Glanvill*, see generally Taylor, 'What Does *Regiam maiestatem* Actually Say'.

72 Bateson, *Borough Customs* (n 69) vol ii 158–159.

73 Simpson and Armstrong, 'Roll of the Burgh Courts of Aberdeen' (n 1) 74–75.

On this occasion, the procedure attributed to the laws of the burghs of Scotland can be traced in the textual *Leges burgorum Scocie*.[74] The witnesses to the text considered here are essentially in agreement. It declared that if an individual was compelled by necessity to sell land that theyheld heritably within a burgh, then they had first to offer it for sale at three head courts of the burgh to their nearest heirs. If the heirs were willing to purchase the land – and therefore presumably alleviate whatever necessity the unfortunate individual faced – then they were also obliged to provide for their sustenance. They were required to feed them as well as they fed themselves and they were also to clothe them (the text even specified that the clothing should be grey or white). If the individual's heirs were unwilling or unable to purchase the lands after they had been offered the opportunity to do so at three head courts of the burgh, then the owner was entitled to sell them.[75] Evidently, this procedure had been observed in Ada's case. She had declared at three head courts of the burgh that she was going to sell her claim in respect of the lands to William of Lindsay, and that if any of her relatives wished to pay off the debt owed to him – and so redeem the lands in accordance with the law – then they should do so. In other words, the clerk of the court was recording that the procedure that was observed when Ada sold her claim to the chamberlain was entirely consistent with the standards laid down in the *leges burgorum Scocie*. Presumably the point was that the court had established that all preconditions for the transfer of Ada's claim to William of Lindsay had been met (i.e. she was of full age and her relatives had not asserted any claim to redeem the lands within the time permitted).

The roll of the burgh courts then proceeded to record the final stage in the transaction – the actual ceremony of transfer of the claim in respect of the lands from Ada to William of Lindsay. The procedure used was said to

74 See NRS Ref PA5/1 f. 63v (c. 35); NRS Ref PA5/2 f. 57r–57v (c. 42); NLS MS 21246 f. 155v–156r (c. 15); Harvard Law Library, MS 164 f. 66r (c.45); *APS*, i (n 2) 340–1; Innes, *Ancient Laws and Customs* (n 2) 20–21. The connection is discussed in P Chalmers, 'Remarks on the law of burghs concerning delivery of lands within burgh' found in J Stuart (ed), *The Miscellany of the Spalding Club Volume* 5, Spalding Club vol 23 (1852) 49–55; Chalmers's perceptive and illuminating remarks will be considered in more detail shortly. It is worth mentioning that Chalmers's work was very helpful to the present writer in reconstructing the details of the procedure.

75 NRS Ref PA5/1 f. 63v (c. 35); NRS Ref PA5/2 ff. 57r–57v (c. 42); NLS MS 21246 f. 155v–156r (c. 15); Harvard Law Library, MS 164 f. 66r (c. 45). For discussion, see also MacQueen and Windram, 'Laws and Courts in the Burghs' (n 2) 220; D B Smith, 'The *Retrait Lignager* in Scotland' (1924) 21 *Scottish Historical Review* 193–206 (who suggests, at 204–205, that the Scottish usages may have derived from the Continent rather than from England). See also Elizabeth Ewan, *Townlife in Fourteenth-Century Scotland* (1991) 94.

adhere to that laid down in the *"leges burgorum"*[76]; however, as Chalmers observed over 150 years ago, it does not seem that all elements of the procedure used can be found in the textual *Leges burgorum Scocie*.[77] Having established her right to transfer her claims to William, she asked the bailies to "read out her charter of infeudation" by which she had "sold the said the land and infeft the said lord William in it in his court".[78] The reference to the sale to William "in his court" ("*in curia sua*") may be significant; this will be discussed further shortly. The bailies agreed; but they did not simply declare William was now entitled to the lands. The bailies, the burgesses present, Ada and William all then left their meeting place[79] and from there they went to the lands in the Gallowgate. The clerk tells us that the bailie, Thomas, son of Roginald, received "the *denarius de intoll* and the *denarius de uttol* from both the parties, the buyer and the seller".[80] Bailie Thomas then gave "sasine" of the lands to William Lindsay.[81] To have received "sasine" of the lands was to have received possession of them from one entitled to give that possession – usually the feudal lord of the lands or, in a burgh, the bailies who represented the king as the burgh's ultimate feudal superior.[82] Most of these stages in the process of transfer were attested in the textual *Leges burgorum Scocie*, and also in another near-contemporary source now known as the Ayr Miscellany.[83] The *Leges burgorum Scocie* provided that a ceremony of conveyance was to be observed when land within a burgh was to be sold. First, the seller was required to stand inside the property at the outset, and the buyer was to stand outside it. Then the seller would leave the property and the buyer would enter it. This was all to be done in the presence of the *"prepositus"* (according to the Ayr MS and the Harvard MS) or the "aldyrman" (according to the Bute

76 The scribe said *"leges burgorum"* and not *"leges burgorum Scocie"*, but it is difficult to discern any real significance in the omission of the word *"Scocie"*.

77 Chalmers, 'Remarks' (n 74) 49.

78 Simpson and Armstrong, 'Roll of the Burgh Courts of Aberdeen' (n 1) 74–77.

79 This may have been the old burgh *tolloneum* – i.e. the place where the burgh tolls were collected; it is possible this was located in the Shiprow by the harbour, a short walk of a few minutes from the Gallowgate. On the early *tolloneum*, see E P Dennison, A T Simpson and G G Simpson, 'The Growth of Two Towns' in E P Dennison, D Ditchburn and M Lynch (eds), *Aberdeen Before 1800: A New History* (2002) 13–43 at 19; see also Dickinson, *Early Records* (n 18) cxxiv–cxxv.

80 Simpson and Armstrong, 'Roll of the Burgh Courts of Aberdeen' (n 1) 76–77.

81 Simpson and Armstrong, 'Roll of the Burgh Courts of Aberdeen' (n 1) 77.

82 See MacQueen, *Common Law and Feudal Society* (n 4) 140; see also A R C Simpson, 'Earth and Stone: History, Law and Land through the Lens of Sasine' in M M Combe, J Glass and A Tindley (eds), *Land Reform in Scotland: History, Law and Policy* (2020) 113–153, in particular at 114–126.

83 For the Ayr Miscellany, see Taylor, *Laws of Medieval Scotland* (n 2) 265–280, 445–481. I am grateful to Professor Taylor for pointing out the significance of the Ayr Miscellany to the discussion presented here.

MS). The seller was to give the *prepositus* a penny for exiting the lands, and the buyer was likewise to give the *prepositus* a penny for entering the lands.[84] Elsewhere these payments were also known as the *denarii de uttoll et intoll*, although only the *intoll* payment seems to have been observed after 1317, save in Aberdeen, where both pennies remained due when conveyances were made.[85] The first chapter of a text labelled as the Ayr Miscellany (the relevant section of which is actually attested in the Bute MS)[86] also made reference to the rule that the *purchaser* had to pay a penny for entry to burgh lands, but it said nothing about the seller having to do the same. However, this may simply have been because the text was to do with how one could prove purchase of lands within burgh. The rules were detailed and attributed to a law allegedly promulgated by David I in 1169 – there is something wrong with this attribution, because David I died in 1153.[87] Regardless, the text provided that no one could prove that they had sasine of lands acquired by purchase within a burgh except through an assize of twelve burgesses and a *prepositus*; and they could only declare that a party had acquired sasine of lands by purchase if one of three sets of criteria were satisfied. First, that "land was given in public at the three chief pleas and made evident to the kin and friends". Secondly, "that the entrant had sasine of the soil in the presence of the above twelve and the grieve [i.e. *prepositus*] and that he gave one penny for entry". Thirdly, "that he held sasine of the said land for one year and one day without challenge from any member of the [seller's] kin".[88] While the court roll did not specify that *twelve* burgesses had been present when Ada transferred her lands to William of Lindsay, and while the conveyance was made in the presence of someone described as a bailie, rather than a *prepositus*, the procedural requirements in the Ayr Miscellany (and indeed the textual *Leges burgorum Scocie*) seem otherwise to have been fully observed.

There was one final explicit reference to the *leges burgorum* in the roll of the burgh courts from 1317; again, it came in the course of the transaction between Ada and William of Lindsay. It was said that,

84 NRS PA5/2 f. 59r (c. 52); NLS MS 21246 f. 157r (c. 28); Harvard Law Library, MS 164 f. 67r (c. 55); *APS*, i (n 2) 342–343; Innes, *Ancient Laws and Customs* (n 2) 25.

85 See Kopacyck, *Legal Language* (n 2) 130–131; see also *Dictionaries of the Scots Language*, 'Uttoll', available at *https://dsl.ac.uk/entry/dost/outtoll* (last accessed 15 July 2022); Dictionaries of the Scots Language, 'intoll' *https://dsl.ac.uk/entry/dost/in_toll* (last accessed 15 July 2022).

86 See Taylor, *Laws of Medieval Scotland* (n 2) 446–447; the relevant section of the text in the Ayr MS is illegible, at least based on the current scans of the document.

87 See Taylor, *Laws of Medieval Scotland* (n 2) 446–447; Chalmers, 'Remarks' (n 74) 50.

88 Taylor, *Laws of Medieval Scotland* (n 2) 446–447. There were also rules to deal with the situation where the *prepositus* and the twelve burgesses who had originally witnessed the giving of sasine had died, but these need not be considered here.

> in the act of handing over the said sasine, the foresaid Ada delivered her completed charter of infeudation to the said lord William with her own hands . . . through that law of the burghs, through which it is said, delivery of lands in burghs ought to be made with charters and with acclamation (*"per illam legem burgorum per quam dicitur, cum cartis et clamore fiat tradicio terrarum in burgis"*).

It was pointed out long ago that the textual *Leges burgorum Scocie* contain no such provision, and this is confirmed by the survey of the witnesses to the text considered here.[89] At the same time, it was noted that texts were not comprehensive codes of what contemporaries called the *leges burgorum Scocie*[90]; and it was suggested that the rule that transfers had to be made *cum cartis et clamore* may ultimately have owed something to certain English and Norman customs regarding the giving of seisin in burgh in cases of necessity. According to those customs, a pre-requisite for the transfer was the *"clameur des ligagners"* – almost literally meaning a call upon the kindred, to be proclaimed at three head courts of the town – whereby they might have a chance to buy the lands on behalf of their indigent relative, at least keeping the property in the family.[91] If this is what was meant, then in one sense the textual *Leges burgorum Scocie* do attest to the basic idea that transfers of land in cases of necessity had to be made *cum clamore* – because they stated the rule that the proposed sale of the lands had to be advertised and proclaimed to the relatives of the landholder at three head courts of the burgh. Yet they do not link this with any notion that the transfer was to be made both *cum clamore* and *cum cartis*. Once again, a provision of the *leges burgorum Scocie* referenced in the burgh court of Aberdeen cannot be found in the textual *Leges burgorum Scocie*.

D: WHAT DID MEDIEVAL ABERDONIANS MEAN BY THE "*LEGES BURGORUM SCOCIE*?"

The evidence surveyed thus far shows that there was significant crossover between the customs and *leges burgorum Scocie* observed in the burgh

89 Chalmers, 'Remarks' 49.

90 Chalmers, 'Remarks' 49.

91 Chalmers, 'Remarks' 49–51. For a similar custom in Waterford (Ireland), dated to ca. 1300, see Bateson, *Borough Customs* (n 69) vol i, 276: *"D'autre part si homme ou femme promet doner ove lour frere ou ove lour seure de son heritage, e il ou ele entre en seysine par chele promesse, cele seisine ne vaut riens, si il ne fust feffé par chartre ou par vive voiz des veysyns. E si le tenant prent rente ou fee de cel feffement, le principal pust porter bref vers lui, come en noun de freche forche."*

courts of Aberdeen, on the one hand, and the textual *Leges burgorum Scocie* witnessed in the Berne MS, the Ayr MS and the Bute MS, on the other. The courts, the court officers, some of the court procedures and even some of the technical rules of pleading attested in the roll dated to 1317 can also be found in the manuscript witnesses to the *Leges burgorum Scocie*. That there was a link between the *leges burgorum Scocie* as they were conceptualised in the burgh courts of Aberdeen and the texts is beyond question. What is more difficult to establish is the nature of that link, because two of the three provisions attributed by a burgh court of Aberdeen to the *leges burgorum Scocie* cannot be traced in the textual *Leges burgorum Scocie*. The latter seem to make no mention of a rule that one had to be fifteen in order to make a transfer of burgh lands; and they also seem to make no mention of a rule that transfers of land in burghs had to be made *cum cartis et clamore*.

This suggests that when the burgh courts of Aberdeen made reference to the *leges burgorum Scocie*, they did not simply mean by this phrase the text witnessed in the Berne MS, the Ayr MS and the Bute MS. But what did they mean? One simple possibility cannot be excluded. Perhaps there was some lost version of the text of the *Leges burgorum Scocie* that contained both of the additional rules just mentioned; perhaps this was faithfully followed in Aberdeen. This reading of the evidence is possible, but of course it depends on an assumption that cannot be proven or disproven. Another reading of the evidence might proceed on the assumption that those in the burgh courts, and those who pleaded before them, had had some legal training, which was commonly available in medieval Scotland. Perhaps they had studied the texts of the *Leges burgorum Scocie*, or a version of the texts preserved at some central location, which was subsequently corrupted in our manuscript traditions. The problem is that there was no centralised system of legal education and training in medieval Scotland at that time.[92] Those who presided over the burgh courts in 1317 were, at base, merchant burgesses; evidence from a later period suggests that they had learned to operate the courts consistently by experience, by participating in its procedures during the course of their careers on the burgh council.[93] It is just

92 For discussion, see Simpson and Wilson, *Scottish Legal History* 56–59; see also MacQueen, *Common Law and Feudal Society* (n 4) 75–84.

93 See A R C Simpson, 'Men of law in the Aberdeen council register? A Preliminary Study, circa 1450–circa 1460' (2019) *Juridical Review* 136–159; see also A R C Simpson, 'Andrew Alanson: Man of law in the Aberdeen Council Register, c.1440–c.1475?' in E Frankot and J Armstrong (eds), *Cultures of Law in Urban Northern Europe: Scotland and its Neighbours c. 1350–c. 1650* (2021) 247–266.

conceivable that there may have been quasi-professional pleaders operating in the burgh courts of Aberdeen in 1317, and perhaps in burgh courts elsewhere in the realm; this possibility will be explored further elsewhere[94] but it is difficult to maintain any notion that they constituted some sort of nascent Scottish legal profession.

It remains possible that what the burgesses of Aberdeen meant by the phrase "*leges burgorum Scocie*" was some lost manuscript of burgh laws, perhaps kept in the town's *tolloneum*. However, this chapter will now explore an alternative possibility, which is based on the evidence that does survive. In essence, this is that the burgesses meant by the *leges burgorum Scocie* a standard that was *attested* in their practice and also in the texts of the *Leges burgorum Scocie*, but nevertheless *independent* of both. To explain this argument, it is necessary to consider again two pieces of evidence that were mentioned briefly above, which strongly indicate that someone with the power to impose common legal standards on the administration of justice within the burghs of Scotland had, in fact, just visited Aberdeen in October 1317 He was, of course, the chamberlain, William of Lindsay. As will be explained, the evidence suggests that his visit was not simply to finalise his private business with Ada. Rather, his visit was in an official capacity, with the purpose of conducting a chamberlain's ayre.

The first piece of evidence that suggests this was the case can be found in a curious detail in the brieve of right issued by Robert I to the *prepositi* of Aberdeen, which is still sewn into the surviving roll of the burgh courts.[95] The brieve purports to have been issued at Aberdeen on 28 July 1317, about ten days before Ada transferred her claim to William of Lindsay in one of the burgh courts. It carries the testing clause "*teste me ipso*" – a form indicating that the king himself had personally witnessed the giving of the brieve. This is puzzling because, as Duncan pointed out, Robert I was almost certainly in southern Scotland at this point.[96] Duncan argued that the brieve was probably issued using the *teste me ipso* clause in Aberdeen by a clerk holding the

94 This possibility was discussed in a paper entitled 'Changing cultures of law in the burgh records, ca. 1310–ca. 1460? Perspectives on the representative work of Alexander Whitleir, Andrew Alanson and Master John Cadiou', which I presented at a seminar held at the Johannes Gutenburg University at Mainz on 27 February 2020. The seminar was led by Professor Jörg Rogge and entitled "Types of Lordship in Comparsion". The paper owed something to a conversation with Brandon Clydesdale, which will be acknowledged in the published version in due course.

95 Simpson and Armstrong, 'Roll of the Burgh Courts of Aberdeen' (n 1) 76–79.

96 *RRS* v (n 60) 140–141 and 262; on the clause *teste me ipso*, see *ibid.*, 108–109.

great seal, which was used to issue such documents.[97] But why would a clerk carrying the great seal of Scotland – which could only be in one place at one time – have been in Aberdeen in the summer of 1317? Duncan suggested that the presence of the brieve of right just mentioned "is best explained as the product of a chamberlain's ayre to Aberdeen, the clerk also carrying the great seal".[98]

What Duncan does not seem to have realised is that the 1317 roll places the chamberlain himself – William of Lindsay – in Aberdeen only about ten days after the brieve of right was issued.[99] In addition, Duncan does not seem to have appreciated that the 1317 roll in fact makes direct reference to a meeting of William of Lindsay's court; this is the second piece of evidence that suggests William of Lindsay had been visiting Aberdeen in the course of a chamberlain's ayre. It will be recalled that part of the process of transferring Ada's claim to the lands in the Gallowgate to William of Lindsay was conducted *in curia sua* – in other words, in his own court. This must have been a reference to the chamberlain's court.[100]

All this suggests that the surviving records of the burgh courts that sat in 1317 are the records of courts that had just been visited and audited by the man who had ultimate responsibility for the administration of justice in the burghs. If anyone had the power – and capacity – to articulate and enforce a common set of *leges burgorum Scocie*, it was him. His visit had facilitated at least some access to the justice that the king offered at common law, in that it had resulted in the issuing of a brieve of right to pursue a claim in relation to lands in the Gallowgate, which remarkably still survives. William's visit had also enabled him to tidy up some business of his own, and, in the process, the clerk of one of the *burgh* courts of Aberdeen was at pains to emphasise that the court in question had been following the *leges burgorum Scocie*.

These last points may make it possible to formulate a fresh way of understanding what the burgh court of Aberdeen may have meant by the term *leges burgorum Scocie*. The link between the surviving textual witnesses of the *Leges burgorum Scocie*, on the one hand, and the customs and *leges* observed in the burgh courts of Aberdeen, on the other, may not have been that one echoed the other. Rather, the link may have been that they *both* echoed, and probably both *shaped*, one of the few things that really had the potential to be actually common in the application of the law within the

97 *RRS* v (n 60) 262.
98 *RRS* v (n 60) 262.
99 Simpson and Armstrong, 'Roll of the Burgh Courts of Aberdeen' (n 1) 70–77.
100 Simpson and Armstrong, 'Roll of the Burgh Courts of Aberdeen' (n 1) 74–77.

burghs.[101] This was the administrative practice of the chamberlain and his clerks when they went on ayre. In July 1317, the visitation of this administrator facilitated access to the justice of the Scottish common law; if Duncan is correct, it was at that point that the surviving brieve sewn into the burgh court roll was issued.[102] At the same time, it was in the course of proceedings involving this administrator that the burgh court had regard to the common laws of the burghs of Scotland; and it did so to underline the effectiveness of a conveyance according to that apparently authoritative standard. Perhaps the visit of the chamberlain provided an opportunity to "refresh the image" of the common law in the minds of those who presided over the burgh courts and in the minds of those who pleaded there. Obviously, the chamberlain was not working with a blank canvas. The echoes of the work of his predecessors would presumably have already found their way into burgh practice, and have shaped the existing – if discordant – manuscript witnesses to the Scottish burgh laws. Indeed, in 1317 a burgh court of Aberdeen resolved a dispute by making reference to an assize held by Stephen of Dunnideer, one of William of Lindsay's predecessors.[103] If the administrative practice of the chamberlain was the ultimate reference point for the "common" laws of the burghs, it was a practice that was articulated and perhaps even negotiated with reference to the collective memories of those who operated the burgh courts *and* with reference to the existing manuscript witnesses to the laws.

E: CONCLUDING REMARKS ON THE "TEXT" OF THE *LEGES BURGORUM SCOCIE*

Admittedly, this is all rather speculative; but it seems to fit the meagre evidence. But if all that is so, what were the common laws of the burghs of Scotland? It is possible to offer a tentative answer using a medieval distinction between "books" and "texts". As Mary Carruthers puts it in her study of memory in medieval culture, "a book is not necessarily the same thing as a text . . . in a memorial culture, a 'book' is only one way among several to

101 It is possible that the so-called *curia quatuor burgorum* also played a role here, although the evidence for its work is extremely limited. See MacQueen and Windram, 'Laws and Courts' (n 2) 214; see also *APS*, i (n 2) 703–704; Innes, *Ancient Customs* 155–158.

102 *RRS* v (n 60) 262.

103 Simpson and Armstrong, 'Roll of the Burgh Courts of Aberdeen' (n 1) 84–87; on Dunideer, see *RRS* v (n 60) 206; see also *PoMS*, 'Stephen of Dunnideer, Master, Rector, Chamberlain of Scotland', *PoMS* no 16400, available at *https://www.poms.ac.uk/record/person/16400/* (last accessed 15 July 2022).

remember a 'text' . . .".[104] The text fundamentally existed not in the books, but in the human *memory*. For the reformer John Wyclif, even God's text was "contained only in a sort of shorthand form in books", which were seen as "the memorial clues and traces of pre-existing truth".[105] These had to be "continually interpreted and adapted to . . . the *liber vitae*, the living book . . . in the actual person of Christ".[106]

Perhaps the common *leges burgorum Scocie* were thought of as "texts" in this medieval sense. The textual *Leges burgorum Scocie* that were in circulation in 1317, and that survive today, would only have been seen as memorial clues guiding one to the "text" of the *leges*, which existed fundamentally in human *memories*. Is it possible that the authoritative "memories" where the texts were fundamentally held to reside were the minds of the senior officials and their clerks whose administrative practices at least had the potential to make the laws of the realm and the burghs truly *common* – men like William of Lindsay?[107] That would fit with the broad crossover, but lack of detailed correlation, between the books of the *leges burgorum* and the practices of the burgh courts, as attested in the 1317 roll. It was not that there was *no* genuinely common "law" between them, but rather it was the case that what

104 M Carruthers, *The Book of Memory: A Study of Memory in Medieval Culture*, 2nd edn (2008) 9–10.

105 Carruthers, *Book of Memory* 11 (n 104) (the second passage – "the memorial clues and traces of pre-existing truth" – is a direct quotation from Wyclif).

106 Carruthers, *Book of Memory* 11 (n 104)

107 On the personnel who staffed the royal administration at this time, see *RRS* v (n 60) 198–214. The suggestion made here draws some inspiration from the ideas expressed in Baker, *Introduction* (n 68) 209, where he speaks about the touchstone for the content of the medieval English common law in the following terms: "Any law which emerged in the course of tentative pleading was not law formally laid down by way of an enrolled judgment, but the accepted learning within the profession: 'common learning', as it is called in the year books. No single precedent could be taken as common learning. Long usage was more sacrosanct, and the courts were unwilling to depart from settled lines of precedent. The authority of accepted doctrine was therefore different from, and more powerful than, a mere judicial decision. Although the judges were the chief repositories of common learning, their collective declarations were received as law not merely because of their judicial office but because they represented the established wisdom in the little intellectual world of Westminster Hall and the inns of court. The common opinion of all the judges and serjeants in the Exchequer Chamber was the highest authority there could be." Of course, there was no common learning with comparable complexity in Scotland at this time, and there was no heterogeneous legal profession to maintain and develop it; but there was, perhaps, the standard of the "established wisdom" of the very small officers and clerks who staffed the royal administration. Might this have lain at the heart of the medieval Scottish common law, at least by the early fourteenth century? If so, it might be possible to conceptualise the medieval Scottish common law as a customary system of law of the sort described in A W B Simpson, *Legal History and Legal Theory: Essays on the Common Law* (1987) 359–382, particularly at 370–382. I am grateful to Hector MacQueen for this reference, and for discussing this point with me.

was truly "common" existed elsewhere and it was echoed, and probably also shaped by, the books and the practice of the courts. That which was truly common was taken to exist as a "text" of laws in the minds of the administrators like William of Lindsay and their clerks, the men who had the capacity to make the laws of the kings of Scots truly "common" in the burghs. Perhaps it was this standard to which the burgh courts of Aberdeen had regard when they claimed to adhere to the *leges burgorum Scocie*.

If this tells us something about the nature of the *leges burgorum Scocie*, it also underlines the challenges inherent in any future attempt to compare burgh laws in Scotland, on the one hand, with town laws in Norway – or elsewhere – on the other.[108] Let it be supposed that the *leges burgorum Scocie* fundamentally existed in the minds of a very small group of royal administrators and their clerks, whose understanding of those *leges* was informed – but not wholly defined – by the textual *Leges burgorum Scocie* and the customary practices of individual courts. If that is so, it follows that significant effort is required to reconstruct what the laws were at any given time only then might meaningful comparison of those laws with others found elsewhere be possible. To reiterate points made earlier in this essay – and indeed by MacQueen and Windram – that act of reconstruction would have to address the fact that many of the individual chapters in the textual *Leges burgorum Scocie* cannot be dated with any confidence. Indeed, they may represent different stages in the development of the law, a point also made by Baird Smith.[109] The evidence of sources such as the 1317 roll would be of central importance to the task of reconstructing such legal development and Baird Smith long ago showed what might be achieved in this regard through the study of monastic registers.[110]

It seems that similar effort is required to reconstruct what courts in Norwegian towns might have meant by the town laws. Of course, historians of Norwegian town law have one advantage over their Scottish counterparts; much more is known about the origins of the Code of the Towns than is understood about the origins of the textual *Leges burgorum Scocie*. As Tveit notes,[111] the Code of the Towns was promulgated by Magnus VI in 1276,

108 What follows is greatly indebted to the discussion in D Ibbetson, 'Comparative legal history: A methodology' in A Musson and C Stebbings (eds), *Making Legal History: Approaches and Methodologies* (2012) 131–345, particularly at 135–143.

109 MacQueen and Windram, 'Laws and Courts in the Burghs' (n 2) 211 and 222; Smith, 'Retrait Lignager' (n 75) 200–202.

110 Smith, 'Retrait Lignager' (n 75) 202–206. See also my forthcoming article, '*Decretum fuit per burgenses*: a fresh perspective on law-making in the medieval Scottish burghs'.

111 For the discussion that follows, see Tveit's contribution to this volume, above at 155–180.

and this makes it possible to talk with confidence about the context in which it was composed and promulgated. Indeed, it also makes sense to consider the possibility that the text was meant to express a coherent and consistent set of rules. Such assumptions simply cannot be made about the textual *Leges burgorum Scocie*, at least in the form in which it survives. Incidentally, this last point underlines the fact that any simplistic attempt to compare the provisions of the Code of the Towns with those of the *Leges burgorum Scocie* in isolation of other sources will run into some serious methodological difficulties.

While it is clearly helpful to understand the origins of the Code of the Towns in such detail, Norwegian historians still face difficulties in reconstructing the "law" as applied in urban centres. Tveit detects significant crossovers between the Code of the Towns and the laws applied in practice. For example, she notes that "town development happened in accordance with the Code of the Towns" in the late-thirteenth century; she cites several examples, including the fact that "[c]rafts involving ovens and the use of fire were ordered to the outskirts of towns".[112] However, she also rejects the "positivistic" argument that the Code of the Towns was simply applied without qualification by the administrations in Bergen, Niðaros, Oslo and Tunsberg. For example, the Code of the Towns assumed that "law was conducted at or by the town assembly", the *mót*, but increasingly legal business was transacted before the town council and the king's appointed judge, the *logmaðr*.[113]

The difficulties in reconstructing the town laws of Norway and the burgh laws of Scotland are evidently daunting but they would need to be addressed before meaningful historical comparison could be possible. Do the essays in this volume give any indications as to what a useful basis of comparison might be in the future? This issue cannot really be considered properly until many more questions about the town laws of Norway, and the burgh laws of Scotland, have been addressed. It has been observed that simply comparing individual provisions in the texts of the *Leges burgorum Scocie* and the Code of the Towns might run into serious methodological difficulties. If the arguments advanced above about the nature of the *leges burgorum Scocie* are correct, any comparison between them and other town laws – including those of Norway – would benefit from exploring one issue in particular. As has been explained, the extent to which there was, in fact, a common law of

112 See Tveit's contribution to this volume, above at 170.

113 See Tveit's contribution to this volume, above at 163–164.

the burghs of Scotland remains unclear. However, in so far as there was such a common burghal law, it arguably owed much of its existence to the work of the small group of royal administrators and clerks, led by the chamberlain, whose collective understanding of the *leges burgorum Scocie* gave some meaning to the term. Is the same at all true for other attempts to articulate town laws that were supposed to be commonly applicable across large territories, such as Norway? Tveit has shown that the Code of the Towns is to some extent consistent with laws that were in fact commonly applicable across urban areas in Norway. But how precisely did this come about? Did it come about through the efforts of a small group of administrators close to the king, whose collective understanding of the text was seen as a touchstone – perhaps not the only touchstone – for what was, and was not, the law? Were they responsible for the legal unity that was achieved? Or was the situation in Norway more complex? Certainly, it cannot have been *very* like the situation in Scotland, where the chamberlain's ayre allowed him to supervise the administration of justice in all of the burghs; there does not seem to have been a comparable institution in Norway. That said, Tveit draws attention to institutional changes in the administration of the law in the late-thirteenth and fourteenth centuries, with a decline in the role of the *mót*, and a rise in the role of the town council and the king's *logmaðr* in deciding disputes. In addition, in his contribution to the present volume, Jørn Sunde has demonstrated the importance of the king's lawmen – who numbered no more than sixteen – in enabling him to achieve a degree of legal unity across Norway.[114] They seem to have effectively negotiated with individual communities how the law was to be understood and applied. Perhaps comparing the work of such royal administrators in Norway with apparent counterparts in Scotland might be fruitful. Perhaps that would provide *some* – but certainly not *all* – of the necessary context to conduct a meaningful comparison of the Scottish and Norwegian legal texts themselves.

114 See Sunde's contribution to the present volume, above at 109–112.

PART 2
THE EARLY MODERN PERIOD, CA. 1500–CA. 1800

7 War and Peace: Scottish-Norwegian Relations in the Early Modern Period (ca. 1520–1707)

Steve Murdoch[*]

A: INTRODUCTION

Relations between Norway and Scotland in the early modern period enjoy a long-established historiography that very often centres on a few key specific themes, whether commerce, migration or war. This can revolve around particular incidents, such as the Scottish-Hanse fracas in Bergen in the 1520s (the "Scottish Incident") or the infamous "Kringen Massacre" (*Skottetoget*) of 1612.[1] Quite often, the focus lies on an incredibly influential individual

* I would like to thank Crispin Gurholt and Nina Østby Pedersen for helping me with some of the older Norwegian language sources used in this chapter, and also ensuring that there are considerably fewer typographical errors in the text than there might have been. Naturally, any extant errors remain my own.

1 For the "Bergen Incident" see N Ø Pedersen, 'Scottish Immigration to Bergen in the Sixteenth and Seventeenth Centuries' in A Grosjean and S Murdoch (eds), *Scottish Communities Abroad in the Early Modern Period* (2005) 135–165. For the 'Kringen Massacre' see T Michell, *A History of the Scottish Expedition to Norway in 1612* (1886).

in Norway, such as the Scottish *lensmann* of Finnmark, John Cunningham til Gjerdrup, or the ethnic Scot, priest and poet, Petter Dass (whose father came from Dundee).[2] Moreover, scholarship commonly centres on the study of the Scottish-Norwegian timber trade, *Skottehandelen*, which certainly began in the sixteenth century and continued well into the eighteenth.[3] This was, however, neither the starting period of Scottish interaction with Norway, nor its end. Indeed, dendrochronological evidence reveals the appetite for Norwegian timber for use in shipbuilding and Scottish buildings of all sizes from an earlier period.[4] Thus a single chapter does not afford enough space to cover the wealth of material to consider. The focus of the present paper will therefore be to review key moments of Scotto-Norwegian interaction, particularly during periods of escalated tension. We can then test the impact of these events against commercial and migratory patterns to see how, or even if, they impacted in any meaningful way upon relations between the two kingdoms.

Of course, the fact that for the majority of the period under consideration, both Scotland and Norway were part of multiple monarchies cannot be ignored. As such, Denmark and England are mentioned where relevant to the argument. Omitting these nations would distort the context of Scottish-Norwegian interaction during this, sometimes tempestuous, period.

2 For John Cunningham see R Hagen, 'On the Edge of Civilisation': Governor John Cunningham in Finnmark' in S Murdoch and A Mackillop (eds), *Military Governors and Imperial Frontiers c. 1600–1800* (2003) 29–51. For Petter Dass see J Simpson, 'Petter Dass (1647–1707)' (1985) 22 *Northern Studies* 52–64; P Dass, *The Trumpet of Nordland*, translated by T Jorgenson (2015). See also the numerous works on Dass by R B Hagen, including most recently R B Hagen 'Katekismesangene hos Petter Dass. Norsk protestantisk demonologi på vers og rim' in *Efter Reformationen: Beyond the Reformation: Rapport til det 29. Nordiske Historikermøde bind 3* (2017) 88–120.

3 A Næss, 'Skottehandelen på Sunnhordland' (1920) VII *Sunnhordland Tidsskrift* 31–86; A Bugge, *Den Norske Trælasthandels Historie II: Fra Freden i Speier til slutten av 1600-tallet* (1925) 268–281; A Lillehammer, 'The Scottish Norwegian Timber Trade in the Stavanger Area in the Sixteenth and the Seventeenth Centuries' in T C Smout (ed), *Scotland and Europe 1200–1850* (1986) 100–106; A Lillehammer, 'Boards, Beams and Barrel-Hoops: Contacts between Scotland and the Stavanger Area in the Seventeenth Century' in G G Simpson (ed), *Scotland and Scandinavia, 800–1800* (1990) 100–106; E Opsahl and S Sogner (eds), *Norske Innvandringshistorie. 1. I kongens tid 900–1814* (2003) 297–315.

4 A Crone and C M Mills, 'Timber in Scottish Buildings, 1450–1800: A Dendrochronological Perspective' (2012) 142 *Proceedings of the Society of Antiquaries of Scotland* 329–369.

B: SCOTLAND AND NORWAY: THE LEGAL AND POLITICAL BACKGROUND

Roots to the early modern relations between Scotland and Norway can be traced right back to the Scottish-Norwegian "Treaty of Perth" (1266). This treaty was subsequently reratified twice, in 1312 and again in 1426, the latter occasion following the formation of the Scandinavian Kalmar Union in 1397.[5] Scotto-Norwegian ties were reinforced when Margaret, daughter of Christian I of the Kalmar Union, became queen to James III of Scotland in July 1469.[6] As well as improved trade relations, the marriage led to specific diplomatic and military opportunities for individual Scots in Scandinavia. A further outcome of the royal union was the Norwegian transfer of the Orkney and Shetland Islands to the Scottish Crown as a pledge for the 4/5ths of Margaret's dowry that remained unpaid.[7] After 1521, however, Scandinavia entered a period of internal turmoil that ended with Gustav Vasa establishing himself as king of an independent Sweden and Frederik I ruling over Denmark-Norway after deposing his nephew, Christian II. The ensuing decades saw a decline in Scottish relations with Denmark-Norway, not least as Scottish support was split between Christian II and his usurping uncle Frederik I. As a result, numerous cases of maritime predation occurred, perpetrated by Scots against the contesting Scandinavian kings and their allies, particularly after Christian landed in Norway in 1531. These privateering episodes spilled over into Norwegian waters, eventually involving the councillors of Bergen and the bishop of Trondheim who were all keen to see the situation resolved.[8] It was in this particular period that the infamous "Scottish Incident" took place, which saw one Scot killed and twelve others attacked in Bergen by Hanse merchants, further souring the view of Scots towards their erstwhile hosts.[9] As Nina Østby Pedersen has established, the impact of this event on Scottish immigration into Bergen was minimal, despite the Hanse merchants claims to Frederik I that the Bergen-Scots had supported Christian II. Regardless, by 1530 Frederik was determined to see the Hanse

5 For recent scholarship, see I P Grohse, *Frontiers of Peace in the Medieval North: The Scottish-Norwegian Frontier, c. 1260–1470* (2017).

6 D Simpson, *Charters and Other Records of the City and Royal Burgh of Kirkwall: With the Treaty of 1468*, Jo Mooney (ed) (1952) 96–102.

7 L Laursen and C S Christiansen (eds), *Danmark-Norges Traktater 1523–1750 11 vols* (1907–1949) iii, 1.

8 These events are fully explored in S Murdoch, *The Terror of the Seas? Scottish Maritime Warfare, 1513–1713* (2010) 92–98.

9 Pedersen, 'Scottish Immigration to Bergen' (n 1) 137–141.

Germans and the Scots reconciled.[10] Pedersen has noted how several prominent Scottish burgesses in the city subsequently became involved in disputes with the archbishop following the seizure of David Falconer of Leith's ship by the archbishop's admiral Kristoffer Trondsen.[11] These burgesses were part of a thriving community and, by 1537, some thirty-six Scottish immigrants had indeed established themselves in Bergen, whilst others had been granted trading rights in Sunnhordland and Ryfylke.[12]

Some have taken this rise in settlement numbers and traders as evidence of a Scottish monopolisation of the timber trade, and not without reason. Arnvid Lillehammer estimated that in 1567 no less than twenty-eight out of the thirty-eight vessels recorded as arriving in Ryfylke were Scottish.[13] Thus, despite "limited political relations", throughout the sixteenth century there was actually a rise in the Scottish population and commercial exchange across Norway, and not a reduction.[14] Towards the end of that century, the large-scale migration of Scots to Norway was aided by the re-establishment of political relations following the 1585 embassy of the House of Oldenburg to Scotland. Negotiations for a new marriage alliance centred on James VI of Scotland and Anna of Denmark, daughter of Frederik II (and sister of Christian IV) arose out of this embassy. Sir Peter Young and Sir William Stewart discussed the more sensitive details of the proposals with the Danes.[15] Further embassies were exchanged until the 1589 conclusion of the marriage agreement. Scottish commissioners sought to ensure that the treaty terms would give Scots the same status as Danes and Norwegians in their home countries with reciprocal rights for Danes and Norwegians in Scotland. The Danes responded, however, that this was already the case under existing agreements between the countries, adding that there was no need for any new agreement on the subject.[16] Anna married James VI

10 Pedersen, 'Scottish Immigration to Bergen' (n 1) 144.

11 Pedersen, 'Scottish Immigration to Bergen' (n 1) 147.

12 Pedersen, 'Scottish Immigration to Bergen' (n 1) 147; N Kolle, A R Nielssen, A Døssland and P Christensen, *Fish, Coast and Communities: A History of Norway* (2017) 90. This source, which notes up to forty Scottish families in Bergen by the mid-sixteenth century, contains the Sunnhordland and Ryfylke information.

13 Lillehammer, 'The Scottish Norwegian Timber Trade' (n 3) 101.

14 S Murdoch and A Grosjean (eds), *The Scotland, Scandinavia and Northern European Biographical Database* [SSNE] (1995–2022) *Institute of Scottish Historical Research,* available at *http://www.st-andrews.ac.uk/history/ssne* (last accessed 15 July 2022).

15 T Riis, *Should Auld Acquaintance be Forgot: Scottish-Danish Relations c. 1450–1707 2 vols* (1988) vol i, 110–111.

16 Danish Rigsarkivet (hereafter DRA), TKUA Skotland A II 5. Scottish proposal to the Danish commissioners, 9 July 1589; DRA, TKUA Skotland A III 7. Danish response to the Scottish proposals, 10 July 1589; *Danmark-Norges Traktater* (n 7) iii 10, 14–21. "Ægteskabstraktat mellem

by proxy in Bergen in 1589. The young groom then set off to collect his new bride, arriving in Norway on 28 October 1589 and marrying Anna in person in Oslo soon after.[17] In December they travelled south to Denmark (via Sweden) where James spent much of his time exchanging ideas with Danish scholars and generally being entertained by Christian IV.[18] One consequence of these discussions included consideration of Danish maritime laws, which were used to nuance the seafaring laws of Scotland thereafter.[19]

C: PROBLEMS IN TRADE AND COMMERCE: "1603 AND ALL THAT!"

The understanding that, in matters of trade, the Scots and Norwegians enjoyed equal status was soon severely tested, particularly after James VI of Scotland also assumed the throne of England in 1603. The Tudor and Oldenburg monarchies had long-held mutual grievances in the late sixteenth century. Specific problems just prior to 1603 had resulted from a policy introduced by Queen Elizabeth in 1598 that forbade Danish-Norwegian traffic from using the most direct route to the Iberian Peninsula through the English Channel because of England's ongoing war with Spain.[20] The Danes responded by letting it be known that they, and their Polish allies, intended to block the Øresund (the Danish Sound at the entrance to the Baltic Sea) and seize English ships as prizes, presumably until the English lifted their ban. This policy simply further provoked the English, especially the merchants from the City of London, who responded by supplying the Turks, who were then at war with Poland, with ammunition and powder.[21] Christian

kong Jacob VI af Skottland og kong Frederik II's datter prinsesse Anna". For more details of the various embassies during the marriage negotiations see D Stevenson, *Scotland's Last Royal Wedding. The Marriage of James VI and Anne of Denmark* (1997) 1–16.

17 P A Munch, 'Samtidig Beretning om Prindsesse Annas, Christian den 4des Systers, Gifter-maal med Kong Jacob d. 6te af Skotland og hendes paa-følgende Kroning' in *Norske Samlinger udgivne af et historisk samfund i Christiania: Første Bind* (1852) 450–512.

18 J T G Craig (ed), *Papers relative to the marriage of King James the Sixth of Scotland with the Princess Anne of Denmark, A.D. MDLXXXIX. And the form and manner of Her Majesty's coronation at Holyroodhouse, A.D. MDXC* (1828) v–ix; J Spottiswoode, *The History of the Church of Scotland* (1655, 1972 reprint) 377–381; Stevenson, *Scotland's Last Royal Wedding* (n 16) 17–39.

19 For discussion of this see J D Ford (ed), *Alexander King's Treatise of Maritime Law*, Stair Society vol 65 (2018) lxxx–lxxxi, lxxxiv and cxx.

20 S Murdoch, *Britain, Denmark-Norway and the House of Stuart, 1603–1660* (2003) 30–31.

21 J D Mackie (ed), *Calendar of State Papers relating to Scotland and Mary, Queen of Scots, 1547–1603* vol 13 (part I) (1969) (hereafter *CSP*, XIII(i)), 127–129. George Nicolson to Sir Robert Cecil, 9 December 1597; *ibid.*, 130–132. Roger Aston to Sir Robert Cecil, 12 December 1597; *ibid.*, 154–155, Roger Aston to James Hudson, 20 January 1598.

IV was outraged and by 1599 he vowed to do the Londoners "great hurt" for their actions.[22] He certainly caused them economic harm by disrupting the staple port of the English Merchant Adventurers at Hamburg and forcing them to move to the more parochial town of Stade, where they remained until 1611.[23]

Further disputes arose over contesting claims to whaling and fisheries in the North Atlantic. The English had been fishing as far across the Atlantic as Newfoundland since the 1490s.[24] The Danes, for their part, had long claimed sovereignty over all the seas between Norway, Shetland, Iceland, Svalbard (Spitzbergen) and Greenland.[25] Although the English had been allowed to fish off Iceland under licence from Copenhagen since the 1490s, this agreement was soon under such pressure that by 1585 tensions between the Oldenburg and Tudor crowns escalated.[26] The English refused to renew their licenses for the Iceland fisheries and claimed to have been whaling in the Northern Seas without competition since 1578. They specifically claimed the area from Svalbard to Greenland as a legitimately acquired possession of the English Crown, though Svalbard was also claimed by the Danes and the Dutch.[27] To add confusion to the mix, the English called Svalbard "Greenland", terming it thus on all their maps. In 1599, a fleet of Danish-Norwegian ships (one carrying Christian IV himself) seized several English vessels near Vardø (Finnmark), including the ship *Charitas of Hull* (William Tellier, master) and escalating the situation to "breaking point" by 1602.[28] These developments, clearly Anglo-Danish in origin, soon impacted

22 *CSP*, XIII (i) (n 21) 546. George Nicolson to Sir Robert Cecil, 1 September 1599.

23 Murdoch, *Britain* (n 20) 32.

24 K J Rankin and P Holm, 'Cartographical Perspectives on the Evolution of Fisheries in Newfoundland's Grand Banks Area and Adjacent North Atlantic Waters in the Sixteenth and Seventeenth Centuries' (2019) 51 *Terrae Incognitae* 195–196.

25 T Fulton, *The Sovereignty of the Sea* (1911) 4 and 108.

26 Fulton, *Sovereignty* (n 25) 109.

27 Fulton, *Sovereignty* (n 25) 164 and 181–183; Murdoch, *Britain* (n 20) 32–33.

28 Fulton, *Sovereignty* (n 25) 110–112; R Hagen, 'Kong Christian IVs tokt til det ytterste nord i 1599; Bakgrunn og konsekvenser' in R B Hagen and P E Sparboe (eds), *Kongens reise til det ytterste nord. Dagbøker fra Christian IVs tokt til Finnmark og Kola i 1599* (2004) 6–9 and 12–14. Hagen notes that all five English ships taken came from Hull. Details of these are recorded in the diaries of Silvert Grubbe and Jonas Carisius. These are reproduced as J Carisius, 'Christian den Fjerdes reisetur til Norge og Vardøhus i Finnmarken' in R B Hagen and P E Sparboe (eds), *Kongens Reise til det ytterste nord. Dagbøker fra Christian IVs tokt til Finmark og Kola I 1599* (2004) 38–44 and S Grubbe 'Kongens sjøreise' in R B Hagen and P E Sparboe (eds), *Kongens Reise til det ytterste nord. Dagbøker fra Christian IVs tokt til Finmark og Kola i 1599* (2004) 70–73. Two small English ships were sent home with the prisoners on board while four English prizes were reported as arriving in Bergen in June, suggesting six were taken in all. For the arrival of the English prizes in Bergen see N Nicolaysen (ed),

directly on Scotto-Norwegian relations, despite an established Scottish presence in Finnmark since the late 1500s.[29] For example, there was a Scottish fishing community operating around Vardø as evidenced by the passes facilitating their activities granted by the Danish-Norwegian authorities as early as 1584.[30]

James Stuart's ascension to the English throne on Elizabeth Tudor's demise in 1603 presented an opportunity to end English and Danish-Norwegian tensions. Christian IV, in an act of good faith, returned the Hull ship *Charitas* to its owner in 1604, with two years' toll-free privileges in the Danish Sound as an additional sweetener.[31] King James wrote to Christian the following year, stating that, "Indeed we do not doubt in the least that the past disputes (whatever they might have been) can easily be put to rest and thoroughly removed owing to our mutual friendship".[32] Christian nevertheless remained sceptical of English intentions and launched new voyages to reclaim his North Atlantic possessions under the direction of the Scot, Sir John Cunningham. These included voyages to Greenland (1605 and 1606), Svalbard (1615) and the Faroes and Iceland (1616).[33] Although numerous Scotsmen were employed in Christian's fleets, when he believed he had been impugned by a subject of any one of the three Stuart kingdoms (particularly the English) he then targeted all of James' subjects irrespective of nationality. Thus, on 12 March 1618, James and his Scottish Council were compelled to issue a proclamation regarding Scottish fishing activities near Faroe.[34] This was in response to Christian IV's complaints that by pursuing their craft in "his" waters, the Scots had seriously interfered with the rights of Danish-Norwegian citizens, supposedly resulting in Christian's fishermen becoming so impoverished that they were unable to pay their taxes. James agreed that the continued Scottish practice of fishing in these areas was in breach of the laws of nations and inconsistent with his special desire to keep on Christian's good terms. Nonetheless, this directly contravened the

Norske Magasin Skrifter og Optegnelser angaaende Norge og forfattede efter Reformationen, II (1868) 171, 21 June 1599.

29 Kolle, Nielssen, Døssland and Christensen, *Fish, Coast and Communities* (n 12) 89.

30 S Petersen and O G Lundh (eds), *Norsk Rigs-Registranter, tildeels i Uddrag, B 2; 1572–1588* (1863) 583. Frederik II, 3 November 1584. With this letter, Frederik answered the request of James VI for six passes for his Scottish subjects to fish around Vardøhus or head into Malmis, Kolmogra or into Russia for trade.

31 Hagen, 'Kong Christian IVs tokt til det ytterste nord i 1599' (n 28) 14.

32 DRA, TKUA, England A 1, 2. James VI & I to Christian IV, 6 May 1605.

33 Hagen, 'At the edge of civilisation' (n 2) 33.

34 J Burton Hill and D Masson (ed), *The Register of the Privy Council of Scotland* (1877–1898) 14 vols (hereafter *RPCS*) XI (1616–1619) 320–330. Proclamation, 12 March 1618.

1589 agreement ensuring parity of status of Scottish, Danish and Norwegian subjects in each other's territories. Severe penalties were imposed and fishermen risked confiscation of their equipment and "further punishment" if they persisted.[35] This was not universally applied; individual Scots resident in Denmark-Norway were still allowed to catch and deal in fish. In particular, John Cunningham, as governor of Finnmark, had total control over the fishing rights in the waters under his jurisdiction.[36] Petter Dass would also later derive part of his income from a generous share in the fishing rights of Nordland.[37] However, as Christian IV demonstrated in 1618, many Scots apparently no longer enjoyed such special treatment despite the legal protection afforded to them under the 1589 agreement, and this was not only in the sphere of fishing.

Scots had, for many years, built ships in Norway largely unhindered, authority being granted to Andrew Watson already by July 1589.[38] Scottish shipbuilders in Norway, whether due to an attempt to gain leverage in Anglo-Danish disputes or not, were frequently molested by the Dano-Norwegian authorities after the Union of Crowns in 1603. Christian IV complained about the Scottish practice of building ships in Norway in July 1604 and fined Christopher Dall 2,000 *rigsdaler* for allowing Scots to build ships on his property. In August 1605, he ordered Styring Boel to confiscate two Scottish ships belonging to Jacob Clerk that had been built in Lister len in Norway.[39] Within a year, King James mediated on behalf of another shipbuilder, William Duncan, who on completing a ship in Norway had been forbidden from sailing it to Scotland. Duncan complained to the Scottish authorities before travelling to London to seek compensation. The case eventually concluded when Duncan, and another Scottish shipbuilder, Richard Weddel,

35 DRA, TKUA England A 1, 2. James VI & I to Christian IV, 27 March 1618. In defence of his slow actions to Christian on the subject James added: "Concerning the complaint about fishing near the Faroe Islands, we could not reply so quickly because we had to wait until the councillors of the kingdom of Scotland, whom this matter especially concerned, could be consulted".

36 See J E Sars and O G Lundh (eds), *Norske Rigs-Registranter, tildeels i Uddrag, B 5: 1619–1627* (1874) 59–60. Christian IV to John Cunningham, 11 December 1619.

37 Simpson, 'Petter Dass' (n 3) 55.

38 J E Sars and O G Lundh (eds), *Norske Rigs-Registranter, tildeels i Uddrag, B 3: 1588–1602* (1865) 49–50. Christian IV to Albert Skeel, 24 July 1589. Others followed suit with permission of Albert Gyldenstjerne, albeit Christian only grudgingly allowed it. See *ibid.*, 140. Christian IV to Axel Gyldenstjerne, 27 September 1590.

39 O G Lundh (eds), *Norske Rigs-Registranter: tildeels i Uddrag: B. 4: 1603–1618* (1870) 79. Christian IV to Laurits Kruse, 24 July 1604 and *ibid.*, 123. Christian IV to Styring Boel, 3 August 1605. For a deeper analysis of Scottish shipbuilders in Scandinavia and Russia see: S Murdoch, 'Surfing the Waves: Scottish Admirals in Russia in their Baltic Context' (2010) 3 *Journal of Irish and Scottish Studies* 59–86.

received permission to collect their ships in September 1606. Christian IV added the punitive condition that they had to pay the costs incurred in impounding and then transporting the ships to Copenhagen.[40] Further incidents followed. In 1612, an Orkney vessel and its cargo belonging to Robert Scoula was arrested in Bergen. The ship had been carrying hides, butter and oil and was the centre of complex litigation for several years, not least since many of the goods on board belonged to King James himself. It was not until 1618 that Christian ordered that the complaint of the Scottish Privy Council be heard.[41] Scoula's treatment may have been catalysed by Orkney privateers perpetrating ongoing attacks on Norwegian shipping and harbours between 1612 and 1617.[42] The motivation for the Orkney raids was rooted in both high and duplicitous policies emanating from the court of King James in London and originating in the Kalmar War (1611–1613).

D: "*SKOTTETOG*": THE KRINGEN MASSACRE OF 1612

When it came to Denmark-Norway's engagement in the Kalmar War against Sweden, King James officially supported Christian IV. The Danish king sought 8,000 British troops for his army and by March 1612 some 4,000 of these were mustering for his service under Andrew Keith, Lord Dingwall, among others.[43] However, Karl IX of Sweden was simultaneously recruiting in Scotland. In January 1611 Colonel James Spens was ordered to raise troops in Scotland to counter the perceived Oldenburg aggression.[44] Spens arrived at the Stuart court in London in November seeking permission to recruit at least 3,000 Scottish soldiers, even though this might contravene the

40 DRA, TKUA England A 1, 2. James VI to Christian IV, 4 April 1606; *Kancelliets Brevbøger, 1606*, 460. Missive to Brede Rantzau anent the Scots William Dunker [sic] and Richard Weddel, 29 September 1606.

41 *Norske Rigs-Registranter, B* 5 728. Christian IV to Knut Urne, 28 August 1618.

42 The National Archives of Great Britain (hereafter TNA), SP75/4, f. 314. Robert Anstruther to James VI, 8 June 1612; *Norske Rigs-Registranter, B* 5 662. Christian IV to Knut Urne, 9 September 1617; *RPCS* (n 34) XI, 1616–1619, 629–630. Scottish Privy Council to Christian IV in favour of Robert Scoula, and against the privateer Simon Stewart, 18 June 1618; A Grosjean, 'Scottish-Scandinavian Naval Links: A case study for the SSNE database', in (1997) 32 *Northern Studies* 111–112.

43 H F Brown (ed), *Calendar of State Papers Relating to English Affairs in the Archives of Venice, Volume 12, 1610–1613* (1905) 239–240, 252, 298. Antonio Foscarini to Doge and Senate, November 1611–March 1612. Specifically letters 316, 342, 355, 372, 373, 387, 446, 452, 583 and 789; Mary Anne Everett Green, *Calendar of State Papers Domestic: James I, 1611–1618* (1858) 124. Chamberlain to Carlton, 25 March 1612; Riis, *Should Auld Acquaintance*, i (n 15) 95–96.

44 Swedish Riksarkiv (hereafter SRA), Anglica 4, unfoliated. Karl IX to James Spens, 24 January 1611. For a detailed analysis see A Grosjean, *An Unofficial Alliance: Scotland and Sweden, 1569–1654* (2003) 33–38.

Stuart-Oldenburg alliance.[45] Spens remained at the Stuart court throughout the first half of 1612, during which time King James informed him that should Christian IV refuse his diplomatic overtures, Gustav II Adolf of Sweden would be allowed to recruit *more* soldiers from Great Britain, thereby confirming that he knew of those already enlisted by Spens.[46] Some 300 of Spens's Scottish recruits were killed in battle or massacred at Kringen (Gudbrandsdalen) in Norway on 26–27 August 1612. This episode is most famously remembered in Edvard Storm's nineteen verse epic *Zinklars Vise* (named after Captain George Sinclair) dating from 1781. Here the poet could not help but inflate the number of the slain at Kringen to 1,400 men, thus exaggerating the event:

Herr Sinclar drog over salten Hav,
Til Norrig hans Cours monne stande;
Blandt Gudbrands Klipper han fandt sin Grav,
Der vanked saa blodige en Pande.
. . .
Ved Romsdals Kyster han styred til Land,
Erklærende sig for en Fjende;
Ham fulgte fjorten hundrede Mand,
Som alle havde Ondt i Sinde
. . .
Med døde Kroppe blev Kringen strøed,
De Ravne fik nok at æde;
Det Ungdoms Blod, som her udfløød,
De Skotske Piger begræde.

Regardless of this epic poem, the truth is that some 2,000 more Scots from Spens's levy successfully landed near Trondheim and crossed into Sweden unmolested.[47] By the time they reached Sweden, the 6,000-strong British force sent to Denmark-Norway had arrived and a truce had already been arranged by Sir James Spens and his step-brother, Sir Robert Anstruther, his

45 SRA, Anglica 4. Gustav Adolf to James Spens, 16 November 1611.

46 SRA, Anglica 3. James Spens to Gustav Adolf, 21 July 1612; Grosjean, *Unofficial Alliance* (n 44) 31–38.

47 Grosjean explains in detail the recruitment and route from Scotland to the Dutch Republic and thence to Norway. See Grosjean, *Unofficial Alliance* (n 44) 31–38. For an English rendering of six of the verses of *Zinklars Vise*, see G Donaldson, *A Northern Commonwealth: Scotland and Norway* (1990) 144–145. Donaldson translates the first of the two verses quoted here as follows: "Herr Sinclair sailed over the salt sea: / His course did stand towards Norway; / Among Gudbrand's rocks he found his grave – / A bloody head was inflicted there . . . On the coast of Romsdal he made his landfall, Declaring himself an enemy. / Fourteen hundred men followed him, / All with evil in their souls". The remaining verse quoted here may be translated as follows: "Krigen was covered with dead bodies / The Ravens had enough to eat; / The spilled blood of the youth, / Was cried over by the Scottish lasses".

opposite number in Danish service.[48] These two men were widely hailed as the authors of the 1613 Knäred Treaty which ended the intra-Scandinavian Kalmar War.[49] From a Norwegian perspective, the Kringen episode continues to feed the heroic notions of Norwegian martial prowess, disregarding their obvious inability to prevent the larger Scottish force from crossing the country. Despite the success of 2,000 Scots making the "Trondheim Traverse", Scottish emphasis is usually placed on Kringen, which is sometimes presented as nothing short of a war crime because most of those killed were executed in cold blood the day after the skirmish.[50] Of greater importance than national sabre-rattling was the fact that the incident had little impact on Scottish-Norwegian relations at all. For example, during the 1612–1613 period at least eight Scots received citizen rights in Bergen, joining an extant Scottish community who continued their business unimpeded.[51] Indeed, following *Skottetoget*, some six Scottish ships loaded timber in Romsdal and sailed for home, while five more sailed the following year.[52] Anders Næss counted a further fifty-six Scottish ships in 1612 alone trading in Sunnhordland, while Arnvid Lillehammer observed seventy more in Ryfylke during the 1612–1613 period.[53] Scrutiny of the port records allow us to give detail to their destinations. The *Aberdeen Shore Work Accounts* record eleven voyages terminating in Aberdeen from Norway in the November 1612 to July 1613 period while the Dundee shipping lists reveal at least a dozen between August 1612 and December the following year.[54] Although

48 TNA, SP75/5, f. 3. Christian IV to Robert Anstruther, 8 August 1612; S Murdoch, 'James VI and the formation of a British Military Identity' in S Murdoch and A Mackillop (eds), *Fighting for Identity: Scottish Military Experiences, 1550–1900* (2002) 17.

49 TNA, SP75/5, f. 63. James VI & I's guarantee of Danish-Swedish peace, 26 January 1613; TNA, SP75/5, f. 73. A copy of the contract of peace procured by the King's most Excellent Majestie of Greate Brittaine and betwixt the Kings of Denmark and Sweden, 26 January 1613; Grosjean, *Unofficial Alliance* (n 44) 38.

50 *The Scotsman*, 25 August 2012, 'Scots invasion of Norway that ended in a war crime'. The issue taken here is that the majority of those who died at Kringen had been killed in cold blood the day after the battle.

51 N Nicolaysen, *Bergens Borgerbog 1550–1751* (1878) 27–28.

52 Bugge, *Den Norske Trælasthandels Historie II* (n 3) 277. Otto Grüner notes seven ships in 1612 and five in 1613, though he does not make a distinction in the 1612 figures for those arriving in Norway before or after *Skottetog*. See O R Grüner, *Hollendertida i Romsdal: sagbruk og trelasthandel på 1600-tallet* (1972) 94–95. I thank Nina Østby Pedersen for passing on this reference.

53 Næss, 'Skottehandelen på Sunnhordland' (n 3) 33; Lillehammer, 'The Scottish-Norwegian Timber Trade' (n 3) 110.

54 L B Taylor (ed), *Aberdeen Shore Work Accounts, 1596–1670* (1972) 73–76; A H Millar (ed), *The Compt Buik of David Wedderburn, Merchant of Dundee, 1580–1630, together with the shipping lists of Dundee 1580–1618* (1898) 231–240. Lillehammer notes seventeen ships originating in Dundee in 1612, but some of these arrived before the outbreak of the war. See Lillehammer,

numerous Scottish merchants and mariners continued their business in Norway they were, unfortunately, never far from conflict. Nearly 14,000 Scots were in Danish-Norwegian service during Christian IV's war against the Habsburgs (*Kejserkrig*), 1625–1629.[55] Though the majority of these men served in Denmark, the Oldenburg Duchies and Baltic German states, some veterans of this conflict would soon find themselves embroiled in yet another conflict and this time from their new homes in Norway. This military episode occurred against the backdrop of the British Civil Wars (1638–1660) and is often overlooked by contemporary scholars.

E: 1645: A SCOTTISH PROXY WAR WITH *HANNIBALSFEIDEN*?

As the Stuart kingdoms became engulfed in civil wars, a peculiar episode arose in which some Scots fled persecution at home only to become embroiled in an intra-Scandinavian conflict pitching Denmark-Norway against Sweden. This led to an event that can best be described as a proxy war fought between Scots in both the Oldenburg and Vasa maritime and military forces during the Torstensson War (1644–1645), particularly the operation known as *Hannibalsfeiden* in 1645.[56]

When Sweden invaded Denmark-Norway in 1644, Christian IV was already employing several Scottish mariners and soldiers in his service. In Norway, these included Tamis Cunningham (a cousin of the aforementioned *lensmann*, John Cunningham), serving as the commander of the Alta Galley Fleet and responsible for the general defence of Finnmark.[57] A long-term veteran of Oldenburg service, Colonel Alexander Seaton, served under Iver Krabbe, receiving an appointment as "Admiral of Marines" – a unit deployed in a squadron of eight ships operating out of Bohuslän in southern Norway.[58] Christian also recruited several Scottish privateers,

'The Scottish-Norwegian Timber Trade' (n 3) 111. For more examples see N Ø Pedersen, 'Skotsk innvandring til Norge i tidlig moderne tid' (2000) Hovedfagsoppgave i historie ved Universitetet i Oslo 54–55 and 60–62.

55 Murdoch, *Britain* (n 20) 202–225.

56 For the full context of maritime participation see Murdoch, *The Terror of the Seas?* (n 8) 214–218. For the context of the land-based operations see S Murdoch and A Grosjean, *Alexander Leslie and the Scottish Generals of the Thirty Years' War, 1618–1648* (2014) 155–160.

57 S Murdoch, 'Scotsmen on the Danish-Norwegian Frontiers c. 1580–1680', in Murdoch and Mackillop (eds), *Military Governors and Imperial Frontiers* (n 2) at 19–20.

58 J O Wahl, *Det Gamle Bergenhusiske Regiments Historie (1628–1720)* (2010) 8–10; A Espeland, *Skottene i Hordaland og Rogaland fra aar 1500–1800* (1921) 34; O H Gjeruldsen, *Defensjonsskipsordingen i Norge, 1630–1704* (2002) 83–87. NB: Gjeruldsen misidentifies Seaton as English.

including Thomas Shearer, William Walker and John Strachan who served together between May and September 1645 in Marstrand, Bohuslän and Christiania (Oslo), thus in the waters under Seaton's command.[59] Of equal significance to these maritime appointments were several of the Norwegian infantry regiments and fortresses under direct Scottish command. Between 1644 and 1645 Colonel George "Jost" Mackenzie commanded the *Akershus* National Infantry regiment and brought his son James into Norwegian service with him.[60] Colonel Andrew Spang commanded a Norwegian regiment bearing his name made up of Scottish officers and foreign recruits.[61] Similarly, Colonel James Wilson formed "Willson's" regiment, recruited from Bohuslän but officered by Scots, including his own son, Captain James Wilson, and kinsman, Ensign Matthew Wilson.[62] The *Smaalenske* National Infantry became the charge of Colonel John Taylor.[63] Another Scot, Colonel James Murray, arrived in Norway in 1644, bearing a testimonial from Charles I confirming his royalist credentials.[64] In November, Christian IV requested still more Scottish officers, which he intended to place as commanders over German mercenaries.[65] In the meantime, those already in place prepared for an attack on Sweden. As early as February 1645, Oxenstierna reported on a series of probing raids directed from Norway into Värmland and ebbing ever closer to Gothenburg.[66] In May Viceroy Hannibal Sehested appointed Colonel Murray as *Stadsoberst* (city colonel) of Marstrand at the mouth of the river Göta, adding to the Scot's command of the Norwegian artillery train.[67] From Marstrand, Sehested pressed towards the River Älv with over

59 Murdoch, *The Terror of the Seas?* (n 8) 217.

60 Norwegian Riksarkiv (hereafter NRA), O Ovenstad, 'Den Norske Hær 1628–1900', unpublished regimental chart collection, pp. 3 and 4; O Ovenstad, *Militærbiografier; den norske hærs officerer fra 18. Januar 1628 til 17. Mai 1841, II: I-Ø* (1949) 148. The rest of this section is drawn from Murdoch and Grosjean, *Alexander Leslie* (n 56) 157–160.

61 NRA, Danske Kanselli: Skapsaker I, 1122/01. Skap IX, pakke 62 A, 4A08326; Ovenstad, *Militaerbiografier*, ii (n 60) 426; Ovenstad, 'Den Norske Hær 1628–1900' (n 60) pp. 3 and 4. The Scottish officers were Lieutenant-Colonel Thomas Gray, Lieutenant-Captain Richard Gordon and Captain William Maitland. Lieutenant Daniel Marchonell was probably from Ireland.

62 Ovenstad, *Militærbiografier* (n 60) ii 571. The other Scots included Captain John Forbes, Captain John Barclay and Lieutenant Alexander Skeen. See NRA, Ovenstad, 'Den Norske Hær 1628–1900' (n 60) p. 3.

63 NRA, Ovenstad, 'Den Norske Hær 1628–1900' (n 60) pp. 3 and 4; Ovenstad, *Militærbiografier* (n 60) ii 478; Wahl, *Det Gamle Bergenhusiske Regiments Historie* (n 58) 10–14.

64 DRA, TKUA, England A I. Charles I to Christian IV, 16 January 1644; Ovenstad, *Militærbiografier* (n 60) ii 192.

65 DRA, TKUA England, A II 15. Instructions to John Henderson from Christian IV to be related to Charles I, 28 November 1644.

66 SRA, Skoklostersamlingen, E 8360. Axel Oxenstierna to Arvid Forbes, 19 February 1645.

67 NRA, Ovenstad, 'Den Norske Hær 1628–1900' p. 4.

4,000 men. They were supported by Colonel Alexander Seaton, serving as commander of a squadron of eight ships with which he prosecuted the "Norwegian" offensive against Gothenburg by sea.[68] Meanwhile, preparing to repel him and the Royalist Scots, the "Swedish" regiments under Scottish command included those of Colonel William Philp (Västmanland infantry), Colonel Hugo Hamilton (Uppland Infantry) and Colonel John Gordon (Närke och Värmland Infantry).[69] Supporting these were the Scots of the Swedish navy, including two admirals, one naval major, three sea captains and four lieutenants at sea in command of ships.[70]

The three Norwegian regiments of Mackenzie, Spang and Wilson appear to have remained within Norway during the assault on Gothenburg. Those of Taylor, Murray and Seaton were deployed and prosecuted much of the "Norwegian" attack on Sweden. Colonel John Taylor of the *Smaalenske* National Infantry was singled out for considerable praise for his role in the assault on Gothenburg.[71] The Murray-Taylor-Seaton offensive illustrates an episode where Gothenburg was bombarded from both maritime assets and land-based Oldenburg territories controlled by Scottish commanders, the majority of whom had only left the British theatre the previous year as refugees. Their actions proved to be in vain. The Treaty of Brømsebro (1645) signalled the defeat of Denmark-Norway. Despite the Norwegians performing the best out of the Oldenburg forces, this treaty resulted in significant territorial losses, including the Norwegian provinces of Jämtland and Härjedalen, to Sweden.

Given Scottish participation on both sides of this war, it would be hard to conclude that the Scots supported Norway. Those who did so apparently did it very well, but the same can also be said of the Scots defending Gothenburg. More importantly, and as in previous periods of tension, this period witnessed an increase in civilian as well as military Scottish presence in Norway. At least seven Scots became burgesses of Stavanger between the outbreak of the civil wars in Scotland (1638) and the Treaty of Brømsebro (1645). A further twenty-eight men also became burgesses of Bergen in the same period, while at least one joined the civic community in Trondheim.

68 Wahl, *Det Gamle Bergenhusiske Regiments Historie* (n 58) 8–10; Espeland, *Skottene i Hordaland og Rogaland* (n 58) 34; Murdoch, *The Terror of the Seas?* (n 8) 216–217.

69 For the number and disposition of the Swedish-based Scots, see Murdoch and Grosjean, *Alexander Leslie* (n 56) 158–160.

70 Grosjean, *An Unofficial Alliance* (n 44) 132–133.

71 NFA, Ovenstad, 'Den Norske Hær 1628–1900' (n 60) 3–4; Ovenstad, *Militærbiografier* ii (n 60) 478; Wahl, *Det Gamle Bergenhusiske Regiments Historie* (n 58) 10–14.

Moreover, many of the soldiers employed during the war chose to remain within Norway after hostilities ceased. Soldiers and civilians alike joined a community of Norwegian-based Scots that, by 1645, was already numerous; according to Nina Østby Pedersen at least thirty-seven Scots were resident in Bergen in that year alone.[72] Many of these were still alive to witness a subsequent major engagement pitting Scots against Norwegians. On this occasion there was no ambiguity as to which side the Scots "should" have been on. Norway was caught up in Frederick III's politics and his unexpected alliance with the Dutch who were at war against England. Due to the dual British monarchy, Norway also found itself at war with Scotland.

F: THE SCOTTISH-NORWEGIAN WAR (1666–1667)

The second Anglo-Dutch war (1665–1667) is a well-understood war in both English and Dutch contexts, largely concerning two major maritime powers trying to establish themselves as the dominant force in global trade. The war, one of the three seventeenth-century Anglo-Dutch Wars, is usually only seen through the lens of the two main combatant powers without thought or recourse to any allies. This particular conflict nevertheless represented not only the first Scotto-Dutch War since the outbreak of the Dutch Eighty Years' War in 1568, but also the first declared war between Scotland and Denmark-Norway since the early mediaeval period. It can be argued that this was a conflict into which the Scots were drawn unwillingly by her larger neighbour, England. Yet once involved there is no doubt that many Scots participated enthusiastically.[73] The Dutch certainly bore the brunt of the Scottish privateering predation, but for the present essay we must ask why Scots would also target Norway?

In July 1665 it seemed likely that Charles II of Great Britain and his cousin Frederik III of Denmark-Norway might form an alliance against the Dutch. A plan was conceived whereby the Scandinavians would seize all Dutch shipping in Norwegian harbours, attack the returning Dutch East India Company (VOC) fleet, and the two kings would divide the spoils.[74]

72 Pedersen, 'Skotsk innvandring til Norge' (n 54) 69–70. More names are found in the SSNE database, which includes the soldiers in the regiments, available at *http://www.st-andrews.ac.uk/history/ssne* (last accessed 16 July 2022). For one of the officers who stayed on with his family after the war see, for example, Sir Thomas Gray (SSNE 45, see *https://www.st-andrews.ac.uk/history/ssne/item.php?id=45* (last accessed 16 July 2022)) – a man with an interesting relationship to Hannibal Sehested.

73 Murdoch, *The Terror of the Seas?* (n 8) 237–281.

74 H L Schoolcraft, 'England and Denmark, 1660–1667' (1910) XXV *English Historical Review*

The plan failed because poor communications between the English and the Danes resulted in the Stuart Royal Navy attacking the Dutch on their own instead of in a concerted operation with their Oldenburg allies. Frederik III apparently felt aggrieved. The situation worsened for the Royal Navy when some of the forts around Bergen fell under Dutch control and bombarded the English ships. Although the Royal Navy successfully took rich Dutch prizes into Leith, the "Bergen Affair" is said to have forced the Danes and Norwegians back into the Dutch camp.[75] The following year Scottish privateers and an English Royal Navy squadron patrolled together between Stavanger and Flekkerøy in Norway. Indeed, some Scottish privateers had attacked Nedstrand on 14 September 1666, a week before Scotland formally declared war against Denmark-Norway.[76]

During the infamous "Nedstrand Raid", Captain Thomas Bennett led a large body of men ashore where they caused both panic and destruction. They plundered the Nedstrand tollbooth (*Ryfylke tollsted*), and the houses surrounding it, then set them all on fire destroying some 7,000 boards, quantities of salted herring, salted and smoked meat and numerous furs. The personal belongings of the chief surveyor of customs, Erik Jorgensen, along with the goods of other merchants, were also pillaged. The Scots then returned to their ship with the customs chest and four customs officers as prisoners.[77] Bennett had told some of the inhabitants of the town that the Royal Navy would follow up his raid by landing some 10,000 men at Vestlandet and Bergen. In a move that gave substance to rumours of this landing, another raid followed at Kristiansand where British privateers liberated goods, including six cannons, while some sixty Norwegians were taken across the North Sea as prisoners.[78] As a result of these raids this whole

471. See also Murdoch, *The Terror of the Seas?* (n 8) 241–246 from which the Norwegian elements here have been abstracted.

75 R Harding, *Seapower and Naval Warfare, 1650–1830* (1999) 87; G Rommelse, *The Second Anglo-Dutch War: International raison d'etat, mercantilism and maritime trade* (2006) 136–137; J D Davies, *Pepys's Navy: Ships, Men and Warfare, 1649–1689* (2008) 21.

76 B Lorentzen, 'Vardevakt og strandvern langs Norges sydvest-kyst i det 17de århundre' (1933) *Historisk Tidsskrift* 305. I would like to express my sincere thanks to Sigmar Myhre, Dagfinn Silgjerd, Lisbet Risa and Rune Blix Hagen who have all discussed the Nedstrand Raid with me.

77 Statsarkivet Stavanger, Tingbok for Ryfylke 1666, Bb3, ff. 35b–37b. Court minute, 8 November 1666; Lorentzen, 'Vardevakt og strandvern langs Norges sydvest-kyst' (n 76) 305; J Elgvin, *En By i Kamp: Stavanger bys historie, 1536–1814* (1956) 165; S I Langhelle, *Tysvær. Slik levde dei, bind 8, fram til 1820* (1997) 209–212.

78 The fact that cannons were taken is suggestive of the ships having come right into port, given the difficulty of moving or loading cannon into ships-tenders that the raiding party would have taken ashore, S Steen, *Kristiansands Historie, 1641–1814* (1941) 120. Steen calls these privateers "English" and provides few sources, though some of the prisoners ended up in Scotland.

area of Norway was put on full alert and Danish-Norwegian ships were diverted from the Sound to protect the coast. This was probably precisely the intended result of Bennett's misinformation. Further raids by British privateers followed, with shots being exchanged in April 1667 between one privateer and a hastily arranged Norwegian shore battery. Bernt Lorentzen believed such activity was in fact very common during this war. Furthermore, the same year, he notes that a group of six Scottish sailors deserted from the Danish-Norwegian warship *Middelborg* then stole a small boat with which they plundered Norwegian coastal communities for several months. They were caught trying to steal a Norwegian galliot by their own former captain, Peder Morsing, and thereafter taken to Bergen, albeit their fate is yet to be determined.[79]

Economic histories contain little or no mention of the Scotto-Norwegian war causing a problem for commerce between the nations. This includes studies dedicated to war and commerce from a Norwegian perspective.[80] Instead, any reduction is blamed on new trading regulations being applied in 1665, at least in Sunnhordland, and specifically in regard to the timber trade.[81] Regardless of these restrictions, four Bergen ships sailed from Sunnhordland to their home port with timber in 1666 before then sailing onto Scotland with their cargo.[82] Another six vessels arrived in Leith in 1667 having embarked from Norway.[83]

While the merchants continued to trade, the soldiers continued to serve. The two refugees from Oliver Cromwell's occupation of Scotland, Lieutenant James Hamilton and Lieutenant Colonel James Hamilton, served throughout the war in the Norwegian army.[84] Major John Forbes served in the *Smaalenske* regiment with no mention having come to light that his country of birth was actually at war with the one in which he lived.[85] Likewise, William Scott received his promotion to lieutenant in the Norwegian army

79 See Lorentzen, 'Vardevakt og strandvern langs Norges sydvest-kyst' (n 76) 306–308.

80 H Salvesen, 'Handelsinteresser og konflikter i Norden 1560–1720' in R B Hagen and E Sparboe (eds), *Kongens reise til det ytterste nord; dagbøker fra Christian IVs tok til Finmark og Kola i 1599* (2004) 105–128.

81 Næss, 'Skottehandelen på Sunnhordland' (n 3) 47.

82 Næss, 'Skottehandelen på Sunnhordland' (n 3) 56.

83 E J Graham, *A Maritime History of Scotland, 1650–1790* (2004) 144.

84 E Marquard (ed), *Kongelige Kammerregnskaber fra Frederik III.s og Christian V.s tid* (1918) 150; I Gulowsen, *Gyldenløvefeiden 1675–1679* (1906) 254; O Ovenstad, *Militærbiografier; den norske hærs officerer fra 18. Januar 1628 til 17. Mai 1841, I: A-H* (1948) 406.

85 A Tayler and H Tayler, *The House of Forbes* (1987) 169 and 201; Riis, *Should Auld Acquaintance*, ii (n 15) 193.

in 1666 and served for years thereafter.[86] There were many more, as well as Scottish women, such as Mary Elisabeth Gray, married to Norwegian soldiers.[87] Indeed, there seems to have been no repercussions against the thriving Scottish communities already spread along the Norwegian coastline so long as they were not directly involved in hostilities. In Bergen, the ethnic-Scot Job Jacobsen Dischington (a burgess since 1665) continued to deal with his partners in Orkney throughout the war.[88] This was not uncommon and nowhere is this more clearly demonstrated than in and around Trondheim. At least five new Scots were operating in Molde from 1664 onwards.[89] More had arrived in the area around Mostadmark.

In 1650 Bernt Brunsmann had discovered a large ore deposit at Mostadmark near Trondheim.[90] The Dutch-based Scottish exile, Sir William Davidson, initially invested heavily in the Mostadmark ironworks and installed the Edinburgh merchant, Alexander Wishart, as his factor for the works.[91] The problems and conflicts that erupted between Brunsmann, Wishart, and Davidson have been thoroughly researched previously.[92] However, it is important to note several aspects about Davidson's involvement, particularly after the outbreak of the 1666 Scotto-Norwegian war. Even after Charles II's declaration of war on his cousin Frederik III in October 1666, the Mostadmark Scots continued with their business, Wishart still living in Mostadmark, and Davidson visiting both Norway and Denmark. During these sojourns he managed to pressure Frederik III to abide by his financial obligations originating in Davidson's loans to the Danish-Norwegian crown. Indeed, Davidson's influence was so strong that he even received permission to break several of the much-vaunted trading regulations established by the London-based monarchy specifically to protect English trade from foreign competition. Despite these extant acts, Davidson organised the export of

86 Ovenstad, *Militærbiografier*, ii (n 60) 390–391.

87 J Sandberg, *Kvinner gift med offiserer i den Norske Hær 1628–1814. Fra stabsfanejunker O. Ovenstads Militærbiografier* (1961) 35.

88 See for example National Records of Scotland, GD 106/224. Obligation by John Scarlatt of Kirkwall to Job Dishingtoune, burgess of Bergen, for seven Rex Dollars. Dated at "Birgan in Norroway", 12 July 1667. For more on Job and his family see Bergen Statsarkiv, Sollied Archive, 'Dischingthun'; D A Bailey, 'An ancient Bible and a Family Record' (1976) XXV *Norsk Slektshistorisk Tidsskrift*, 169–171.

89 Pedersen, 'Skotsk innvandring til Norge' (n 54) 80.

90 L Halse 'Mostadmarkens Jernverk' in *Malvik Bygdebok* 3 vols (1957–1959) vol i 239; B Sogner, *Trondheim bys historie. II. Kjøpstad og stiftsstad 1537–1807* (1962) 190.

91 Halse, 'Mostadmarkens Jernverk' (n 90) 240.

92 S Murdoch, *Network North: Scottish Kin, Commercial and Covert Associations in Northern Europe, 1603–1746* (2006) 193–204.

Norwegian timber aboard Dutch ships to the English colonies in America in December 1666.[93] The granting of this permission is astonishing. As a Scot, Davidson had no rights to trade with English colonies under the terms of the English Navigation Acts. Moreover, no Dutch ships should have been allowed to sail to English colonies, especially during time of war between the English and Dutch nations. Equally, with Norway as a belligerent ally of the Dutch, Norwegian goods were subject to confiscation! Nevertheless, Davidson had the support of Charles II and Frederik III and both monarchs ensured there would be no hindrance to Davidson's unorthodox trade across the Atlantic.

G: CONCLUDING REMARKS

The intention of this brief survey of Scottish-Norwegian relations in times of peace and war has been to highlight that the focus on moments of episodic conflict is not necessarily the best way of understanding historical relations between the two nations in the sixteenth and seventeenth centuries. When one reflects on the 1523 "Scottish Incident" in Bergen, *Skottetoget* in 1612, or indeed the Nedstrand Raid in 1666 (and the wider Scotto-Norwegian War), what we see are but brief moments that impacted on particular individuals. They did not resound across the nations and they were probably hardly known about in the wider Scottish-Norwegian communities, even in their own time. Though undoubtedly traumatic for those killed, injured or financially damaged, the truth is that life continued pretty much as before and undisturbed. War apparently provided no legal obstacle to the continuation of trade and the expansion of ethnic Scottish communities in Norway and, indeed, the Scots remained legally protected by the 1589 Stuart-Oldenburg alliance in pursuit of their activities. Moreover, as the case of Sir William Davidson shows, subsequently imposed legal restrictions, such as the Navigation Acts, could even be overruled by the monarchs of Scotland and Norway to ensure that trade continued and even increased.

Nevertheless, it often remains the intermittent moments of conflict that often draws the attention of popularising scholars, as evidenced in Gordon Donaldson's *A Northern Commonwealth*. That volume flits across spectacular events from one century to the next without consideration of the

93 For the export of Norwegian deals of timber only months later see M A Everett Green, *Calendar of State Papers Domestic: Charles II, 1666–1667* (1864) 384. License for Davidson, 'West Indies and Norway Merchant', December 1666.

wider context. Indeed, it moves from *Skottetoget* to the twentieth century from one page to the next, missing out the greater impact of migration and commerce in either direction, let alone the other wars.[94] However, in the intervening period, the Scottish community in Norway continued to grow. Some 300 individual citizens in Bergen, forty-five in Stavanger, and thirty in Trondheim, have been identified to date.[95] These individuals, whether burgesses or soldiers, also had families and it is clear that many of the transient maritime population felt at home on both sides of the North Sea.

According to Lillehammer, the Scottish timber trade ended in 1717, though that conclusion is somewhat erroneous. What actually happened was *Skottetiden*, or the period that saw the end of Scottish dominance in the trade in southern Norway, came to an end.[96] However, neither migration nor commercial exchange concluded abruptly between the two nations in 1717. Indeed, Scottish migrants and merchants continued to arrive in Norway well into the eighteenth century. Similarly, the wars mentioned above were not the last that Scots would fight in, either for or against Norway. Indeed, "Duncans krig", an assault launched from Norway against the Swedes in 1679 is named after James Duncan. Duncan had actually come into Danish-Norwegian service from Sweden in 1671 with his brother David, but soon found himself fighting his former colleagues. From February 1679, he campaigned against Sweden with his cavalry troop and some 1,500 infantry.[97] Duncan, like the Scottish colonels and mariners of the 1640s, is somewhat forgotten by modern scholarship, which tends to offer yet another rendition of *Zinklars Vise*. There are, of course, exceptions: the older scholarship of Næss, Bugge, and Lillehammer still stand up to scrutiny especially on the economic relations. They offer starting points to move beyond myth and truly get to grips with Scottish-Norwegian relations in the early modern period. More recently, Nina Østby Pedersen's encyclopaedic work has significantly moved our understanding along and has been built on by Opsahl and Sogner.[98] From this corpus we find that Scotland and Norway continued to engage in commercial and cultural exchange beyond "epoch dates" such as 1707. In that year, Scotland became part of the unitary British state and

94 Donaldson, *A Northern Commonwealth* (n 47) 145–146.

95 SSNE Database, available at: *http://www.st-andrews.ac.uk/history/ssne* (last accessed 16 July 2022). See also Pedersen, 'Skotsk innvandring til Norge' (n 54) 65–89.

96 Lillehammer, 'The Scottish Norwegian Timber Trade' (n 3) 109.

97 I Gulowsen, *Gyldenløvefeiden 1675–1679* (1906) 246; D Schnitler, *Blade af Norges Krigshistorie* (1895) 156, 166 and 168–169; A F Jensen, *Kavaleriet i Norge, 1200–1994* (1995) 145–175.

98 Opsahl and Sogner, *Norsk Innvandringshistorie*, vol 1 (n 3) 297–315.

the cultural icon Petter Dass died – though the two events are, obviously, unrelated. But neither of these events changed much at that particular moment. Rather, it would be impossible to find a period where there was no interaction between these two North Sea neighbours whether at war or not, or before or after the formation of the unitary state of Great Britain. Moreover, we must be extremely careful not to build a false narrative that seeks to create the impression of some kind of special relationship. One need only think of the Scottish communities in Sweden, Poland-Lithuania or the Dutch Republic to find ethnic enclaves of equivalent status to anywhere in Denmark-Norway.[99] Similarly, as shown in the works of numerous scholars such as Grüner, Opsahl and Sogner, it is equally possible to view the period in hand as one of Dutch as well as (or instead of) Scottish importance.[100] Thus, it is incumbent upon the scholars of any age to avoid the myopic draw of the spectacular event, or the confines of one limited source-base to create a particularistic narrative. Only then can we determine a relationship that sometimes found itself tested and yet continues to evolve to this day.

99 See, for example, P Bajer, *Scots in the Polish-Lithuanian Commonwealth, 16th–18th Centuries: The Formation and Disappearance of an Ethnic Group* (2012); D Catterall, *Community Without Borders: Scots Migrants and the Changing Face of Power in the Dutch Republic, c. 1600–1700* (2002); S Murdoch, 'Community, Commodity and Commerce: The Stockholm-Scots in the Seventeenth Century' in David Worthington (ed), *British and Irish Emigrants and Exiles in Europe, 1603–1688* (2010) 31–66.

100 Grüner, *Hollendertida i Romsdal* (n 52) passim; Opsahl and Sogner, *Norsk Innvandringshistorie*, vol 1 (n 3) 297–305.

8 Traders and Immigrants: A Norwegian perspective on Scottish-Norwegian economic relations from the fifteenth to the early seventeenth century

Per G. Norseng[*]

[*] The article was completed while fellow at the project *Social Governance through legislation* at the Centre for Advanced Studies, Oslo, Norway.

A: INTRODUCTION

By ca. 1600, trade between Scotland and Norway was extensive, and remained so throughout the seventeenth and into the eighteenth century. In particular, a great number of Scottish ships and merchants are known to have been calling regularly on harbours in rural areas of south-western and western Norway. With regular trade followed cultural influences, personal relations and migration, especially Scottish immigration to Norway. Drawing mostly on Norwegian primary sources and secondary literature, this chapter will outline the origins, early development, character, extent and impact of the Scottish-Norwegian trade relations up to the early 1600s.

In many respects, the resource geographies of Scotland and south-western and western Norway were quite similar. In this sense, Norway and Scotland were not an obvious match as partners in trade.[1] The most important exception in our context, however, was access to timber. With growing demand and deforestation in coastal areas, Scotland increasingly needed to import timber. More than anything else, Scottish ships came in ever greater numbers to Norway for lumber in the sixteenth and early seventeenth century. What they could offer their Norwegian trade partners in return, though, was not solely based on Scottish natural resources but was also to a large extent based on Scotland being a more advanced mercantile economy with extensive international commercial connections.

B: SOURCES AND LITERATURE

It may come as a surprise how limited our knowledge is as regards Norwegian-Scottish economic relations. This is due partly to a rather fragmentary Norwegian source material prior to ca. 1600, both chronologically and geographically, and partly to a modest interest for the topic in modern academic research, with exceptions mostly of a limited geographical scope. From a Norwegian point of view, more attention has been paid to other aspects of the countries' international trade in this epoch, particularly the trade with members of the Hanseatic League and the Dutch.

Late medieval sources in Norway mainly consist of individual charters – property deeds, royal ordinances and instructions, privileges for Norwegian

1 Cf. A Lillehammer, 'The Timber Trade and The Ryfylke Farmers c. 1500–1700', in A Lillehammer, J Bruijn, T C Smout, S I Langhelle, *Timber and Trade: Articles on the Timber Export from the Ryfylke Area to Scotland and Holland in the 16th and 17th Century* (1999) 21–22.

towns and foreign merchants, diplomatic correspondence – and a few cadasters, mostly ecclesiastical. Extant sources bearing upon our topic pick up in the sixteeenth century, both in quantitative and qualitative terms. Starting from ca. 1500 and gradually improving towards the end of the sixteenth century, they now also include: public records and account books for some years and some areas; expense and income accounts for the archiepiscopal see of Trondheim and royal castles, mostly in Bergen and Oslo; inventories for royal castles; customs and tax registers, etc.; a citizen register from ca. 1550 onwards in Bergen; contemporary topographical literature; Danish customs accounts for the Sound toll from 1497 onwards; correspondence between the German *Kontor* in Bergen and the Hanseatic League and other German and Dutch sources. To some extent toponymical and archaeological evidence may also contribute. More extensive and coherent customs accounts, as well as court rolls that can illuminate amongst other things the trade with Scotland, are only extant from the turn of the sixteenth and the seventeenth centuries onwards and customs records remain fragmented for great parts of the seventeenth century.[2]

Compared to England, Germany and the Netherlands, the Norwegian archival sources in this period do not amount to very much. Scottish primary sources are far more diverse and plentiful from the late middle ages, including, for example, court rolls and customs registers. Even so, Scottish research on trade relations between Scotland and Europe in the middle ages, including Scandinavia, reflects that information on trade with Norway prior to ca. 1500 is very limited. This also applies to Scottish sources from the sixteenth and early seventeenth centuries. Although extensive customs registers are available, they do not reveal the destinations of Scottish ships engaging in foreign trade. Moreover, only imports from England and Ireland were taxed, and most export commodities were also exempt. Hence, the still rather meagre Norwegian sources in fact yield more on Scottish-Norwegian trade relations than Scottish sources. On both sides of the North Sea, however, we have to take the possibility of considerable tax evasion into account, maybe especially for trade with small ships and for trade between Norway and the still Norwegian-speaking populations in the Scottish Northern Isles and Norway. Traders from Shetland and Orkney were not treated as foreigners in Norway until 1580, and therefore appear in the Norwegian customs

2 See, e.g. O A Johnsen, *Innføring i kildene til Norges historie inntil det 19. århundre* (1939) 55–90.

accounts only from the late sixteenth century onwards.[3] At the same time, for trade in rural districts, it is an additional source of error that sawmills and forests on manors belonging to the nobility and the clergy were exempt from taxation, including customs duties.[4]

The good news is that the accessibility of the extant Norwegian sources is generally very good. Up to ca. 1570, almost all extant Norwegian primary sources have been transcribed and published in print by the National Archives and other institutions over the last almost two centuries. Some have also been published and made searchable online. Furthermore, in recent years the National Library has digitised and made available online most Norwegian printed publications. The increasing archival sources from the late sixteenth and the seventeenth centuries have to some extent also been transcribed and published in a way that now allows free search via the National Library or otherwise, and others have been scanned and made available online in non-searchable modes.[5]

Alexander Bugge's two monumental works from the 1920s on the history of medieval and early modern Norwegian shipping and lumber exports, respectively, are still the standard general reference works on the Scottish-Norwegian commercial relations.[6] To some extent Bugge, who collected foreign sources for the *Diplomatarium Norvegicum*, also consulted Scottish archival sources. Later nationwide outlines of the development of Norwegian shipping, foreign trade or economic history more generally, are

3 See, in particular, I Guy, 'The Scottish Export Trade, 1460–1599', in T C Smout (ed), *Scotland and Europe 1200–1850* (1986) 62; C T Smout, 'The Norwegian Timber Trade before 1707, from the Scottish Perspective', in J Bruijn, T C Smout, S I Langhelle, A Lillehammer, *Timber and Trade: Articles on the Timber Export from the Ryfylke Area to Scotland and Holland in the 16th and 17th Century* (1999) 42–43; D Ditchburn, *Scotland and Europe: The Medieval Kingdom and its Contacts with Christendom, c. 1215–1545*. Vol 1. *Religion, Culture and Commerce* (2001) 193; J Ø Sunde, *Vegen over havet. Frå Mowatane på Shetland til Baroniet Rosendal/ Across the Sea. The Mowats from a Shetland Lairdship to a Norwegian Barony* (2010) 68; cf. also E Frankot, *'Of Laws of Ships and Shipmen': Medieval Maritime Law and its Practice in Urban Northern Europe* (2012) vol 20 Scottish Historical Review Monograph Series.

4 See Sunde, *Across the Sea* (n 3) 71; cf. A Næss, 'Sagbruk i Søndhordland indtil 1750' (1919) vol 6 *Sunnhordland. Årsskrift frå Bygdemuséet og Sogelaget i Sunnhordlandsbygdene* 10, 15–17; A Næss, 'Skottehandelen på Sunnhordland' (1920) vol 7 in *Sunnhordland. Årsskrift frå Bygdemuséet og Sogelaget i Sunnhordlandsbygdene* 26, 40 and 44; A Espeland, *Skottene i Hordaland og Rogaland' fraa aar 1500–1800* (1921) 23.

5 See *https://www.arkivverket.no/om-oss/vare-publikasjoner/arkivverkets-bokhandel*; *https://www.nb.no/search?mediatype=b%C3%B8ker*; *https://www.digitalarkivet.no/en/*; *https://media.digitalarkivet.no/db/browse* (all last accessed 17 July 2022).

6 A Bugge, 'Skibsfarten fra de ældste tider til omkring aar 1600' (1923) vol 1 *Den norske sjøfarts historie* 8–369; cf. R Tank, 'Fra hollændervældet til handelsempiren', *ibid.*, 373–591; A Bugge, *Den norske trælasthandels historie* vols I–II (1925).

less comprehensive and largely rely on Bugge, directly or indirectly, for trade relations.[7] More recent comprehensive works on Norwegian foreign trade of this epoch focus on Germans and Hollanders trading in Norway. Some of these, especially Arnved Nedkvitnes' impressive monograph on the German Hansa in Bergen 1100–1600, are nevertheless useful in our context as well.[8]

There is, moreover, in Norway a long and very strong tradition of local history, both urban and rural, earlier often conducted by schoolteachers, parish priests and other learned amateurs in the craft of the historian, but increasingly also by professional historians. The most important Norwegian towns in the middle ages and sixteenth century are covered by extensive and often multi-volume monographs by academically trained historians, often in recent decades.[9] This also applies to many rural communities, some of which in the seventeenth and eighteenth centuries developed into towns because of their trade with foreigners.[10] Such local studies brings us closer to the

7 See e.g. O A Johnsen, *Norwegische Wirtschaftsgeschichte* (1939); S Dyrvik (ed), *Norsk økonomisk historie 1500–1970: Band 1: 1500–1850* (1979); B Berggren, A E Christensen and B Kolltveit (eds), *Norsk sjøfart: Bind 1* (1989).

8 J Schreiner, *Hanseatene og Norges nedgang* (1935); J Schreiner, *Hanseatene og Norge i det 16 århundre* (1941); M Løyland, *Hollendartida i Noreg 1550–1750* (2012); A Nedkvitne, *The German Hansa and Bergen 1100–1600* (2014); cf. J Wubs-Mrozewicz, *Traders, Ties and Tensions. The Interaction of Lübeckers, Overijsslers and Hollanders in late Medieval Bergen* (2008). See also F Forfang, 'Sagbruksproduksjon I Noreg 1610–63' (2021) *Heimen* 58/4: 315–342.

9 See E Bull, *Oslos historie. Kristianias historie: bind 1* (1922); O A Johnsen, *Tønsbergs historie bind 1–3* (1929–1952); I Seierstad, *Skiens historie: Bind 1* (1958); A O Johnsen, *Tønsberg gjennom tidene* (1971); K Helle, *Bergen bys historie: bind 1* (1982); A B Fossen, *Borgerskapets by: 1536–1800. Bergen bys historie: bind 2* (1979); G A Blom, *Trondheim bys historie: Bind 1* (1956); B Sogner, *Trondheim bys historie: bind 2* (1962); G A Blom, *St. Olavs by. Middelalder til 1537. Trondheims historie 997–1997: bind 1* (1997); S Supphellen, *Trondheims historie: 997–1997: bind 2: Innvandrernes by* (1997); A Nedkvitne and P G Norseng, *Oslo bys historie bd. 1: Byen under Eikaberg* (1991); K Sprauten, *Oslo bys historie: bind 2: Byen ved festningen: Frå 1536 til 1814* (1992); G A Ersland og A Solli, *Stavangers bys historie: bind 1* (2012); J Elgvin, *En by i kamp 1536–1814. Stavanger bys historie: bind 2* (1956); K Helle, *The History of Stavanger from its Origins to 2015* (2016); E Johansen, L Opstad, M Dehli, *Sarpsborg før 1839* (1976); cf. K Helle, F-E Eliassen, J E Myhre, O S Stugu, *Norsk byhistorie: Urbanisering gjennom 1300 år* (2006).

10 In our context see e.g. A Næss, O Kolltveit, *Strandebarm og Varaldsøy: i gamal og ny tid: 1. Bandet: Bygdesoga* (1947); A Lillehammer, *Soga om Sauda: tredje bandet: Bygdesoga før 1880* (1991); M Løyland, *Fjordfolk. Fedas historie fra de eldste tider og fram til 1963* (1999); E Holberg, K Dørum, *Arendal før kjøpstaden fram til 1723. Arendal by- og regionhistorie, Del 1* (2018); K Steffens, *Kragerøs historie 1666–1916* (1916); I B Knudsen, O Teige, *Kysten Skogen Byen. Kragerøs historie: Bind I* (2015); T Pedersen, *Drammen. En østlandsbys utviklingshistorie: bind I* (1961); S Steen, *Kristiansands historie 1641–1814* (1941); J Skeie, O G Moseng, *Kristiansand står og faller med sin havn. Kristiansand havns historie* (2009); F-E Eliassen, *Mandal bys historie. Den førindustrielle byen: ca. 1500–1850* 2 vols (1995); M Ringard, *Flekkefjords historie* (1942); O A Abrahamsen, *Farsund bys historie: En by blir til: Fra stedets oppkomst til 1850: Bind 1* (1997); B Dannevig, *Grimstads sjøfarts historie* (1971); L T Andressen, *Moss bys historie: Bind 1: Frem til 1700* (1984); M Dehli, *Kjøpstad og festningsby 1567–1767. Fredrikstad bys historie:*

extant archival sources. Especially since the 1980s, a substantial number of regional histories have also widened and deepened our understanding of the economic connections between Norway and Scotland in our period and the subsequent centuries.[11] This is the case even if the "Skottehandel" (trade with the Scots) is not everywhere treated as a specific topic. Some local and regional studies have, however, since the early twentieth century been specifically dedicated to this topic and are consequently particularly useful for the present purpose.[12]

C: NORWEGIAN-SCOTTISH TRADE AND THE NORWEGIAN TOWNSCAPE OF THE MIDDLE AGES UP TO THE SIXTEENTH CENTURY

To fully understand the nature of the trade relations between Scotland and Norway and its impact on early modern Norwegian economy, society and culture, it is important to bear in mind some crucial characteristics of the commercial infrastructure of Norway: in spite of its extensive territory and long coastline, there were very few towns in the middle ages compared to other countries. At any given time before 1500 no more than between twelve

bind 1 (1960); J M Tønnessen, *Porsgrunns historie: bind 1: Fra lasteplass til kjøpstad 1576–1807* (1956); O G Moseng, *Byen i emning. Porsgrunns historie: Bind 1*(2006); S G Eliassen, *Haldens historie: Bind 1 1665–1826*; N de Seve, *Molde bys historie: I: Før året 1838. Ladested og kjøpstad* (1962); A O Johnsen, *Kristiansunds historie: 1. bind 1. halvbind* (1942); K Bugge, *Aalesunds historie: bind 1* (1923); cf. I Bull, *Lokalsamfunnet i verden. Norske lokalsamfunns plass i den første globaliseringen på 1600- til 1800-tallet* (2020).

11 E Hovland, H E Næss (eds), *Fra Vistehola til Ekofisk. Rogaland gjennom tidene: bind 1* (1987); J Sulebust, *Strilesoga: bind 1* (1997); A Døssland, *Strilesoga: bind 2* (1998); K Helle (ed), *Vestlandets historie,* bind 1–3 (2006); J R Myking, J R Ugulen, B G Økland, *Hardanger. Ei regionhistorie til 1750* (2015); I Fløystad, *Agders historie: bind 3: Bønder, byvekst og borgarar 1641–1723* (2007); B E Johnsen, G Sætra, *Sørlandsk skipsfart 1600–1920* (2016); Ø Rian (ed), *Telemarks historie: bind 1* (2014), P G Norseng, S G Eliassen, *I Borgarsysle. Østfolds historie: bind 2* (2005); A Dybdahl, *Fra pest til poteter: 1350–1850. Trøndelags historie: bind 2* (2005); A Døssland, *Med lengt mot havet. Fylkeshistorie for Møre og Romsdal: bind 1* (1990); E Holberg, M Røskaft; *Nordlands historie: bind 1* (2015); H J Krøvel, H E Tafjord, *Folk i fjordriket før 1763. Soga om Sogn og Fjordane: bind 1* (2017); cf. E. Lönnrot (ed), *Bohusläns historia* (1963).

12 See e.g. Næss, 'Sagbruk i Søndhordland' (n 4) 3–40; Næss, 'Skottehandelen' (n 4) 3–86; Espeland, *Skottene* (n 4); O. Kolltveit, 'Skogen og trelasthandelen i Strandebarm', *Hardanger* (1934) 54–63; A Lillehammer, 'Skottehandelen og Rogaland. By mot land på 1600-talet', in *Ætt og heim* (1987) 39–55; A Lillehammer, 'Skottar og hollendarar på Agder- og Rogalandskysten', in K A Andersen (eds), *Kontakten mellom Agder og Holland på 16- og 1700-talet: Flekkefjord museum 30. juni–1.juli 2000* (2001) 4–24; B. Slettan, *Skogbrukspolitikk og trelasthandel. En artikkelsamling* (Kristiansand 1997); J Bruijn, T C Smout, S I Langhelle, Lillehammer, 'The timber trade' (n 3); J Ø Sunde, *Vegen over havet/Across the Sea* (n 3).

and fifteen places may be called towns – in some cases only with considerable terminological leeway.[13]

The Norwegian towns all suffered heavily from the agrarian crisis of the late middle ages, although some, especially Bergen, apparently somewhat less than others. Some of the smaller ones lost much of their economic and administrative functions as towns and were abandoned. Only one new town – "Oddevald" (Uddevalla) – was granted town privileges in the late middle ages. By 1500, a mere eleven towns remained. With one exception, the episcopal see of Hamar, they were all coastal towns. According to rough estimates, only four of them had a population of more than a few hundred inhabitants – Oslo and Tønsberg probably between 1,000 and 1,500, Trondheim (Nidaros) maybe between 1,500 and 2,000, and Bergen possibly more than 5,000.[14]

North of Bergen, Trondheim, which had lost much of its position in Norwegian foreign trade to Bergen during the thirteenth century, was granted a royal privilege to trade all over Norway in 1455. During the fifteenth century, it seems to have regained some of its former position as a commercial centre, amongst other things by trading in stockfish from northern Norway.[15]

The Oslo fjord area was the most urbanised region in the country, counting, in addition to Oslo and Tønsberg, the medieval towns Sarpsborg (Borg), Skien, Marstrand, Oddevald and Konghelle. These latter three are situated in Bohuslän in the far southeast and have since 1658 belonged to Sweden. Between Skien in Telemark and Stavanger in the southwest, between Stavanger and Bergen, and between Bergen and Trondheim, there were no towns at all at the turn of the fifteenth and sixteenth centuries, and none north of Trondheim. Only one "new" town was granted town privileges between 1500 and the 1640s – Fredrikstad, which replaced nearby Borg in 1567 due to a devastating fire in Borg and more favourable harbour conditions in Fredrikstad.[16]

13 Helle et al, *Norsk byhistorie* (n 9) 41–42, 80–84 and 145–148; cf. P G Norseng, 'The Trade in Painters' Materials in Norway in the Middle Ages. Part 1: The "Silent" Trade in Painters' Materials in the High Middle Ages', in J Kirby, S Nash, J Cannon (eds), *Trade in Artists' Materials: Markets and Commerce in Europe to 1700* (2010) 50–63.

14 See K Helle, *Bergen bys historie* (n 9) 687–688 and 692–693; Helle et al, *Norsk byhistorie* (n 9) 12[illegible]–128; A Nedkvitne og P G Norseng, *Oslo bys historie* (n 9) 356–357; Sprauten, *Oslo bys historie* (n 9) 16–17; Blom, *St. Olavs by* (n 9) 325; Supphellen, *Trondheims historie* (n 9) 9.

15 See Bugge, 'Skibsfarten' (n 6) 274; Blom, *St. Olavs by* (n 9) 285–287, 327; cf. Helle et al, *Norsk byhistorie* (n 9) 83.

16 See Helle et al, *Norsk byhistorie* (n 9) 127 and 152.

From the high middle ages, it had been the policy of the Norwegian kings, and later the Danish kings, to prohibit foreign merchants to call on ports and trade north of Bergen or in their overseas possessions, and more generally also to concentrate both domestic and foreign trade in the towns, aiming to control commercial activities, safeguard customs revenues and protect the economic interests of the townspeople. During the late middle ages and sixteenth century, this policy became increasingly difficult to enforce, amongst other things due to the growing exports of timber. From a practical point of view, it made no sense to transport timber or lumber from the vast coastal and rural districts of western and eastern Norway to the scattered towns for export via intermediaries there.[17] This is important to keep in mind when the rather modest evidence in Norwegian sources for shipping and trade between Norwegian towns and Scotland in the sixteenth century, as well as in the late middle ages, is to be interpreted below.

From the twelfth century onwards, trade between Norway and the British Isles can be seen to have been conducted both by English and Scottish as well as Norwegian merchants and ships. For obvious geographical reasons, but probably partly also due to more extant sources for Norway's largest and most important commercial town, this trade is better documented for Bergen than for other Norwegian medieval towns. In the thirteenth century, more and more of the trade between Bergen and England, as well as between Bergen and the continent (both the Baltic and the Netherlands), was taken over by Germans. By 1280, the Germans had become quite dominant, and in the early fourteenth century merchants from the Hansa towns seem to have completely replaced the Norwegians in the Anglo-Norse trade in Bergen, to a large extent conducted as part of a triangular trade between Norway, England and Flanders, or between the Baltic, Bergen and Flanders. To some degree, a similar development took place in the lesser towns of eastern Norway, and the native Norwegian merchant class was eroded.[18]

The trade of English merchants and ships with Norway, on the other hand, although stagnating instead of expanding like the German trade, did not suffer the same serious decline as did the Norwegian active trade in the fourteenth century, and continued after the Black Death into the late middle

17 Cf. Helle et al, *Norsk byhistorie* (n 9) 80 and 128–129; cf. e.g. Johnsen, *Norwegische Wirtschaftsgeschicte* (n 7) 159–174 and 240; Bugge, 'Skibsfarten' (n 6) 331–332. See also S Koch's chapter, Chapter Nine, in this volume.

18 Nedkvitne, *The German Hansa* (n 8) 55–66 and 80–87; cf. Helle, *Bergen bys historie* (n 9) 378–390; Helle et al, *Norsk byhistorie* (n 9) 85–86.

ages [19] Scottish merchants also seem to have continued visiting Bergen throughout the high middle ages. Among them was probably a Roberto Pellipario, or Robert the Skinner, who according to the accounts of the great chamberlain of Scotland in January 1307 received sixty shillings in Aberdeen for his expenses carrying a letter from the king to Norway.[20] Some may even have engaged in trade between England and Norway. According to the customs rolls for King's Lynn, a Willem "Scot" in 1306 brought stockfish there from Bergen and exported cloth and caps.[21]

Unlike in England and Norway, the Germans engaged in direct trade with Scotland to a much more modest degree. If Berwick-upon-Tweed is left out, they apparently did not establish permanent trading posts in Scotland. This left more space both for Scottish and Norwegian active shipping and trade between the two countries even after the German expansion. Moreover, unlike Norwegian merchants, Scottish merchants continued an extensive trade with the Netherlands in the late middle ages.[22] People like Willem Scot may have engaged in a triangle or even quadrangle trade between Norway, Scotland, England and the continent.

O A Johnsen, in his outline of Norwegian economic history in 1939, was of the opinion that in spite of the Hanseatic dominance, trade with Scotland and Shetland as well as with the Atlantic islands, Denmark and Holland was being conducted from all medieval towns of Norway. He also concluded that the Scottish trade in Norway probably never ceased entirely. However, as had earlier also been pointed out by Alexander Bugge, Johnsen maintained that it picked up considerably in the fifteenth century, especially towards the end of the century, due to the growing need in Scotland for importing timber. Bugge assumed that the 1455 privileges amongst other things brought Trondheim back into the business of trade with Scotland. Nevertheless, both the Scottish and Dutch trade with Norway, according to Johnsen, still amounted to little compared to the dominant Hanseatic trade, until the sixteenth century.[23]

19 Nedkvitne, *The German Hansa* (n 8) 66–69.

20 A Bugge (ed), *Diplomatarium Norvegicum*, vol XIX (1914) no 455 (henceforth DN); cf. S Bagge and A Nedkvitne (eds), *Regesta Norvegia*, vol III (1983) no 376 (henceforth RN).

21 "De Willelmo Stot de Northberge (. . .)"; see Bugge (ed), DN, vol XIX (n 20) 514 (*https://www.dokpro.uio.no/cgi-bin/middelalder/diplom_vise_tekst.cgi?b=16411&s=&str=* (last accessed 17 July 2022)); cf. however Helle, *Bergen bys historie* (n 9) 378; Bagge and Nedkvitne (eds), RN, vol III (n 20) no 365; Nedkvitne, *The German Hansa* (n 8) 606.

22 See e.g. Ditchburn, *Scotland and Europe* (n 3) 138–196.

23 Johnsen, *Norwegische Wirtschaftsgeschicte* (n 7) 159–161; cf. Bugge, 'Skibsfarten' (n 6) 274.

Sources are scarce, however, both for Scottish trade with Norway in the late middle ages and vice versa. To a large extent, the assessments of earlier historians seem to have been based on circumstantial evidence and common sense until the very end of the fifteenth century, but they seem fair, and are not entirely unsubstantiated. A few examples, scattered throughout the fourteenth and especially the fifteenth century, will have to suffice in our context.

Active Norwegian trade with Scotland towards the middle of the fourteenth century is suggested by an entry in the customs records for Aberdeen 1341 concerning a Norwegian merchant who was remunerated for a duty he had paid. Furthermore, according to an account of Pietro Querini, a Venetian who suffered shipwreck on a voyage from his hometown to Flanders and, in a miraculous way, ended up in Lofoten in Northern Norway in 1432 with some of his crew, he was told by the local fishermen that Bergen at this time was visited on a regular basis by numerous ships from different countries, including Scotland.[24]

Sources for Aberdeen have in recent years been made especially easy to consult through Aberdeen Records online. In general, they seem to yield disappointingly little information for our purpose, and astonishingly little for Bergen in particular.[25] One court case, from 1450, is worth mentioning, however. A ship from Aberdeen apparently had called both in a Flemish and Norwegian port on the same voyage.[26] This is a further indication of Scottish triangular trade between Scotland, the continent and Norway in the late middle ages.

D: RESIDENT SCOTS, GERMANS, AND NORWEGIANS IN LATE MEDIEVAL SCOTTISH-NORWEGIAN TRADE

In 1341, a letter from bishop Håkon of Bergen to his colleague in Stavanger, mentioning a tailor named "Jon Skotr",[27] may indicate the presence of Scottish immigrant craftsmen in Bergen, which would also imply trading connections. However, one swallow does not make a summer. The same can be said for the first mention of a resident Scottish merchant in Bergen.

24 Bugge (ed), DN, vol XIX (n 20) no 560; H A Wold, *Querinis reise – Il Viaggio di Querini* (2004) 185–186 and 198–199.

25 See Search Aberdeen Registers, available at *https://sar.abdn.ac.uk* (last accessed 17 July 2022).

26 Search Aberdeen Registers, "Norwegiam", *https://sar.abdn.ac.uk/search?q=Norwegiam&r=5&m=0&o=1&sm=0* (last accessed 17 July 2022).

27 C R Unger and H J Huitfeldt (eds), (DN, vol IX) (1878) no 131.

Grievances from the citizens of Bergen on extensive misconduct of the Hansa *Kontor* there in 1440 included complaints about a "nordfar", Jon or Jørgen "Skott", who in his house had stored 1,400 stockfish that were unlawfully seized by the Germans. He most likely was a Scottish immigrant of some economic means who had settled and gained citizenship in Bergen, had his own warehouse in the town and was engaged in direct trade in dry cod with northern Norway.[28]

With this exception, the first hard evidence of Scottish residents in Bergen appears in the early 1500s, but a Scottish supreme court case from 1491, referring to some lost property that had been retrieved on behalf of several Scottish men in Norway, may indicate immigration from Scotland towards the end of the fifteenth century, possibly to Bergen.[29] However, we also know a "Tord Skott" who served as "radman" or member of the town council in Oslo in the late 1490s.[30] The first name is Norwegian; the surname or nickname, nevertheless, indicates that Tord may have been Scottish or of Scottish descent, or otherwise had a connection with Scotland. By the end of the fifteenth century, moreover, more direct evidence for trade connections between Scotland and Norway also surfaces in Norwegian as well as in Scottish sources from the middle of the fifteenth century.

Two charters issued in Oslo in 1445 refer to merchants with typically German names, but apparently citizens in the town, who traded with Scotland. Prior to 1468 this must have meant mainland Scotland, not Shetland or Orkney.[31] Another citizen of Oslo who was probably born in Germany, or the son of a German, was Herman Kremer, who died on a voyage to Scotland in 1494.[32] In one of the 1445 cases, a Norwegian skipper, Hans Eriksson, accounted to 'Clawes Reppyn' (also called 'Clawes backer') and "Hans Wysendorp" for both the ship and the cargo he had sailed from the coast of Agder in the south of Norway via Bergen to Scotland where he sold both ship and cargo on their behalf. With Agder as the point of depar-

28 A Bugge (ed), *Norges gamle Love* 2. Række, vol I (1912) 246 (§ 2) (henceforth NgL), cf. Schreiner *Hanseatene og Norge* (n 8) 64.

29 Bugge, 'Skibsfarten' (n 6) 319; Bugge, *Den norske trælasthandels historie: I* (n 6) 276–277.

30 Chr C A Lange and C R Unger (eds), DN, vol II (1852) no 991 (1496), C R Unger and H J Huitfeldt-Kaas (eds), DN, vol VII (1869) no 518 (1499).

31 Lange and Unger (eds), DN, (DN, vol II) (n 30) nos 764 and 765; cf. Nedkvitne, *The German Hansa* (n 8) 183. Before 1468, a reference to Scotland must have been to the Scottish mainland, and not Shetland or Orkney.

32 Lange and Unger (eds), DN, vol II (n 30) no 978; cf. Nedkvitne and Norseng, *Oslo bys historie* (n 9) 373.

ture for the voyage, at least part of the cargo was, by all probability, timber bought there.[33]

Alexander Bugge pointed out that import of timber for building castles and other purposes is frequently mentioned in the accounts of the Scottish treasury in the latter half of the fifteenth century. This import is initially attributed to "Dutchmen", i.e. Germans in this context, and probably to a large extent refers to Baltic timber. But among these "Dutchmen" in 1496 appears a man called "Bend Ollufesone", in Norwegian spelling Bent Olavsson. The assumption that he was Norwegian is corroborated by the information that he had sold "rachteris" and "sparris", both clearly referring to Norwegian terms for lumber ("rafter" and "sperrer"). In 1501, furthermore, these Scottish accounts for the first time explicitly mention timber bought from Norwegians (Nordwaymen), according to Bugge.[34] In this context the trade treaties between Denmark-Norway and Scotland of 1492 and 1496 should likewise be mentioned.[35]

Some of the timber imported to Scotland by Germans could also be Norwegian. Hansa merchants may have engaged in the trade with Scotland to a greater extent than is commonly believed. With the Germans in Oslo trading with Scotland in 1445 in mind, some of the German timber merchants appearing in the accounts of the Scottish treasury in the latter half of the fifteenth century may have been citizens of Oslo or other Norwegian towns (except probably for Bergen, where the Hansa, contrary to politics elsewhere in Norway, quite effectively prohibited German merchants or craftsmen from registering as citizens there until the early 1500s).[36] German ships visiting harbours in eastern Norway may also have been chartered to bring timber to Scotland. More likely, ships belonging to citizens of German extraction in Norwegian towns may have been chartered by Scottish importers of timber from Norway.[37]

33 Lange and Unger (eds), DN, vol II (n 30) no 764; cf. Nedkvitne and Norseng, *Oslo bys historie* (n 9) 373.

34 Bugge, 'Skibsfarten' (n 6) 274–275; Bugge, *Den norske trælasthandels historie: I* (n 6) 258–260; Ditcburn, *Scotland and Europe* (n 3) 159.

35 See Bugge, 'Skibsfarten' (n 6) 296.

36 See e.g. O A Johnsen, *Tønsbergs historie: bind 1* (n 9) 406–407; cf. Schreiner, *Hanseatene og Norges Nedgang* (n 8) 59: Schreiner, *Hanseatene og Norge* (n 8) 126–127 and 284–288; Nedkvitne, *The German Hansa* (n 8) 486–487.

37 See e.g. Johnsen, *Tønsbergs historie: bind 2* (n 9) 40 (1611–1612).

E: THE TRADE RELATIONS BETWEEN SCOTTISH AND NORWEGIAN TOWNS IN THE SIXTEENTH CENTURY

In 1509 Scottish merchants appear for the first time in extant Bergen sources in a way that beyond any reasonable doubt demonstrates that they had become quite usual visitors there. That year, the citizens of Bergen were granted by King Hans the right of first refusal for all goods that were being imported by English and Scottish merchants, while Hansa traders were supposed to wait for two weeks before they were allowed to buy any such merchandise.[38] Investigations of the earliest extant customs accounts from Bergen, from 1518–1521, reveal the following picture[39]:

Table 8.1 Number of foreign ships paying customers in Bergen, 1518–1523

Captain's hometown	1518 after 4 April 1518	1519	1520	1521 before 30 November	1522/1523 20 April–2 May
Baltic towns	52	63	40	60	0
North Sea Hansa towns	10	10	19	20	22
Holland/Friesland	4	3	7	5	2
Hansa or Holland	0	3	1	2	2
Scotland	6	5	4	4	2
England	1	1	1	0	0
All foreign ships	73	85	72	91	22

In our context, the most interesting aspects of these records is that the presence of Scottish ships, although quite modest compared to the dominant Hansa trade in Bergen, is on a par with ships from Holland and Friesland, and significantly higher than the English presence. This may suggest that the English in the later middle ages had almost completely let their commercial contacts with Bergen be taken over by the Germans, whereas the Scots continued to trade actively with Bergen.

The accounts for the payment of "ship toll" in Bergen, a fixed duty that in the second half of the sixteenth century was collected from ships loading or unloading cargoes in Bergen, show a slightly different picture[40]:

38 G.A. Blom and F-L Næshagen (eds), NgL 2. vol III:1 (1966) no 213; cf. Nedkvitne, *The German Hansa* (n 8) 183.

39 Helle, *Bergen bys historie* (n 9) 775; cf. Nedkvitne, *The German Hansa* (n 8) 105.

40 Nedkvitne, *The German Hansa* (n 8) 251–252; cf. Bugge, 'Skibsfarten' (n 6) 346 and 356.

Table 8.2 Number of foreign ships paying "ship toll" in Bergen, 1567–1599

Skipper's hometown	1567	1577	1597–1599 (average)
Baltic Hansa towns	44	43	110
North Sea Hansa towns	47	44	93
Holland/Friesland	16	1	9
England	2	5	1
Scotland	10	2	8
France	0	2	1
All foreign ships	119	97	222

These scattered and shifting numbers do not significantly change our view on the role of the Scottish active trade in Bergen, but we should note that while Scottish skippers accounted for about 8 per cent of the number of ships calling at Bergen in 1567 and paying toll, they were down to less than 4 per cent of the much higher overall numbers for 1597–1599. Apparently, as far as the limited sources can tell, growing foreign trade in Bergen in the last decades of the sixteenth century did not prompt a corresponding growth of Scottish trade there.

We will return to how this should be interpreted and more fully explained. Part of the explanation, however, may be that a significant number of Scottish traders as well as craftsmen from early in the sixteenth century settled permanently in Bergen and became citizens there, causing the Germans at the *Kontor* in Bergen to complain.[41] As local citizens they did not have to pay customs duties and hence do not appear in the customs registers. The Scottish influx to Bergen should not be exaggerated, however. The first extant citizen register from ca. 1550 onwards shows a total of about 500 entries before 1600. Of these new citizens from the latter half of the sixteenth century, eighteen were explicitly said to be Scottish, six explicitly from Shetland and Orkney and maybe another ten of Scottish descent, judged by their names.[42]

Early indications of active Scottish trade in Trondheim are to be found in two charters from 1528. In one of these, two Scots in the service of David Falconer in Leith testified in Trondheim that they, with his permission, had sold his ship "Peter" to the archbishop and received full payment.

41 See e.g. Chr C A Lange and C R Unger (eds), DN, vol V (1861) no 1039 (1523); cf. Helle, *Bergen bys historie* (n 9) 756 and 774–775; Fossen, *Bergen bys historie* (n 9) 25–26 and 43–45; Nedkvitne, *The German Hansa* (n 8) 183–184.

42 N Nicolaysen (ed), *Bergens Borgerbog 1550–1751* (1878).

The second charter states that the archbishop of Trondheim had seized a ship named "Bonaventura", belonging to two citizens of Dysart, the merchant John Lanchrisk and *Walterus Scot*, who therefore authorised Thomas Boswell of Kinghorn and James Makesson of Dundee to seek and receive compensation for the loss on their behalf in Bergen, Trondheim or elsewhere in Norway.[43]

The extent of the Scottish trade in Trondheim in the sixteenth century is difficult to assess, but here as well as in Bergen some Scottish immigrants occur in the records in the first half of the century. From 1528 onwards, a few Scots appear in the service of the archbishop, undertaking travels abroad and trading with Scotland, England and elsewhere on his behalf. Some of these apparently became citizens of Trondheim. A tax list from 1548 includes two or three men with the nickname "Skott" of a total of 379 taxpayers in Trondheim. Two of them seem to have been in the archbishop's service earlier.[44]

In the towns to the south and east of Bergen, i.e. Stavanger and the towns in the Oslo fjord area and the coast of Skagerrak, evidence for Scottish traders is even more slim in the first half of the sixteenth century. However, in the accounts for Akershus castle 1531–1533, a purchase of Scottish salt is mentioned, and among the urban tenants of St Mary's church in Oslo three men are registered on a property called "Skotthegardt" in 1542.[45] It is hard to tell if these men were all Scots. More importantly the name of this property clearly hints at Scottish residents in the town. Among the foreign merchants, Dutch traders dominated, but a few Scottish merchants and ships also appear. In Oslo, the commander of Akershus castle in 1550 is known to have confiscated a ship from Leith and put the skipper in jail.[46] In 1560, the largest single exporter who paid customs duties there, was "Hanns Skotte", who loaded lumber.[47]

Although at first in very small numbers, people of Scottish origins from

43 C R Unger and H J Huitfeldt-Kaas (eds), DN, vol VIII (1874) (1871–1874) nos 569 and 573; cf. Bugge, 'Skibsfarten' (n 6) 324.

44 See J A Seip (ed), *Olav Engelbrektssons rekneskapsbøker 1532–1538* (1936) 12, 18, 32, 37, 40, 51, 57, 71, 72, 78, 89, 93, 115, 118, 124, 144, 147, 148, 159; C R Unger and H J Huitfeldt-Kaas (eds), DN, vol XI (1884) no 680 and vol XII (1888) 593, 628; A Bugge and F Scheel (eds), *Liste over dem som betalte leding I Trondhjems by i aaret 1548* (1917) X, XII–XIII, 3, 11; cf. Supphellen, *Trondheims historie* (n 9) 31.

45 H J Huitfeldt-Kaas (ed), *Norske Regnskaber og Jordebøger fra det 16de Aarhundrede,* vol IV (1903–1906) 565 (henceforth NRJ).

46 Bugge, 'Skibsfarten' (n 6) 366.

47 See *Norske lensrekneskapsbøker 1548–1567* vol II (1940) 125 (henceforth NLR); Bugge, 'Skibsfarten' (n 6) 339.

then on also appear as citizens, taxpayers and tenants of urban properties both in Stavanger in the southwest and especially in Oslo and other towns of eastern Norway.[48] In 1591, the king instructed the master of the castle in Oslo to see to it that Hollanders, Frenchmen, Scotsmen and other nations paid customs duties for wine, salt, herbs and other commodities that they were bringing to the town.[49] The extent of the Scottish trade with Oslo, as well as Oslo's trade with Scotland, cannot however be more fully assessed before the first extant customs books appear there from 1599. In the early 1600s, in addition to Danish ports, Oslo seems to have had its closest active trade with Scotland, France and Spain. The Scottish ports that were most frequently visited by the growing Oslo merchant fleet were Dundee, Leith, and St Andrews.[50]

However, Norwegian sources from the sixteenth century do not account for Norwegian ships sailing to Scotland to the same extent. As mentioned above, in some cases, ships owned by Norwegians, or foreigners who had settled in Norwegian towns, may have been chartered by Scottish merchants.[51] During this century, the active trade of Bergen citizens and other Norwegian merchants with Scotland seems to have been increasing. During the war between England and Scotland in the late 1540s, several Norwegian ships were seized by the English near Leith and the Firth of Forth. Bugge was implying that these ships were mainly from eastern Norway, with active trade with Scotland from Bergen and Trondheim picking up in the 1570s and 1580s respectively.[52] Even so, Scottish trade with Norway seems to have been more significant than Norwegian trade with Scotland throughout the sixteenth century. In extant ship lists for Dundee from the 1580s of numerous ships arriving from Norway, all were Scottish, except for one ship from Oslo owned by a Scottish resident.[53] In the early seventeenth century, nevertheless, more local ships in Tønsberg, for example, can be seen sailing to Scotland than Scottish ships visiting there.[54]

48 See e.g. NLR, vol II (n 47) 25, 130, 157, 281; cf. Johnsen, *Tønsbergs historie: bind 2* (n 9) 38–39; Sprauten, *Oslo bys historie* (n 9) 83–84; Opstad et al, *Sarpsborg gjennom tidene* (n 9) 233 and 237; Elgvin, *En by i kamp* (n 9) 40.

49 O G Lundh og J E Sars (eds), *Norske Rigs-Registranter*, vol III (1865) 207 (henceforth NRR).

50 Bull, *Oslos historie* (n 9) 439.

51 See e.g. NLR, vol II (n 47) 130–131.

52 See Bugge, 'Skibsfarten' (n 6) 364–366.

53 Bugge, 'Skibsfarten' 366.

54 Johnsen, *Tønsberg gjennom tidene* (n 9) 98.

The presence of Scottish visiting and resident merchants in Bergen, Oslo and other Norwegian towns, and the number of ships and skippers from Norway calling on ports in Scotland, are far from reflecting the true scope and nature of the Scottish-Norwegian economic relations in this period. Scottish commercial activities from the first half of the sixteenth century onwards in fact figure more prominently in sources from rural districts and ports outside the towns than they do in the towns.

F: SCOTTISH TRADERS IN NORWEGIAN RURAL DISTRICTS IN THE SIXTEENTH AND SEVENTEENTH CENTURIES

With growing timber export from the high middle ages onwards, royal authorities had from ca. 1380 more or less accepted that foreigners bought timber in harbours in rural districts, directly from the producers; thus, for most practical purposes, the timber trade was exempt from the general ban on trade outside the towns. Going back to the fourteenth and fifteenth centuries, in some sources even to the thirteenth century, we know of quite a few such harbours visited by German merchants and other foreigners, especially in eastern Norway.[55]

For the collection of customs duties and control of the trade, this lenient policy was a challenge. In some regions the authorities had already adjusted to the situation in the late middle ages by putting up local customs controls outside the towns rather than insisting on upholding the trade monopolies of the medieval towns and their burghers. This policy was, to a large extent, continued in the sixteenth century and large parts of the seventeenth century. Some old towns were granted new royal privileges, starting with the 1508 privileges for Oslo, that, amongst other things, aimed at giving the burghers control of the timber trade that was going on in the surrounding rural districts and in proto-urban harbour settlements that developed there, in Norwegian named "ladested". The much more rapidly expanding timber trade boosted both by growing demand abroad and the gradual introduction of water-powered sawmills from ca.1500 onwards, which eventually revolutionised the industry, was nevertheless allowed a considerable degree of free development in rural districts, only partly with the burghers acting as middlemen. This occurred in some places until the second half of the

55 See e.g. Bugge, *Den norske trælasthandels historie: I* (n 6) 207–237 and 254–255; K Helle, A Nedkvitne, 'Norge. Sentrumsdannelser og byutvikling i norsk middelalder', in G A Blom (ed), *Middelaldersteder. Urbaniseringsprosessen i Norden* vol 1 (1977) 250–251 and 276–277; cf. also Søren Koch's chapter in the present book.

seventeenth century, in other places even to the early eighteenth century.[56] From a modest start ca.1500, the number of registered sawmills in Norway by 1610 had grown to about 1,000 mills scattered along the coast of southern Norway, from the Oslo fjord to the Trondheim fjord region.[57]

Admittedly, some timber was nevertheless transported to Bergen and other towns for customs clearance and export in the sixteenth century.[58] As a consequence of the rapid development of the sawmilling industry and the continued royal leniency towards a decentralised trade with timber and lumber, however, it is not in the towns, but in the rural districts of western and eastern Norway that the Scottish traders are most visible in the sixteenth century, appearing there from the 1520s with the earliest extant account books for the royal administration in the Bergen and Oslo castles. In some regions they became not only more numerous than in the towns, but also dominant among the foreign traders. This applies especially to the coastal regions Hardanger-Sunnhordland, south of Bergen, and eventually also to the adjacent Ryfylke (including the present time Haugalandet region north and northeast of Stavanger).[59]

In Sunnhordland, the first foreign ships known to have exported timber from the region, and also the first Scottish ships, appear in the 1521 accounts for Bergen castle. This year four foreign ships called at Halsnøy monastery, two Dutch and two from Scotland. One of the Scottish skippers paid duties for importing five barrels of salt ("skottesalt") and loading 'bordwith' or planks at the monastery. The number of foreign ships calling at Sunnhordland harbours was steadily growing throughout the sixteenth century. Thirty-two ships were registered in 1563 and forty-five in 1567. As far as the Scots are concerned this, much more than in Bergen, is where the real action was in the latter half of the sixteenth century. Allegedly, the decreasing number of Scottish ships between 1567 and 1577 registered in Bergen was due to a separate customs station having been put up at Eldøy in Sunnhordland in this period.[60] At some point in the 1590s the customs station was moved to Lervik on the island of Stord, strategically located for

56 See e.g. Bugge, *Den norske trælasthandels historie: I* (n 6) 207–237, 254–255; Helle and Nedkvitne, 'Norge', 276–277; Helle et al, *Norsk byhistorie* (n 9) 157–163; A Lillehammer, 'The timber trade' (n 3) 7–8.

57 Forfang, 'Sagbruksproduksjon i Noreg' (n 8) 322; for a geographic overview, see also e.g. Bugge, *Den norske trælasthandels historie* II (n 6) 332–334.

58 See e.g. Fossen, *Borgerskapets by* (n 9) 33–34.

59 See e.g. Johnsen, *Norwegische Wirtschaftsgeschichte* (n 7) 227; Bugge, *Den norske trælasthandels historie* II (n 6) 142–47, 190–199; cf. II 205–281.

60 Espeland, *Skottene* (n 4) 20–21.

all foreign ships exporting timber from the entire region to be able to call there on their way home and pay their duties instead of reporting to Bergen (or evade the customs). In the 1580s, the commander of Bergenshus castle was also instructed to appoint harbour masters in the many harbours in this region.[61] The first extant accounts for the Stord customs station, from 1597, reported no less than eighty foreign vessels. Half of these were from mainland Scotland and eleven from Shetland and Orkney. Only one ship was from England, five from Germany and the rest from Holland.[62] In addition, a fair number of ships may have called and traded at manor farms that were exempt from customs duties.

According to the 1610 customs accounts for Sunnhordland, fifty-six ships out of a total of 112 entries were from mainland Scotland and seventeen from the Shetland and Orkney Isles.[63] This Scottish dominance in the Sunnhordland timber and lumber export continued throughout the seventeenth century. Typically, the ships would stay in the area for a considerable time to be able to buy timber and lumber from several sawmills and farmers, due to the small-scale structure of production and ownership. Often the skippers would be quite regular visitors in the same region for years, developing close contacts and building trust in the local communities. Some Scots settled there. For instance, in 1563 a 'Joen Schott' paid tax to the king as co-owner of a sawmill.[64]

Further south, in the Ryfylke region, there are indications that the timber export started with Dutch traders early in the sixteenth century. However, the first sawmill here is not documented before 1554, but the number of sawmills seems to have picked up quickly, to sixty-four in 1606. In the extant sources, the first Scottish ships also appear later in Ryfylke than in Sunnhordland. Otherwise the development was quite similar. In 1567, of a total of thirty-eight foreign ships calling in the Ryfylke fjords, between twenty-five and twenty-eight were Scottish. There too, the Scottish dominance among ships exporting timber and deals continued in the seventeenth century.[65] The

61 Næss, 'Skottehandelen' (n 4) 30: Espeland, *Skottene* (n 4) 20–21.

62 See e.g. Bugge, *Den norske trælasthandels historie* II (n 6) 190–199; Myking et al, *Hardanger* (n 11) 224; Espeland, *Skottene* 32.

63 For example, Espeland, 'Skottene' (n 4) 21.

64 Myking et al, *Hardanger* (n 11) 224; Bugge, *Den norske trælasthandels historie: I* (n 6) 148–164; Næss, 'Sagbruk i Sørhordaland' (n 4) 9–10; cf. Espeland, *Skottene* (n 4); Næss, 'Skottehandelen' (n 4); Kolltveit, 'Skogen og trelasthandelen' (n 12).

65 See e.g. Lillehammer, 'The timber trade' (n 3) 12–15; S I Langhelle, 'The Timber Export from the Tysvær-area in the 16th and 17th century', in J Bruijn et .al , *Timber and Trade* (n 3) 25–26; Elgvin, *En by i kamp* (n 9) 38–39; cf. Bugge, *Den norske trælandshandels historie* II (n 6) 143–147.

Ryfylke fjords were within the trade district of Stavanger. According to the privileges granted to this town by the king in 1579, the burghers there should enjoy a trading monopoly within its bounds. In the early seventeenth century, to some extent the timber export from Ryfylke can be seen to have been carried out by skippers and ships from Stavanger, in some cases chartered by Scottish and other foreign traders.[66] In practice, however, here too it was impossible to direct all timber business via the town and avoid direct trade between foreign merchants and farmers. Like Sunnhordland, Ryfylke got its own customs station and its own customs officer in 1630.[67]

Admittedly, both in Sunnhordland and Ryfylke many of the Scottish ships have been shown to be very small, compared to ships from other foreign nations. According to Arnvid Lillehammer, in the decades towards 1639 the average size of the calling Scottish ships in Ryfylke may have been between ten and fourteen lasts (ten to twenty-eight tons), whereas the Frisians and the Dutch seldom averaged less than twenty lasts (forty tons). Therefore, the Scottish contribution to the overall export from these parts of Norway, although still impressive, for a long time was far less dominant in terms of tonnage and volume of trade than in number of callings, until the Dutch from around 1630 withdrew from the Ryfylke timber trade.[68] However, as mentioned above, Scottish traders also exported timber on chartered ships, belonging to other foreigners or Norwegians. For Sunnhordland, this has in fact been shown to constitute a considerable part of the Scottish trade in the early 1600s. In 1597 Scottish traders counted for 736 lasts, or 48.5 per cent of the registered tonnage, most of which were Scottish vessels. In 1610 the Scots counted for 1989 lasts or 71.5 per cent, of which more than 700 lasts were on chartered non-Scottish ships. In 1614, although with lower total figures, the Scots were even more dominant, with 89 per cent of the registered export tonnage.[69]

The Scottish ships came from most parts of Scotland's North Sea coast as well as from Shetland and Orkney, but less frequently from Sutherland and Caithness and very occasionally from Glasgow. In this main area for the "Scottish trade" in Norway, however, there seems to have been a "division of labour", with contacts being particularly strong between the small burghs in Fife, between the Firth of Tay and the Firth of Forth, and Ryfylke, on

66 Bugge, *Den norske trælastandels historie* II (n 6) 141–142.

67 Lillehammer, 'The Timber Trade' (n 3) 7–8.

68 See Lillehammar, 'Skottar og hollendarar' (n 12) 16; Lillehammer, 'The timber trade' (n 3) 16; cf. Elgvin, *En by i kamp* (n 9) 38–39.

69 Næss, 'Skottehandelen' (n 4) 33–34.

the one hand, and on the other hand between the towns further north in Scotland, including Shetland and Orkney, and Sunnhordland – a picture that makes good sense geographically.[70]

In other parts of western Norway and in the Trondheimsfjord region, too, numerous sawmills had been established by the turn of the sixteenth and seventeenth centuries. Foreign ships, from 1294 until the middle of the sixteenth century, had quite consistently been prohibited to sail north of Bergen. Once they were permitted to do so, they were at first apparently expected to pay customs duties in Bergen (and in Trondheim) and there are no extant customs records for the rural districts there from the sixteenth century. From the early seventeenth century this would gradually change.[71] Although Scottish ships were eventually calling there on a regular basis as well, they were mostly greatly outnumbered by the Dutch (including the Frisians) in western Norway north of Bergen, and only during the seventeenth century came to play an important role further north.[72]

The same goes for the coast of Agder, to the southeast of Stavanger, although the Scottish trade there is less thoroughly researched. Scottish skippers appear in customs accounts before 1530 and the first water-powered sawmills appear in accounts from the subsequent decade, but sawmilling and lumber exports apparently only very gradually picked up in this region and became a major industry. The Scots, not surprisingly, were far more numerous in the westernmost part of Agder, closest to Ryfylke, than in the eastern part. However, nowhere in Agder can their presence be seen to have been as significant as the Dutch in the sixteenth or early seventeenth century.[73]

Further east, a few Scots also appear in the extant account books from the late 1520s, some of them in contexts that indicate that they at least temporarily were residents in rural districts there. A Thomas "Skott" at Eiker north

70 Lillehammer, 'Skottar og hollendarar' (n 12) 22; Langhelle, 'The Timber Export" (n 65) 26.

71 See e.g. Bugge, *Den norske trælasthandels historie: II* (n 6) 200–203; Fossen, *Borgerskapets by* (n 9) 213–214.

72 See e.g. Bugge, *Den norske trælasthandels historie: II* (n 6) 271–72; Krøvel and Tafjord, *Folk i fjordriket* (n 11) 223–224; Bugge, *Aalesunds historie* (n 10) 33–34; Seve, *Molde bys historie* (n 11) 41, 59, 64, 74 and 117; Johnsen, *Kristiansund bys historie* (n 10) 97; Dybdahl, *Fra pest til poteter* (n 11) 172–173 and 337.

73 See e.g. Huitfeldt-Kaas (ed), NRJ, vol IV (n 45) 310; Lillehammer, 'Skottar og hollendarar' (n 12) 18–23; Fløystad, *Agders historie* (n 11) 136–137 and 228; Johnsen & Sætra, *Sørlandsk skipsfart* (n 11) 12–13; Løyland, *Fjordfolk* (n 10) 120; Holberg & Dørum, *Arendal før kjøpstaden* (n 10) 230–231; Abrahamsen, *Farsund bys historie* (n 10) 23–25; Skeie & Moseng, *Kristiansand står og faller med sin hamn* (n 10) 30; Dannevig, *Grimstads sjøfarts historie* (n 10) 34–36; cf. Bugge, *Den norske trælasthandels historie: I* (n 6) 292–295, *II* (n 6) 129–135, 273–275, 330–332.

of Drammen, in an important timber exporting area, in 1528 paid a fine for the permission to "sail with the Hollanders", and "Hans Skotte" paid taxes in the coastal parish and fishing community of Eckerö in southern Bohuslän in 1528.[74] Occasionally from the late 1530s, Scottish skippers and ships also occur in the account books, paying customs duties and being involved in court cases, etc. in rural districts.[75] Other Scots can be seen to have rented property, like "Willum Skotte" and "Jacop Skotte" who according to the 1557–1558 and 1560–1561 accounts, respectively, paid rent for warehouses at Moss, a harbour or "ladested" some seventy kilometres south of Oslo. The same Wilhelm shortly afterwards seems to have been serving as sailor in the Danish-Norwegian navy.[76]

Timber and lumber were the main exports from rural districts in present time eastern as well as western Norway. Particularly during a great influx of annual North Sea herring shoals 1556–1589, however, the herring fisheries on the coast of Bohuslän caused both Norwegian and foreign fishermen, traders and ships to visit there in the thousands. A contemporary topographer, the reverend Peder Claussøn Friis (born 1545), mentions Scots among several nations who visited "Viksiden" (Bohuslän) to buy and export herring in this era that he describes in a manner that resembles our image of the gold rush in Klondyke.[77] In this setting, the authorities not very surprisingly worried about foreign ships evading customs control by not sailing to Marstrand, the centre of the herring trade, but calling in other harbours instead, and trading not only in herring there. A royal ordinance in 1586 seems to attribute a prominent role in this nuisance specifically to people from Scotland, by forbidding "pedlars, vagrants, Scots and other nations to travel about Bohuslän, robbing, stealing and selling their miscellaneous merchandise".[78]

74 Huitfeldt-Kaas (ed), NRJ, vol IV (n 45) 171 and 325.

75 See e.g. Huitfeldt-Kaas (ed), NRJ, vol IV (n 45) 334 and 507; NLR, vol II (n 47) 17, 125, 130–31, 157, 281; cf. e.g. Bugge, 'Skibsfarten' (n 6) 366; Tønnessen, *Porsgrunns historie* (n 10) 48–52; Pedersen, *Drammen* (n 10) 105.

76 H J Huitfeldt-Kaas (ed), NRJ, vol I (1887) 6, 196, and H J Huitfelt-Kaas (ed), NRJ, vol II (1896) 2, 8.

77 G Storm (ed), *Samlede Skrifter af Peder Claussøn Friis* (1881) 94–97, 269–270 and 273–275; cf. Norseng and Eliassen, *Østfolds historie bind 2* (n 11) 134–135; cf. E Lönnroth (ed), *Bohusläns historia* (1963) 149–170.

78 S Petersen and O G Lundh (eds), NRR, vol II (1963) 660; cf. Bugge, 'Skibsfarten' 353.

G: EXPORTS FROM NORWAY IN THE SIXTEENTH AND EARLY-SEVENTEENTH CENTURY SCOTTISH-NORWEGIAN TRADE

Timber and lumber indisputably constituted the main Norwegian commodity on the Scottish market, both for Scottish and Norwegian merchants and skippers. But what kind of timber and deals did the Scots buy, and what other goods were exported there from Norway?

According to Alexander Bugge, the Scots in the sixteenth century were particularly interested in importing oak.[79] More recently, these questions have been studied in greatest detail and most systematically with the Scottish trade in mind for south-western and western Norway south of Bergen. In the early seventeenth century, when extant sources are more numerous, it has been shown for Ryfylke by Arnvid Lillehammer that the following four processed commodities were most important for the timber traders from Scotland; in terms of value and volume, boards or deals of pinewood loomed highest, but also considerable quantities of beams or baulks, likewise mostly pinewood. Barrel hoops of hazel and firewood from birch constituted most of the remaining timber export here, with firewood as the least important. Unlike the Germans and the Dutch, who bought great quantities of firewood from Norway, the Scots had good access to alternative fuel, like coal and peat. Lillehammer suggests that the usually very modest quantities of firewood recorded on the Scottish ships indicate that this wood was mostly used to fill up the ships after the other and more important commodities had been loaded. Furthermore, unprocessed trees or logs occur infrequently in the customs records and the Scots seem to have bought their mast timber elsewhere, mostly from the Baltic, where the quality of the timber was considered to be better for this purpose.[80]

What can be shown to be the case for Ryfylke in these respects also seems to apply to Sunnhordland, according to regional and local studies that have been conducted there. The same probably goes for the coast north of Bergen and south and east of Stavanger – Agder and the Oslo fjord region – as far as can be judged from the less researched sources and more scanty information in secondary literature on the Scottish-Norwegian timber and lumber trade there.[81]

79 Bugge, *Den norske trælasthandels historie: II* (n 6) 216–221.

80 Lillehammer, 'The Timber Trade' (n 3) 17–18; cf. Espeland, *Skottene* (n 4) 21.

81 See e.g. Næss, 'Skottehandelen' (n 4) 21–22, 24–25 and 35–37; Espeland, *Skottene* (n 4) 21 and 23; Løyland, *Fjordfolk* (n 10) 117–119; Rian (ed), *Telemarks historie* (n 11) 265–266; Krøvel

These findings also reflect that the export of timber, especially oak, had been subject to periodical restrictions in the sixteenth century and a total ban from 1602, to secure sufficient supplies of oak for use in the Danish-Norwegian navy.[82] For lack of sufficient Norwegian sources prior to ca. 1600, it is hard to assess the extent of oak exported from Norway to Scotland in the sixteenth century. Oak beams were, however, among the obviously Norwegian commodities on one of the ships that were seized by the English off Leith in 1547, as pointed out by Bugge, and in the early 1560s a general rise in Norwegian custom tariffs and a ban on the export of oak from Agder and elsewhere in Norway caused the Scottish Parliament to send an envoy to King Fredrik II in Copenhagen to negotiate a repeal of both these measures, but to no avail.[83] Before 1602, however, the export bans were often enforced only for a few years and also mostly limited to specific regions or sizes of oak timber.[84] Moreover, occasional export licences were granted in spite of the bans, in the latter decades of the century apparently most frequently to Scots, especially after the marriage of James VI of Scotland to the sister of Christian IV in 1589.[85] Smuggling, or evasion of the export ban, did of course also take place, probably to a quite large extent.[86] Bugge examined the customs accounts for Dundee, finding considerable amounts of oak imported from Norway in the late sixteenth century.[87] But the oak forests in Ryfylke and elsewhere seem to have been retreating in the seventeenth century in spite of the export bans. Oak was hardly as significant a part of the Scottish timber imports from Norway in the first decades of the seventeenth century as it had been in the previous century.[88]

With growing deforestation, for the towns of the east coast of Scotland it must have been easier and cheaper to import timber by ship from across the North Sea than to transport it overland from the forests of the Scottish

and Tafjord, *Folk i fjordriket* (n 11) 224; cf. Bugge, *Den norske trælasthandels historie: I* (n 6) 292–314, *II*, 99–100, 183–219, 230–240, 251–265, 337–361.

82 See e.g. Lillehammer, 'The Timber Trade' (n 3) 17–19; Næss, 'Skottehandelen' (n 4) 20–22, 25–26 and 42; Kolltveit, 'Skogen og trelasthandelen' (n 12); Ringard, *Flekkefjords historie* (n 10) 16–18; Johnsen and Sætra, *Sørlandsk skipsfart* (n 11) 12–13; Løyland, *Fjordfolk* (n 10) 118; cf. Bugge, *Den norske trælasthandels historie: II* (n 6) 17–38 and 221.

83 Bugge, 'Skibsfarten' (n 6) 365; Bugge, *Den norske trælasthandels historie: II* (n 6) 220–221 and 242.

84 See note 80 above; cf. also e.g. Espeland, *Skottene* (n 4) 13–14.

85 See E O Heiberg and S Petersen (eds), *Norsk Rigsregistranter*, vol I (1861) 382; Petersen and Lundh (eds), NRR, vol II (n 78) 619; Lundh and Sars (eds), NRR, vol III (n 49) 73 and 451; e.g. Espeland, *Skottene* (n 4) 13–14; Bugge, *Den norske trælasthandel historie: II* (n 6) 221.

86 See e.g. Løyland, *Fjordfolk* (n 10) 117–118.

87 Bugge, *Den norske trælasthandels historie: II* (n 6) 221, 248, 250–264; cf. 232–240.

88 Lillehammer, 'The Timber Trade' (n 3) 17–19.

Highlands.[89] The timber trade was obviously the main reason, maybe also the only reason, why Scottish skippers would flock to western Norway and elsewhere on the Norwegian coast in the sixteenth century and early seventeenth century.

Nevertheless, timber was not the only commodity the Scottish ships would bring back to Scotland, or Norwegian ships would take there. Among the frequent grievances towards the Scots from the German *Kontor* in Bergen in the first half of the sixteenth century were complaints about Scottish traders purchasing victuals in Sunnhordland and other rural districts, causing deficits in Bergen.[90] From Ryfylke and Sunnhordland in the seventeenth century they are also known to have exported horses, hides and fish.[91] Moreover, according to the accounts, the castle commander in Bergen in the 1520s was selling tar, other Norwegian forest products, bees wax imported from the Baltic and copper to Scottish merchants.[92] We should also bear in mind that not only royal officials, but both Scottish resident merchants and Norwegian merchants, especially in Bergen and other Norwegian towns, had access to a whole range of foreign commodities there that they could re-export to Scotland, as demonstrated in 1523 in an incident with the German *Kontor*. The Scottish residents in Bergen were attacked by the Germans and were afterwards seeking compensation for a great variety of goods, indicating that they were not only importing Scottish and exporting Norwegian commodities, but were also dealing in commodities from all over northern Europe.[93] This point is also illustrated by the fact that, in addition to typical Norwegian goods like timber, fish oil, tar and pitch, both beer, in this context probably German beer, and Swedish iron ("Osmundjern") are among the commodities on Norwegian ships that were seized off the coast of Scotland in the late 1540s while apparently heading for Scottish harbours.[94]

Consequently, most of the Norwegian commodities in the trade with Scotland were processed raw materials, with one exception in particular that seems to have been especially important in some coastal communities in Sunnhordland. In 1597, export duties were paid there for thirty-four boats, in 1610 for no less than seventy-two boats, probably all small vessels typi-

89 Cf Bugge, *Den norske trælasthandels historie: II* (n 6) 230.

90 See e.g. Schreiner, *Hanseatene og Norge* (n 8) 122.

91 Lillehammer, 'The Timber Trade' (n 3) 17; cf. e.g. Næss, 'Skottehandelen' (n 4) 64.

92 Huitfeldt-Kaas (ed), NRJ, vol I (n 76) 339, 341, 420, 443, 544; cf. Nedkvitne, *The German Hansa* (n 3) 183; cf. Espeland, *Skottene* (n 4) 9.

93 Nedkvitne, *The German Hansa* (n 8) 183–184 and 484–485.

94 See Bugge. 'Skibsfarten' (n 6) 365.

cally with two or three pairs of oars. These "mass produced" boats were to a large extent sold to Scots, apparently mostly to skippers from Shetland and Orkney.[95] Although with annual variations in numbers, this seems to have been a quite regular trade. Occasionally in the extant customs accounts from this region we also come across references to export of what seems to have been ready-made "IKEA style" log houses.[96]

By ca. 1550, it had apparently also become a habit for Scots and other foreigners to buy ships in Norway – sometimes specifically built for export – as an alternative to buying timber for shipbuilding at home. This could be seen as a way of evading customs duties, other restrictions on timber exports or both. Unlike the export of small boats, this trade was consequently opposed by the authorities. In 1554 the Dano-Norwegian king issued a prohibition forbidding ships to be built in Norway for immediate sale to foreigners. Second-hand ships were only permitted to be sold for export after ten years of domestic use. The odd export license was nevertheless granted, at least on one occasion in 1590 on request from the king of Scotland.[97]

Probably likewise to evade export restrictions, in the latter half of the sixteenth century it seems to have been quite common for Scots to buy timber in these regions and the adjacent parts of the Agder coast, where access to oak timber was more ample, in order to build ships of their own there and bring them back to Scotland. This practise was also strongly opposed and prohibited by the king from 1562 but continued into the seventeenth century, no doubt to a large extent illegally, sometimes however with licences to individual Scots, occasionally on request from the Scottish king or queen.[98]

H: NEW CONSUMER GOODS – IMPORTS TO NORWAY IN THE SCOTTISH-NORWEGIAN TRADE IN THE LONG SIXTEENTH CENTURY

We have seen above that one of the two very first Scottish ships registered in the early sixteenth century customs records for Bergen, harbouring at

95 Næss, 'Skottehandelen' (n 4) 36 and 46; Næss and Kolllveit, *Strandebarm og Varaldsøy* (n 10) 205; Espeland, *Skottene* (n 4) 21 and 23.

96 Næss, 'Skottehandelen' (n 4) 24–25; Espeland, *Skottene* (n 4) 21.

97 See e.g. Næss, 'Skottehandelen' (n 4); Bugge, *Den norske trælasthandels historie: II* (n 6) 135–136; cf. Lundh and Sars (eds), NRR, vol III (n 49) 139.

98 See e.g. Lundh and Sars (eds), NRR, vol III (n 49) 49–50, 119–120, 140, 211, 412, 557–558, 562, O G Lundh (ed), NRR, vol IV (1870) 129; Bugge, 'Skibsfarten' (n 6) 366; Næss, 'Skottehandelen' (n 4) 21 and 25–26; Espeland, *Skottene* (n 4) 13–14 and 25; Ringard, *Flekkefjords historie* (n 10) 18; cf. Bugge, *Den norske trælasthandels historie: II* (n 6) 17–38.

the monastery at Halsnøy in Sunnhordland, declared five barrels of salt for import duties. Furthermore, referring to information from Scottish Privy Council records from 1574–1575, Alexander Bugge, rather sweepingly, stated that the Scots in particular exported salt to Norway, especially so-called small salt, for conservation of fish.[99] But to what extent is this statement representative of Scottish-Norwegian trade in the sixteenth century in general?

Admittedly, as pointed out by Arnved Nedkvitne (amongst others), the accounts for Scottish ships visiting Bergen from the 1520s and throughout the rest of sixteenth century, give the impression that salt was the main article imported there by Scottish ships. Contemporary topographic literature points in the same direction. The Bergenhus castle was obviously a great consumer of salt, which was acquired from Scottish ships by purchase as well as in payment of customs duties. Sometimes Scottish salt was referred to as "white salt".[100] Purchases of "skottesalt" also appear in sixteenth century accounts for Akershus castle in Oslo but more rarely, and never in the extant sixteenth century sources as payment for customs duties like in Bergen.[101]

Scottish salt was also imported in rural areas. A charter from 1592, for example, mentions salt among several commodities that the vicar of Strandebarm parish in Sunnhordland got from Scottish traders in exchange for planks and timber that they needed for shipbuilding. Salt imported by Scottish ships also appears in the customs accounts from the fjord district both south and north of Bergen in the subsequent decades, but not very frequently in Sunnhordland.[102]

Salt extraction from seawater was becoming a significant industry in Scotland at the time. Although considered being of "the coarse variety", the plentiful Scottish salt was an important part of Scottish foreign trade with east England, the Baltic, western Sweden and the Low Countries.[103] But

99 Bugge, *Den norske trælasthandels historie: II* (n 6) 212.

100 Nedkvitne, *The German Hansa* (n 8) 183, 250 n 3; cf. N Nicolaysen (ed), *Norske Magasin*, vol II (1868) 51–53, 72–73, 81, 89; Espeland, *Skottene* (n 4) 9 and 21.

101 For a quick overview of mentions of Scottish salt, Norwegian salt, Lüneburger salt, Biscaya salt, etc. in the extant Norwegian account books from the first half of the sixteenth century, see the key words "salt" in the indexes of matters in H J Hiitfelt-Kaas (ed), NRJ, vols 1–4, or search electronically for these terms in the online versions of this publication and the NLR.

102 See Næss, 'Skottehandelen' (n 4) 28 and 48; Krøvel and Tafjord, *Folk i fjordriket* (n 11) 224.

103 D M Pallister (ed), *Cambridge Urban History of Britain: volume 1* (2000) 716; cf. C A Whatley, *The Scottish Salt Industry 1570–1850. An Economic and Social History* (1987); J Dow, 'Scottish trade with Sweden 1512–1580' (1969) 48 *Scottish Historical Review* 71, 75–78; J Dow, 'Scottish Trade with Sweden 1580–1622' (1969) 48 *Scottish Historical Review* 125–130; Ditchburn, *Scotland and Europe* (n 3) 186.

salt was also being extracted from the sea all along the Norwegian coast as well. Two areas stand out in the Norwegian context with a particularly extensive salt production; the Hardanger fjord south and east of Bergen, and the Inner Oslo fjord.[104]

Based on firewood, not coal like in Scotland, the Norwegian salt production was, however, on a smaller and less industrial scale. It is also a commonly held opinion by Norwegian historians and archaeologists that the domestically produced salt was of such inferior quality that it was not much used for preserving food, but mostly fed to livestock and merely used as table salt by humans, in addition to preserving hides. Nevertheless, charters, cadasters and accounts from these regions demonstrate that the salt production was of great economic interest to landowners here, especially in the Oslo fjord area. In the sixteenth century land rent, tithes and taxes were extensively being collected in salt, even along trade routes in the interior of south-eastern Norway, and salt is known to have been exported to western Sweden both in the high middle ages and in the first half of the sixteenth century. Salt production remained an important side occupation for the rural population along the Hardanger fjord and the Oslo fjord well into the seventeenth century until imported salt of finer quality from southern Europe became more easily and cheaply available and factories for refining coarse imported salt were established by royal initiative.

Against this background, I find it hard to believe that the domestically produced salt, especially in the Hardanger and Oslo fjord regions and the adjacent regions – which are also some of the regions most affected by the timber trade of Scottish and other foreign merchants and ships – was not also to a great extent being used in the sixteenth century to preserve fish and meat, although the low quality of the salt may have affected the durability and quality of the salted foods. Bringing large quantities of salt from Scotland to these regions would at least at first sight seem to be like shipping coals to Newcastle.

The frequent occurrence in the accounts of salt being used by Scottish skippers as payment for customs duties in Bergen or bought from them for

104 For this and the next paragraphs, see e.g. Bugge, 'Skibsfarten' (n 6) 329–334; Myking et al, *Hardanger* (n 11) 127–129; Norseng and Eliassen, *I Borgarsysle* (n 11) 121–123; P G Norseng, 'Middelalderbyen Oslo og fiskeressursene i Indre Oslofjord', in L-M B Johansen, E L Bauser, J Brendalsmo and K Paasche (eds), *En aktivist for Middelalderbyen Oslo* (2015) 224; P G Norseng, 'Kirke, prest og kirkesogn i Rygge i katolsk tid', in B Bandlien (ed), *Arvegull: Rygge kirke* (2019) 198; K Loftsgarden, 'Salt – ressurs og handelsvare i middelalderen' (2018), in *Heimen* vol 55/1 50–61.

the castle there in the sixteenth century may in part reflect that Scottish salt, maybe especially the "white salt", was of higher quality and hence better suited for some preservation purposes than domestic salt. But it may also simply reflect that salt was a suitable form of ballast because it was heavy and could also, rather than just being disposed of in the port of call, be sold or used as currency in the so-called commodity money system. This was still in operation in a sixteenth century Norwegian economy that was less monetised than the Scottish economy.[105] Furthermore, the royal castle in Bergen, with numerous soldiers and servants, no doubt needed particularly great quantities of salt to preserve food for their extensive households. This may also apply to the odd mentions of Scottish salt being bought by royal officials in Oslo as well.

The demand for imported salt – including Scottish salt – may also, particularly in Bergen, have been of some significance among the townsmen. Ships from the still modest Bergen fleet are known to have sailed with timber to Spain to buy salt.[106] In 1542, the *Kontor* reported that the burghers, in line with the right of first refusal that the king had granted them in 1509 and confirmed in 1541, insisted that a cargo of salt on a ship from Scotland should be sold to them, and not at *Bryggen*, the German wharf.[107]

By the middle of the sixteenth century, Norwegian and immigrant burghers in Bergen were encroaching on the Hansa monopoly in the fish trade from northern Norway. Drying cod without salt to produce stockfish was, for climatic reasons, not a good option except during the winter fisheries in northern Norway. In the early sixteenth century, judging from castle accounts and inventories, salting cod from northern Norway, the western coast or elsewhere, must have been quite usual. During that century a new practice also emerged in northern Norway. To be able to preserve the cod that was caught in the summer, which could not be dried without adding salt, a primitive kind of "klippfish" apparently was produced, probably for the domestic market, by drying salted cod.[108]

In general, the market for Scottish salt in the sixteenth century elsewhere in Norway was hardly as great as it was in Bergen, particularly not in the

105 Cf. G I Pettersen, *Priser og verdiforhold i Norge ca. 1280–1500* (2013) 8–101.

106 See e.g. Johnsen, *Norwegische Wirtschaftsgechichte* (n 7) 254; Schreiner, *Hanseatene og Norge* (n 8) 356.

107 For example, Schreiner, *Hanseatene og Norge* (n 8) 146, 134 and 145–146.

108 See G Storm (ed), *Historisk-topografiske skrifter om Norge og norske landsdele, forfattede i Norge i det 16de Aarhundrede* (1895) 204; Schreiner, *Hanseatene og Norge* (n 8) 346–48; Nedkvitne, *The German Hansa* (n 8) 494–495.

regions that were most frequently visited by Scottish traders. The only other context where a more extensive Scottish export of salt to Norway is likely to have taken place on a regular basis, is the herring fisheries in the Bohuslän region in modern-day western Sweden, which from 1556 to 1589 must have caused an extreme rise in the demand for salt. The presence both of Scottish traders and Scottish salt in Bohuslän in this period is well attested. The scale and importance of this is, however, more obscure in Norwegian primary sources as well as secondary literature, but the dominant role played by salt – from Scotland or elsewhere – in Scottish imports recorded in the 1570s to the then Swedish border town Nya Lødöse (from 1624 replaced by Gothenburg), may serve as an indication of the great need for imported salt on both sides of the border.[109]

In the Bergen accounts, in addition to salt, malt is also recorded as payment of customs duties from Scots in Bergen, and charters from the 1520s testify to Scottish export of grain to Norway. In 1567, the Germans were making complaints about excessive Scottish supplies of malt to Bergen causing the prices to drop. In 1577, however, only one of eight Scottish ships registered in Bergen can be seen to have carried grain – representing, according to Nedkvitne, only 0.5 per cent of the total imports of grain there that year.[110]

According to the extant castle accounts, customs duties from Scottish skippers in Oslo and nearby harbours were mainly being paid in cash, but in one instance malt was used as payment instead.[111] Both malt and beer can otherwise be seen to have been imported to eastern Norway by Scottish visiting or resident skippers, with malt also on one occasion being imported by Scottish traders arriving on a Danish ship.[112]

The cargoes of seven Norwegian ships seized by the English off the Firth of Forth in 1549 may give us an indication of what were the most common exports from Scotland to Norway on board Scottish as well as Norwegian vessels. Among the returned commodities were flour, malt, beer, biscuits and hemp.[113] Different kinds of Scottish cloth and canvas from the Scottish islands are frequently mentioned in the castle account books both in Bergen and Oslo.[114]

109 Dow, 'Scottish trade with Sweden 1512–1580' (n 103) 75–76; cf. for Bohuslän, e.g. S Petersen and O G Lundh (eds), NRR, vol II (n 78) 198 and 580–581.

110 Schreiner, *Hanseatene og Norge* (n 8) 306–307; Nedkvitne, *The German Hansa* (n 8) 303.

111 Huitfeldt-Kaas (ed), NRJ, vol IV (n 45) 334; cf. e.g. Bugge, 'Skibsfarten' (n 6) 329–330.

112 See e.g. H J Huitfeldt-Kaas (ed), NRJ, vol II (n 76) 131, cf. vol IV (n 45) 336.

113 See Bugge, 'Skibsfarten' (n 6) 365.

114 See e.g. key words "klæde" in the indexes of matter in Huitfeldt-Kaas (ed), NRJ, vols 1–4.

In Bergen, in addition to salt and grain, cloth and lime can also be seen to have been imported by Scottish skippers, as well as commodities that were definitely not of Scottish origin, but imported from elsewhere, like wine. This is yet another hint of rather complex trade patterns in some of the Scottish-Norwegian economic exchange, reminding us also of how the Scottish residents in Bergen after the German attacks in 1523 were seeking compensation for the loss of a great variety of commodities from all over northern Europe.[115]

For the towns of western and eastern Norway, the Scottish import of cereals was clearly less significant than the import of Baltic grain by the German merchants. In general, the grain export from Scotland was, for climatic reasons more unreliable and subject to great fluctuations.[116] Neither the Scottish traders nor their customers in Norwegian towns depended on it. Import of grain on Scottish ships in the sixteenth and early seventeenth century was probably far more essential, both to the Scots and their trading partners, in coastal areas outside the towns, especially in western Norway. Here the influx of Scottish ships was particularly great; here there was a demand that neither the Germans, nor for the time being the burghers of Bergen and Stavanger, catered for; and here grain from Scotland or elsewhere could be exchanged for timber.

Although less visible and harder to assess in the extant sources than the exports, from the late-sixteenth century we also get a fairly clear impression of the import commodities that Scottish traders brought to rural districts in Norway. It has been most thoroughly investigated in the two main areas of the so-called Scottish trade in Norway, Sunnhordland and Ryfylke.

For Ryfylke, information on Scottish imports is available in the customs registers from the very beginning of the seventeenth century, reflecting no doubt also the situation in the preceding last decades of the sixteenth century. Arnvid Lillehammer has demonstrated that the Hollanders and other foreigners very often seem to have sailed in ballast to Norway to collect timber, paying in cash rather than in kind, and this appears to have been the case to a much lesser degree with the Scots. Payments are at first mostly made in cereals and cereal products – grain, flour, malt and bread, in great quantities. While oat was the most common cereal crop on Ryfylke farms, the Scots brought barley, rye and wheat. In addition, textiles, espe-

115 Nedkvitne, *The German Hansa* (n 8) 183–84 and 485; cf. Næss, 'Skottehandelen' (n 4) 9; Huitfeldt-Kaas (ed), NRJ, vol I (n 76) 139, 202.

116 See Ditcburn, *Scotland and Europe* (n 3) 149–142; cf. Smout, 'The Norwegian Timber Trade' (n 3) 41–42.

cially linen cloths, were common Scottish imports and means of payment, as well as shoes. Only later, by the middle of the seventeenth century, a development towards a wider range of commodities can be seen, including industrial and handicraft products like liquor, bar iron, iron pans, knives and soap, as well as foods like peas and beans. As Lillehammer points out, some of these Scottish imports to Ryfylke must have originated elsewhere than in Scotland, like the rye that was probably a re-export from the Baltic.[117] It has been suggested that Scottish ships sailing to Norway to a large extent may have been engaged in triangular trade with the Netherlands, partly as a means of financing purchases of timber in Norway to bring back to Scotland.[118] The same may have been the case with Scottish ships sailing to the Baltic.

These diversified Scottish imports facilitated dramatic changes in local consumer patterns, introducing the local population in Ryfylke to new eating and drinking habits, fashions, etc. The same evidently happened in Sunnhordland and other rural areas that were visited by Scottish ships. For example, the Scots who traded with the vicar in Strandebarm in 1592, in addition to salt, provided him with both grain, textiles and "other commodities that he needed".[119] Royal writs from the late sixteenth century onwards and early seventeenth century customs accounts reveal the same pattern as in Ryfylke; the Scots mostly brought cereal products – malt, flour, grain, beer – but also peas, fish, spirits, wine, canvas, woollen cloth, silk, shoes and other commodities, and they paid for much of their timber purchases in kind. From ca. 1650, tobacco and sugar also appear – tobacco, at least, had probably been known for a while even in these parts.[120]

Some of the Scots' merchandise may have been bought in Bergen or other towns from other visiting foreigners or resident traders there.[121] Most

117 Lillehammer, 'The Timber Trade' (n 3) 22–23.

118 Smout, 'The Norwegian Timber Trade' (n 3) 42. For examples north of Bergen in the seventeenth century, cf. Seve, *Molde bys historie* (n 11) 117.

119 See Næss, 'Skottehandelen' (n 4) 28.

120 See e.g. Næss, 'Skottehandelen' (n 4) 26–28 and 47–50; Sunde, *Across The Sea* (n 3) 65. For the less researched Scottish imports in rural areas north of Bergen and in the Agder and the Oslo fjord regions, see e.g. Krøvel and Tafjord, *Folk i fjordriket* (n 11) 224, Seve, *Molde bys historie* (n 11) 117; Fløystad, *Agders historie* (n 11) 121; Løyland, *Fjordfolk* (n 10) 123–124; Rian (ed), *Telemarks historie* (n 11) 265–266; Seierstad, *Skiens historie* (n 9) 138 and 267. For the introduction of tobacco in Norway, see e.g. J Johannessen, 'En arkeologisk undersøkelse av krittpiper som kilde til når tobakkskonsum ble vanlig i Oslo' (2016) *Årbok for Norsk Maritimt Museum 2015* 11–27.

121 Cf. e.g. Næss, 'Skottehandelen' (n 4) 33–34.

of it, nevertheless, was probably imported by the Scottish skippers themselves, from Scotland, Ireland, England or the Continent.[122]

The Scottish-Norwegian trade was not a one-way traffic, as we have seen above. The Norwegian shipping to Scotland was by all probability more extensive than the extant sources reveal.[123] Although the sources are biased, we nevertheless have reason to believe that it was on a much smaller scale than the Scottish trade with Norway. In the sixteenth century, the Norwegian towns were few and small. The Germans in Bergen did not show much interest in the timber trade, nor in trade with Scotland. The indigenous merchant classes there and in other towns were not numerous and were only gradually gaining strength after two centuries of German domination of Norwegian foreign trade. Still, with the kind of small and medium sized ships that seem to have been typical for the Scottish trade in the Norwegian fjords, one may wonder if the sawmill owners and other people in the rural districts to some extent organised trade expeditions of their own to Scotland with timber. This may certainly have occurred, but one should also bear in mind that since the late middle ages it was forbidden for ordinary farmers to build real ships for foreign trade, or boats of more than between three and four lasts, partly to protect the trade of the nobility and the town burghers, and partly because it was a concern that the farmers might neglect their farms if they engaged in trade and shipping. To the extent that it was effectively enforced, this also favoured Scots when the trade between Scotland and Norway took off in the sixteenth century.[124]

I: THE SCOTTISH TRADE – TRADE WITH FEW TENSIONS?

Scottish traders and immigrants in Bergen in the first half of the sixteenth century apparently were regarded as a serious threat to the interests of the German merchants there, not merely by competing in the import trade with grain. In the attack, orchestrated in 1523 by the German *Kontor*, on local residents at *Stranden*, opposite the German wharf (*Bryggen*), Scots seem to have been particularly targeted. The Germans were complaining about Scottish traders engaging in local trade in the city. In the late 1540s,

122 For outlines of Scottish foreign trade, see Ditchburn, *Scotland and Europe* (n 3) 138–196; Smout (ed), *Scotland and Europe* (n 3).

123 Bugge, *Den norske trælasthandels historie: II* (n 6) 241–245.

124 Lange and Unger (eds), DN, vol 2 (n 30) no 963; cf. e.g. Johnsen, *Norwegische Wirtschatftsgescichte* (n 7) 158–159; Næss and Kolllveit, *Strandebarm og Varaldsøy* (n 10) 194–195.

they also made complaints about Scots trading outside Bergen and buying victuals there instead of timber. Furthermore, Scottish piracy and privateering off the coast of Norway was also an issue mostly brought forward by the Germans in the early sixteenth century.[125]

In contrast, the presence of Scottish traders in Bergen, other Norwegian towns and rural districts in general seems to have caused little tension with the indigenous population and the local and royal authorities throughout the sixteenth century. Complaints of pirates and privateers from Scotland occur on and off, but this in general does not seem to have created any hostility against Scots. The authorities apparently were more concerned with the French in this respect.[126]

Of course, on an individual basis, legal and other conflicts also occurred between the natives and Scottish visiting traders and immigrants. In the castle accounts, occasionally Scots appear as victims or perpetrators of acts of violence or other offences. One particularly ugly case is reported from the Bohuslän region by the scribe of the bishop of Oslo. During a visitation there in 1594 the bishop's retinue passed by the remains of two Scots, who apparently some years earlier had killed a local priest and subsequently were executed on the breaking wheel.[127] In all, however, the extant sources to a very limited extent bear witness of conflict between Norwegians and visiting Scots in this epoch.[128]

In the towns, the royal authorities also seem to have welcomed not only Scottish, Dutch and other foreign visiting merchants, but also immigration, from Scotland and elsewhere, especially in Bergen as a counterbalance to the resident Germans at the *Kontor* who dominated the trade without being citizens, and as a means to strengthen the emerging native merchant class in the efforts to break the virtual German monopoly in the stockfish trade there.[129] Probably for the same reasons, the Scottish presence does not seem to have caused serious grievances or opposition from native traders. There are, however, no signs in extant sources of any long-lasting local opposition

125 For example, Næss, 'Skottehandelen' (n 4) 28 and 47–49; Schreiner, *Hanseatene og Norge* (n 8) 64 and 67; Nedkvitne, *The German Hansa* (n 8) 479, 484–485.

126 See e.g. Heiberg and Petersen (eds), NRR, vol 1 (n 85) 118, 179, 186–187; cf. Espeland, *Skottene* (n 4) 12.

127 Y Nielsen, *Biskop Jens Nilssøns visitasbøger og reiseopptegnelser 1574–1597* (1885) 173 and 175.

128 See, however, Langhelle, 'The Timber Export' (n 70) 35.

129 See e.g. Nedkvitne, *The German Hansa* (n 8) 471–496; N Bjørgo, Ø Rian and A Kaartvedt, *Norsk utenrikspolitikks historie: bind 1: Selvstendighet og union* (1995) 161–165; Johnsen, *Norwegische Witschaftsgeschichte* (n 7) 184, 228 and 230; Schreiner, *Hanseatene og Norge* (n 8) 8–9, 57–58, 64–69, 119–120 and 127.

to Scottish or other urban immigration, except from the Germans at the *Kontor*, who were now struggling to close ranks and prevent fellow Germans from settling outside *Bryggen* as burghers.[130]

Repeated prohibitions on the export of timber, especially of oak, were obviously not popular with the foreign traders who called on Norwegian harbours. These export prohibitions, as well as efforts to limit exports by raising customs duties instead, caused diplomatic interventions on behalf of the Dutch from the emperor Charles V and his son Philip II of Spain. In contrast, Scottish authorities apparently did not engage in similar active diplomacy on their behalf with some minor exceptions already mentioned, although Scots were heavily involved in the timber export especially from western and south-western Norway.[131] In several other respects, however, the Scottish traders in Norway in the sixteenth century in fact benefited from a quite lenient political and legal regime for foreign traders who called in Norwegian ports to collect timber.

Throughout this century and well into the next, the Danish-Norwegian kings for most practical purposes continued their pragmatic policy of exempting the timber trade from the general ban on trade outside the towns, allowing Scottish as well as other visiting foreigners to purchase timber and lumber in the rural districts directly from the local population, without intermediaries.[132] During the sixteenth century, they more or less gave up on enforcing the old and repeatedly confirmed ban on foreigners sailing north of Bergen. Scots and other foreigners started to purchase timber and trade with the locals in the northern fjords of western Norway as well as in the Trondheim fjord region, and to some extent even engaged both in the fish trade and with fisheries in northern Norway.[133]

Royal measures to restrict the number of sawmills remained at best half-hearted and ineffective until the latter half of the seventeenth century. Except from the Trondheim fjord region, most sawmills were still small, with limited production capacity, in the early 1600s. This allowed a decentralised ownership structure where ordinary farmers could take part in the business along with noblemen and royal officials, until deforestation in the coastal

130 See Schreiner, *Hanseatene og Norge* (n 8) 120–122 and 126–127; cf. Nedkvitne *The German Hansa* (n 8) 471–496.

131 See e.g. Bugge, *Den norske trælasthandels historie: II* (n 6) 219–221; Næss, 'Skottehandelen' (n 4) 21–22, 25–26; Bjørg et al, *Selvstendighet og union* (n 128) 165–168.

132 See also Koch's chapter in the present volume.

133 See Johnsen, *Norwegische Wirtschaftsgescichte* (n 7) 250; Krøvel and Tafjord, *Folk i fjordriket* (n 11) 224; Bugge, *Aalesunds historie* (n 10) 34; Seve, *Molde bys historie* (n 11) 41, 59, 64 and 74; Dybdahl, *Fra pest til poteter* (n 11) 172–173.

areas gradually changed the sawmilling industry, making it more capital intensive and in need of more complex organisation to transport timber from the interior.[134]

Efforts to make the foreign traders in the rural districts buy and sell for cash were apparently also ineffective. As long as they did not otherwise engage in local trade, or in trade between town and countryside, the foreigners were allowed to pay for their purchases in whatever commodities of decent quality they were importing.[135] To draw a distinct line between paying in kind for purchases of timber and other Norwegian products, on the one hand, and illegal trading in the rural districts on the other, cannot have been easy.

Traders in the towns were evidently not very happy with the direct trade that was going on between Scottish skippers, other foreigners and local farmers and landowners in the rural districts. In the case of Stavanger, for example, it was a source of tension that, although the burghers there owned quite a lot of land and forests in the Ryfylke region, local farmers owned many of the best locations for putting up sawmills. These tensions do not, however, seem to have reflected on the Scottish skippers, who for obvious reasons were welcomed both by the burghers and the rural population.[136] More generally, the burghers sought to control the trade with the Scots and other foreigners and act as intermediaries. During the sixteenth century, the kings gradually adopted a more active policy of protecting the trade interests of the burghers at the expense of visiting foreign traders and royal officials, as well as local farmers, by granting new and more extensive privileges. This policy seems to have had some effect from the 1560s with growing timber exports over Bergen. More generally, the long reign of Christian IV (1588–1648) was a breakthrough for the towns in this respect. For instance, in 1607 Stavanger was granted a trade monopoly within a circumference or radius of about thirty-four kilometres from the town. However, the lumber trade was exempt from this monopoly. Nevertheless, from ca. 1620 more and more lumber from Ryfylke was being transported via Stavanger on its path to Scotland and other foreign markets, although never surpassing 50 per cent

134 See Forfang, 'Sagbruksproduksjon i Noreg' (n 8) 315–342; cf. e.g. Bugge, *Den norske trælasthandels historie: II* (n 6) 50–63 and 145; Næss, 'Sagbruk i Sønderhordland' (n 4) 18 and 26–27; Bull, *Oslos historie* (n 9) 401–402; Ø Vestheim, *Fløting gjennom århundrer: Fløtingas historie i Glomma- og Mjøsvassdraget* (1998).

135 Lundh and Sars (eds), NRR, vol III (n 49) 61–64, Lundh (ed), NRR, vol IV (n 98) 24–25; cf. e.g. Næss, 'Skottehandelen' (n 4) 27, 47–49; Tønnessen, *Porsgrunns historie* (n 10) 55.

136 Lillehammer, 'The Timber Trade' (n 3) 13; cf. Lillehammer, 'Skottehandelen og Rogaland' (n 12) 51–52; Elgvin, *En by i kamp* (n 9) 121–124.

of the total exports. In 1662 the towns won their final victory over the rural population when King Fredrik II issued new privileges for all the Norwegian towns, granting them a trade monopoly in the timber trade as well, within trading districts that effectively divided the entire Norwegian countryside between them, and also reduced rivalry between towns, like between Bergen and Stavanger over trading rights in Sunnhordland and Ryfylke.[137]

The Danish-Norwegian kings' long-lasting inability, or even reluctance, to impose and enforce effective measures to restrict the direct trade between foreigners and the local population in the sawmilling and timber exporting districts hence paved the way for the extensive Scottish trade, especially in the Hardanger-Sunnhordland and Ryfylke regions. This situation may be explained by a series of dilemmas caused by the dramatic expansion of the sawmilling industry and influx of Scots and other foreign traders that the kings had to try to balance.

On the one hand, the growing timber exports offered incomes from taxation of the owners of sawmills and forests and their workers as well as customs duties from the traders. On the other side, overexploitation and deforestation were conceived of as threats to the supplies of timber to the Danish-Norwegian navy[138]; perhaps to the long-term fiscal basis as well.

Insisting more effectively on transactions in the rural areas being carried out with cash, not in kind, would have been beneficial for tax collection. This was probably the most important motivation for the legislation that was passed to that effect, although both the kings and the town burghers propagated such measures by referring to the low quality and uselessness of much of the merchandise that the foreigners brought, cheating the locals of much of the incomes they deserved from the trade.[139] On the other hand, the Scots were important purveyors of cereals and other necessities to the rural population. It is symptomatic that when the young Christian IV in 1589 prohibited payment in kind, he made an exception for good merchandise, like wine, peas, silk cloth and other commodities that the nobility and the burghers needed. It is equally symptomatic that when a temporary ban on all timber export in the region north of Bergen was introduced in 1590, the

137 See Helle et al, *Norsk byhistorie* (n 9) 158–60; Fossen, *Borgerskapets by* (n 9) 42–43, 149–154, 212–214, 365–370; Lillehammer, 'Skottehandelen og Rogaland' (n 12) 51–52; Næss, 'Skottehandelen' (n 4) 26–28; cf. e.g. Johnsen, *Kristiansunds historie* (n 10) 97; Ringard, *Flekkefjords historie* (n 10) 20–21.

138 See Johnsen, *Norwegische Wirtschaftsgeschichte* (n 7) 119.

139 See Johnsen, *Norwegische Wirtschaftsgescichte* (n 7) 250; Krøvel and Tafjord, *Folk i fjordriket* (n 11) 224; Bugge, *Aalesunds historie* (n 10) 34; Seve, *Molde bys historie* (n 11) 41, 59, 64 and 74; Dybdahl, *Fra pest til poteter* (n 11) 172–173.

locals protested that they suffered from the absence of foreigners who would come for timber and bring flour, malt and other commodities that they needed. The king hence instructed the burghers of Bergen to provide the rural population with such things in their place.[140]

With the commodities that Scotland's agriculture and industries could offer, and its extensive foreign trade networks, the arrival of the Scots must, in most respects, have been conceived of as a blessing to the local rural population. The direct trade with the Scots offered good income opportunities both for sawmill-owners and their workforce, by extensive purchases of timber and deals, as well as victuals and other provisions during their often prolonged stays in the fjords. They would typically stay for several weeks, even months, due to the decentralised structure of the sawmilling industry that forced even the skippers of the many small Scottish ships to load timber from numerous mills. Sometimes the stays were prolonged by repair works on the ships. The Scots brought a variety of imported goods that would otherwise less conveniently have had to be purchased in the towns, probably at higher prices, in spite of allegations of the opposite from complaining townspeople who were jealous of the Scottish traders. By buying timber, deals and other local products, and by paying in kind rather than in cash, the Scots brought the inhabitants of the fjord districts into more direct contact with the outside world and an international market economy. The Scots carried with them foreign consumer goods as well as immaterial culture, enhancing the local inhabitants' standard of living.[141]

J: THE SCOTTISH LEGACY

Especially in Agder and the Langesund and Oslo fjord regions, urbanisation was spreading in this period, with numerous timber harbours in the rural districts growing to become little towns, at first as "ladesteder" under the jurisdiction and economic control of the older towns or "kjøpsteder", from the 1640s onwards in many cases gaining town privileges as "kjøpsteder" in their own right. Many of Norway's most important shipping towns in later centuries emerged in this way.[142]

With increasing deforestation in the coastal areas, the timber in the seventeenth century had, to a greater and greater extent, to be collected in the

140 Lundh and Sars (eds), NRR, vol III, 218; cf. Næss, 'Skottehandelen' (n 4) 26–27.
141 See e.g. Lillehammer, 'The Timber Trade' (n 3) 22–23; Langhelle, 'The Timber Export' (n 70) 34.
142 See e.g. Helle et al, *Norsk byhistorie* (n 9) 202–206.

interior and floated to the coast. This not only gradually enabled the burghers to take over the control of the timber trade; it also caused the geographical centre of gravity in the timber trade south of the Trondheim fjord region to move from the western coast to eastern Norway, where the interior of the country offered more timber and more rivers where it could be floated.[143] Nevertheless, Scottish traders to some extent continued to visit the inner parts of the long fjords, like the Hardanger fjord, in search for timber at least until the latter half of the eighteenth century.[144]

To a large extent, this development excluded the ordinary farmers in the coastal areas from the export sawmilling business. New town privileges and regulations of the timber trade from the latter half of the seventeenth century onwards added to this effect, granting the town burghers a monopoly on the timber trade.[145] In parts of Ryfylke, Arnvid Lillehammer suggests that the long-term effect of the farmers' once very lucrative trade with the Scots and the deforestation was a growing dependency on cereal imports, and eventually also growing poverty.[146]

In the fjord areas between Bergen and Stavanger, where the timber trade was once most extensive and boosted the local economy the most in the sixteenth and seventeenth centuries, the forest resources in the interior that could be mobilised for the coastal sawmills were at the same time more limited. The incomes from timber trade in these areas dropped considerably towards the end of the seventeenth century, as we have seen, and the long-term economic effect was different than in Agder and eastern Norway.[147] Further urbanisation in this epicentre of the Scottish-Norwegian trade is mostly a more recent phenomenon, connected partly to the rich herring fisheries from the early nineteenth century and partly to modern industrialisation based on ample access to hydroelectric power from some of the numerous waterfalls that once made the timber trade flourish from the early sixteenth century.[148]

However, the Scottish legacy is also cultural. With Scottish skippers often staying for long periods of time in the timber exporting regions of western and south-western Norway, in many cases making two or three annual trips to the same places over several years, meeting with the same people there,

143 See e.g. Lillehammer, 'The Timber Trade' (n 3) 11.
144 Næss, 'Skottehandelen' (n 4) 57–63.
145 See e.g. Helle et al, *Norsk byhistorie* (n 9) 159–160.
146 Lillehammer, 'The Timber Trade' (n 3) 23; cf. Langhelle, 'The Timber Export' (n 70) 32–35.
147 See e.g. Lillehammer, 'The Timber Trade' (n 3) 14–21; cf. Næss, 'Skottehandelen' (n 4) 57–61.
148 See e.g. Helle et al, *Norsk byhistorie* (n 9) 157–165 and 202–206.

close personal relations and cultural influences would follow. This impact of the Scottish trade was reinforced by immigration.

We have met with Scottish immigrants not only to Norwegian towns, but also to the rural districts in the sixteenth century. Some of the immigrants were prominent people, like the nobleman Andrew Mowat from Shetland who married into a rich Norwegian noble family and first settled on the island of Tysnes in Sunnhordland in the late sixteenth century. His granddaughter Karen Mowat was allegedly the richest heiress in Norway when she married a poor nobleman, Ludvig Rosenkrantz, ca. 1658. Her fortune became the foundation of the only barony in the country, Rosendal, which after her death was erected by her husband in 1678.[149]

Other immigrants to Sunnhordland include members of Scottish families like Sinclair, Stuart, Cunningham, Durham and Erskine, also doing well in marriage, and some in military service. Most of the Scottish immigrants are unknown to us. In the early stages many of them served as soldiers and officers. More Scottish immigrants arrived in the seventeenth century. They tried to make new careers in Norway in the military, in royal administration or in crafts and trade, in Hordaland and elsewhere. Quite a few succeeded and by the late seventeenth or early eighteenth century a fair number of families of Scottish ancestry held prominent positions all over Norway. With them they brought military, maritime, commercial, industrial and spiritual knowhow.[150]

The memory of the Scottish immigration survives not only in family names but also in folk traditions and numerous placenames related to the Scottish presence along the Norwegian coast.[151] It has even been suggested that the double stringed Hardanger fiddle, an icon in the Norwegian folk music tradition, is an import from Scotland, inspired by the viola d'amore.[152]

149 Sunde, *Across the Sea* (n 3) 59–60.

150 See e.g. Espeland, *Skottene* (n 4) 14–20; Næss and Kolllveit, *Strandebarm og Varaldsøy* (n 10) 34, 194–198, 466; E Opsahl, S Sogner and K Kjeldstadli (ed), *I Kongenes tid. Norsk innvandringshistorie: bind 1* (2003) 185–191, 213, 231–232, 254–255, 290, 307–312 and 322.

151 See e.g. Næss, 'Skottehandelen' (n 4) 80–86; Næss, 'Sagbruk i Søndhordland' (n 4) 38–42.

152 See e.g. Ø Strømmen, 'Hardingfela – Noreg sitt nasjonalinstrument' (2002) *Kvam herad*, available at *https://www.kvam.no/velkomen-til-kvam/fakta-om-kvam/hardingfela/* (last accessed 3 August 2022).

9 Norm and Fact: Timber trade in early modern western Norway (1530–1730)

Sören Koch

A: INTRODUCTION

From the late medieval period, all timber trade from western Norway to Scotland, England and the European continent was supposed to be subject to monopolies held by trading posts such as the cities of Bergen and Stavanger. However, most timber trade was carried out in such a way as to avoid the cities and often to evade taxation. The court rolls of the rural areas around Bergen document the authority's fruitless efforts to regulate a market contrary to the interests of the involved economic actors until the end of the seventeenth century. This paper attempts to answer the question why the legal framework for the North Sea trade failed to realise the legislator's intention. In other words, why did norm and fact fall apart?

It is often said that legal regulation of trade is a key factor of economic growth and success.[1] Law is supposed to provide predictability, which in turn would facilitate efficiency of transactions. A sufficiently clear legal framework is a precondition for legal certainty. However, trade regulations contrary to the interest of most of the actors involved are doomed to be ineffective unless sufficiently enforced by authorities. Where such authorities are lacking, or are not capable of efficiently enforcing the law, market forces will prevail. Frequent attempts to regulate timber trade against the interests of producers, merchants and end consumers in early modern Norwegian-Scottish timber trade provide an example illustrating the point.

Since the thirteenth century, royal legislation was recognised as an effective means of regulating social behaviour and trade relations.[2] However, the legal regulations concerning the trade with foreigners in the rural areas of western Norway, especially regarding timber, were strikingly different from trading practice.[3] In other words, there was a considerable gap between the normative order and the trade reality.

To render the paper relevant for the topic of this volume and to limit the rich source material concerning the timber trade in western Norway, we will focus on the timber trade with Scotland, which flourished in this region especially from the sixteenth century to the early eighteenth century.[4] The

1 See e.g. B Ginting, R Sembiring, M Siregar and A Abduh, 'The Role of Law in Economic Development: To Develop a Special Economic Zone in Order to Build a National and Regional Economy' (2017) 1 *Proceedings of MICoMS* 209–214.

2 J Ø Sunde, 'In Daughters of God and counsellors of the judges of men: changes in the legal culture of the Norwegian realm in the High Middle Ages' (2014) in S Brink and L Collinson (eds), *New Approaches to the Early Law in Scandinavia* (2014) 134 ff.

3 The geographical area (western Norway) included in this survey extends from Stavanger (*Rogaland, Sunnhordaland*) in the south via Bergen to the district of *Sunnmøre* north of Bergen; this area is not completely identical with the administrative entity of Bergenhus-lehn, which at times also included territories in northern Norway and other parts of the country.

4 For an overview of the Norwegian timber trade with Scotland, England and the Low Countries in the same period, see J Ø Sunde, *Vegen over havet. Frå Mowatane på Shetland til Baroniet Rosendal* (2010); Ø G Gryt '"Trelastnæringa på Sunnmøre 1600–1660": Frå "skiønne Fyrreskove" Til "fattig og Udtømmet"', *Master Thesis, University of Bergen* (2008); A Lillehammer (1988) 'Skottehandelen og Rogaland: By mot land på 1600-talet' (1987) *Ætt Og Heim* 39–55; J Bruijn, T Smout, S Langhelle and A Lillehammer, *Timber and trade: Articles on the timber export from the Ryfylke-area to Scotland and Holland in the 16th and 17th century: Fagrapport* vol 1 (1999); A Næss, *Skottehandelen på Sunnhordaland* (1959); A Espeland and Voss sogelag, *Skottene i Hordaland og Rogaland: Fra aar 1500–1800* (1921); S Tveite, *Engelsk-Norsk Trelasthandel 1640–1710* (1961); H S K Kent, 'The Anglo-Norwegian Timber Trade in the Eighteenth Century' (1955) New Seriens 8 no 1 *The Economic History Review* 62–74, stressing the high degree of dependence on Norwegian timber for the English and Scottish industry in the 1730s. Kent

scope of the paper is limited to fir timber, deals and battens, as these constituted the largest volumes of the timber exported to Scotland.[5]

In the first part of the paper, I will give a concise overview of the lawmakers' attempts to enforce a particular model of trade, and of their failure to do so. In the second part, I will explore some reasons causing the disparity between the normative and the factual. The explanation is apparently based on a rather complex interplay of very different factors, highly dependent on the historical context at a given point in time. However, in my view, the *economic* interests of the social groups involved and their impact on the regulation of the timber trade can be identified as a crucial and constantly relevant factor when trying to understand the relationship between the law and the reality it is supposed to regulate. A crucial factor is that it was difficult to enforce the legal rules against the interests of the parties involved in early modern times – resembling the situation on the supranational level today.

Based on a critical analysis of the arguments put forward in relevant legal sources,[6] I will identify the economic interests of the following five social groups and then explain the extent to which the law addressed them. First, I will consider the rural population, such as peasants, local tradesmen, innkeepers and local citizens. Secondly, I will examine the interests of the lower nobility, actively involved in the timber trade. Thirdly, reference will be made to the foreign merchants, such as the Hanseatic League, the English, Dutch and, most importantly in the context of this paper, the Scots. Fourthly, the paper will consider the citizens of the cities such as Bergen and Stavanger. Finally, reference will be made to the interests of the king and his representative in Bergen – the minister of Bergenhus. As the first two social

refers to the fact that the Board of Trade rebutted the recommendation of the British envoy in Denmark-Norway to put higher duties on Norwegian imports with the argument that Norwegian imports were essential and could not be replaced from other sources (cf. p. 62 note 1). The same will certainly have applied for Scotland (cf. Kent, 'The Anglo-Norwegian Timber Trade' 67). See also H S K Kent, *War and Trade in Northern Seas; Anglo-Scandinavian Economic Relations in the Mid-Eighteenth Century* (1973). Older literature: L J Vogt, *Om Norges Udførsel af Trælast i Ældre Tider* (1885). On the impact the trade relations had on the terminology used by the merchants, see M Lorvik, 'Mutual Intelligibility of Timber Trade Terminology in the North Sea Countries during the Time of the "Scottish Trade"' (2003) 2 *Nordic Journal of English Studies* 223–243. From an interdisciplinary perspective R Hutchison, 'The Norwegian and Baltic Timber Trade to Britain 1780–1835 and Its Interconnections' (2012) 37 *Scandinavian Journal of History* 578–599.

5 R Hutchison (n 5) 579.

6 Such as legal codes, ordinances, royal letters, charters, privileges, petitions, complaints, but also administrative documents such as tax and custom registers as well as court rolls both from Bergen and the districts of South Hordaland and Sunnmøre.

groups had negligible influence on the establishment of the legal framework, it is essential to study how their interests were perceived, articulated and taken into consideration by the other groups. In this context, the townspeople's perceptions and opinions are especially important, as their vested interests in organising the trade was a driving factor in the development of the legal framework.

The underlying hypothesis for the paper is that an effective legal regulation of inter-regional trade requires that sufficient consideration is given to the interests of all social groups involved – or at least most social groups, including those not actively participating in norm production.[7]

B: NORWEGIAN-SCOTTISH TIMBER TRADE REALITY/ PRACTICE

Despite a continuous legislative and administrative struggle to channel all west Norwegian timber trade through the major trading posts of Bergen and Stavanger, Scottish merchants in particular often seem to have traded timber directly with the local producers.[8] Interestingly, the gap between the normative and the factual was not ignored, but was constantly subject to complaints, negotiations, regulations and court rulings. A statement by a commission of royal officials (*stiftsamtsmænd*), which had to consider the economic situation of both towns and rural districts, illustrates the underlying problems. In their report to the crown from 1735 we can read:

> Here in the bishopric of Bergen, seven miles south of the city, is the island of Stort, where various families have settled down, . . . and where the well-known custom-post for the region Sunnhordland is located. Despite the fact that this custom-post is no trade-post, and a custom-post is not supposed to collect taxes for other products than timber, one can observe that neither the inhabitants of this island nor those of the neighbouring districts purchase any products from Bergen. Instead they receive all they need, from foreigners, especially from Scotland, which here in the fjords buy and load their timber, as well as from the

7 P O'Brien, 'European Economic Development: The Contribution of the Periphery' (1982) 35 no 1 *The economic history review* 1–18, has shown that the inter-regional trade and the inter-regional markets were a crucial factor for the pre-industrial growth in Europe, thereby rebutting the World System Theory promoted by writers such as Immanuel Wallenstein and Grunder Frank who emphasis the importance of colonial peripheries.

8 See A Bugge, *Den norske trælasthandels historie: Fra freden i Speier til slutten av 1600–tallet*: II (1925) 178. Another example where the Danish-Norwegian authorities seem to have failed to change a practice was with regard to the import of Swedish timber into Norway, floating the Norwegian sawmills, particular in the area of Fredrikshald, see the rescript of 21 April 1745, in J A S Schmidt (ed), *Reskripter, Resolusjoner og kongelige Brev for Kongerike Norge*, vol I (1847) 313.

English and Dutch who buy lobster from them. It may not be proven, but it has to be assumed that a not inconsiderable amount of Tobacco, Alcohol and the like is imported by these foreign traders deliberately bypassing customs and violating the well-established privileges and customs as well as the precepts of our Norwegian Laws. Also other products are often not declared properly. And this will continue unless the custom post is abandoned as it is impossible for the customs officers (as many as they may be) to control such an enormous region efficiently. Considering your own economic loss, your highness, and also the devastating consequences for Bergen's inhabitants, who suffer from this illegitimate trade, so do we feel obliged to recommend the abolishment of the custom-post Sunnhordland. At the same time, we recommend to prohibit all trade except with Bergen. These measures will increase your tax revenue and the welfare of Bergen. Furthermore, it will preserve the forests in the district of Sunnhordland, where the trees for many years have been lumbered before sufficiently grown and have been sold to foreigners for an unreasonably low price, without conferring your majesty any considerable benefit or profit.[9]

The claims put forward here are hardly new. Attempts to implement such an economic model had already been proposed in the early fourteenth century. According to this model, all direct trade between the rural areas and foreign tradesmen was prohibited. Instead, timber (as all other products produced in these areas) were supposed to be transported, registered and taxed in Bergen. The king had a pre-emptive right in respect of timber sold in the town.[10] The rest should be sold to the townspeople who could use the timber or sell it to foreigners. Despite constant attempts by the citizens of the cities to further regulate and enforce such a trade model, the timber trade followed a very different pattern in practice. Scottish, English, German and Dutch merchants sailed directly into the fjords and traded timber and some other products such as fur and fish for corn, salt, cloth, spices and many more.[11] Sometimes they even ordered ships that

9 Bergen Museum Manuscript Collection – in the Department of Special Collection – Manuscripts and Rare Book Collection; no 243, 27 ff. Transcription by Næss, *Skottehandelen* (n 4) 36 f (my translation). Similar reports have been received from the region Sunnmøre north of Bergen, the natural scientist and topographer H Strøm, *Physisk og Oeconomisk Beskrivelse over Fogderiet Søndmør, beliggende i Bergens Stift i Norge* vol 1 (1762) 79, explained the deforestation of this area as follow: "This deforestation was in particular caused by the timber trade activities with the Scottish, which was here more excessive than in any other part of the country, since they had easy access to the production sides by sailing down the Breesund, which is well known by sailors" – Original: *"Hvilket man i sær tilstkriver den stærke Træe-handel med Skotterne, som her skal havt sin Fart, mere end paa noget andet Stæd, I anledning ad det korte og rene Indløb igjennem Breesund, some r Søefarende saa vel bekient"*.

10 See King Magnus the Lawmender's Code of the Towns, Book VI ch 18.

11 Cf. Protocol by the Bergen Town council (byråd) (1607), referring to close, fabric, liquor, gingerbread and very little money (*egne klæde, lerret, brendeuin, lerpotter, frandzuin, peberkager, og nogle faa penge*).

were built in Norway and sailed them to Scotland.[12] Historians disagree on the extent to which the timber trade happened without being reported and declared to the tax authorities.[13] The low degree of consistency regarding the amount of timber exports in the tax records and a survey of court practice, including cases in which merchants were convicted for tax fraud, indicate that a rather high percentage of timber exports were not declared properly.[14] The high degree of deforestation in the area can hardly be explained by a combination of the recorded legitimate exports and the relatively low demand for timber products in Norway. Hence, both the crown and the townspeople had a very strong interest in regulating the timber trade efficiently.

C: THE NORMATIVE FRAMEWORK

(1) Introduction

In 1299 King Håkon Magnusson announced a decree (*rettarbot*) prohibiting trade with peasants, excepting only trade among farmers themselves.[15] All goods produced in rural areas were now supposed to be transported to Bergen from where they could be resold. As this decree did not produce sufficient results, Håkon V enacted another decree in 1302, this time more specifically stating: "No foreigner has the right to buy timber at any other place than at royal yards or from house-owners in the cities".[16] The prohibition was renewed and even expanded several times, often due to the

12 We know of fifty-two new ships and boats in 1664 built and delivered in the district of South Hordaland in 1664 alone, Næss, *Skottehandelen* (n 4) 23 with reference to the Stat Archive in Bergen; Sorenskrivaren i Sunnhordland, *Court Record for Sunnhordland*, A12 (1665) 14.06.1665; and thirteen boats built with reference to a complaint to the council of the realm by the minister of Bergenhus from 1590; O G Lundh and I E Sars (eds), *Norges Rigs-Registranter*, vol III (1865) 155 (henceforth NRR).

13 Næss, *Skottehandelen* (n 4) 34 refers to a considerable amount of unregistered exports; Lorvik, 'Mutual Intelligibility' (n 4) 226 indicates the same, but points out that the often long visits of the Scottish merchants would hardly have been completely unrecognised by the authorities. For a similar argument, see Gryt, 'Trelastnæringa på Sunnmøre' (n 4) 12. On the other hand, constant complaints concerning smuggling and avoiding taxes throughout the sixteenth and seventeenth century indicate that an effective custom control of the vast landscapes of western Norway with thousands of miles coastline was almost impossible.

14 See e.g. Tveite, *Engelsk-Norsk Trelasthandel* (n 4) 42. Bugge, *Den norske trælasthandels historie*, II (n 8) 189 observed that "Bergen's share in the timber trade was insignificant" (my translation).

15 R Keyser and P A Munch (eds), *Norges Gamle Love*, vol III (1849) no 12 (henceforth (NgL).

16 Næss, *Skottehandelen* (n 4) 7, with reference to Keyser and Munch (eds), NgL vol III (n 15) no 53.

complaints of individual tradesmen, the Hanseatic League in Bergen or the lord of Bergenhus in 1366, 1414, 1444 and 1560.[17]

As far as can be reconstructed from the surviving manuscripts, the reason for the prohibition was that foreign traders would buy the timber for unreasonably low prices, which would endanger both the functioning of the local market and the welfare of the rural population. Bergen's city council and the lord of Bergenhus, often backed by the king's council, pretended to act in the best interest of a functioning market and in the interest of the rural population, which needed protection from greedy and ruthless foreigners.[18] Furthermore, it was emphasised that foreign interference would endanger the king's interests in controlling trade activities and ruin his tax revenue.[19] In other words, these fourteenth-century arguments were basically the same as those which were put forward by the commission in 1735.

Be that as it may, the surviving source material provides us with little evidence as to what extent merchants and farmers complied with the royal orders.[20] The fact that the prohibition was renewed in 1316, 1331 and 1360 indicates that trade practice was still not in accordance with royal commands and may not have greatly changed over this period.[21] After the Black Death had a devastating effect on the Norwegian economy, including the timber trade, the legislative efforts to regulate this area became scarce.

(2) The role of the Hanse

The gap between the normative and the factual situation becomes apparent again in the fifteenth and sixteenth centuries when the Hanseatic League[22]

17 Cf. Næss, *Skottehandelen* (n 4) 7 ff with further reference.

18 For example, Keyser and Munch (eds), NgL vol III (n 15) no 111.

19 Keyser and Munch (eds), NgL vol III (n 15) no 53 and 70.

20 Næss, *Skottehandelen* (n 4) 7: "the prohibition was of little effect" – *"forbodi var lite akta"*.

21 See Keyser and Munch (eds), NgL vol III (n 15) no 70, 91 and 114. King Håkon V explicitly expresses his frustration with the limited effect of the legislative precepts. In the fourteenth century we find several complains put forward by the local authorities, the lawmen in Bergen and Norwegian tradesmen against the practice of German tradesmen doing business with peasants especially on the way to and from Bergen (cf. Keyser and Munch (eds), NgL vol III (n 15), no 47 and 70). Both the king and local authorities issued regulations prohibiting these trade practices, obviously with very little success. This caused a shortage of highly needed timber products in Bergen, more complaints by the royal ombudsmen and new precepts obliging all inhabitants of the region to offer their timber to the royal yard first Næss, *Skottehandelen* (n 4) 7.

22 Some historians regard the lack of interest in trading timber on the part of the Hanseatic League as one of the reasons why the Norwegian timber trade was relatively insignificant until the middle of the sixteenth century (timber was shipped to Lübeck and other Hanseatic cities from Prussia, the Baltics and Russia because of better quality and lower transportation costs). The Hanseatic League was cautious to reinforce the royal order prohibiting any foreigner trading

became important players in west Norwegian Trade.[23] As early as 1377, we find a royal decree that admonishes the Hanseatic merchants for breaking their privileges when directly trading with peasants.[24] In an ordinance of 1444 enacted by King Kristoffer of Bavaria, the Hansa were even accused of cutting down trees illegally.[25] Even if such incidents may have taken place, they cannot have happened particularly regularly. Quite the opposite seems likely. One of the reasons that timber trade in Norway did not become an important and significant branch of business before the late sixteenth century was that the Hanseatic cities had very limited interest in trading timber with Norwegians. They drew their timber supplies from the Baltic states, where they could purchase timber of better quality and with lower transport expenses. As long as they dominated the trade with Norway, the *Kontor* and the Hanseatic cities had a vital interest in monopolising all trade in Bergen and other trading posts. Their dominance relied on them being the main provider of essential grain supplies and on their being able to exclude merchants from other nations from gaining access to the Norwegian market. Allocating trade in the most important trade posts made it easier to achieve that goal. True, they traded other goods with the local peasants and let them even build houses for them, both strictly prohibited by Norwegian law.[26] However, again the amount of trade involved was not nearly at the level it reached after the influence of the Hanseatic League had declined and after English and Dutch merchants in particular started coming more regularly to the western parts of Norway.

From an analytical point of view, the defence of the Hanseatic League as a reaction to the above-mentioned ordinance of 1444 is particularly interesting.[27] The Hanseats argued that they would cut timber only with

activities north of Bergen. The decline of the Hanseatic League's economic and political power made it possible for both tradesmen from Holland and Scotland to sail into the fjords. See e.g. Bugge, *Den norske trælasthandels historie: II* (n 8) 188; Gryt, 'Trelastnæringa på Sunnmøre' (n 8) 16 with further reference. At the same time, we need to acknowledge that the new water-driven saw technology, which had been established along the Norwegian coast from ca. 1530, made the timber products in Norway much more interesting for the international market and made it much more profitable for the Norwegians to sell timber.

23 See e.g. for English-Norwegian timber trade relations Kent, 'The Anglo-Norwegian Timber Trade' (n 4) 61 ff emphasising that until the late seventeenth century the timber trade was comparably free from English regulation and characterised by low duties on timber import from Norway. We can assume that the same is true for Scotland.

24 Keyser and Munch (eds), NgL, vol III (n 15) no 111.

25 S Bagge, S H Smedal, K Helle (eds), Norske Middelalderdokumenter (1973) 439.

26 See Magnus the Lawmender's Code of the Norwegian Realm of 1274 Book VII ch 52.

27 This ordinance was based on a more or less unaltered legislative implementation of the allegations brought forward by the citizens of Bergen and the council of the realm in 1441. Kristoffer

the approval of the local population and, in this case, they would pay a fair price. The argument continues by stating that the poor peasants would benefit from the possibility of gaining access to necessary goods. In other words, they would act in concordance with and to further the common good (*gemene beste*), that is the interests of the rural population.[28] Serious doubts concerning this intention arise from the fact that the German merchants protested several times against Scottish and Dutch merchants engaging in direct local trade. These protests forced King Christian I to renew the prohibition on trading outside the cities twice in 1469 and 1471.[29] In both degrees the prohibition was legitimised with a reference to the "old law" (*olden loueliken*) and customs (*vnde wonheiden*). Interestingly, the king too argued that this prohibition would be beneficial for the common good (*gemene beste*) and would protect the rural population.[30]

(3) Scottish timber trade in western Norway

A first legal document primarily aimed at regulating the activities of Scottish timber traders in western Norway can be found in a royal letter addressed to all vassals (*lensmen*) along the west coast from 1547, explicitly prohibiting all Norwegians from trading with Scottish "pirates".[31] This encompassed a prohibition on the export of timber, renewed in 1562.[32] Due to constant complaints, the absolute prohibition was lifted in 1564.[33] However, this did not imply any right to trade timber freely. Rather, the citizens of the west Norwegian towns Stavanger and Bergen were granted a trade privilege guar-

of Bavaria, who needed the support of the Norwegian council and the citizens, to enforce his claim to the Danish-Norwegian throne was more than willing to meet their demands. Once elected king, he was almost immediately forced to repeal the drastic restriction that were imposed on the German tradesmen by the ordinance.

28 Keyser and Munch (eds), NgL, vol II (n 25) 254, see also Næss, *Skottehandelen* (n 4) 9.

29 C R Unger and H J Huitfeldt (eds), *Diplomatarium Norvegicum*, vol VII (1874) no 468, 463 and 471 (henceforth DN, vol VII).

30 *Ibid.*

31 Langhelle and Lillehammer, *Timber and trade* (n 4) 26.

32 H Jørgensen and Tolldirektoratet, *Det Norske tollvesens historie: Fra middelalderen til 1814* (1969) 17.

33 Grøt, 'Trelastnæringa på Sunnmøre' (n 4) 42 ff. Some local historians such as B J Dahle, 'Eit Borgerskap i vekst, Handel og Kjøbmannskab på Sunnmøre 1550–1700' (1994) in S U Larsen and J Sulebust (eds), *I Balansepunktet: Sunnmøres Eldste Historie. Ålesund*, 339 argue that the timber trade in the sixteenth century was completely "free". As shown here, this is not the case, at least from a legal perspective. We must need not base our assessment of the legal framework on an evaluation of the factual situation.

anteeing them the exclusive right to export all goods, including timber.[34] Still, in practice most of the timber trade was conducted directly between local producers and Scottish tradesmen.[35] Frequent complaints brought forward by the Norwegian council on behalf of the citizens of Bergen and Stavanger, as well as attempts to re-establish royal control by more active ministers of Bergenhus such as Erik Rosenkrantz seem to have been fruitless. Directly trading with the rural communities had become a widely accepted practice and the tax records document a constantly increasing amount and value of exported timber between the 1530s and 1560s.[36]

As the normative order did not manage to change practiced customs, the only way to avoid a permanent divergence between norm and fact was to adapt the law. This did not happen by amending legislation, but through case law. In a trial from 1561, the king's governor Erik Rosenkrantz had the most prominent judges of the country review the legitimacy of the current trade practice. These judges were the appellate court judges assembled in a court that later was called higher appellate court – *overlagting*.[37] The charters, privileges and royal letters referred to in court were apparently regarded as being of a more political than legal nature.[38] The four lawmen in Bergen judging on the proceeding initiated by Rosenkrantz apparently understood that very well. In their verdict, they interpreted the royal ordinance of 1302 restrictively, one might even state *contra legem*. They argued that the trade limitation concerning foreigners covered only the eventuality that the tradesmen were not willing to pay the official fees and taxes (*"at de ikke må kiøbe saadant tømmer af bønderne tollfri . . ."*).[39] This is remarkable for several reasons. First, this is the only indictment among thirteen others in which the court did not fully support Rosenkrantz's position. Secondly, the most prestigious body of judges in the Norway at that time (*overlagting*) apparently acknowledged – at least to some extent – the

34 H Paus, *Samling Af Gamle Norske Love: Gamle Kongelige Forordninger Og Privilegier: Udgivne for Kongeriget Norge*, vol 2 (1751) 286 and 299 ff.

35 Gryt, 'Trelastnæringa på Sunnmøre' (n 4) 24 ff; Næss, *Skottehandelen* (n 4) 11.

36 Cf. H J Huitfeldr-Kaas, *Norske Regnskaber og Jordeböger fra det 16de Aarhunderde*, vol III (1901) 78, 564, 570 and 658 (henceforth NRJ). Local variations as well as external factors such as war, blockades etc. do not impact the general trend.

37 On this court, see J A Seip, *Lagmann og Lagting i senmiddelalderen og det 16de århundre* (1934) 123; S Koch, 'Consequences of changing expectations to law and its institutions' (2015) 83 *Tijdschrift voor Rechtsgeschiedenis* 461–486.

38 See S Koch, E Rosenkrantz und das Kontor in Bergen – Ein politischer Rechtsstreit und seine weitreichenden Folgen, Hanseatic History Review (forthcoming).

39 N Nicolaisen, *Norske Magazin*: Skrifter og Optegnelser angaaende Norge og forfattede efter reformation, vol I (1860) 461.

established trade practice as normatively relevant. Finally, one may speculate whether Rosenkrantz himself accepted this view, as the only reason we know of this trial is because it is mentioned in his memorials. This outcome, even though contradictory to the interests of the citizens in Bergen, might have been in concordance with the royal interests. It seems no coincidence that the prohibition to trade timber with foreigners was officially lifted only three years later in 1564.[40] Jørgensen argued that the crown's financial interests were decisive. The crown intended to increase the tax revenue from the local peasants and the export taxes on timber.[41] The judgment of 1561 had paved the way for a more liberal interpretation of the medieval trade restrains on timber export. In the following years, several new proposals were made to control the scope of the timber trade and to secure efficiently the crown's tax revenue.[42] Standardising the tax revenue rates for timber and regulating the size of the different timber products were among the more efficient measures.

All that contributed to the notion that the practice of trading timber directly with Scottish merchants was legitimate and based on a legally acknowledged custom. The establishment of a separate tax post at Eldøyvågen, on the island of Stort south of Bergen, around 1590 is also important in this regard. The oldest recovered tax register dates back to 1597. Already in the 1580s, the lord of Bergenhus had ordered that a good man, in this case the harbour bailiff (*havnefogt*), would register the foreign vessels at their local residences. The apparent intention was to claim the newly established tenth (tithe) more efficiently. This tax was raised on all timber products from 1547. It can be assumed that this fee was originally paid to the church and that it continued to be imposed by the crown after the Reformation. However, in contrast to the church, the crown had no representatives on the local level with a similarly good overview over the ongoing trade. This tax post enabled merchants to register their cargo and pay taxes without sailing to Bergen, consequently further undermined the city's trade privilege and monopoly.

The citizens of Bergen would not accept this and fought back. They tried to reinforce the medieval order. In 1631, the high council of Norway

40 See n 34.

41 Jørgensen and Tolldirektoratet, *Det Norske tollvesens historie* (n 32) 18.

42 See Paul Hvitfelt's recommendations, in S Petersen and O G Lundh (eds), *Norges Riges Registranter*, vol II (1863) 93–95; and Lundh and Sars (eds), NRR, vol III (n 12) 658–659: 9 May 1602 a royal degree (*Forordning om Tømmertold udi Norge*) unified the duties owed to the crown when exporting specified types of timber.

(*Herredag*) discussed the situation (again in reaction to a complaint by Bergen citizens).[43] The *Herredag* functioned as the highest instance of appeal in the Norwegian court system and was packed with high-ranking officials and a varying number of appeal court judges. The old rules and privileges were confirmed, but without proposing more specific measures to enforce them in practice. Three years later a royal degree strictly prohibited all barter transactions,[44] but this commandment seems to have been as fruitless as all legal measures before.

This is surprising. The complains that were discussed at the council (*Herredag*) were not only based on the citizens' desire to control the timber trade but also informed by a very real danger that uncontrolled deforestation would cause the collapse of the whole business in many regions in western Norway.[45] Tax and shipping records from all west Norwegian districts of Bergenhus seem to indicate that timber exports were drastically being reduced, and indeed came to an end in some areas in the mid-seventeenth century.[46] Several independent sources document a high degree of deforestation in almost all parts of western Norway.[47] The remaining forest was too difficult to reach to continue the high level of timber production that had taken place in the first decades of the century. As trees grow slowly in the Scandinavian climate, it would be almost a century before the western Norwegian timber production could recover. However, we can also register some differences among the different areas. It seems that the districts south of Bergen were governed by a more sustainable policy than the northern districts. This might be explained by the lack of experience when interacting with foreign traders in the northern regions. Foreigners had been forbidden to travel north of Bergen for centuries. When the Hanseatic League dominated the trade with Bergen this prohibition was mostly upheld, but as

43 P Groth (ed), Norske Herredags-Dombøger: Tredje Række 4: (1625–1646) Afsigtsbog for 1631 (1929) 43 ff.

44 O G Lundh (ed), *Norske Rigs-Registranter*, vol IV (1870) 526 f.

45 Gryt, 'Trelastnæringa på Sunnmøre' (n 4) 38 ff who makes an argument for increasingly strict rules by comparing relevant provisions in the Code of the Norwegian Realm of 1274, Book VII ch 52, Christian IV's Norwegian Code of 1604, Book VI ch 50, and Christian V's Norwegian Code of 1687, Book III ch 14 Art. 35–37.

46 For references see Gryt, 'Trelastnæringa på Sunnmøre' (n 4) 24 ff.

47 Næss, *Skottehandelen* (n 4) 17; Gryt, 'Trelastnæringa på Sunnmøre' (n 4) 25 ff with reference to Hans Strøm's reports from 1723, see A Nedkvitne, *'Mens Bønderne Seilte Og Jægterne For' Nordnorsk Og Vestnorsk Kystøkonomi 1500–1730* (1988) 665. Already in 1613 Peder Claussøn Friis presents a different picture, at least for the district of Sunnmøre north of Bergen speaking of *'sciøne Furescoufue oc gode Træ'*. Deforestation became a severe problem in the early seventeenth century.

their influence started to decrease, Dutch, Scottish and English traders also started to sail directly into the fjords in these districts.[48]

(4) The 1661 petition and its consequences

A more serious attempt to stop the established trade practice was made after the implementation of absolutism. In 1661, a delegation of twenty-three representatives of the citizenships of the eight largest cities in Norway delivered a catalogue of thirty-seven, often very specific, recommendations to the king.[49] This document is interesting also because it contains some very progressive ideas such as the establishment of a Norwegian Supreme Court (*Hofret*), a commerce collegium and a university.[50] However, for our purpose the first recommendations are most interesting.

In the very first section, the representatives recommended the abolition of all small ports and harbours, which could potentially provide competition for the major trading cities. In addition, they explicitly refer to relevant sections in King Christian IV's Norwegian Code of 1604.[51] This provision prohibits penniless people from settling in rural areas, where they were forced to make a living by unlawfully lumbering the forest. It is based on a provision of the Code of the Realm from 1274.[52] However, the part of this provision regarding the protection of the forest came into the code when revising it in 1604, and it is based on a compilation of older provisions originally dating back to the sixteenth century, when deforestation became an increasingly urgent problem in this region.[53] In contrast to the 1604 Code, the Code of the Realm only prohibited impecunious persons from engaging

48 In 1607 Bergen's council complained that "*Tidske, hollandske oc engelske skibe løber Norden for Bergen til Nummeldal, Normør, Romsdal och Sundmør under det skin attj ville købe deler, men saa obkiøber de . . .*", cited from (Gryt (n 4)) 34.

49 "Andragende fra Kjöpstædernes Deputerede 8th august 1661", original manuscript on four pages printed in *Meddelelser fra det norske Rigsarchiv indeholdende Bidrag til Norges historie af trykte Kilder*, vol I (1870) 30 ff.

50 *Meddelelser fra det norske Rigsarchiv indeholdende Bidrag til Norges historie af trykte Kilder* no 18 Commerce collegium, no 19 Establishment of a Norwegian Supreme Court and no 32 Establishment Norwegian University.

51 *Meddelelser fra det norske Rigsarchiv indeholdende Bidrag til Norges historie af trykte Kilder* no 49, art 1 p 32 f.

52 The Code of the Realm of 1274 VII-23.

53 Norwegian Code of 1604 VI-50 "*dog at hand icke hugger skowen til skade*" based on provisions in a Recess from 1568, confirmed Ordinance 1584 art 18, cf. Ordinance 7. October 1578 art 30. However, it seems the nobility was exempt from this limitation, see Bjelke comment: "Denne Restrix eller Limitation er Adelen fri for i Norge" Privilege 21 July 1591 art 11. Cf. Ordinance 1578 art 14. See also the Code of 1604 VI-20 s 3.

in trade in the summer months. The new regulation was thus much stricter. The underlying assumption appears to have been that the poorest were particularly vulnerable to foreigners, who would use them as decoys to conduct unsustainable timber trade practices.

In the opinion of the representatives of the trade cities, the norms concerning the timber trade should now be invoked to force poor people to leave the countryside and to move to the cities. Also, all craftsmen should be forced to move into cities. Taking into consideration that the 1661 petition's opening section explicitly concerned the timber trade, it is highly likely that this recommendation aimed to stop rural communities running their own sawmills.[54] These had been common in western Norway from the sixteenth century onwards and had boosted a flourishing industry of timber production.[55] Ships, construction elements and even complete houses were produced in the Sunnhordland region south of Bergen, and other rural parts of the country, especially in the first part of seventeenth century. This had caused the deforestation of considerable parts of the country. Transferring the control over the mills to burghers was presumably regarded as an efficient counter-measure.

Most significant, however, is the third section of the recommendation of 1661, stating initially that the current trade practice between the rural population and foreign tradesmen is ruinous for the whole country.[56] The foreign tradesmen, the argument continues, would take advantage of the inexperience and dependency of the local population, and would not pay a reasonable price. Partly due to their inner affection towards these foreigners (*den Fremmede geneiget*), the farmers were willing to accept half the timber's value, which in turn would reduce the profit for domestic traders. Finally, the deforestation was directly linked to the current illegal trading and to the low tax revenue produced by this business.[57]

54 Several other legislative initiatives seem to have had a similar aim. In 1662, the Norwegian governor proposed to establish a taxation of mills not based on the production but an evaluation of good men. This evaluation would determine the annual fees for the future. Such a regime burdens the risk of economic fluctuations exclusively on the owners of the mill.

55 Sunde, *Vegen over havet* (n 4) 35 ff; Lillehammer, 'Skottehandelen og Rogaland' (n 4) 99 f.

56 "Andragende fra Kjöpstædernes Deputerede" (n 49) 33.

57 "Andragende fra Kjöpstædernes Deputerede" (n 49) 33 no 3 "*Eftersom Bøndernes Lastebrug og Kjøb med Fremmede er almindelig Lands Fordærv for Alle, som udig Kjøbstederne nogen Handel og Brug haver; thi først ere de Fremmede Bondens Vilkaar bekandt, og giver hannem som et sat* (sic!) *Marked ikke epter hans Arbeide eller Lastens Værd, mens hvad hna af Miskundhed vil, hvorefter Borgerne maa gaae eller lade Lasten ligge til Forraadelse. Bondene er og saa tilsinds og den Fremmede geneiget, at han før det til dennem for halv Værd afhænder, end Indlændiske derpaa den ringste Skillings Fortjeneste forunder, hvor Skovene i stor Mængde udhugges, efterdi*

The obvious solution proposed in 1661 was that all farmers and all other landowners, apparently also encompassing the lower nobility,[58] would be obliged to exclusively sell timber to the burghers (*"borgerskap"*).[59] In return, the rural population would receive a reasonable price (*billig og ret*). The interesting question was who was regarded part of the *"borgerskap"* in this context. Already in the sixteenth century, citizens of the cities of Trondheim, Bergen and Stavanger engaged more extensively in trading activities in the rural areas and, according to Bugge, Dahle and Gyte, managed to get control over the timber trade with foreigners in the 1620s in many districts.[60] Eventually, they owned many sawmills and huge tracts of land producing timber. However, these Norwegian tradesmen, holding the citizenship in one of the above-mentioned cities, were not changing the nature of the trade considerably. Nor did they transport timber to the cities before selling their products to the foreign traders. They continued to trade directly with the Scottish, Dutch and English merchants.[61]

Despite the crown's continuous attempts to abandon all forms of barter trade and to replace it with a monetised economy, in accordance with the law, the extent of monetary payments was not significantly affected by the engagement of burghers in local timber trade. The term *"borgerskap"* (citizenship) in the abovementioned petition of 1661 therefore is to be interpreted narrowly as merchants operating and residing in the major trading posts. In a manner that was consistent with this general position, the petition claimed that all men involved in timber trading (*"skippere, styremænd, Tømmermænd og Baadsmænd maate residere og boe udi Kjøbstædene"*) should be obliged to live in a city.[62] The petition further demanded severe

Bonden derfore saa lidet bekommer, at det Intet kan forslaaes, enten til hans Skatters Betaling eller Levnets Ophold."

58 Cf. "Andragende fra Kjöpstædernes Deputerede" (n 49) no 11: *"At al Monopolia og egennyttig Handel maatte afskaffes, og Eders Kongl. Majst. Naadelig ville lade sig behage, ingen særdeles Frihed Nogen at give paa indførende eller udførende Vare, som Kjøbstæderne kunde være til Skade eller Præjudits . . ."*. The nobility was traditionally exempted from paying any taxes for their economic activities, including timber trade.

59 "Andragende fra Kjöpstædernes Deputerede" (n 49) 33 no 3: *"Hvorfore vi underdaningsten begjærer, at Sligt maatte afskaffes, og Bønderne samt Alle (af Handling og Upriviligerte) af hvad Stand det er tilholdes, deres Last og Vare til ingen Anden end Borgerskabet at sælge, og de pligtig derfore at give dennem Skjel and Fyldest som billig og ret kan være, endog epterhaanden forhøie, som de Tid epter anden den til de Fremmedes Forhandling kunde opdrive."* See also no 8: *"Og endog Landlougen samt Kjøbstædernes Privilegier tilholder, at alle Vare, som Landet giver, skulle sælges i Kjøbestæderne paa Torvet . . ."*

60 Gryt, 'Trelastnæringa på Sunnmøre' (n 4) 92; Bugge II (n 8) 243; see also, Dahle, 'Eit Borgeskap' (n 35) 340 ff.

61 Gryt, 'Trelastnæringa på Sunnmøre' (n 4) 92.

62 "Andragende fra Kjöpstædernes Deputerede" (n 49) no 9.

punishments for all violations of these precepts, in particular the infringement of the trade monopoly of the cities.[63] Finally, the petition recommended the limitation of export and the establishment of standards for quality and measures of timber products to maintain a sustainable use of the forest.[64]

These *recommendations* were reviewed in Copenhagen. It was presumably the king's chancellor, Hannibal Sehested, who agreed in principle to many of these proposals.[65] He even considered the demolition of all small ports in a radius of thirty kilometres around each city.[66] However, concerning the regulation of trade, he recommended that it should be the townspeople's responsibility to acquire timber from rural providers. He argued that the cities should be obliged to build ships to sail to the farmers and give them what they needed in return for a fair price, so that they have no grounds to complain.[67] This mutual obligation was manifested in the second section of the privilege that was given to the burghers on 30 July 1662.[68]

It seems that the new rules were obeyed, at least initially. However, the surviving tax registers show that this caused a considerable decline in tax revenue for the first year all export was organised via Bergen. Just fifteen rigsdaler, that is 1 per cent of the usual annual tax revenue, which in average stood at between 1,500 and 2,000 rigsdaler, was declared in Bergen that year.[69] The king and his administration reacted immediately. With an

63 "Andragende fra Kjöpstædernes Deputerede" (n 49) no 8: "... *Saa er det dog kommen i den Misbrug, at det* [the cities' privileges] *er ei lenger agtes, med mindre Eders Kongl. Majst. Derover ville lade stille saadan alvorlig Bud og Forbud under høieste Peen og Straf, saa Enhver (derimot særsindig og egenvillig) deraf kunde have Avsky.*" See also no 13 demanding that violations are brought to court by the competent royal officials and that wrongdoers would be sentenced according to the law and privileges of the cities.

64 "Andragende fra Kjöpstædernes Deputerede" (n 49) no 4–7. The problem was regarded as so severe that the Kings's chancellor recommended the establishment of an expert commission. The report of this commission is another important document for this survey.

65 "Erklæring over Köbstædernes Supplication", printed in *Meddelelser fra det norske Rigsarkiv* (n 49) 44.

66 Manuscript without date and signature printed in *Meddelelser fra det norske Rigsarkiv* (n 68) 48 no 2; "*Alle Havner inden de 3 Mile paa alle Sider af Byerne at maatte afskaffes, samt hvis Last og Vare inden forbe*[te.] *Mile falder at maatte føres til Byene*"; no 3: "*Alle andre Smaalast-Havner og Indviger uden forbe*[te] *3 Mile, de store Laststeder undtagen, ogsaa at maatte afskaffes.*" See also verdict of the Norwegian council (*Herredag*) from 15 August 1631 explicitly referring to this privilege *Norske Herredags-Dombøger*. Tredje Række 1–4: (1625–1646) Afsigtsbok for 1631 (1929) 3 f.

67 "Andragende fra Kjöpstædernes Deputerede" (n 49) 44.

68 Ordinance of 20 April 1665, in Paus, *Samling Af Gamle Norske Love* (n 34) 994 para 3.

69 Næss, *Skottehandelen* (n 4) 27 f and table on 29.

ordinance from 20 April 1665, the strict prohibition of trading with foreigners locally was lifted and it was replaced by a rule stating that where the burghers are not willing to give the peasant or local citizens a fair and reasonable price *(lige og fuldkommen værd)* for their timber cargo, or buy a reasonable quantum from them, they (the farmers or local citizens) are allowed to sell the goods to foreigners.[70] As these very abstract preconditions were hardly ever contested in practice, the trade with the foreign tradesmen was soon flourishing as before. The tax registers bear witness that the absolutist regime also failed to implement effectively what had been intended by legislators since the late medieval times. Local communities, and not the cities and their citizens, remained in charge of the timber trade with foreign merchants, particularly from Scotland and the Netherlands.

This is still the situation that was described by the above-mentioned report by the 1735 commission. For more than 400 years, the regulation of trade in western Norway and the underlying reality were far from being in concordance.

D: NORM AND OBEDIENCE: THE SPECIFIC CONCERNS OF THE ACTORS INVOLVED

(1) The rural population

Taking a closer look at the specific economic interest of the involved social groups might contribute to explaining why the normative order was only partially obeyed, if at all. Starting at the local level, it seems apparent that the rural population had a very strong interest in selling timber in exchange for goods and products that were urgently needed and to which they otherwise had very limited access. Timber was a renewable resource and could be harvested and even processed into building materials and ships at the local level. As a result of water-driven sawmills, which were established in the region from around the 1530s, the quality and quantity of timber products increased, rendering the Norwegian market attractive for foreign merchants.[71] However, the peasants had neither experience nor the resources to

70 Ordinance of 20 April 1665 in Paus, *Samling Af Gamle Norske Love* (n 34) 993 f.

71 Lillehammer, 'Skottehandelen og Rogaland' (n 4) 39 f; S G E Lythe, *The Economy of Scotland in its European Setting 1550–1625* (1960/1976) 147: "In both countries the geographical and economic conditions facilitated the expansion of this sea-born timber trade. For a timber user in Edinburgh or Aberdeen it was certainly simpler and probably cheaper to arrange a direct ship-

organise the trade efficiently themselves. Apart from a few noble families,[72] the rural population did not ship their goods abroad and only occasionally shipped them to Bergen or Stavanger. They were therefore depending on a constant and reliable import of those goods. The sources indicate that the citizens of Bergen, even though they were willing to control the trade, had no ambition or ability to provide the rural population with the same quantity or quality of goods that they gained from foreigners.

The narrative used by the citizens of Bergen to legitimise their trade monopoly, saying that the foreigners would take advantage of the specific economic situation of the local population, may have had some truth in it. Still, if the alternative to selling under price or bartering for goods of dubious quality with foreign merchants was selling nothing at all, or selling goods for even lower prices to the Norwegian merchants, it seems comprehensible why they would prefer trading with foreign merchants. Despite regular complaints about the quality of tobacco, which it was illegal to import anyway, we find little evidence that the quality of goods provided by the foreigners was especially poor. In contrast to Bergen, where this apparently was a problem, we find no complaints regarding the quality of imported goods in the local court records. The Scottish traders generally seemed to have fulfilled their end of the bargain. We even have examples where a Scottish tradesman, Thomas Green, uses the local court to redeem his reputation after being offended by a Norwegian farmer, *inter alia*, by stating the merchant's goods were rotten and of the worst quality.[73]

The records from Sunnhordland district court, particularly in the years following the renewed privilege for Bergen in 1662, demonstrate that both the central administration and local officials started to understand that enforcing a trade monopoly for Bergen without taking into consideration the demands of the rural community was unrealistic.[74] However, as long as Bergen's citizens could not satisfy these economic demands and the infrastructure for

ment from a Norwegian port, for the alternative involved a devious cross-country haul from a forest in a remote glen."

72 For example, the family Mowat, which was heavily involved in timber trade with Scotland via the Shetland Isles, see Sunde, *Vegen over havet* (n 4) for an overview of the main actors in the district of Sunnmøre see, Gryt, 'Trelastnæringa på Sunnmøre' (n 4) 88 ff.

73 The Stat Archive in Bergen; Sorenskrivaren i Sunnhordland, *Court Record for Sunnhordland*, A13 (1666) 24 ff.

74 The Stat Archive in Bergen; Sorenskrivaren i Sunnhordland, *Court Record for Sunnhordland*, A14 (1667) 367 ff.

domestic trade was still very poor,[75] there was no alternative to trading with foreigners, even if it was in violation of the law.

Another priority for the rural population was maintaining contact with the foreigners, as they would be guests in inns and would also bring cultural exchanges through fashions, news, music, etc. to the rural areas. By way of illustration, in the year the Scots were effectively banned from coming to the ports in the region, the local court granted dispensation to two innkeepers from the annual tax of two rigsdaler because the absence of foreign guests had almost bankrupted them.[76]

An interest the farmers shared with the traders, independently of their origin, was avoiding taxes. As early as the thirteenth century, we find regulation concerning the punishment for tax avoidance, and the court rolls hold several examples of both foreigners and domestic traders being sentenced accordingly.[77] However, as the abovementioned ordinance of 1665 bears witness, there was constant discussion on what was owed and of how, when and to whom the tax was to be paid.[78]

From 1545, shortly after implementation of the Reformation, the crown had imposed a fee of 10 per cent – the tenth – on certain timber products.[79] After the introduction of absolutism and the enactment of the privilege for the trading cities in 1662,[80] the local tax officer announced the applicable rules in court and publicly warned the rural population of the consequences of disobeying the law.[81] In order to enforce this more effectively, he summoned all farmers whose land was forested to court the following year.[82] They were forced – under oath – to report how much timber they had produced and sold in the year 1664.[83] The court records of this year give us both a unique insight into how the trade was organised and also at least a rough idea of its scope.[84] It became clear that of the fifty-two persons testifying in

75 Therefore, Chancellor Sehested frequently demanded a strengthening extension of the internal trade and supply routines in Denmark-Norway. This seems to have changed in the early years of the eighteenth century, when the local customs rolls provide evidence of Norwegian ships increasingly being involved in timber trade. The Great Nordic War (1700–1721) put a limit on this development.

76 Court record (n 74) 367 ff, 369.

77 Court record (n 74) 373.

78 Ordinance of 20 April 1665 in Paus, *Samling Af Gamle Norske Love* (n 36).

79 Grøt, 'Trelastnæringa på Sunnmøre' (n 4).

80 See n 68 above.

81 The Stat Archive in Bergen; Court Record for Sunnhordland, A11 (1664) 251 ff.

82 Court record (n 81) 252.

83 Court record (n 81) 253.

84 Court record (n 81) 255 ff.

court, only a few had paid their dues.[85] The farmers defended themselves in these proceedings by stating that they were in general willing to pay, but that the applicable law was unclear on whether this obligation was owed by them or the foreigners.[86] They complained about the unreliability of the Bergen people. The latter would deliver rotten products and pay less than the foreigners.[87] The tax officer Anders Rasmussen Rasch and the district judge (*sorenskriver*) were not open to considering such complaints and pursued a strict application of the law. They argued the rural communities had been sufficiently "reminded and warned", but they had deliberately ("*drumdristig . . . overhørig*") ignored the law.[88] Some were sentenced to pay the due tenth, and in addition a considerable penalty. Others were reminded that they could risk punishment for refusing to give their accounts under oath.[89]

The report from the local tax officer and the judge, which was sent to the central administration in Copenhagen, seems to have had consequences. The royal ordinance of 1665, mentioned earlier,[90] explicitly referred to the "unsteadiness among our subjects" and regulated the issues in question in a very pragmatic and plain way. First, it obliged the timber producers to render the tenth *in natura* by delivering thirteen planks whenever they sold twelve. In other words, every thirteenth plank should be provided to the local tax authorities. Secondly, the ordinance allowed local producers to sell their timber to foreigners if Norwegian merchants would not offer to buy it, or if they would only offer to buy it for an unjust price.[91]

To sum up, the interests of the local producers lay in maintaining a constant demand and a fair price for their timber products, as well as in maintaining access to goods that were either inaccessible or difficult to import into Norway. The sources indicate that the townspeople were unable or unwilling to meet any of these demands. The demand for timber in the western Norwegian cities was limited – except in the aftermath of some devastating fire. Constant complaints implied that the citizens were not willing to pay a reasonable price or provide the local population with the goods they

85 This gives rise to the question of the extent to which the hypothesis of some historians regarding the obedience of tax and custom rules by local timber traders (both foreign and local) can be upheld. It rather seems that their arguments were guided by the burning desire to prove that the tax records were a complete and reliable source for their analysis of the scope and direction of the timber trade in Norway.

86 Court record (n 81) 261.

87 Court record (n 81) 264.

88 Court record (n 81) 264.

89 Court record (n 81) 264.

90 Ordinance of 20 April 1665 in Paus, *Samling Af Gamle Norske Love* (n 34).

91 *Ibid.*

could barter with foreign tradesmen. The ordinance of 1665 was supposed to redress these concerns through legislation.

(2) The foreign merchants

The foreign tradesmen's main economic concern was to get easy and cheap access to timber supplies. Trading with the producer instead an intermediary is feasible providing that the transport expenses are not disproportionately increased. This precondition was met. Another important consideration for merchants is predictability. Scottish tradesmen, in particular, had established long-lasting relationships with specific communities and would come to the same harbours over many years. A mutually beneficial relationship with the rural population is implied also in the replies of the Hanseatic tradesmen to the complaints by the Bergen population in the fifteenth and sixteenth century. They argued that they would in fact guarantee that the necessary supplies would reach these parts of the realm and would provide this "service" for the common benefit (*gemene beste*).[92] Indeed, they claimed they were suffering losses rather than making a profit in doing so.[93] They even threatened to stop trading with the local population. This last argument may have been the most effective as it was rather clear that their supplies were absolutely necessary.[94] On the other hand, the German merchants had both their ships and houses built in the villages around Bergen. We know that the Scots from the sixteenth century onwards did not just buy planks, masts and other timber products, but ordered complete ships that were built by farmers over the winter.[95] Interestingly, the farmers were explicitly prohibited from building ships for sale.[96] This seems to have been another legal provision with very limited effect, at least in times of prospering timber trade in the sixteenth and seventeenth centuries. Preserving a mutually beneficial relationship was hence in the interest of both social groups, i.e. the local timber producers and the Scottish merchants.

92 Næss, *Skottehandelen* (n 4) 45 f.
93 Næss, *Skottehandelen* (n 4) 46.
94 Næss, *Skottehandelen* (n 4) 47.
95 Næss, *Skottehandelen* (n 4) 47.
96 The Code of the Towns of 1276 VII-17; the Code of the Realm of 1274 VII-23 and see (n 57).

(3) Nobility and local officials

I will just briefly touch upon the interests of the nobility and local officials. Both groups were actively involved in the timber trade. Originally, they were freed from taxation and could organise the trade themselves. However, the crown gradually repealed these privileges, especially after 1660. The long-lasting legal conflict between Ludvig Rosenkrantz and the tax authorities in the second half of the seventeenth century bears witness to this change.[97] The difference between the rural population and foreign merchants on the one hand and the nobility and officials on the other, was that the latter groups had at least some influence on normative order. The correspondence of Axel Mowat, Bernt Orning, Ludvig Rosenkrantz or Hans Lauritzen, just to name some examples, with high standing officials in Copenhagen provides us with several examples of their attempts to legitimise local trade practices.[98] Interestingly, they often advocated their interests by referring to the benefit for the local communities and the necessity for the rural producers to barter timber products directly with foreign merchants.

(4) The townspeople

The townspeople's elite, more precisely the Norwegian merchants acting from Bergen and Stavanger, had for centuries shaped the normative order. Due to their direct influence on the Norwegian council, with the king's administration and not least the king himself being frequently dependent on the citizens' support both economically and politically, they managed again and again to codify their interests. All trade, including the timber trade, was supposed to be channelled exclusively through the major trading points. Foreigners' access to smaller ports was supposed to be strictly restricted or entirely prohibited and local producers were to be obliged to transport their goods to the cities and offer them to the crown and townspeople. Regardless of their successful domination of the normative order, in the eyes of a range of powerful interest groups they still were unable or unwilling to engage sufficiently with the interests of the timber producers. The citizens of the towns therefore failed to realise their goal of dominating the timber trade in

97 Næss, *Skottehandelen* (n 4); Sunde, *Vegen over havet* (n 4) 54 ff.

98 For details see Sunde, *Vegen over havet* (n 4) 32 ff, 52 ff and Gryt, 'Trelastnæringa på Sunnmøre' (n 4) 96 ff.

practice. Without additional support from the king, they could not enforce the normative order either.

(5) The crown's interests

At first glance, the constant flow of regulation and the repeated attempts to limit or even prohibit foreigners from directly trading with the rural population seems to indicate that the interests of the crown and of the citizens in Bergen and Stavanger were aligned. Still, detailed analysis reveals that even though the regulations enacted in the name of the king adopt the arguments and narratives from the citizens' complaints, the interests of the crown are slightly different; the interests of the crown are, first and foremost, to benefit economically from the trade,[99] to organise it in a sustainable and predictable manner, and then to control it by monopolising it in Bergen. This argument is supported both by the fact that Erik Rosenkrantz tacitly accepted the *contra legem* interpretation of the 1302 ordinance by the appellate court in Bergen in 1561, and also by the king's abolition of the privileges given to the cities in 1662 in the ordinance of 1665. Indeed, the establishment of the tax station in Sunnhordland is the clearest proof of the king' interest in a prospering timber trade including the export from rural areas. Despite constant complaints by the citizenry throughout the seventeenth century and the first half of the eighteenth century,[100] the station was not abolished before 1754.

It seems the royal administration eventually recognised that effective regulation and control of the timber trade required that the economic interests of the rural population should be considered adequately.[101] However, the

99 Gryt, 'Trelastnæringa på Sunnmøre' (n 4) 29.

100 See "Erklæring om Norges Indkomst og Vilkaar 1662" in *Medelelser fra det Norske Risarkiv* (n 49) 317 no 9: "*Sammeledes udi Bergenhus Lehn eragtes ingen mere Toldsted end Bergen alene fornøden, og Sundhordalands Told sammesteds . . . afskaffes, al Trelast med all andre Vare, ingen undtagen, igjen at føres til Byen, og ingen Ladning der i Lehnet uden Bergen alene tilstedes.*" The local historian Anders Næss held that these plans were stopped by an intervention of the King himself. I did not manage to find the royal letter he refers to in this context. What is documented is that in 1662 the Norwegian delegation in Copenhagen for the first time recommends the abolishment of the tax post in Sunnhordland and recommends the prohibition of all direct trade with foreigners. However, not all members of the commission agree on this conclusion. The tax officer Daniel Knoff states in a dissenting reply that he is concerned about the lack of consideration of the rural populations. He therefore recommends the establishment of a commercial *concillium*, which recognises both the requirements of commerce and the country's nature, with a particular focus on understanding the needs of each place in connection with the negotiations and the regulations of the timber trade.

101 In 1735, the leader of the land commission L D Ferry notes: "Reason teaches us that it is

crown was neither able nor willing to guarantee a sufficient and predictable domestic supply of goods in the rural areas. Therefore, the 1662 city privilege (*kjøbstadsprivilegiet*) imposed this obligation on the townspeople.[102] In addition, the cities should provide ships to transport timber and other goods to the markets.[103] The king's councillors Gyldenløve and Bjelke proposed even the establishment of so-called "companies" that could monopolise the timber trade based on fixed prices. These companies were also supposed to organise the distribution and sale of all timber products.[104] To further protect the peasant's interests, Gyldenløve recommended that prices should be fixed annually for almost all rural products that had to be sold to the crown or citizens.[105] In addition, his memorandum suggested that peasants should be freed from the prohibition against selling their products to foreigners; this would apply in the situation that neither the crown nor the burghers would buy their goods.[106] This proposition was integrated in the Ordinance of 1665, effectively abolishing the trade monopoly for the cities pursuant to the privilege given three years earlier.

This amendment became necessary because the citizens had neither the means nor intention to provide a service that would make it attractive for the rural population to trade exclusively with Bergen and the other trading cities. Against this background, the crown was willing to accept imperfect

impossible for a single customs officer to efficiently control an area of between 300 and 400 kilometers of coast where twenty to thirty ships sail into as many different ports" (my translation). See Næss, *Skottehandelen* (n 4) 36.

102 Cf. section 2.1 of the city privilege of 1662.

103 Gyldenloves and Bjelkes Betænkning 1670, in *Meddelelser fra det norske Rigsarkiv* (n 49) 429 f: "*At alle Kjöbestæder ved deres Privilegiers Fortabelse skulde være forpligtet at holde ved deres Byer en viss antal egene Skibe og Fartøig . . . hvormed de deres Varer sielv og ingen fremmede kunde udføre og deres Fornødenhed derimot indbringe, i sær Henseende iblandt Annet, at al Trælast, som i Kjøbenhavn forbruges, mest udi svensk Skiberumme udi Norge avhentes og her indbringes.*"

104 *Ibid.*, 430 Nr. 10: "*At opprette visse Compagnier til Trelast og andre saadanne Varers Forhandling eller Udskibning, paa det des Pris kunne komme under Consideration og Isteden Frembede nu Prisen sætter, det dennem til Billighed maate paalægges.*"

105 "Statholder U.F. Gyldenlöves Forslag angaaende Justitien, Militsen, Indkomsterne og Handelen i Norge 1666", in *Meddelelser fra det Norske Rigsarkiv* (n 49) 347 ff on 348: "*Eftersom Bonden er obligert at forföre hans Vare til Kjøbsstederne og handle med Borgerne og ikke Fremmede, daa paa det de derimot ogsaa kunde nyde billig Skjel og betaling af Borgerne for deres Vare, og at Bonden dermed ei heller, naar han kommer til Byen, vorder forlegen: 1. Da er höilig fornöden, at hver Stiftsamtmand . . . skulle sætte og gjöre en vis og tilbörligTaxt og Kjöb immellem Borgere og Fremmede samt mellom Borgere og Bonden paa alle Landets Vare, ingen untagen, . . . Og hvis Kjøpstedsmanden ikke inden forelagte Tid handlede med Bonden, daa Bonden være fri for Varene til Fremmede selv at selge og afhandle . . .*"

106 *Ibid.*, 348: "*Og hvis Kjøpstedsmanden ikke inden forelagte Tid handlede med Bonden, daa Bonden være fri for Varene til Fremmede selv at selge og afhandle.*"

control and eventually loss of some tax revenue. The alternative, that is to take measures to enforce a different regime, was apparently economically unsustainable.

E: CONCLUDING REMARKS

When we try to explain why timber trade was not effectively regulated by law prior to the second half of the eighteenth century in western Norway, what stands out is the normative order's failure to acknowledge the central concerns of the social groups involved. This paper has proven that we need to be careful in assuming that trading privileges and regulations were either always operational or legally enforceable. Rather, one needs to see privileges and legislation in operation in the broader economic context and as a matter of historical research this will necessitate consideration of taxation records as well as local court records. Understanding the underlying commercial concerns and, in particular, the interplay between law and competing individual, collective and public interests, may contribute to predicting the effects, acceptance and efficiency of legislation in a constantly more globalised and internationalised world, with overlapping and often competing legal regimes.

10 The Law and Economy of Shipwreck in Scotland during the Sixteenth Century

J D Ford

A: INTRODUCTION

The title above specifies the spatial as well as the temporal limitations of this essay, which examines evidence of shipwrecks in Scotland during the sixteenth century alone.[1] During this period many ships sailing out of Scottish ports were wrecked in other countries, including Norway, and these disasters sometimes had repercussions at home.[2] The concern here, however,

1 On the fifteenth century see E B I Frankot, 'Maritime Law and Practice in Late Medieval Aberdeen' (2010) 89 *Scottish Historical Review* 136, at 145–148, and *'Of Laws of Ships and Shipmen': Medieval Maritime Law and Its Practice in Urban Northern Europe* (2012) 175–176.

2 R K Hannay (ed), *Acts of the Lords of Council in Public Affairs, 1501–1554* (1932) 77, 285 and 489; J H Burton and D Masson (eds), *Register of the Privy Council of Scotland*, 14 vols (1877–98) vol 2, 584–585, and vol 14, 201–202 and 246; T C Wade (ed), *Acta curiae admirallatus Scotiae, 1557–1562* (1937) 7, 10, 12, 29, 37–38 and 72; R L Mackie (ed), *The Letters of James the Fourth, 1505–1513* (1953) 147; R K Hannay and D Hay (eds), *The Letters of James V* (1954) 7, 155, 189 and 369; H J Smit (ed), *Bronnen tot de Geschiedenis van der Handel met Engeland, Schotland en Ierland*, 2nd ser., 2 vols (1942–1950) vol 1, 535; J S Brewer, J Gairdner and R H Brodie (eds), *Letters and Papers, Foreign and Domestic, of the Reign of Henry VIII, 1509–1547*, 21 vols (1862–1910) vol 7, 414–415; A Clifford (ed), *The State Papers and Letters of Sir Ralph Sadler*, 2 vols (Edinburgh, 1809) vol 1, 582–583; J Bain, W K Boyd, H W Meikle, A I Cameron, M S Giuseppi and J D Mackie (eds), *Calendar of the State Papers Relating to Scotland and Mary Queen of Scots, 1547–1603*, 13 vols (1898–1969) vol 1, 264 and 502, and vol 10, 272, 318, 393, 461, 475–476, 515–517 and 525–528; J Stevenson, A J Crosby, A J Butler, S C Lomas, A B Hinds and R B Wernham (eds), *Calendar of State Papers, Foreign Series, of the Reign of Elizabeth*, 23 vols (1863–1950) vol 2, 107, 113–114, 116, 131 and 256, vol 4, 114, 346

is with the legal and (to a lesser extent) the economic consequences of the shipwrecks that often occurred on the coasts of Scotland. More precisely, the concern is with the rights and duties people were believed to have when they were involved in recovering the remains of ships – including their equipment and cargoes – after they were destroyed while navigating near Scotland. Two main types of evidence are considered, both of which must be handled cautiously. In the first place, access to the subject is eased by the existence of several treatises touching on the legal aspects of shipwreck, written by lawyers during the last quarter of the century.[3] The caveat requiring to be attached to this material is that its writers tended to draw their information from other books, and may not have provided an accurate account of how wrecks were dealt with in practice. In the second place, records survive of litigation relating to the subject, sometimes in burgh courts sitting in coastal towns, sometimes in central courts sitting in Edinburgh. The caveat requiring to be attached to this material is that for much of the century the expectation was that litigation relating to navigation would be dealt with in specialised admiralty courts, from which scarcely any records have survived.[4] Since the treatise writers usually wrote about the law applicable in the admiralty courts, they may be taken to compensate to some extent for the absence of these records, just as the availability of records from other courts may be taken to compensate to some extent for the theoretical tendencies of the treatise writers. If viewed from the different perspectives provided by these two bodies of material, the consequences

and 376–377, vol 5, 148, and vol 6, 122, 421 and 550; J Bain (ed), *The Border Papers: Calendar of Letters and Papers Relating to the Affairs of the Borders of England and Scotland*, 2 vols (1894–1896) vol 2, 819–820, and vol 9, 670; J R Dasent, E G Atkinson, J V Lyle, R F Monger and P E Penfold (eds), *Acts of the Privy Council of England*, 46 vols (1890–1964) vol 17, 41–42, 77–79, 81, 86, 106, 156, 179–182 and 350–351; J Stuart (ed), *Extracts from the Council Register of the Burgh of Aberdeen*, 2 vols (1844–1848) vol 1, 331–333; L B Taylor (ed), *Aberdeen Council Letters*, 6 vols (1942–1961) vol 1, 4; J D Marwick (ed), *Extracts from the Records of the Burgh of Edinburgh*, 1st ser., 5 vols (1869–92) vol 4, 545; W Angus (ed), *Protocol Book of Mr Gilbert Grote, 1552–1573* (1914) 84; Aberdeen City Archives (ACA), council register of Aberdeen, CA1/1/24, pp. 79 and 402, CA1/1/25, pp. 546, 568 and 586, CA1/1/26, pp. 78, 144 and 151, and CA1/1/29, pp. 20–21; Dundee City Archives (DCA), burgh court minute book of Dundee, BCMB (mostly unfoliated), vol 19, 14 January 1596.

3 Not all the treatises referred to were completed, let alone published, before the end of the century.

4 Burton and Masson (eds), *Register of the Privy Council of Scotland* (n 2) 242–243; Bain et al (eds), *Calendar of the State Papers Relating to Scotland and Mary Queen of Scots* (n 2) vol 4, 300; A Maxwell, *Old Dundee, Ecclesiastical, Burghal and Social, prior to the Reformation* (1891) 318–319; DCA, BCMB, vol 1, ff 119v–120r and 139v; National Records of Scotland (NRS), register of the privy seal, PS1/71, f 148. The only surviving court book, covering a period of less than five years, is cited in n 2 above.

of shipwrecks in Scotland during the sixteenth century may come into view fairly clearly, but it needs to be remembered that there is a significant gap in the evidence available.

B: THE RIGHT TO "WRAK" AND THE "AULD LAWES"

The earliest account of the relevant law is found in a compilation of sources known as the "practicks" of Sir James Balfour of Pittendreich, who seems to have followed instructions issued by a Scottish parliament in 1575 to a commission set up to compare, condense and consolidate "the bukis of the law, actis of parliament and decisionis befoir the sessioun".[5] In dealing with the consequences of shipwrecks, Balfour drew attention to one item from each of these categories. According to the first, it had been "statute and ordanit" that if a ship was wrecked and any creature "cum living and quick to the land", the ship should not be treated as "wrak", but rather all "gudis and geir" washed ashore should be gathered and preserved by the local authorities, in order to be restored to anyone who appeared within a year and a day and established title to them.[6] It was added that if no one claimed salvaged property within the prescribed period, it would "pertene to the king", unless "wrak" had already been granted to someone else. Both in the compilation known as Balfour's "practicks" and in two surveys of "the bukis of the law" used in its production, these provisions were ascribed to a collection of regulations called the *Leges forestarum*.[7] It may be wondered what they had to do with the regulation of activities in forests, and they are indeed absent from modern editions of the collection, which are limited to provisions on the hunting of game, the straying of livestock, the gathering of wood and similar matters.[8] Yet the provisions on shipwreck do appear in a longer version of the *Leges forestarum* found in many manuscripts containing the

5 K M Brown, G H MacIntosh, A J Mann, P E Ritchie and R J Tanner (eds), with A Grosjean, A R MacDonald, K F McAlister, D J Patrick, L A M Stewart et al, *The Records of the Parliaments of Scotland to 1707* (St Andrews, 2007) available at *http://www.rps.ac.uk* [*RPS*], A1575/3/7; T Thomson and C Innes (eds), *The Acts of the Parliaments of Scotland* [*APS*], 12 vols (1814–1875) vol iii, 89.

6 P G B McNeill (ed), *The Practicks of Sir James Balfour of Pittendreich*, 2 vols, Stair Society vols 21–22(1962–1963) vol 2, 623–624 (here and in other quotations from primary sources, the punctuation and capitalisation of the original are sometimes adjusted, but not the orthography).

7 National Library of Scotland (NLS), Adv. MS 25.4.11, f 33v (in Latin), and NRS, GD112/71/5, f 41r (in Scots).

8 *APS*, i, 687–692; M L Anderson, *A History of Scottish Forestry*, 2 vols (1967) vol 1, 150–154; J M Gilbert, *Hunting and Hunting Reserves in Medieval Scotland* (1979) 291–307.

medieval texts known as the "bukis of the law" or "auld lawes".[9] Perhaps the confusion resulted from the widespread association of the word "wrak" with the word "waith", which seems to have come from the Old Norse term "veiðr", meaning hunting or fishing, and to have been wrongly identified with the English term "waif", more suggestive of straying.[10] In any case, it was from the longer version of the *Leges forestarum* that Balfour (or one of his assistants) had extracted these provisions.

Towards the end of the century they were ascribed to the *Leges forestarum* again by Sir John Skene of Curriehill, who may have been familiar with the surveys of "the bukis of the law" used by Balfour.[11] In a dictionary of the technical and archaic terms encountered in the old laws, Skene explained that the word "wrek" meant the "power, libertie and prerogative competent to the king, or to ony person to quhome the samin is granted be him, be infeftment or ony uther disposition, to intromet and up-take sik guds and geare as are schip-broken".[12] After adding that the right enjoyed by a landowner "infeft with wreck" would be as extensive as the right enjoyed by "the king himself, giver theirof", Skene made reference to "*L. forest.* c. *Inter antiqua* 56". It may be significant that unlike Balfour, who cited the relevant article by its number alone, Skene also drew attention to its opening phrase, which indicated that the provisions on shipwreck had been "found written among old royal statutes".[13] He moved on at once to rehearse the terms of a statute attributed to the English king Edward I, and it was not until this point that he took his readers through the provisions Balfour had reproduced from the *Leges forestarum*. As a matter of fact, the terms of the

9 For instance, NRS, PA5/3, f. 116; NLS, Adv. MS 7.1.9, f 406v, Adv. MS 25.4.12, ff 250v–251r, Adv. MS 25.5.6, ff 233v–234r, and MS 16497, ff 127v–128r; St Andrews University Library (SAUL), msKF51.R4, ff 124v–125r.

10 W Craigie, A J Aitken, J A C Stevenson, H D Watson and M G Dareau (eds), *A Dictionary of the Older Scottish Tongue from the Twelfth Century to the End of the Seventeenth*, 12 vols (1931–2002) vol 11, 619–620, and vol 12, 320–323. Brian Smith has kindly drawn attention to an illuminating account of the derivation of "waith" in his *Toons and Tenants: Settlement and Society in Shetland, 1299–1899* (2000) 58–63.

11 J Buchanan, 'The MSS of *Regiam Maiestatem*: An Experiment' (1937) 49 *Juridical Review* 217, at 220–221; J W Cairns, T D Fergus and H L MacQueen, 'Legal Humanism and the History of Scots Law: John Skene and Thomas Craig', in J MacQueen (ed), *Humanism in Renaissance Scotland* (1990) 48, at 51. Skene may have assisted in compiling the surveys and working on them may have led him to compose his dictionary, which was first circulated as an appendix to Balfour's practicks. These possible connections will be explored elsewhere.

12 J Skene, *De verborum significatione* (1597) sigg S4v–5r (the word "are" has been inserted at the end of this quotation, where it surely belongs).

13 As the numbering of the articles in the manuscripts is variable, and sometimes differs even internally between tables of contents and the articles themselves, this suggestion must be made with some hesitation.

fourth chapter of the first Statute of Westminster, enacted in 1275, were almost identical to the terms of the article cited from the *Leges forestarum*, differing mostly in the order of their presentation.[14] In the English statute the aim had been to codify the law of shipwreck emerging from previous legislation and the thinking of lawyers.[15] Skene went on to close his discussion by mentioning the statute *De praerogativa regis*, supposedly enacted during the reign of Edward II, which extended "wreck of the sea" to encompass "whales and great sturgeons taken in the sea or elsewhere within the realm, except in certain places privileged by the king".[16] If Skene suspected, and may have been trying to suggest to his readers, that the "old royal statutes" among which the provisions on shipwreck had been "found written" by the compilers of the *Leges forestarum* were actually Acts passed in the parliaments of England, he did not make his thinking explicit. He was forced to admit that in Scotland too "wrek" was "ane worde specified in the lawes and sindrie infeftments".[17] Quite apart from being found in many copies of the *Leges forestarum*, the word continued to appear throughout the sixteenth century in feudal charters.[18]

Whatever Skene may have been thinking when he wrote his dictionary, he changed his mind shortly after it was printed in 1597. The provisions on shipwreck were omitted from a draft edition of the old laws he produced, in which a short version of the *Leges forestarum* was included.[19] Then, in

14 *The Statutes of the Realm*, 11 vols (1810–1828) vol 1, 28.

15 H T Riley (ed), *The Annals of Roger de Hoveden*, 2 vols (1853) vol 2, 170–171; H C Maxwell Lyte and C G Grump (eds), *Calendar of the Charter Rolls Preserved in the Public Record Office*, 6 vols (1903–1927) vol 1, 220; S E Thorne (ed), *Bracton on the Laws and Customs of England*, 4 vols (Cambridge, MA) vol 3, 339–340.

16 *Statutes of the Realm* (n 14) vol 1, 226.

17 *De verborum significatione* (n 12) sig S4v.

18 *RPS*, A1504/3/147, 1567/4/14, 1579/10/57, 1581/10/90 and 94, 1584/5/54, 1587/7/144, 1592/4/196, 1592/4/203 and 1592/4/209; *APS*, ii 271–273 and 562–565, and vol 3, 154–157, 254–256, 263–267, 323–325, 510–516, 629–636, 645–648 and 650–656; J H Ballantyne and B Smith (eds), *Shetland Documents*, 3 vols (1999–2016) vol 1, 98, 147, 165, 171, 181 and 238; J Balfour Paul, J M Thomson, J H Stevenson and W K Dickson (eds), *Registrum magni sigilli regum Scotorum: The Register of the Great Seal of Scotland*, 11 vols (1984) vol 4, 727–728, and vol 5, 263–264, 467–468, 516, 565 and 590.

19 NLS, Adv. MS 7.1.10, ff 164r–166v. Skene claimed to have transcribed at least some of the twenty-two articles he listed from an "antiquus codex" belonging to Sir David Lindsay of Edzell, adding that they were said there to date from the reign of William I (1165–1214). Gilbert, *Hunting and Hunting Reserves in Medieval Scotland* (n 8) 272–273, has identified NLS, Adv. MS 25.9.7(1) ff 30–35, as Lindsay's copy, though why is not entirely clear. Someone had written on it in pencil that it came from the "Edzell Charter Chest", and it does contain twenty-two articles. However, they are not identical with Skene's articles, they are manifestly not from an old transcription, since the last two are based on sixteenth century legislation, and there is no indication at any point that the rest date from the reign of William I.

revising his draft for the press, he reintroduced the provisions, but as part of another medieval text, called the *Statuta regis Alexandri*.[20] Now presented as an Act passed by a Scottish king during the first half of the thirteenth century, they appeared without the statement that they had been found *inter antiqua statuta regia*, and in the slightly different order recorded in the Statute of Westminster, although in substance they remained the same.[21] In a marginal annotation to his Latin edition of the old laws, Skene claimed to have found these provisions in a manuscript he labelled the *liber Perthensis*, but what this signified is hard to tell.[22] There is no known manuscript in which the shipwreck provisions appear in the *Statuta regis Alexandri*. There is one in which they are separated from the *Leges forestarum*, but they are not attached there to any other medieval text, nor is the manuscript connected in any discernible way with Perth.[23] Alice Taylor, who has recently published a reliable edition of the *Statuta regis Alexandri* from which these provisions are absent, has plausibly proposed that awareness of the presence in the longer version of the *Leges forestarum* of other articles that did actually derive from Alexander II's legislation may have encouraged the belief that these provisions came from the same source.[24] For a patriotic Scot, determined to defend the authenticity of the old laws, the belief would have been attractive.[25] As Habakkuk Bisset, who assisted both Balfour and Skene in the late sixteenth century, was to point out in the early seventeenth century, it implied that it was an English king who had copied a Scottish legislator, not vice versa.[26]

Skene may possibly have known that the shipwreck provisions had already been attributed to Alexander II by another author, for that author had been

20 NLS, Adv. MS 25.5.8, f 197; J Skene (ed), *Regiam maiestatem: Scotiae veteres leges et constitutiones* (1609) pt 2, f 28; J Skene (ed), *Regiam maiestatem: The Auld Lawes and Constitutions of Scotland* (1609) pt 2, f 19r.

21 The king to whom the Act was attributed was Alexander II, the immediate successor of William I.

22 A Taylor (ed and tr), *The Laws of Medieval Scotland: Legal Compilations from the Thirteenth and Fourteenth Centuries*, Stair Society vol 66 (2019) 13–14. Although NLS, Adv. MS 25.5.10, originated in the priory of Chartreux at Perth, it was certainly not Skene's source (*Laws of Medieval Scotland*, 393–402).

23 NLS, Adv. MS 25.4.15, ff 198v–199r.

24 Cf. Taylor (ed), *Laws of Medieval Scotland* (n 22) 127 and 350–351.

25 H L MacQueen, '*Glanvill* Resarcinate: Sir John Skene and *Regiam maiestatem*', in A A MacDonald, M Lynch and I B Cowan (eds), *The Renaissance in Scotland: Studies in Literature, Religion, History and Culture* (1994) 385, at 385, and '*Regiam maiestatem*, Scots Law and National Identity' (1995) 74 *Scottish Historical Review* 1, at 16–17.

26 P J Hamilton-Grierson (ed), *Habakkuk Bisset's Rolment of Courtis*, 3 vols (1920–1926) vol 2, 214–216.

appointed to the chair of civil law at the University of St Andrews previously held by his brother.[27] In a treatise on maritime law apparently written around 1587 (of which an abbreviated version was printed three years later without the attribution), William Welwod had also compared the laws of Scotland and England, although he had not confined his comparison to those laws, and had been intent on making a different point.[28] In the year of his appointment to the St Andrews chair, the earl of Bothwell had received a new charter as admiral of Scotland, in which the officials who staffed his courts had been instructed to follow the example of the maritime laws of "France, Spain, England, Denmark or other foreign nations".[29] With this perhaps in mind, Welwod cited a document entitled *De officio admiralitatis Angliae*, along with "statut. Alexa. 2", in support of the proposition that "quhair admiralities ar constitut and allowit", if a ship was sunk without survivors and no one appeared within a year and a day to claim salvaged goods, "the half belangis to the admirall, the rest to the finder".[30] The English document, unlike the provisions contained in the first Statute of Westminster or attributed to Alexander II, did mention this division into two parts, but it was another distribution that had been adopted in Scotland. "And agane in uther countries", Welwod continued, "a third to the king, a thrid to the admiral, and a thrid to the finder, as in France". He cited in support of this proposition a French edict issued by Henry III in 1584, which had renewed an edict issued by Francis I in 1544, subject to the qualification that the king's share had sometimes been transferred to the owners of land where goods were recovered.[31] The Scottish admiral's new charter assigned him two thirds of "*wrak* et *weth gudis*", with the other

27 It was from his elder brother William that Skene had received the copy of the old laws now known as the Bute manuscript, but it does not have the shipwreck provisions among either the *Leges forestarum* or the *Statuta regis Alexandri* (Taylor (ed), *Laws of Medieval Scotland* (n 22) 52–53). Whether there was any personal contact between John Skene and William Welwod is unclear, but it may be significant that they had both been encouraged to study at the University of Wittenberg, an unusual destination for Scottish students at this time.

28 J D Ford (ed), *Alexander King's Treatise on Maritime Law*, Stair Society vol 66 (2018) 371. For an examination of the relationship between the manuscript and printed versions see J D Ford, 'William Welwod's Treatises on Maritime Law' (2013) 34 *Journal of Legal History* 171.

29 *Registrum magni sigilli regum Scotorum* (n 18) vol 5, 449–50; NRS, PS1/55, ff 190v–193.

30 T Twiss (ed), *The Black Book of the Admiralty*, 4 vols (1871–76) vol 1, 241.

31 J M Pardessus (ed), *Collection de lois maritimes antérieures au XVIIIe siècle*, 6 vols (1828–1845) vol 4, 300; F-A Isambert, M Jourdan and M Decrusy (eds), *Recueil général des anciennes lois françaises*, 29 vols (1822–1833) vol 12, 854, and vol 14, 561. On the origins of the distribution see J Darsel, *L'Amirauté en Bretagne: Des origines à la fin du XVIIIe siècle*, ed. G Le Bouëdec (2012) 160, and F Trivellato, 'Amphibious Power: The Law of Wreck, Maritime Customs and Sovereignty in Richelieu's France' (2015) 33 *Law and History Review* 915 at 931–932.

third assigned to the finders.[32] Welwod surmised that "in Scotland the prince hes quatt his thrid to the admirall", but neglected to consider what would happen if the king's share had been transferred to a landowner. With reference to provisions added to some French copies of the *Rôles d'Oléron*, a compilation dating from the twelfth century, he had already limited the rights of landowners to items "found without fludemark" and had hinted at an adjustment to the "custome" underpinning their rights when admiralties were constituted across Europe.[33]

C: THE CONFISCATION OF WRECKS AND THE CIVIL LAW

According to the 1587 charter, "*wrak* et *weth gudis*" were "bona eiecta et pro derelictis habita" – that is, items washed ashore from a wreck were "regarded as" abandoned things. In the theory of the civil law taught by Welwod, had they been genuinely abandoned things (*res derelicta*) they would have been ownerless (*res nullius*) and open to acquisition by the finders who took possession of them (*occupatio*), whereas merely regarding them as abandoned things served to justify a different mode of acquisition.[34] In a treatise dealing with the "droit de varech" or "droit de bris" recognised in France, Christophle du Bois-Gelin explained how this worked by drawing attention to three texts from the books of the civil law.[35] In the first, an extract from the juristic writings of ancient Rome, which had been preserved in the *Digest* compiled at the behest of the emperor Justinian, it was observed that unclaimed goods (*bona vacantia*) were assigned in certain circumstances to the imperial treasury (*fiscus*) in order to prevent things from remaining without an owner for a long time.[36] In the second, a passage from the twelfth century compilation known as the *Libri feudorum*,

32 The myth that the distribution in thirds of whales driven ashore in the Northern Isles derived from "udal law" has been exploded in B Smith, 'Pilot Whales, Udal Law and Custom in Shetland: Legal Red Herrings' (2003) 23 *Northern Scotland* 85. The response noted in R Houston, 'Custom in Context: Medieval and Early Modern Scotland and England' (2011) 211 *Past and Present* 35 at 44, is simply bizarre.

33 Pardssus (ed), *Collection de lois maritimes* (n 31) vol 1, 348–349 and 351–354. Although the *Rôles d'Oléron* were often included in copies of the old laws of Scotland and were consequently regarded by Welwod as part of the "common law" of the land, these particular provisions were not among those transcribed.

34 P Birks and G McLeod (trs), *Justinian's Institutes* (1987) 2.1.47; A Watson (ed), *The Digest of Justinian*, 4 vols (1985) 41.1.9.8. How much teaching Welwod really did at St Andrews, where students were not admitted to read for law degrees, is unclear.

35 *Traité des droits royaux de bris et de brefs* (1595) 44–45.

36 *Digest of Justinian* (n 34) 38.9.1.pr. The circumstances envisaged were not the recovering of goods from wrecks.

which had been incorporated into the books studied in the schools of civil law, *bona vacantia* were listed among the peculiar privileges of the ruler (*inter regalia*).[37] In the third text, again from Justinian's *Digest*, things open to acquisition by the ruler were described quite literally as goods deserving of assignment to the treasury (*bona confiscanda*).[38] In England, similarly, Christopher St German remarked that "the lawe must nedes reduce the propertye of all goodes to some man".[39] If goods retrieved from a shipwreck were not claimed, he explained, "it shold not be knowen who ought to take them, and so might they be distroyed and no profite com of theym". It was therefore "resonable" for the law to "appoynt who ought to have them", and it was "not unreasonable" for them to be "forfet to the kyng", since he incurred "great charge" in clearing the sea of "pyrates". In Scotland the same line of argument was rehearsed by Thomas Craig of Riccarton, who commented that the king had "granted the greatest part of the goods known as wrack to the admiral, so that he may keep navigation safe for his people".[40] Craig was unsure how consistent the custom (*consuetudo*) that had grown up around this grant was with the grants often made to coastal landowners.

The charter granted to the Scottish admiral in 1587 was unusually precise in its terms, but there is some evidence that the "privileges" or "profits" vaguely referred to elsewhere were taken in practice to encompass a customary right to the remains of wrecked vessels.[41] In 1549 the admiral rewarded someone with a gift of a pinnace wrecked at St Monans, "now pertening to us be resoun of eschete throw rycht and privilege of admiralite grantit to us and our predecessouris".[42] It was clearly expected that the recipient of the gift would obtain items recovered from the wreck by certain named individuals, who remained in possession of them, but whether it was expected that those individuals would retain a portion is unclear. In 1581 a landowner who was ordered by the privy council to surrender ordnance recovered from a wreck at Scoughall was prepared to do so only on receiving a discharge of

37 *Volumen legum quod parvum vocant* (1604) cols 117–118 ("Libri feudorum", 2.56); K Lehmann, *Das Langobardische Lehnrecht* (1896) 182.

38 *Digest of Justinian* (n 34) 48.21.3.7.

39 T F T Plucknett and J L Barton (eds), *St German's Doctor and Student* (1974) 291–292.

40 L Dodd (tr), *Jus feudale tribus libris comprehensum, Book I* (2017) 496–497. As will be revealed by an edition of David Chalmers' compendium of Scots law, being prepared for publication by Winifred Coutts, Julian Goodare and Andrew Simpson (who kindly provided a preview of the relevant entries), it was under the rubric "Escheit" that the provisions on "wrak", as found in the *Leges forestarum*, were cited there.

41 *RPS*, 1581/10/91; *APS* iii, 256–9; NRS, Morton papers, GD150/2278; B Seton, 'The Vice Admiral and the Quest of the "Golden Pennie"' (1923) 20 *Scottish Historical Review* 122, at 123.

42 W Fraser (ed), *Memorials of the Family of Wemyss of Wemyss*, 3 vols (1888) vol 2, 177–178.

liability to the admiral, without which she would have been "in danger to be persewit for the samin".[43] In 1596 landowners on the coast of Fife were summoned before an admiralty court to answer for timber, tackle and other things they had recovered from a wreck there.[44] When the case was transferred to the College of Justice, the highest civil court in the country, one of the defenders objected that his family had been infeft in their lands "as ane frie barone, with privilege of wrak, wathe and wier guidis arryving within the boundis of the said baronie", and long before "ony infeftment grantit to the said admerall and his predicessouris in the said office of admeralitie".[45] Advocates appearing on behalf of the admiral resisted this objection on the two grounds adumbrated in the manuscript version of Welwod's treatise, to which they may conceivably have had access, although there is no evidence that it had been put into circulation. In the first place, they argued that the objects at issue had been found "within the sie merk be the said defender, to the quhilk the privilegis contenit in his said infeftment can na wayes be extendit". Any claim founded on ownership of land, they reasoned, would have to depend on items from a wreck being washed by the waves onto the land granted, beyond the foreshore retained by the crown. In the second place, they argued that no infeftment in land could possibly "derogat the richt privileges, commoditeis and casualiteis of the said admeralitie, without the said admerall or his predicessours haid gevin thair express consent and assent to the said infeftment". Despite the "allegit anteraitie" of the grant of the land, they insisted, it could not undermine the right exercised by the admirals of Scotland "past memorie of man". The lords of council and session, as the judges of the court were known, dismissed the landowner's objection "in respect of the said answer and replye", but whether both arguments were considered equally convincing is not revealed by the records of the case.[46]

The admiral whose interests were defended in the 1596 case was presumably unaware that one of the lawyers selected to represent him had

43 Burton and Masson (eds), *Register of the Privy Council of Scotland* (n 2) vol 3, 367–368; NRS, register of the privy council, PC1/10, p. 547.

44 NRS, register of acts and decreets of the lords of council and session, CS7/159, ff 193v–194r and 283v–284.

45 It is a source of some uncertainty that the word "wrak", like the word "wair", with which it was associated in many charters and other documents, could signify a right to gather seaweed for use as manure on land (Craigie et al, *Dictionary of the Older Scottish Tongue* (n 10) vol 11, 613–614).

46 NRS, CS7/159, ff 356r and 385. Although the significance of the brief entry in DCA, BCMB, vol 8, 5 March 1565, is obscure, it may be that a landowner had claimed title to a "wrak schip that brak" on his property.

written critically about his immediate predecessor's grant of "*wrak* et *weth gudis*" in another unpublished treatise.[47] Alexander King, a judge in the central admiralty court sitting in Edinburgh as well as an advocate in the College of Justice, had drawn attention to civil law texts in which the Roman emperors had refused to take advantage of the misfortunes of others by claiming wrecked goods for their treasury, and had similarly denied coastal landowners the right to benefit from maritime disasters.[48] Both a medieval emperor and a pope, it was further pointed out, had threatened those who plundered wrecks with condign punishment.[49] King had devoted much of his chapter "De naufragiis" to discussion of various procedures provided by the civil law for the protection of the victims of shipwrecks, conscious that they did not form part of the law of Scotland, yet eager for them to exert some influence on the handling of shipwrecks in the admiralty courts.[50] In particular, he had argued that while "the letter of the law" conferred on the admiral a share of unclaimed goods retrieved from wrecks, "equity" required him to abstain from exploiting such a "corrupt custom". Although Welwod had been less dismissive of the admiral's privilege, he had drawn attention to other civil law sources suggesting that unclaimed goods should be donated to the poor or the church.[51] Furthermore, he had prefaced his account of "wrak" with an account of the civil law procedures protecting the victims of shipwrecks, and it was only this part of his discussion that survived in the printed version of his treatise, from which several passages defending the admiral's privileges were omitted.[52] Skene too drew attention to some of the civil law sources in annotating the provisions he had come to attribute to Alexander II, beginning with the axiom that *fiscus ex naufragio et aliena*

47 The second duke of Lennox had replaced the fifth earl of Bothwell as admiral in 1591 and had immediately removed the author of the treatise from office as an admiral depute.

48 B W Frier (ed), *The Codex of Justinian*, 3 vols (2016) 11.6.1; *Digest of Justinian*, 47.9.7.

49 *Codex Iustiniani* (1559) col. 1192 (authentic "Navigia", between C.6.2.18 and 19); L Weiland, W Stürner, I Schwalm, R Bork, W Eggert, K Zeumer, R Salomon, M Kühn and W D Fritz (eds), Monumenta Germaniae historica, *Constitutiones et acta publica imperatorum et regum*, 11 vols (1893–2003) vol 2, 109; A Friedberg (ed), *Corpus iuris canonici*, 2 vols (1879–1881) X 5.17.3; G D Mansi, P Labbe, G Cossart and N Coleti (eds), *Sacrorum conciliorum nova et amplissimo collectio*, 56 vols (1759–1927) vol 22, cols 230–231. These threats were echoed in the provisions from the *Rôles d'Oléron* in which Welwod had found evidence of the demands typically made by "the men quha hes the superioritie on the coistis" (n 33 above).

50 Ford (ed), *Alexander King's Treatise on Maritime Law* (n 28) 186–207.

51 I Faber, *Commentaria super Institutis* (1527) f 25v (ad J.2.1.47); *Codex Iustiniani* (n 49) col. 1485 (authentic "Omnes peregrini", between C.6.59.10 and 11).

52 Ford (ed), *Alexander King's Treatise on Maritime Law* (n 28) 370–371; William Welwod, *The Sea-Law of Scotland* (1590) sigg C5–6r.

calamitate compendium sectari non debet.[53] He left his readers to draw their own conclusions from comparison of these sources with the Statute of Westminster, to which he referred in the margins of his Latin edition of the old laws, alongside the *Statuta regis Alexandri*.[54]

Welwod and Skene both referred further to an Act passed by the Scottish parliament in 1430, which was another of the three sources gathered together by Balfour in his treatment of the law of shipwreck.[55] The Act opened by confirming that when wrecks occurred in Scotland, "the schip and the gude salbe eschete to the king gif thai be of tha cuntreis the quhilkis oysis and kepis the samyn law of brokyn schippis".[56] It was well known, for instance, that Scottish ships destroyed on the coasts of England would be treated as "just wrack" unless claims were promptly made for the return of anything salvaged from them.[57] Accordingly, since the same law of shipwreck was used and kept in England as in Scotland, English vessels destroyed on the coasts of Scotland would be treated in the same way there. However, the Act proceeded to provide that if ships broken in Scotland came from "ony lande that kepis nocht that law, thai sal hafe the sammyn favor her as thai kep to schippis of this lande brokyn with thaim". There were other countries where the civil and canon laws had been more influential and where no rights to "wrak" had been either asserted by rulers or granted to landowners.[58] The innovation in the 1430 Act was to exempt vessels from these countries from the law of "wrak". King did not mention the Act in his treatise, but nor did he refer directly to the provisions found in the *Leges forestarum* or added to the *Statuta regis Alexandri*. He reasoned instead, on the strength of his civilian learning, that the privilege introduced by "corrupta nostra aliorumque con-

53 The axiom put into a more pithy and emphatic form the sentiment expressed as a rhetorical question in the *Codex of Justinian* (n 48) 11.6.1: "what right has the treasury in another's calamity in order to seek profit from so lamentable an affair?" The other sources to which Skene drew attention at this point were the *Digest of Justinian*, 47.9.1.pr.–1, and the standard gloss "Criminibus" on that text, in *Digestum novum* (1569) col. 1358.

54 Skene (ed), *Regiam maiestatem: Scotiae veteres leges et constitutiones* (n 20) pt 2, f 28.

55 McNeill (ed), *Practicks of Sir James Balfour* (n 6) vol 2, 624. Chalmers (see n 40 above) cited the act as well, under the rubric "Scheippis".

56 *RPS*, 1430/19; *APS*, ii, 19.

57 J S Brewer et al (eds), *Letters and Papers of the Reign of Henry VIII* (n 2) vol 17, 95; Bain et al (eds), *Calendar of the State Papers Relating to Scotland and Mary Queen of Scots* (n 2) vol 2, 272, and vol 9, 547; M M Meikle, *A British Frontier? Lairds and Gentlemen in the Eastern Borders, 1540–1603* (2004) 255.

58 R A Melikan, 'Shippers, Salvors and Sovereigns: Competing Interests in the Medieval Law of Shipwreck' (1990) 11 *Journal of Legal History* 163; cf. A H Krappe, 'Le droit de bris' (1943) 5 *University of Toronto Law Journal* 113.

suetudo" should be allowed to fall into disuse.[59] Balfour and Skene merely made reference to the Act, which was accessible in print elsewhere, while reproducing the provisions from the old laws in their entirety.[60] Welwod, on the other hand, began his whole discussion of the law of shipwreck not only by summarising the terms of the Act, but also by turning them back to front. "Strangeris incurring schipwrak in Scotland", he wrote, "suld have the same favour of us that our peopill usses in sic caisses to receave of thame on thair coistis, sua that na confiscatioun sould be maid thairof, except thay use to da sa to us".[61] On this basis, he was able to maintain that the law of Scotland prohibited the plundering of wrecks and encouraged the salvaging of goods for the benefit of their current owners. It helped, of course, that the provisions from the old laws themselves required goods to be "saisit and keipt at the sicht of the schiref or coroner or of the kingis baillies or officiaris", and to be retained for a year and a day "in the handis of the indwellaris of the town quhair thay wer fund".[62] As Welwod pointed out, even the period of time prescribed was consistent with the civil law procedures designed to assist the victims of shipwrecks.[63]

D: THE SALVAGING OF WRECKS AND FORENSIC CUSTOM

The third source referred to by Balfour was a note summarising a decision delivered by the lords of council and session in the later 1520s.[64] The court had ruled that when a vessel was driven ashore by a storm in Scotland, "not beand just wrak be the lawis of this realme", everything recovered from it was to be restored to the owners or their representatives as soon as they provided the salvors with a guarantee against liability for "intromissioun

59 Ford (ed), *Alexander King's Treatise on Maritime Law* (n 28) 206–207.

60 *The Actis and Constitutiounis of the Realm of Scotland* (1566) was available by the time Balfour was writing – indeed, he had been personally involved in its editing – and Skene had himself edited *The Lawes and Actes of Parliament* (1597).

61 Ford (ed), *Alexander King's Treatise on Maritime Law* (n 28) 370; Welwod, *Sea-Law of Scotland* (n 52), sig C5r.

62 McNeill (ed), *Practicks of Sir James Balfour* (n 6) vol 2, 624; Skene (ed), *Regiam maiestatem: Scotiae veteres leges et constitutiones* (n 20) pt 2, f 28; Skene (ed), *Regiam maiestatem: The Auld Lawes and Constitutions of Scotland* (n 20) pt 2, f 19r.

63 *Codex of Justinian* (n 48) 11.6.2. On the originally limited scope of the procedures referred see A J B Sirks, *Food for Rome: The Legal Structure of the Transportation and Processing of Supplies for the Imperial Distributions in Rome and Constantinople* (1991) 213–217.

64 McNeill (ed), *Practicks of Sir James Balfour* (n 6) vol 2, 623–624 (the precise date provided here is misleading). On the origins of Balfour's notes summarising decisions of the lords of session see W M Gordon, *Roman Law, Scots Law and Legal History: Selected Essays* (2007) 283–296.

thairwith, at all handis havand or pretendand to have interes thairto".[65] Records relating to the case reveal in more detail that "ane greit schip" belonging to the king of Denmark, Norway and Sweden, called the *Peter de Hulle* or *Peter van Hulle*, had been wrecked near Aberdeen, where various local dignitaries and others had taken possession of a considerable quantity of equipment and wares.[66] An ambassador sent from Denmark had raised an action against them for "the wranguis, violent and maisterfull spoliatioune, away taking, intrometting and withhalding" of the things obtained, they had been ordered to restore the things to the ambassador, and he had been required to provide "sufficient cautioun to keip all the intromettours witht the saids guds recoverit, and all uthers our soverane lords liegis, harmless and skaithless thairof as law will".[67] In another case heard around the same time the lords of session had confirmed that the appropriate course of action for victims of shipwreck to take in Scotland was to "rais summondis apoun the spulzearis and intromettouris".[68] Complaints of "spuilzie", which were linked in the minds of learned lawyers with the *actio spolii* of the canon law, were widely used in Scotland as a means of recovering possession of property.[69] In 1530, after "ane schip of Danskin" called the *Jhesus* was wrecked near Aberdeen, dignitaries and others there were warned by the central authorities that if they did not restore everything they had salvaged from the ship to its owners, "thai suld be accusit as intromettors and spulzears of the haile guds".[70] Eventually, several summonses for spuilzie were raised in the

65 Nothing in the surviving records of the case supports the first phrase quoted, which may have been added to the note by Balfour in order to emphasise the difference between the ground covered by this entry and by his previous extract from the *Leges forestarum*.

66 *Acts of the Lords of Council in Public Affairs* (n 2) 254–255, 264, 272 and 314–315; NRS, register of acts and decreets of the lords of council and session, CS5/36, ff 154r, 157v and 159, CS5/37, f 229r, CS5/38, ff 46v–47r, and CS5/40, f 98v; *RPS*, 1526/6/13 and 1526/6/15; *APS* ii, 302; R K Hannay and D Hay (eds), *Letters of James V* (n 5) 130, 134, 151 and 198; C A Lange, C R Unger, H J Huitfeldt-Kaas and G Storm (eds), *Diplomatarium Norvegicum*, 23 vols (1847–1992) vol 8 (2) 562–563, vol 9, 550–553, and vol 18, 585–586.

67 The particular decreet summarised in Balfour's book is recorded at NRS, CS5/38, ff 46v–47r.

68 *Acts of the Lords of Council in Public Affairs* (n 2) 296, 308 and 352; NRS, CS5/40, ff 8v–9r and 139, and CS5/42, f 122; M Livingston, G Donaldson, J Beveridge and D H Fleming (eds), *Registrum secreti sigilli regum Scotorum: The Register of the Privy Seal of Scotland*, 7 vols (1908–66) vol 2, xx and 47.

69 A M Godfrey, *Civil Justice in Renaissance Scotland: The Origins of a Central Court* (2009) 239–247.

70 *Acts of the Lords of Council in Public Affairs* (n 2) p. 356; NRS, CS5/42, ff 181v–2r; ACA, CA1/1/13, pp. 15–23, 70, 103, 105–107, 113–117, 134–139 and 141–144. At an early stage in the affair, the owner of the land on which the ship was driven aground claimed that they were "on his land as wrak", but this was clearly a misunderstanding (*Acts of the Lords of Council in Public Affairs* (n 2) 345; CS5/41, f 150v).

case.[71] Fifty years later it was the turn of some shipowners from Aberdeen to raise a summons for "spoliatioun" after timber and tackle from a ship destroyed at North Berwick was found in the possession of people living all across East Lothian.[72] At the end of the century a shipowner from Bergen – a burges of the town, but with the Scottish surname Dewar – was pursuing various inhabitants of Easter Ross before the privy council to satisfy "ane decreit obtenit be him befoir his hienes admirall aganis thame for spoliatioun of ane schip".[73] It seems likely that traces of other actions for spuilzie raised before the admiral have been lost along with the records of his courts.

The language of "wranguis, violent and maisterfull spoliatioune" may be misleading. For example, there is no evidence anywhere in the records of the *Peter de Hulle* case that the parties pursued intended to retain the goods they had "wone or recoverit within the say, sand or uther placis", still less that they had resorted to violence and force in taking them.[74] On the contrary, the dignitaries summoned had been appointed agents by the king's ambassador "to ressave and intromett witht the saids guds to his behuf", and they had "intromettit witht" (or taken possession of) the remains of the ship at his direction.[75] The problem was that while the ambassador represented Christian II, a claim to the items recovered was also being made by representatives of Frederick I.[76] Understandably, the "spulzearis and withhaldaris of the gudis and stuff" were reluctant to surrender them to one claimant to the throne of Denmark, Norway and Sweden unless they received effective

71 This episode is examined in some detail in A R C Simpson, 'Spuilzie and Shipwreck in the Burgh Records' (2018) 9 *Journal of Irish and Scottish Studies* 70.

72 NRS, CS7/97, f 358, CS7/98(1) ff 328v and 331v, and CS7/98(2) f 245v.

73 Burton and Masson, *Register of the Privy Council of Scotland* (n 2) vol 5, 643–644, and vol 6, 48–49, 54, 120 and 175; NRS, PC1/17, 170–171, 183–184 and 326–327, and PS1/71, f 148; R J Adam (ed), *The Calendar of Fearn: Text and Additions, 1471–1667* (1991) 184; W MacGill (ed), *Old Ross-Shire and Scotland, as Seen in the Tain and Balnagown Documents*, 2 vols (1909–11) vol 1, 269; T Brochard, 'The Socio-Economic Relations between Scotland's Northern Territories and Scandinavia and the Baltic in the Sixteenth and Seventeenth Centuries' (2014) 26 *International Journal of Maritime History* 210, at 223–224.

74 *RPS*, 1526/6/15; *APS*, ii, 302.

75 NRS, CS5/38, ff 46v–47r. As Skene's definition of "wrek" (quoted at n 12 above) shows, the word "intromet" could be used in a neutral or even positive sense.

76 *Acts of the Lords of Council in Public Affairs* (n 2) 254–255 and 272; NRS, CS5/36, f 159, and CS5/38, ff 46v–7r. Having already lost power in Sweden, Christian had been deposed by the Danish nobility in favour of his uncle in 1523 (P D Lockhart, *Denmark, 1513–1660: The Rise and Decline of a Renaissance Monarchy* (2007) 18–20). His ambassador reported that the Scots were relying on Frederick's claim as an "excuse" for not returning the equipment and wares, but this comment in a defensive letter to his principal is as close as any source comes to suggesting that the Scots meant to retain the goods (R K Hannay and D Hay (eds), *Letters of James V* (n 5) 151; Lange et al (eds), *Diplomatarium Norvegicum*, vol 18, 585–586). That they never were returned to Christian, who never recovered his throne, is scarcely surprising.

protection against an action by the other claimant. Similarly, at least some of the defenders in the *Jhesus* case seem to have been quite innocent. The master of the ship had asked for assistance from the local dignitaries, "promittand thame faithfully the thrid of the haile guds that hapint to be wone, kepand the twa part to thame that has just tytill thairto".[77] Both the master and the Hanseatic merchants whose cloth the ship was carrying had appointed the dignitaries as their agents to "resave and ouptak all maner of claitits and gudis" preserved in Aberdeen.[78] One local man insisted that "he, at the marinars command, had intromettit and wone ane part of thair guds", another maintained that he had become involved at the request of one of the local dignitaries, who had promised "to reward him for his labours", while a third professed himself willing to hand over cloth as soon as he was paid "for his labours, coists and expensis he maid in the first wynyng of the said claith".[79] An assise was left to decide whether the third man had been promised "ony maner of thing for his labors in the wyning of the said claitht, or gif he aucht to have ony thing thairfor".[80] There is no doubt that some people in Aberdeen took advantage of the misadventure of the *Jhesus*, but others took part in a consensual salvage operation and retained possession of goods only to ensure that they received the recompense to which they believed they were entitled for the efforts they had made.[81]

Salvage agreements are mentioned in other records of cases heard in the burgh courts. The language of spuilzie is absent from these cases, in which there was no intervention by the central authorities.[82] Sometimes reference was made to an agreement, but not always. In 1528, for example, the master of a German ship wrecked at Aberdeen promised a local man fifteen pounds Scots, "or thane samekle gudis of the said schip as will corespond to the said xv *lib.* money forsaid, and that for the sanite of himself and his childer, and bringing tham, the said schip and the merchandis gudis to ane

77 ACA, CA1/1/13, p. 16.
78 ACA, CA1/1/13, pp. 113–114 and 134–135.
79 ACA, CA1/1/13, pp. 19, 106–107 and 116.
80 ACA, CA1/1/13, pp. 136–137 and 143.
81 Details of a salvage contract requiring mariners from Anstruther to use their boats and cables to recover goods belonging to merchants of Edinburgh from a ship "sunkyn and drownit" off Port Seton, in exchange for payment of an agreed sum of money, can be found in NRS, register of acts and decreets of the lords of council and session, CS6/3, f 121v.
82 The language of spuilzie is lacking from the records of a case initially handled by a burgh court in Ayr after a ship was wrecked at Dunure, even though it ended up being handled by the lords of council and session (*Acts of the Lords of Council in Public Affairs* (n 2) 487; NRS, CS6/12, ff 157v–158r). Presumably the tone had already been set before the case was drawn to the attention of the central court.

havin".[83] Similarly, in 1565 the master of a French ship run aground at Balmedie promised to pay some local people "for thair labours taikynd in, saifeing and winning of the said schipe and the geir being in hir and pertening to hir".[84] In 1554, on the other hand, when two men appeared before the bailies of Dundee and admitted that the master of a wrecked ship to whom they had restored tackle had "contentit us for oure saiffing of the said guds", no mention was made of a prior agreement.[85] In 1583 the same court found that the master and owners of a ship wrecked at Orkney were obliged to reward a mariner "for his gryt labors, travellis and expensis maid in the saiftie of thair schipis geir and mercheands geir", as well as for "aventering of his lyff in saiftie thairof".[86] Again, no mention was made of a prior agreement, though the mariner could have been a member of the crew. An article of the *Rôles d'Oléron* obliged the mariners of a wrecked vessel "to save as much as they can of the vessel and goods", and obliged the master to give those who fulfilled their responsibility "as much as will get them home", if necessary by using the salvaged goods to raise funds.[87] Some versions of the code added advice to judges that if "the master and merchants should promise folk who helped them to save the said goods and vessel a third part or a half of the vessel and wares", it would be misguided to pay strict attention to the agreement when the emphasis ought to be on ensuring that the salvors' labours were adequately recompensed.[88] Unlike the articles cited by Welwod to illustrate the avarice of landowners, the first of these provisions was included in a version the *Rôles d'Oléron* found in some copies of the old laws of Scotland.[89] While the people who appeared as litigants or served as judges and jurors in the burgh courts may not have had much familiarity with these or any other written sources, a vague awareness of the provisions they contained may nonetheless have informed a popular belief that rewards ought to be paid to salvors, and that things recovered from wrecks might be used to provide the rewards.[90]

83 ACA, CA1/1/12/1, p. 317.
84 ACA, CA1/1/25, pp. 531–532 and 570.
85 DCA, BCMB, vol 3, 3 September 1554.
86 DCA, BCMB, vol 16, 18 February 1583.
87 Twiss (ed), *Black Book of the Admiralty* (n 30) vol 1, 90–91.
88 Pardssus (ed), *Collection de lois maritimes* (n 31) vol 1, 325–326.
89 E Frankot, 'The Scottish Translations of the *Rôles d'Oléron*: Edition and Commentary', in A M Godfrey (ed), *Stair Society: Miscellany Eight* (2020) 13, at 29–30.
90 Masters, mariners and merchants in Scotland were probably not familiar with the *Nomos Rhodion nautikos*, which Welwod took to be fundamental to the rights of salvors (*Alexander King's Treatise on Maritime Law* (n 28) 371; W Ashburner (tr), *The Rhodian Sea-Law* (1909), 37–38 and 117–119).

Although it was stipulated in the *Rôles d'Oléron* that a master must not sell equipment recovered from a wreck without the express permission of the shipowners, the remains of the German ship wrecked at Aberdeen in 1528 were sold there by its master without the apparent involvement of its owners.[91] In fact, there are many examples in the burgh records of masters selling the remains of ships as well as goods to local purchasers, and in no case is it specified that the master had been authorised to do so by the owners.[92] In 1526, for instance, the master of a ship from Stralsund was content to record in the council register of Aberdeen that he had been paid by two local men for "all and haill the wrak of the said schip, witht maists, takillis, cabillis, ankors and all and sindry uthir thingis pertenend to hir".[93] The purchase of equipment from wrecks must have benefited the maritime economy of Scotland, where it was not always easy to find essential items, yet it would be rash to presume that masters were forced to sell at discounted prices.[94] In a later case entered in the Aberdeen council register, after a Dutch ship was "cassin be storme off wedder on the sandis of this burgh", the master, "thinking thairby that scho suld have wrackit", sold his "boit" to a local man.[95] When it transpired that the ship could be refloated, the purchaser promptly agreed to let the master buy the boat back for "the same price as he sauld hir". The parties ended up in dispute, but the local man had not tried to take advantage of the master's predicament by driving a hard bargain. Another Dutch master, whose ship actually was "wrackit on the sandis" at Aberdeen, professed himself "thankfullie receavit and interteneit be the provest, bailleis, consall and inhabitantis of the said burgh", in particular through "bying, selling, dettis and utheris contractit be the said burgh or ony off the inhabitantis thairoff, be ressone off the said schip".[96]

91 Twiss (ed), *Black Book of the Admiralty* (n 30) vol 1, 90–91; ACA, CA1/1/12/1, p. 323. The remains of the ship run aground at Balmedie in 1565 were also sold, but with the consent of the mariners, who were understood to be the owners of the ship.

92 Stuart (ed), *Extracts from the Council Register of the Burgh of Aberdeen* (n 2) vol 1, 428; ACA, CA1/1/8, pp. 86–87, CA1/1/12/1, p. 358, CA1/1/16, pp. 316 and 538, CA1/1/27, p. 738, CA1/1/32, p. 496, CA1/1/35, p. 341, and CA1/1/36, pp. 17–18; SAUL, B10/8/6, pp. 526–527.

93 ACA, CA1/1/12/1, p. 66.

94 In 1538, for example, the master of a damaged ship who was forced to put into Aberdeen found that "thair was nether takill nor sails to be gottin within this burgh" (ACA, CA1/1/16, pp. 104–105). For the benefit derived from even modest findings from wrecks see T Johnson, 'Medieval Law and Materiality: Shipwrecks, Finders and Property on the Suffolk Coast, ca. 1380–1410' (2015) 120 *American Historical Review* 406, and 'The Economics of Shipwreck in Late Medieval Suffolk', in J P Bowen and A T Brown (eds), *Custom and Commercialisation in English Rural Society: Revisiting Tawney and Postan* (2016) 121.

95 ACA, CA1/1/34/2, p. 602.

96 ACA, CA1/1/34/2, p. 532. See too R L Mackie (ed), *Letters of James the Fourth* (n 2) 103–104.

Someone representing the crew of a third Dutch ship wrecked at Aberdeen simply thanked the local inhabitants for "the greit humanite doune to tham", while the same people were urged by the bailies of Dundee, after a ship from that burgh was wrecked near Aberdeen, to provide assistance "as ye wald that we did siclik to your nychtbours, and ony utheris, for mericy and zeal of justice".[97] When shipwrecked sailors were found to be destitute, with nothing they could sell to raise funds for their passage home, subventions were made to them from burgh funds, "for making thair chairges hamewart, and for thair present support".[98] It was indeed suspected that the burghs were in danger of being taken advantage of by "maisterfull and ydle beggaris" who pretended to be "schipbrokin".[99]

E: THE PLUNDERING OF WRECKS AND POPULAR CUSTOM

It should not be imagined, however, that the victims of shipwreck invariably received charitable treatment in Scotland. If the master of the *Jhesus* was grateful to the authorities and people of Aberdeen for the recovery of goods from his vessel, "confessand him richt honestlie and humanlye tretit amangis thame", it is not without significance that the provost of the town had felt the need to contact the most powerful nobleman in the area and urge him "to cum to defend and caus the saids guds be keipit fra violance and spulze, quhilk he dred of gentilmen of the cuntretht".[100] The language of spuilzie was sometimes used quite aptly. When the lords of council and session advised that spuilzie was the appropriate form of action for the victims of shipwreck to employ in Scotland, they were dealing with a case in which the pursuers were able to allege "the spoliatioun, down breking, distructioun, away taking and withthalding" of their ship and goods by the defenders.[101] Likewise, the Aberdonian shipowners who appeared before the same judges

97 ACA, CA1/1/11, p. 155, and CA1/1/18, pp. 316–317.

98 Stuart (ed), *Extracts from the Council Register of the Burgh of Aberdeen* (n 2) vol 2, 115–116; *Extracts from the Records of the Burgh of Edinburgh* (n 2) vol 4, 338, 531–532, 542 and 546; M Wood and H Armet (eds), *Extracts from the Records of the Burgh of Edinburgh*, 2nd ser., 9 vols (1927–1967) vol 1, 35–36, 48, 74, 133, 176 and 199; G S Pryde (ed), *Ayr Burgh Accounts, 1534–1624* (1937) 161; Bain et al (eds), *Calendar of the State Papers Relating to Scotland and Mary Queen of Scots* (n 2) vol 9, 624; M A S Hume (ed), *Calendar of Letters and State Papers Relating to English Affairs, Preserved in or Originally Belonging to the Archives of Simancas*, 4 vols (1899) vol 4, 547–548; ACA, CA1/1/36, 302; Edinburgh City Archives (ECA), minute book of the town council of Edinburgh, SL1/1/7, f 161v, and SL1/1/8, f 114r.

99 *RPS*, 1575/3/5 and 1579/10/27; *APS*, iii, 86–89 and 139–142.

100 ACA, CA1/1/13, pp. 18 and 115.

101 NRS, CS5/40. f 139.

to recover their property from inhabitants of East Lothian were able to allege "the dimolesching and cutting downe of the said schip", after it was driven in a tempest onto "the sands of North Berwick", from which it could perhaps have been refloated.[102] A pursuer in an admiralty court used the equally robust language of "brekking and distroying", while another case apparently heard there concerned a "shipe hewed asunder with axis and other weapons, whiche otherwise might have bene made mony of".[103] In diplomatic correspondence and contemporary histories, complaints were made about "rude and ravenous people" in Buchan who "rifled, spoyled and caried away" everything left of a ship driven onto the rugged coastline there, about the burning of a vessel run aground at Mull "by treacherie of the Irishe, and almost all the men within it consumed with fire", and about the "spoliatioun" at an unspecified location of a "schip and gudis, and murthour of the personis for the maist pairt being in the same schip, committit be certane Scottismen".[104] Another well documented case of "wrangous, violent and maisterfull spoliatioun and awaytaking" related to a vessel that was stripped of its equipment and torn apart after its whole crew went ashore in Shetland to search for provisions.[105] No clearer example of the destroying of a ship by "wreckers", as opposed to the plundering of ships wrecked by storms, has been found.[106]

102 NRS, CS7/98(1) ff 328v and 331v.

103 Wade (ed), *Acta curiae admirallatus Scotiae* (n 2) 172; Bain et al (eds), *Calendar of the State Papers Relating to Scotland and Mary Queen of Scots* (n 2) vol 4, 159, 178, 258, 293–294, 300 and 303; National Archives at Kew (NAK), state papers (domestic) of the reign of Elizabeth, SP52/23/1, f 42.

104 Burton and Masson (eds), *Register of the Privy Council of Scotland* (n 2) vol 1, 251–252; A I Dunlop (ed), *The Warrender Papers*, 2 vols (1931–1932) vol 1, 30–32; Bain et al (eds), *Calendar of the State Papers Relating to Scotland and Mary Queen of Scots* (n 2) vol 9, 635; Dasent et al (eds), *Acts of the Privy Council of England* (n 2) vol 6, 27, 51–52, 54 and 56–57; R Lindesay of Pitscottie, *The Historie and Cronicles of Scotland*, 3 vols, A J G Mackay (ed) (1899–1911) vol 2, 117; J Leslie, *De origine, moribus, et rebus gestis Scotorum libri decem* (1578) 528–529, and *The Historie of Scotland*, tr. J Dalrymple, 2 vols, E G Cody (ed) (1888–1895) vol 2, 367; R Hakluyt, *The Principal Navigations, Voyages, Traffiques and Discoveries of the Englis Nation*, 16 vols, E Goldsmid (ed) (1885–1890) vol 3, 141–151; NAK, SP52/42, f 119.

105 Burton and Masson (eds), *Register of the Privy Council of Scotland* (n 2) vol 5, 153 and 195–197; R Pitcairn (ed), *Ancient Criminal Trials in Scotland*, 3 vols (1833) vol 1(2) 336; Ballantyne and Smith (eds), *Shetland Documents* (n 18) vol 2, 95–96 and 102–103; W F Skene (ed), *Memorials of the Family of Skene of Skene* (1887) 164–165; NRS, miscellaneous papers (foreign), RH9/5/21, and PC1/15, p. 308; D M Ferguson, *Shipwrecks of Orkney, Shetland and the Pentland Firth* (1988) 29–30.

106 No example has been found of ships being lured to their destruction with false lights, which according to H Henningsen, 'Legends about "Wreckers"' (1985) 71 *Mariner's Mirror* 215, was a mythical activity existing only in the minds of people who read written sources like the *Digest* uncritically, assuming that legislators only dealt with abuses that actually existed.

Given that rewards could be earned by people living on the coasts if they participated in salvage operations, that in lieu of payment salvors were sometimes permitted to retain part of the goods they recovered, that goods recovered from wrecks could often be purchased, and that if goods recovered from a ship lost with all hands remained unclaimed after a year and a day, the finders may have been able to claim a share, it may be suspected that the people who plundered wrecks believed they were acting within their rights. Popular investigations of "wrecking" in the western and northern isles of Scotland during the twentieth century have revealed that the people involved were inclined to resent any imputation of wrongdoing.[107] Their attitude was that the sea, to which they were in danger of losing their lives or livelihoods, occasionally included among the rich bounty it returned the remains of other people's property.[108] A scholarly study of wrecking in England in the eighteenth century has brought to light a great deal of evidence of similar attitudes at that place and time.[109] The author discovered that people residing in coastal communities did not draw a clear distinction between legal "salvage" and illegal "wrecking", but believed they were entitled to appropriate anything retrieved from the sea. He found more instructive the historian Edward Thompson's distinction between the "political economy" of the wealthy, which was supported by the laws written down in books, and the "moral economy" of the poor, which was sustained by popular usages and customs.[110] Comparison might be made with Eric Hobsbawm's use of the phrase "social criminality" to describe behaviour that is condemned by an "official" system, favoured by the rich and powerful, yet sanctioned by an "unofficial" system, favoured by the poor and vulnerable.[111] The evidence available from England in the eighteenth century reveals not only that ordinary people who plundered wrecks did not think

107 R Hutchinson, *Polly: The True Story behind Whisky Galore* (1990) 53 and 94; B Bathurst, *The Wreckers: A Story of Killing Seas, False Lights and Plundered Ships* (2005) 61–101. It seems more than a little outrageous for the latter author, after pointing out that the northern isles are closer to Norway than England, to attribute the wrecking activities of their inhabitants to "the fishy stink of their Viking past".

108 Cf. A M Richmond, '"The Broken Schippus He Ther Fonde": Shipwrecks and the Human Costs of Investment Capital in Middle English Romance' (2015) 99 *Neophilologus* 315, at 315–316.

109 J G Rule, 'Wrecking and Coastal Plunder', in D Hay, P Linebaugh, J G Rule, E P Thompson and C Winslow, *Albion's Fatal Tree: Crime and Society in Eighteenth-Century England* (1975) 167.

110 E P Thompson, *Customs in Common* (1991) 271 and 336–340 especially.

111 E J Hobsbawm, 'Social Criminality' (1972) 25 *Bulletin of the Society for the Study of Labour History* 5, at 5–6 especially.

they were really doing anything wrong, but also that they adhered to certain norms governing the plundering process, such as respect for each other's acquisitions when made in particular ways.[112] No such evidence has come to light from Scotland in the sixteenth century. All the evidence discussed so far suggests that a distinction was recognised between legal salvage and illegal wrecking.[113] The people who were accurately described as "violent and maisterfull spuilzearis" appear to have accepted that they were wrongdoers. Yet this evidence is derived almost entirely from books written by lawyers or records compiled by the clerks of various courts. It may be wondered what chance there is of the moral economy of the poor ever being represented in sources of these types, and whether an unofficial system of norms could possibly have found its way into the repositories of an official system.

An answer begins to emerge if attention is finally paid to two exceptional cases noted in the council register of Aberdeen, in which ordinary people did assert rights to things salvaged from wrecks. In the first case, heard in 1548, several local men proved that they were present "at the wynninge of the geir of the Ingliss schip quhilk brak laitly in the raid", and were consequently awarded as much of the things retrieved "as the laif of the wynnars of the same gat".[114] In the second case, heard two years later after equipment was salvaged from an "Inglis schip that brak one the bar", an anchor and cables were claimed by two local men who sought to prove that they were "the princypall laborars and wynnars thairof".[115] What sets these cases apart from all the other salvage disputes encountered in the records of the burgh courts is that the masters of the wrecked ships were not present, nor any other Englishmen for that matter. Instead of claiming rewards for their labours from the master, mariners, merchants or owners of the ships wrecked, the pursuers were demanding appropriate shares of the things recovered from the other parties involved in their recovery. They were claiming to be entitled to things salvaged from wrecks, which were to be distributed evenly among everyone who took part in the salvage operation, and were not to be returned, even in part, to their original owners. The explanation cannot be that the ships had been lost without survivors, because a year and a day had not elapsed since they were wrecked, after which claims would have been

112 Cf. M Rediker, *Between the Devil and the Deep Blue Sea: Merchant Seamen, Pirates and the Anglo-American Maritime World, 1700–1750* (1987) 285.

113 In the case of the *Jhesus*, for instance, it was this distinction that was being applied.

114 ACA, CA1/1/20, pp. 9, 13, 15 and 18.

115 ACA, CA1/1/20, pp. 368, 371, 374, 378–379, 407 and 410.

expected from the admiral or landowners.[116] Yet the explanation cannot be that salvors were generally reckoned to be entitled to keep what they took either, for then all the other records of salvage disputes (as well as the spuilzie cases and the legal treatises) would make little sense. The crucial point about these two cases would appear to be that they were heard at a time when Scotland was at war with England.[117] According to the theory taught in universities throughout Europe, things pertaining to enemies (*res hostium*) were not only to be regarded as, but were equated with, things that had no owner (*res nullius*) and therefore became the property of anyone who took effective possession of them (*occupatio*).[118] It was this theory that underpinned the litigation over prize acquisition that is often encountered in the records of the burgh and other courts in sixteenth-century Scotland.[119] It is important to note, however, that no express mention was made in either of these cases of the theory of the law schools, with which the parties present are unlikely to have had much acquaintance.[120] Instead, the parties seem to have shared a belief that in practice things taken from enemies became the property of the takers, without necessarily knowing where the belief originated.

In fact, no express mention of the learned laws, or of written sources generally, has been found in any of the entries from the burgh court records cited in this essay, in which the connections occasionally drawn between theory and practice have necessarily been vague and imprecise. The claims made in practice to "wrak" did not fit neatly with the written sources referred to by the lawyers in their treatises, although the practice may ultimately have been founded on those sources, just as the claims made by salvors to rewards, and the use of salvaged property to provide rewards, may ultimately have been founded on provisions of the *Rôles d'Oléron*, although the terms of the provisions in question were not adhered to exactly. The sources referred to by the lawyers may have come to influence the practice of the courts sitting in coastal towns, but it was practice itself, or the accepted way of doing things, that was considered obligatory by the people who litigated there.[121]

116 It may be recalled that a landowner did register an interest in the *Jhesus* case (n 70 above).

117 G Phillips, *The Anglo-Scots Wars, 1513–1550* (1999) 201–255.

118 *Justinian's Institutes*, 2.1.17; *Digest of Justinian* (n 34), 41.1.5.7, 41.2.1.1 and 41.2.3.21.

119 This material will be returned to in a book entitled *The Emergence of Privateering*, but see in the meantime Ford (ed), *Alexander King's Treatise on Maritime Law* (n 28) 259–266.

120 The same might be said in relation to the prize cases.

121 For a preliminary investigation of this subject see J D Ford, 'Telling Tales: Maritime Law in Aberdeen in the Early Sixteenth Century', in J Armstrong and E Frankot (eds), *Cultures of Law in Urban Northern Europe: Scotland and Its Neighbours, c. 1350–c. 1650* (2021) 23.

When his account of the moral economy of the poor was reprinted, Edward Thompson remarked that custom lies at the interface between law and practice.[122] His remark is instructive, provided it is properly understood.[123] For one thing, it indicates that when law takes the form of custom it may look rather different when viewed from the perspectives of authors expert in the law and of lay people engaged in practice.[124] The authors in sixteenth-century Scotland who dealt with the law of shipwreck in their treatises tried not only to connect the practice of the courts with the books they had been reading, but also to use their reading as a basis for reappraising, and sometimes reforming, practice.[125] To Thomas Craig, for example, it seemed that the "custom" of assigning wrak to the admiral was defensible in the light of the feudal law, which was in keeping with certain civil law texts, whereas to Alexander King, the same "custom" seemed indefensible when compared with other civil law texts, which were more consistent with the canon law. Both King and Welwod wanted actions of spuilzie and disputes over salvage to be handled in Scotland in accordance with the written sources they studied.[126] Their attempts to marry theory with practice are interesting, but their treatises cannot simply be read as reliable accounts of the law applied in practice.

For lay people – the ordinary people whose voices can in fact be heard in the records of the burgh courts – practice became law when it was established as custom, regardless of how closely it might have accorded with the law written down in books. In the burgh courts lay people claimed things to which they believed they had customary rights, not things to which lawyers told them they had rights in accordance with written sources of law.[127] The other thing Thompson's remark about custom indicates, however, is that just as written law need not be reflected perfectly in the customs it informs, so

122 *Customs in Common* (n 110) 97.

123 F J Blakemore, 'The Legal World of English Sailors, c. 1575–1729', in M Fusaro, B Allaire, F Blakemore and T Vanneste (eds), *Law, Labour and Empire: Comparative Perspectives on Seafarers, c. 1500–1800* (2015) 100, at 101–103.

124 Legal historians typically make this point by distinguishing between the legal customs of communities and the customary laws into which they were often turned by lawyers.

125 There is a difference, of course, between the practice or "practick" of the courts, developed especially in the minds of the lawyers who represented litigants there, and the practice or settled behaviour of those litigants. In the burgh courts parties were sometimes represented by university graduates, who made clever procedural moves on their behalf but it was the practices of the parties themselves that were often treated as customs.

126 The broad aims of these authors are examined more fully in Ford (ed), *Alexander King's Treatise on Maritime Law* (n 28) xc–xcvii.

127 When they were represented by university graduates, the discussion of procedure typically became more technical, but not the discussion of the substantive law applied.

practice need not pass through custom into law.[128] The efforts made by central authorities and local dignitaries to prevent the plundering of wrecks are suggestive of a popular practice of plunder, which might even have extended at times to deliberate wrecking. Yet even if it had been normal for people to help themselves to whatever could be recovered from wrecks, and even if the practice had been in some sense normative – even if people had believed they had some sort of right to the things they recovered – it would only follow that the practice was considered legal if the relevant norms were regarded as the kind of customs that counted as laws. People were not slow to assert their rights before the courts when they considered them to be legal, and to do so they made use of the language of custom or usage. We hear the voices of lay people asserting rights to things taken from enemy ships, as well as to rewards for salvaging things from other ships, and we hear them insisting that these rights were customary. But we do not hear them asserting rights to keep things taken from wrecks more generally. If there was an unofficial and unrecorded system of plunder, it appears to have been regarded neither by lawyers nor by lay people as a system of legal norms. The moral economy of shipwreck, if there was one in sixteenth-century Scotland, must have been of a different nature.[129]

128 See too M Weber, *Economy and Society: An Outline of Interpretive Sociology*, 2 vols, G Roth and C Wittich (eds) (1978) vol 1, 319–325.

129 For further examples of shipwrecks in Scotland not touched on above see Wade (ed), *Acta curiae admirallatus Scotiae* (n 2) 8–9, 39–40, 44 and 46; W Mackay, H C Boyd and G S Laing (eds), *Records of Inverness*, 2 vols (1911–1924) vol 1, 126 and 209; Ballantyne and Smith (eds), *Shetland Documents* (n 18) vol 1, 249–250; *Bronnen tot de Geschiedenis van der Handel met Engeland, Schotland en Ireland* (n 2) 1st ser., vol 1, 160; Bain et al (eds), *Calendar of the State Papers Relating to Scotland and Mary Queen of Scots*, vol 2, 395, vol 4, 54, and vol 8, 354; T Thomson (ed), *A Diurnal of Remarkable Occurrents that Have Passed within the Country of Scotland since the Death of King James the Fourth till the Year 1575* (1833) 122–123; Sir James Melville of Halhill, *Memoirs of His Own Life* (1827) 186 and 369–370; NRS, PS1/56, f 25r, and James Brown Craven bequest, GD106/135; DCA, BCMB, vol 12, 23 April 1573, and vol 14, 14 September 1579; SAUL, burgh court book of Crail, B10/8/4, pp. 419–420; ACA, CA1/1/8, p. 132, CA1/1/9, p. 328, CA1/1/10, p. 286, CA1/1/11, p. 675, CA1/1/18, pp. 308, 582 and 595, and CA1/1/27, pp. 197, 303, 473–474 and 517; Dumfries Archive Centre (DAC), burgh court book of Dumfries, WC4/8, f 184v; D M Ferguson, *Shipwrecks of North East Scotland, 1444–1990* (1991) 1; P D Anderson, *Robert Stewart, Earl of Orkney, Lord of Shetland, 1533–1593* (1982) 55, 72 and 120, and *Black Patie: The Life and Times of Patrick Stewart, Earl of Orkney, Lord of Shetland* (1992) 40 and 45; C Martin, *Scotland's Historic Shipwrecks* (1998) 11–45; T M Y Manson, 'The Fair Isle Spanish Armada Shipwreck' in G W S Barrow (ed), *The Scottish Tradition: Essays in Honour of Ronald Gordon Cant* (1974) 121.

Index

EU Authorised Representative:
Easy Access System Europe Mustamäe tee 50, 10621 Tallinn, Estonia
gpsr.requests@easproject.com

Printed and bound by CPI Group (UK) Ltd, Croydon, CR0 4YY
17/09/2026
02218450-0001